10th International Conference on Tree Adjoining Grammars and Related Formalisms 2010 (TAG+10)

New Haven, Connecticut, USA
10 – 12 June 2010

Editors:

Srinivas Bangalore
Robert Frank
Maribel Romero

ISBN: 978-1-5108-2681-6

Proceedings of the 10th International Conference
on Tree Adjoining Grammars and Related Formalisms (TAG+10)
Yale University

Srinivas Bangalore, Robert Frank & Maribel Romero (eds.)

June 10–12, 2010

Credits:
Program Co-Chair: Srinivas Bangalore
Program Co-Chair: Maribel Romero
Local Arrangements Chair: Robert Frank
Editor: Marc Novel
using LaTeX's 'confproc' class

Preface

The papers in this volume were presented at the Tenth International Workshop on Tree Adjoining Grammars and Related Formalisms. TAG+10 continues the long tradition of exploring the relations between Tree-Adjoining Grammars and related formalisms along mathematical, linguistic, and computational perspectives. TAG+10 includes 11 papers that were selected on the basis of submitted abstracts for oral presentation and 8 papers that were selected for poster presentation. Each paper was reviewed by three reviewers. The oral presentations were organized into the following sessions: Syntax/Semantics, Formalisms, Parsing/Generation, Corpora and Broad Coverage Grammars. The quality of the technical program presented in this volume is due in large part to the rigor and enthusiasm of the TAG+10 program committee for maintain high scientific standards. The authors of the papers have indicated that they have greatly benefited from the reviews they have received. Many thanks to the the members of the program committee, whose names are listed here, for their time and efforts.

Tilman Becker	Emily Bender	Pierre Boullier
John Chen	David Chiang	Eric de la Clergerie
Claire Gardent	Chung-hye Han	Karin Harbusch
Aravind Joshi	Laura Kallmeyer	Marco Kuhlmann
Alessandro Mazzei	David McDonald	Martha Palmer
Owen Rambow	James Rogers	Anoop Sarkar
Sylvain Schmitz	Hiroyuki Seki	Vijay Shanker
Mark Steedman	Amanda Stent	Matthew Stone
Bonnie Webber	Fei Xia	Naoki Yoshinaga

As in previous years, TAG+10 included invited speakers drawn from outside of the TAG community, to stimulate cross-framework interactions and cross-pollination. This year's speakers, to whom we are grateful for their paricipation, were Ed Stabler (UCLA) and Chris Barker (NYU). We are pleased to be able to include Barker's contribution in this volume. TAG+ workshops have emphasized tutorials, designed to help students and interested researchers quickly catch up with the state of the art. TAG+10 included a wonderful selection of illustrious tutorial speakers on a wide range of topics. We are thankful to our tutorial speakers for accepting our invitations to educate workshop participants: Rajesh Bhatt (UMass Amherst), Alexander Clark (Royal Holloway), Marco Kuhlmann (Uppsala), and William Schuler (Minnesota/Ohio State).

A special feature of this year's workshop was our ability to provide financial support to student authors and participants to help them attend the workshop. This was possible in great part to the National Science Foundation's financial support, to whom were are very grateful. We would also like to express our appreciation to the Yale University Department of Linguistics and Program in Cognitive Science for their financial and logistical support, without which this workshop would not have been possible.

Welcome to TAG+10!

Srinivas Bangalore (Program Co-Chair)
Maribel Romero (Program Co-Chair)
Robert Frank (Local Arrangements Chair)

Conference Program

Thursday, June 10

9:00-9:15   Welcome and Introduction to TAG+10

9:15-10:45   *Tutorial 1*
Rajesh Bhatt

10:45-11:15   Coffee Break

11:15-12:45   *Tutorial 2: Relating TAG and Dependency Grammar. A Tree-Based Approach*
Marco Kuhlmann

12:45-2:15   Lunch Break

2:15-3:45   *Tutorial 3: Grammar Induction and "Empiricist" Representations*
Alexander Clark

3:45-4:15   Coffee Break

4:15-5:45   *Tutorial 4: Incremental Parsing in Bounded Memory*
William Schuler

5:45-6:45   Refreshments

Friday, June 11

9:00-10:00   **Invited Speaker**
Incremental Parsing
Edward Stabler

10:00-10:30   Coffee Break

10:30-11:00   *Non-local Right Node Raising: an Analysis using Delayed Tree-Local MC-TAG*
Chung Hye-Han, David Potter and Dennis Ryan Storoshenko

11:00-11:30   *Unifying Adjunct Islands and Freezing Effects in Minimalist Grammars*
Tim Hunter

11:30-12:00   *Reevaluating Gapping in CCG: Evidence from English & Chinese*
Nathaniel Little

12:00-2:00   Lunch Break

2:00-2:30   *Well-Nested Tree Languages and Attributed Tree Transducers*
Uwe Mönnich

2:30-3:00   *On Calculus of Displacement*
Glyn Morrill and Oriol Valentín

3:00-3:30   Coffee Break

| 3:30-5:00 | **Poster Session** |

Dependency Structures and Unavoidable Ill-nestedness
Joan Chen-Main and Aravind K. Joshi

Generating LTAG grammars from a lexicon/ontology interface
Philipp Cimiano, Felix Hieber and Christina Unger

Restricting Inverse Scope in STAG
Michael Freedman and Robert Frank

Surprisal Derives the Recent Filler Hypothesis in Mildly Context Sensitive Grammars
Kyle Grove

From Partial VP Fronting towards Spinal TT-MCTAG
Timm Lichte

Gapping through TAG derivation trees
Timm Lichte and Laura Kallmeyer

Control Verb, Argument Cluster Coordination and Multi Component TAG
Djamé Seddah, Benoit Sagot and Laurence Danlos

Building factorized TAGs with meta-grammars
Éric Villemonte de la Clergerie

Saturday, June 12

10:00-10:30 *Discontinuity and Non-Projectivity: Using Mildly Context-Sensitive Formalisms for Data-Driven Parsing*
Wolfgang Maier and Laura Kallmeyer

10:30-11:00 *Sentence Generation as Planning with Probabilistic LTAG*
Daniel Bauer and Alexander Koller

11:00-11:30 Coffee Break

11:30-12:30 **Invited Speaker**
Cosubstitution, Derivational Locality and Quantifier Scope
Chris Barker

12:30-2:00 Lunch Break

2:00-2:30 *Binding Variables in English: An Analysis Using Delayed Tree Locality*
Dennis Ryan Storoshenko and Chung-Hye Han

2:30-3:00 *TAG Analysis of Turkish Long Distance Dependencies*
Elif Eyigöz

3:00-3:30 Coffee Break

3:30-4:00 *A TAG-derived Database for Treebank Search and Parser Analysis*
Seth Kulick and Ann Bies

4:00-4:30 *Automated Extraction of Tree Adjoining Grammars from a Treebank for Vietnamese*
Phuong Le Hong, Thi Minh Huyen Nguyen, Phuong-Thai Nguyen and Azim Roussanaly

Table of Contents

Incremental Parsing in Bounded Memory

William Schuler
Department of Lingustics
The Ohio State University
schuler@ling.osu.edu

Abstract

This tutorial will describe the use of a factored probabilistic sequence model for parsing speech and text using a bounded store of three to four incomplete constituents over time, in line with recent estimates of human short-term working memory capacity. This formulation uses a grammar transform to minimize memory usage during parsing. Incremental operations on incomplete constituents in this transformed representation then define an extended domain of locality similar to those defined in mildly context-sensitive grammar formalisms, which can similarly be used to process long-distance and crossed-and-nested dependencies.

1 Introduction

This paper will describe the derivation of a factored probabilistic sequence model from a probabilistic context-free grammar (PCFG). The resulting sequence model can incrementally parse input sentences approximately as accurately as a bottom-up CKY-styple parser, incrementally estimating the contents of a bounded memory store of intended constituents, consisting of only three to four working memory elements, in line with recent estimates of human short-term working memory capacity (Cowan, 2001). The detailed derivation of this model is intended to illustrate how probabilistic dependencies from an original PCFG (or other types of syntax-derived dependencies) can be preserved in a processing model with human-like working memory constraints.

1.1 Notation

This paper will associate variables for syntactic categories c, trees or subtrees τ, and string yields $\bar{x}$ with constituents in phrase structure trees, identified using subscripts that describe the path from the root of the tree containing this constituent to the constituent itself. These paths may consist of left branches (indicated by '0's in the path) and right branches (indicated by '1's), concatenated into sequences η (or ι or κ). Thus, if a path η identifies a constituent, that constituent's left child would be identified by $\eta 0$, and that constituent's right child would be identified by $\eta 1$. The empty path ϵ will be sued to identify the root of a tree.

The probabilistic parsers defined here will also use an indicator function $[\![\cdot]\!]$ to denote deterministic probabilities: $[\![\phi]\!] = 1$ if ϕ is true, 0 otherwise.

2 Parsing

For a phrase structure subtree rooted at a constituent of category c_η with yield $\bar{x}_\eta$ (a sequence of individual words x), the task of parsing will require the calculation of the inside likelihood probability or Viterbi (best subtree) probabilities. When the domain X of words x is a subset of the domain C of category labels c, these can be calculated using rule probabilities in a probabilistic context-free grammar (PCFG) model θ_G, notated:

$$P_{\theta_G}(c_\eta \to c_{\eta 0}\, c_{\eta 1}) = P_{\theta_G}(c_{\eta 0}\, c_{\eta 1} \mid c_\eta) \qquad (1)$$

Any yield $\bar{x}_\eta$ can be decomposed into prefix $\bar{x}_{\eta 0}$ and suffix $\bar{x}_{\eta 1}$ yields:

$$\bar{x}_\eta = \bar{x}_{\eta 0}\bar{x}_{\eta 1} \qquad (2)$$

Therefore, inside likelihood probabilities can be defined by marginalizing over all such decompositions:

$$
P_{\theta_{\text{Ins(G)}}}(\bar{x}_\eta \mid c_\eta) =
\begin{cases}
\text{if } |\bar{x}_\eta| = 1 : [\![\bar{x}_\eta = c_\eta]\!] \\
\text{otherwise} : \displaystyle\sum_{\bar{x}_{\eta 0} c_{\eta 0}, \bar{x}_{\eta 1} c_{\eta 1}} P_{\theta_G}(c_\eta \rightarrow c_{\eta 0}\, c_{\eta 1}) \\
\qquad\qquad \cdot P_{\theta_{\text{Ins(G)}}}(\bar{x}_{\eta 0} \mid c_{\eta 0}) \\
\qquad\qquad \cdot P_{\theta_{\text{Ins(G)}}}(\bar{x}_{\eta 1} \mid c_{\eta 1})
\end{cases}
\tag{3}
$$

and Viterbi scores (the probability of the best tree) can be defined by maximizing over all such decompositions:

$$
P_{\theta_{\text{Vit(G)}}}(\bar{x}_\eta \mid c_\eta) =
\begin{cases}
\text{if } |\bar{x}_\eta| = 1 : [\![\bar{x}_\eta = c_\eta]\!] \\
\text{otherwise} : \displaystyle\max_{\bar{x}_{\eta 0} c_{\eta 0}, \bar{x}_{\eta 1} c_{\eta 1}} P_{\theta_G}(c_\eta \rightarrow c_{\eta 0}\, c_{\eta 1}) \\
\qquad\qquad \cdot P_{\theta_{\text{Vit(G)}}}(\bar{x}_{\eta 0} \mid c_{\eta 0}) \\
\qquad\qquad \cdot P_{\theta_{\text{Vit(G)}}}(\bar{x}_{\eta 1} \mid c_{\eta 1})
\end{cases}
\tag{4}
$$

From these, it is possible to obtain the probability of a sentence $\bar{x}_\epsilon$:

$$
P(\bar{x}_\epsilon) = \sum_{c_\epsilon} P_{\theta_{\text{Ins(G)}}}(\bar{x}_\epsilon \mid c_\epsilon) \cdot P(c_\epsilon)
\tag{5}
$$

and the most likely tree:

$$
\hat{\tau}_\epsilon = \operatorname*{argmax}_{\tau_\epsilon} P_{\theta_{\text{Vit(G)}}}(\bar{x}_\epsilon \mid c_{\tau_\epsilon}) \cdot P(c_{\tau_\epsilon})
\tag{6}
$$

3 Incremental Parsing using Incomplete Constituents

Note that any prefix of a yield $\bar{x}_\eta$ can be rewritten as an 'incomplete yield' consisting of the complete yield lacking some suffix of that yield $\bar{x}_{\eta\iota}$:

$$
\bar{x}_\eta = (\bar{x}_\eta / \bar{x}_{\eta\iota}) \bar{x}_{\eta\iota}
\tag{7}
$$

It is therefore possible to decompose any inside likelihood or Viterbi probability into two parts: first, an 'incomplete constituent' probability of generating this incomplete yield $\bar{x}_\eta / \bar{x}_{\eta\iota}$ along with an *awaited* constituent of category $c_{\eta\iota}$, given an *active* constituent of category c_η; and second, an ordinary inside or Viterbi probability (or 'complete constituent' probability) of generating $\bar{x}_{\eta\iota}$ given $c_{\eta\iota}$:

$$
P_{\theta_{\text{Ins(G)}}}(\bar{x}_\eta \mid c_\eta) = \sum_{\iota \in 1^+, \bar{x}_{\eta\iota}, c_{\eta\iota}} P_{\theta_{\text{IC(G)}}}(\bar{x}_\eta / \bar{x}_{\eta\iota},\, c_{\eta\iota} \mid c_\eta) \cdot P_{\theta_{\text{Ins(G)}}}(\bar{x}_{\eta\iota} \mid c_{\eta\iota})
\tag{8}
$$

This decomposition can be represented graphically as a transformation of the structure of a recurrence from the standard PCFG recurrence above, corresponding to PCFG dependencies, to one involving incomplete constituents (in particular, this will transform the end of a right-expanding sequence into the beginning of a left-expanding sequence of incomplete constituents):

$$
\tag{9}
$$

This decomposition gives incomplete constituent probabilities that can then be decomposed into other incomplete constituent probabilities (this will transform the middle of a right-expending sequence into the middle of a left-expanding sequence of incomplete constituents):

$$
\begin{aligned}
& P_{\theta_{\text{IC(G)}}}(\bar{x}_\eta / \bar{x}_{\eta\iota 1},\, c_{\eta\iota 1} \mid c_\eta) \\
& = \sum_{\bar{x}_{\eta\iota}, c_{\eta\iota}} P_{\theta_{\text{IC(G)}}}(\bar{x}_\eta / \bar{x}_{\eta\iota},\, c_{\eta\iota} \mid c_\eta) \\
& \qquad \cdot P_{\theta_{\text{IC(G)}}}(\bar{x}_{\eta\iota} / \bar{x}_{\eta\iota 1},\, c_{\eta\iota 1} \mid c_{\eta\iota}) \\
& = \sum_{\bar{x}_{\eta\iota}, c_{\eta\iota}} P_{\theta_{\text{IC(G)}}}(\bar{x}_\eta / \bar{x}_{\eta\iota},\, c_{\eta\iota} \mid c_\eta) \\
& \qquad \cdot \sum_{\bar{x}_{\eta\iota 0}, c_{\eta\iota 0}} P_{\theta_G}(c_{\eta\iota} \rightarrow c_{\eta\iota 0}\, c_{\eta\iota 1}) \cdot P_{\theta_{\text{Ins(G)}}}(\bar{x}_{\eta\iota 0} \mid c_{\eta\iota 0})
\end{aligned}
\tag{10, 11}
$$

represented graphically:

$$
\tag{12}
$$

or into the product of a grammar rule probability and an inside probability at the end of a sequence of such decompositions (this will transform the beginning of a right-expanding sequence into the end of a left-expanding sequence of incomplete constituents):

$$
P_{\theta_{\text{IC(G)}}}(\bar{x}_\eta / \bar{x}_{\eta 1},\, c_{\eta 1} \mid c_\eta) = \sum_{\bar{x}_{\eta 0}, c_{\eta 0}} P_{\theta_G}(c_\eta \rightarrow c_{\eta 0}\, c_{\eta 1}) \cdot P_{\theta_{\text{Ins(G)}}}(\bar{x}_{\eta 0} \mid c_{\eta 0})
\tag{13}
$$

represented graphically:

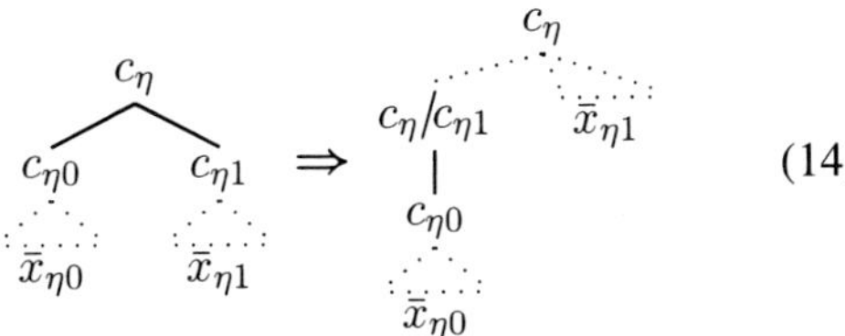

$$(14)$$

Essentially this transformation turns right-expanding sequences of constituents (with subscript addresses ending in '1') into left-expanding sequences of incomplete constituents, which can be composed together as they are recognized incrementally from left to right. The decompositions of Equations 8–13, taken together, are a model-based right-corner transform (Schuler, 2009).

This transformation can then be defined on depth-specific rules, allowing the sequence model to keep track of a bounded amount of center-embedded phrase structure.

$$P_{\theta_{\text{Ins(G),d}}}(\bar{x}_\eta \mid c_\eta) = \sum_{\iota \in 1^+, \bar{x}_{\eta\iota}, c_{\eta\iota}} P_{\theta_{\text{IC(G),d}}}(\bar{x}_\eta / \bar{x}_{\eta\iota}, c_{\eta\iota} \mid c_\eta)$$
$$\cdot P_{\theta_{\text{Ins(G),d}}}(\bar{x}_{\eta\iota} \mid c_{\eta\iota}) \quad (15)$$

$$P_{\theta_{\text{IC(G),d}}}(\bar{x}_\eta / \bar{x}_{\eta\iota 1}, c_{\eta\iota 1} \mid c_\eta)$$
$$= \sum_{\bar{x}_{\eta\iota}, c_{\eta\iota}} P_{\theta_{\text{IC(G),d}}}(\bar{x}_\eta / \bar{x}_{\eta\iota}, c_{\eta\iota} \mid c_\eta)$$
$$\cdot P_{\theta_{\text{IC(G),d}}}(\bar{x}_{\eta\iota} / \bar{x}_{\eta\iota 1}, c_{\eta\iota 1} \mid c_{\eta\iota}) \quad (16)$$
$$= \sum_{\bar{x}_{\eta\iota}, c_{\eta\iota}} P_{\theta_{\text{IC(G),d}}}(\bar{x}_\eta / \bar{x}_{\eta\iota}, c_{\eta\iota} \mid c_\eta)$$
$$\cdot \sum_{\bar{x}_{\eta\iota 0}, c_{\eta\iota 0}} P_{\theta_{\text{G-R},d}}(c_{\eta\iota} \to c_{\eta\iota 0}\, c_{\eta\iota 1})$$
$$\cdot P_{\theta_{\text{Ins(G),d+1}}}(\bar{x}_{\eta\iota 0} \mid c_{\eta\iota 0}) \quad (17)$$

$$P_{\theta_{\text{IC(G),d}}}(\bar{x}_\eta / \bar{x}_{\eta 1}, c_{\eta 1} \mid c_\eta) =$$
$$\sum_{\bar{x}_{\eta 0}, c_{\eta 0}} P_{\theta_{\text{G-L},d}}(c_\eta \to c_{\eta 0}\, c_{\eta 1}) \cdot P_{\theta_{\text{Ins(G),d}}}(\bar{x}_{\eta 0} \mid c_{\eta 0})$$
$$(18)$$

Estimating probabilities for the beginning and ending of these transformed left-expanding sequences will require the estimation of expected counts for repeated recursive decompositions of yet-unrecognized incomplete constituents according to Equation 8, marginalizing over values of $\bar{x}$. Since left children and right children are decomposed differently, the expected counts $\theta_{\text{G-RL}^*,d}$ will use PCFG probabilities $\theta_{\text{G-R},d}$ and $\theta_{\text{G-L},d}$ that are conditioned on whether the expanding constituent is a right or left child, and on the center-embedding depth d of the expanding constituent. The expected counts $\theta_{\text{G-RL}^*,d}$ are of constituent categories $c_{\eta\iota}$ anywhere in the left progeny of a right child of category c_η:

$$E_{\theta_{\text{G-RL}^*,d}}(c_\eta \xrightarrow{0} c_{\eta 0} \ldots) = \sum_{c_{\eta 1}} P_{\theta_{\text{G-R},d}}(c_\eta \to c_{\eta 0}\, c_{\eta 1})$$
$$(19)$$

$$E_{\theta_{\text{G-RL}^*,d}}(c_\eta \xrightarrow{k} c_{\eta 0^k 0} \ldots) = \sum_{c_{\eta 0^k}} E_{\theta_{\text{G-RL}^*,d}}(c_\eta \xrightarrow{k-1} c_{\eta 0^k} \ldots)$$
$$\cdot \sum_{c_{\eta 0^k 1}} P_{\theta_{\text{G-L},d}}(c_{\eta 0^k} \to c_{\eta 0^k 0}\, c_{\eta 0^k 1}) \quad (20)$$

$$E_{\theta_{\text{G-RL}^*,d}}(c_\eta \xrightarrow{*} c_{\eta\iota} \ldots) = \sum_{k=0}^{\infty} E_{\theta_{\text{G-RL}^*,d}}(c_\eta \xrightarrow{k} c_{\eta\iota} \ldots)$$
$$(21)$$

$$E_{\theta_{\text{G-RL}^*,d}}(c_\eta \xrightarrow{+} c_{\eta\iota} \ldots) = E_{\theta_{\text{G-RL}^*,d}}(c_\eta \xrightarrow{*} c_{\eta\iota} \ldots)$$
$$- E_{\theta_{\text{G-RL}^*,d}}(c_\eta \xrightarrow{0} c_{\eta\iota} \ldots)$$
$$(22)$$

In practice the infinite sum is estimated to some constant K using value iteration (Bellman, 1957).

These expected counts can then be used to calculate left progeny probabilities:

$$P_{\theta_{\text{G-RL}^*,d}}(c_\eta \xrightarrow{*} c_{\eta\iota} \ldots) = \frac{E_{\theta_{\text{G-RL}^*,d}}(c_\eta \xrightarrow{*} c_{\eta\iota} \ldots)}{\sum_{c_{\eta\iota}} E_{\theta_{\text{G-RL}^*,d}}(c_\eta \xrightarrow{*} c_{\eta\iota} \ldots)}$$
$$(23)$$

which can be used to calculate forward or Viterbi probabilities for all incomplete constituents in the memory store, along with their yields:

$$P_{\theta_{\text{Fwd}}}\left((\bar{x}_{\eta d}/\bar{x}_{\eta d\iota_d 1})_{d=1}^D, (c_{\eta d})_{d=1}^D, (c_{\eta d\iota_d 1})_{d=1}^D\right) =$$
$$\prod_{d=1}^D P_{\theta_{\text{G-RL}^*,d}}(c_{\eta d-1 \iota_{d-1} 1} \xrightarrow{*} c_{\eta d} \ldots)$$
$$\cdot P_{\theta_{\text{IC(G)}}}(\bar{x}_{\eta d}/\bar{x}_{\eta d\iota_d 1}, c_{\eta d\iota_d 1} \mid c_{\eta d}) \quad (24)$$

Putting all the pieces together, probabilities for stores of incomplete constituents can now be defined in terms of transitions from possible previous stores of incomplete constituents (set apart by parentheses in the equation below) and reductions of incomplete constituents and terminal symbols into complete constituents (set apart by square brackets). These transitions either:

- add a layer of structure below an awaited constituent at some depth level (the first case below),

- add a layer of structure to the top of an active constituent at some depth level (the second case below), or

- carry forward the probability of an incomplete constituent at a depth at which no transition takes place (the third case below):

$$
\mathsf{P}_{\theta_{\mathrm{Fwd}}}\left(\left(\bar{x}_{\eta_d}/\bar{x}_{\eta_d \iota_d 1}\right)_{d=1}^{D}, \left(c_{\eta_d}\right)_{d=1}^{D}, \left(c_{\eta_d \iota_d 1}\right)_{d=1}^{D}\right) =
$$

$$
\prod_{d=1}^{D}
\begin{cases}
\text{if } c_{\eta_{d+1}} = \bar{x}_{\eta_{d+1}}, \iota_d \neq \epsilon : \\[4pt]
\quad \sum_{\bar{x}_{\eta_d \iota_d},\, c_{\eta_d \iota_d}} \\[4pt]
\quad \cdot \left(\begin{array}{l} \mathsf{P}_{\theta_{\mathrm{G\text{-}RL}^*,d}}\left(c_{\eta_{d-1}\iota_{d-1}1} \xrightarrow{*} c_{\eta_d}\ \ldots\right) \\ \cdot \mathsf{P}_{\theta_{\mathrm{IC(G)},d}}\left(\bar{x}_{\eta_d}/\bar{x}_{\eta_d\iota_d},\, c_{\eta_d\iota_d} \mid c_{\eta_d}\right) \end{array} \right) \\[10pt]
\quad \cdot \sum_{\bar{x}_{\eta_d\iota_d 0},\, c_{\eta_d\iota_d 0}} \sum_{\kappa\ s.t.\ \bar{x}_{\eta_d\iota_d 0\kappa}=c_{\eta_d\iota_d 0\kappa}} \\[4pt]
\quad \left(\begin{array}{l} \mathsf{P}_{\theta_{\mathrm{G\text{-}RL}^*,d+1}}\left(c_{\eta_d\iota_d} \xrightarrow{*} c_{\eta_d\iota_d 0}\ \ldots\right) \\ \cdot \mathsf{P}_{\theta_{\mathrm{IC(G)},d+1}}\left(\bar{x}_{\eta_d\iota_d 0}/\bar{x}_{\eta_d\iota_d 0\kappa},\, c_{\eta_d\iota_d 0\kappa} \mid c_{\eta_d\iota_d 0}\right) \end{array} \right) \\[10pt]
\quad \cdot \left[\dfrac{\mathsf{P}_{\theta_{\mathrm{G\text{-}RL}^*,d+1}}\left(c_{\eta_d\iota_d} \xrightarrow{0} c_{\eta_d\iota_d 0}\ \ldots\right)}{\mathsf{P}_{\theta_{\mathrm{G\text{-}RL}^*,d+1}}\left(c_{\eta_d\iota_d} \xrightarrow{*} c_{\eta_d\iota_d 0}\ \ldots\right)} \cdot \llbracket \bar{x}_{\eta_d\iota_d 0\kappa} = c_{\eta_d\iota_d 0\kappa} \rrbracket \right] \\[10pt]
\quad \dfrac{\mathsf{P}_{\theta_{\mathrm{G\text{-}R},d}}\left(c_{\eta_d\iota_d} \to c_{\eta_d\iota_d 0}\ c_{\eta_d\iota_d 1}\right)}{\mathsf{E}_{\theta_{\mathrm{G\text{-}RL}^*,d+1}}\left(c_{\eta_d\iota_d} \xrightarrow{0} c_{\eta_d\iota_d 0}\ \ldots\right)} \\[12pt]
\text{if } c_{\eta_{d+1}} = \bar{x}_{\eta_{d+1}}, \iota_d = \epsilon : \\[4pt]
\quad \sum_{\bar{x}_{\eta_d 0},\, c_{\eta_d 0}} \sum_{\kappa\ s.t.\ \bar{x}_{\eta_d 0\kappa}=c_{\eta_d 0\kappa}} \\[4pt]
\quad \left(\begin{array}{l} \mathsf{P}_{\theta_{\mathrm{G\text{-}RL}^*,d}}\left(c_{\eta_{d-1}\iota_{d-1}1} \xrightarrow{*} c_{\eta_d 0}\ \ldots\right) \\ \cdot \mathsf{P}_{\theta_{\mathrm{IC(G)},d}}\left(\bar{x}_{\eta_d 0}/\bar{x}_{\eta_d 0\kappa},\, c_{\eta_d 0\kappa} \mid c_{\eta_d 0}\right) \end{array} \right) \\[10pt]
\quad \cdot \left[\dfrac{\mathsf{P}_{\theta_{\mathrm{G\text{-}RL}^*,d}}\left(c_{\eta_{d-1}\iota_{d-1}1} \xrightarrow{+} c_{\eta_d 0}\ \ldots\right)}{\mathsf{P}_{\theta_{\mathrm{G\text{-}RL}^*,d}}\left(c_{\eta_{d-1}\iota_{d-1}1} \xrightarrow{*} c_{\eta_d 0}\ \ldots\right)} \cdot \llbracket \bar{x}_{\eta_d 0\kappa} = c_{\eta_d 0\kappa} \rrbracket \right] \\[10pt]
\quad \cdot \dfrac{\mathsf{P}_{\theta_{\mathrm{G\text{-}RL}^*,d}}\left(c_{\eta_{d-1}\iota_{d-1}1} \xrightarrow{*} c_{\eta_d}\ \ldots\right)}{\mathsf{P}_{\theta_{\mathrm{G\text{-}RL}^*,d}}\left(c_{\eta_{d-1}\iota_{d-1}1} \xrightarrow{+} c_{\eta_d 0}\ \ldots\right)} \\[10pt]
\quad \cdot \mathsf{P}_{\theta_{\mathrm{G\text{-}L},d}}\left(c_{\eta_d} \to c_{\eta_d 0}\ c_{\eta_d 1}\right) \\[8pt]
\text{if } c_{\eta_{d+1}} \neq \bar{x}_{\eta_{d+1}} : \\[4pt]
\quad \left(\begin{array}{l} \mathsf{P}_{\theta_{\mathrm{G\text{-}RL}^*,d}}\left(c_{\eta_{d-1}\iota_{d-1}1} \xrightarrow{*} c_{\eta_d}\ \ldots\right) \\ \cdot \mathsf{P}_{\theta_{\mathrm{IC(G)},d}}\left(\bar{x}_{\eta_d}/\bar{x}_{\eta_d\iota_d},\, c_{\eta_d\iota_d} \mid c_{\eta_d}\right) \end{array} \right)
\end{cases}
\tag{25}
$$

Note that the left progeny probabilities above cancel out over time, leaving only the relevant original PCFG probabilities at the end of each sentence.

4 Parsing in a Factored Sequence Model

Store elements can now be abstracted away from (i.e. marginalized over) individual constituent structure addresses. Store elements are therefore defined to contain the only the active and awaited ($c_{s_t^d}^A$ and $c_{s_t^d}^W$) constituent categories necessary to compute an incomplete constituent probability:

$$
s_t^d \overset{\mathrm{def}}{=} \langle c_{s_t^d}^A, c_{s_t^d}^W \rangle \tag{26}
$$

$$
\overset{\mathrm{def}}{=} \langle c_{\eta_d}, c_{\eta_d\iota_d} \rangle \ s.t.\ \iota_d \in 1^+, \eta_d \in \eta_{d-1}\iota_{d-1}0^+ \tag{27}
$$

Reduction states are defined to contain only the complete constituent category $c_{r_t^d}$ necessary to compute an inside likelihood probability, as well as a flag $f_{r_t^d}$ indicating whether a reduction has taken place (to end a sequence of incomplete constituents):

$$
r_t^d \overset{\mathrm{def}}{=} \langle c_{r_t^d}, f_{r_t^d} \rangle \tag{28}
$$

$$
\overset{\mathrm{def}}{=} \langle c_{\eta_d}, \llbracket \bar{x}_{\eta_d} = c_{\eta_d} \rrbracket \rangle \tag{29}
$$

Since $\iota_d \in 1^+$, it follows that:

$$
x_{1..t} = \left(\bar{x}_{\eta_d}/\bar{x}_{\eta_d\iota_d}\right)_{d=1}^{D} \tag{30}
$$

This allows store elements to be abstracted away from (marginalized over) tree addresses in the calculation of forward or Viterbi probabilities:

$$
\mathsf{P}_{\theta_{\mathrm{Fwd}}}\left(x_{1..t}, s_t^{1..D}\right) =
$$
$$
\sum_{\eta_{1..D},\, \iota_{1..D}} \mathsf{P}_{\theta_{\mathrm{Fwd}}}\left(\left(\bar{x}_{\eta_d}/\bar{x}_{\eta_d\iota_d}1\right)_{d=1}^{D}, \left(c_{\eta_d}\right)_{d=1}^{D}, \left(c_{\eta_d\iota_d}1\right)_{d=1}^{D}\right)
\tag{31}
$$

Forward probabilities can then be factored into contributions from previous store states (θ_{Fwd} at $s_{t-1}^{1..D}$ below, parenthesized in Equation 25), reductions of terminal symbols (θ_{B} below, bracketed in Equation 25), and transition operations (θ_{A} below, not set apart in Equation 25):

$$
\mathsf{P}_{\theta_{\mathrm{Fwd}}}\left(x_{1..t}, s_t^{1..D}\right) =
$$
$$
\sum_{s_{t-1}^{1..D}} \mathsf{P}_{\theta_{\mathrm{Fwd}}}\left(x_{1..t-1}, s_{t-1}^{1..D}\right) \cdot \mathsf{P}_{\theta_{\mathrm{A}}}\left(s_t^{1..D} \mid s_{t-1}^{1..D}\right)
$$
$$
\cdot \mathsf{P}_{\theta_{\mathrm{B}}}\left(x_t \mid s_t^{1..D}\right) \tag{32}
$$

Probabilities for recognized sequences of incomplete constituents (Equations 8 through 13), and expected left progeny counts for unrecognized sequences of incomplete constituents (Equations 19 through 22) can be combined in a probabilistic push-down automaton with a bounded pushdown store (to simulate the bounded working memory store of a human comprehender). This is essentially an extension of a Hierarchical Hidden Markov Model (HHMM) (Murphy and Paskin, 2001), which obtains a most likely sequence of hidden store states $\hat{s}^{1..D}_{1..T}$ of some length T and some maximum depth D, given a sequence of observations (e.g. words) $x_{1..T}$:

$$\hat{s}^{1..D}_{1..T} \stackrel{\text{def}}{=} \underset{s^{1..D}_{1..T}}{\operatorname{argmax}} \prod_{t=1}^{T} \mathsf{P}_{\theta_A}(s^{1..D}_t \mid s^{1..D}_{t-1}) \cdot \mathsf{P}_{\theta_B}(x_t \mid s^{1..D}_t) \tag{33}$$

The model generates each successive store only after considering whether each nested sequence of incomplete constituents has completed and reduced:

$$\mathsf{P}_{\theta_A}(s^{1..D}_t \mid s^{1..D}_{t-1}) \stackrel{\text{def}}{=}$$
$$\sum_{r^1_t..r^D_t} \prod_{d=1}^{D} \mathsf{P}_{\theta_R}(r^d_t \mid r^{d+1}_t s^d_{t-1} s^{d-1}_t) \cdot \mathsf{P}_{\theta_S}(s^d_t \mid r^{d+1}_t r^d_t s^d_{t-1} s^{d-1}_t) \tag{34}$$

The model probabilities for these store elements and reduction states can then be defined (from Murphy and Paskin 2001) to expand a new incomplete constituent after a reduction has taken place ($f_{r^d_t} = 1$), transition along a sequence of store elements if no reduction has taken place ($f_{r^d_t} = 0$):

$$\mathsf{P}_{\theta_S}(s^d_t \mid r^{d+1}_t r^d_t s^d_{t-1} s^{d-1}_t) \stackrel{\text{def}}{=}$$
$$\begin{cases} \text{if } f_{r^{d+1}_t} = 1, \ f_{r^d_t} = 1 : \mathsf{P}_{\theta_{S\text{-}E,d}}(s^d_t \mid s^{d-1}_t) \\ \text{if } f_{r^{d+1}_t} = 1, \ f_{r^d_t} = 0 : \mathsf{P}_{\theta_{S\text{-}T,d}}(s^d_t \mid r^{d+1}_t r^d_t s^d_{t-1} s^{d-1}_t) \\ \text{if } f_{r^{d+1}_t} = 0, \ f_{r^d_t} = 0 : [\![s^d_t = s^d_{t-1}]\!] \end{cases} \tag{35}$$

and possibly reduce a store element (terminate a sequence) if the store state below it has reduced ($f_{r^{d+1}_t} = 1$):

$$\mathsf{P}_{\theta_R}(r^d_t \mid r^{d+1}_t s^d_{t-1} s^{d-1}_{t-1}) \stackrel{\text{def}}{=}$$
$$\begin{cases} \text{if } f_{r^{d+1}_t} = 0 : [\![r^d_t = \mathbf{r}_\perp]\!] \\ \text{if } f_{r^{d+1}_t} = 1 : \mathsf{P}_{\theta_{R\text{-}R,d}}(r^d_t \mid r^{d+1}_t s^d_{t-1} s^{d-1}_{t-1}) \end{cases} \tag{36}$$

where $s^0_t = \mathbf{s}_\top$ and $r^{D+1}_t = \mathbf{r}_\top$ for constants $\mathbf{s}_\top$ (an incomplete root constituent), $\mathbf{r}_\top$ (a complete lexical constituent) and $\mathbf{r}_\perp$ (a null state resulting from the

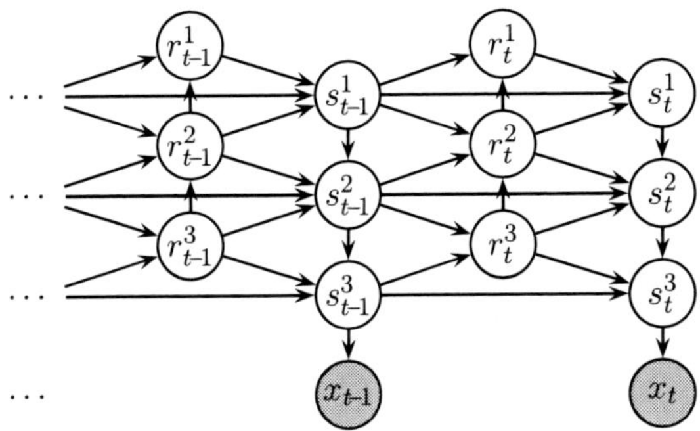

Figure 1: Graphical representation of the dependency structure in a standard Hierarchic Hidden Markov Model with $D = 3$ hidden levels that can be used to parse syntax. Circles denote random variables, and edges denote conditional dependencies. Shaded circles denote variables with observed values.

failure of an incomplete constituent to complete). The model is shown graphically in Figure 1.

These pushdown automaton operations are then refined for right-corner parsing (from Schuler 2009), distinguishing active transitions $\theta_{S\text{-}T\text{-}A,d}$ (in which an incomplete constituent is completed, but not reduced, and then immediately expanded to a new incomplete constituent in the same store element) from awaited transitions $\theta_{S\text{-}T\text{-}W,d}$ (which involve no completion):

$$\mathsf{P}_{\theta_{S\text{-}T,d}}(s^d_t \mid r^{d+1}_t r^d_t s^d_{t-1} s^{d-1}_t) \stackrel{\text{def}}{=}$$
$$\begin{cases} \text{if } r^d_t = \mathbf{r}_\perp : \mathsf{P}_{\theta_{S\text{-}T\text{-}A,d}}(s^d_t \mid s^d_{t-1} r^{d+1}_t) \\ \text{if } r^d_t \neq \mathbf{r}_\perp : \mathsf{P}_{\theta_{S\text{-}T\text{-}W,d}}(s^d_t \mid s^{d-1}_t r^d_t) \end{cases} \tag{37}$$

$$\mathsf{P}_{\theta_{R\text{-}R,d}}(r^d_t \mid r^{d+1}_t s^d_{t-1} s^{d-1}_{t-1}) \stackrel{\text{def}}{=}$$
$$\begin{cases} \text{if } c_{r^{d+1}_t} = x_t : \mathsf{P}_{\theta_{R\text{-}R,d}}(r^d_t \mid s^d_{t-1} s^{d-1}_{t-1}) \\ \text{if } c_{r^{d+1}_t} \neq x_t : [\![r^d_t = \mathbf{r}_\perp]\!] \end{cases} \tag{38}$$

These right-corner parsing operations then construct a full inside probability decompositions, using Equations 8 through 13 and Equations 19 through 22, marginalizing out all constituents that are not required in each term:

- for expansions:

$$\mathsf{P}_{\theta_{S\text{-}E,d}}(\langle c_{\eta\iota}, c'_{\eta\iota} \rangle \mid \langle -, c_\eta \rangle) \stackrel{\text{def}}{=}$$
$$\mathsf{E}_{\theta_{G\text{-}RL^*,d}}(c_\eta \stackrel{*}{\to} c_{\eta\iota} \ldots) \cdot [\![x_{\eta\iota} = c'_{\eta\iota} = c_{\eta\iota}]\!] \tag{39}$$

a) binarized phrase structure tree:

b) result of right-corner transform:

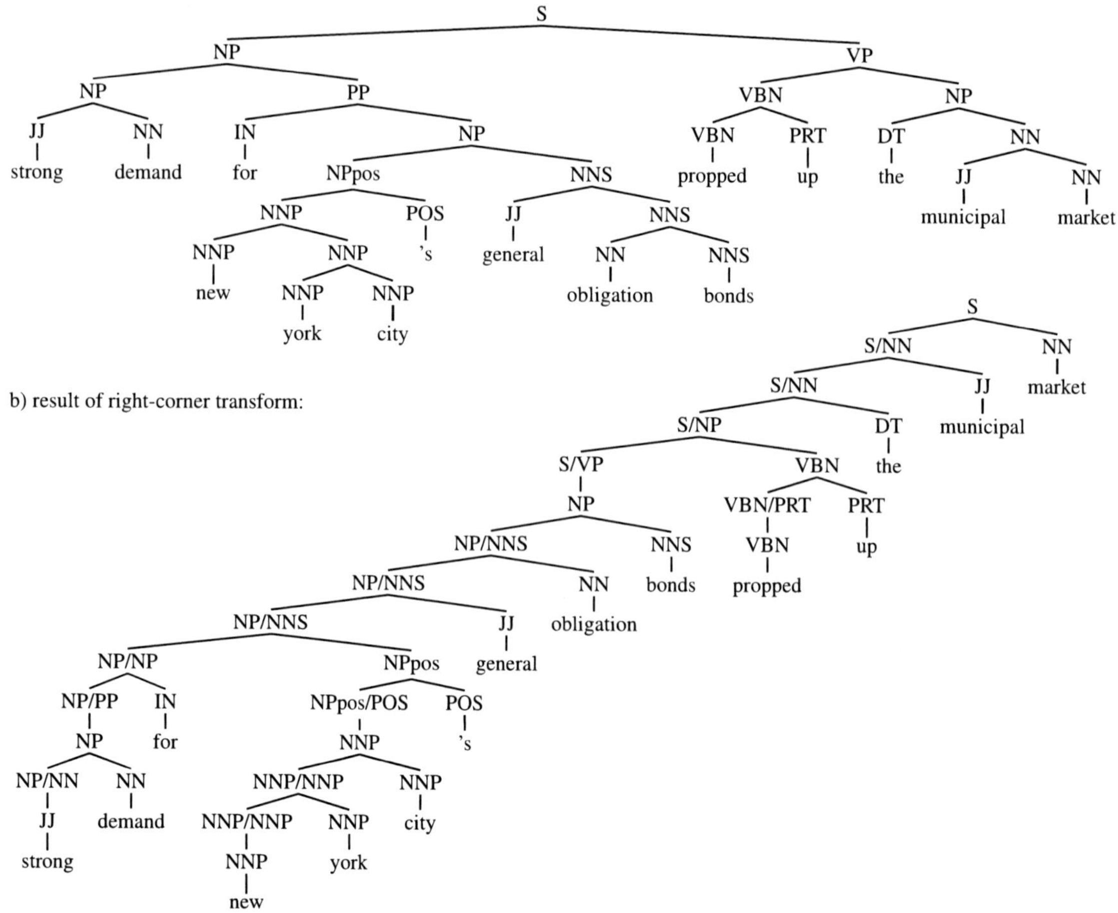

Figure 2: (a) Sample binarized phrase structure tree for the sentence *Strong demand for New York City's general obligations bonds propped up the municipal market,* and (b) a right-corner transform of this binarized tree.

- for awaited transitions, from Equation 11:

$$P_{\theta_{\text{S-T-w},d}}(\langle c_\eta, c_{\eta\iota 1}\rangle \mid \langle c'_\eta, c_{\eta\iota}\rangle\, c_{\eta\iota 0}) \overset{\text{def}}{=}$$

$$[\![c_\eta = c'_\eta]\!] \cdot \frac{P_{\theta_{\text{G-R},d}}(c_{\eta\iota} \to c_{\eta\iota 0}\, c_{\eta\iota 1})}{\mathsf{E}_{\theta_{\text{G-RL}^*,d}}(c_{\eta\iota} \overset{0}{\to} c_{\eta\iota 0}\ \ldots)} \quad (40)$$

- for active transitions, from Equations 8 and 13:

$$P_{\theta_{\text{S-T-A},d}}(\langle c_{\eta\iota}, c_{\eta\iota 1}\rangle \mid \langle -, c_\eta\rangle\, c_{\eta\iota 0}) \overset{\text{def}}{=}$$

$$\frac{\mathsf{E}_{\theta_{\text{G-RL}^*,d}}(c_\eta \overset{*}{\to} c_{\eta\iota}\ \ldots) \cdot P_{\theta_{\text{G-L},d}}(c_{\eta\iota} \to c_{\eta\iota 0}\, c_{\eta\iota 1})}{\mathsf{E}_{\theta_{\text{G-RL}^*,d}}(c_\eta \overset{+}{\to} c_{\eta\iota 0}\ \ldots)}$$

$$(41)$$

- for cross-element reductions:

$$P_{\theta_{\text{R-R},d}}(c_{\eta\iota}, 1 \mid \langle -, c_\eta\rangle\, \langle c'_{\eta\iota}, -\rangle) \overset{\text{def}}{=}$$

$$[\![c_{\eta\iota} = c'_{\eta\iota}]\!] \cdot \frac{\mathsf{E}_{\theta_{\text{G-RL}^*,d}}(c_\eta \overset{0}{\to} c_{\eta\iota}\ \ldots)}{\mathsf{E}_{\theta_{\text{G-RL}^*,d}}(c_\eta \overset{*}{\to} c_{\eta\iota}\ \ldots)} \quad (42)$$

- for in-element reductions:

$$P_{\theta_{\text{R-R},d}}(c_{\eta\iota}, 0 \mid \langle -, c_\eta\rangle\, \langle c'_{\eta\iota}, -\rangle) \overset{\text{def}}{=}$$

$$[\![c_{\eta\iota} = c'_{\eta\iota}]\!] \cdot \frac{\mathsf{E}_{\theta_{\text{G-RL}^*,d}}(c_\eta \overset{+}{\to} c_{\eta\iota}\ \ldots)}{\mathsf{E}_{\theta_{\text{G-RL}^*,d}}(c_\eta \overset{*}{\to} c_{\eta\iota}\ \ldots)} \quad (43)$$

A sample phrase structure tree is shown as a right-corner transformed recursive structure in Figure 2,

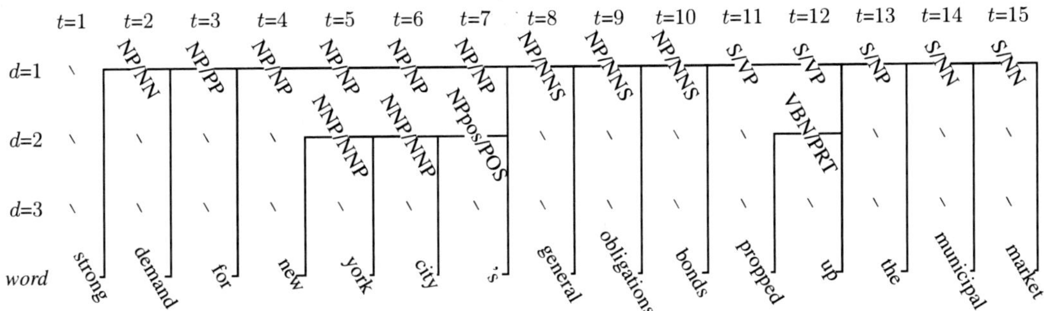

Figure 3: Sample tree from Figure 2 mapped to s_t^d variable positions of an HHMM at each depth level d (vertical) and time step t (horizontal). This tree uses at most only two memory store elements. Values for reduction states r_t^d are not shown.

5 Discussion

This paper has presented a derivation of a factored probabilistic sequence model from a probabilistic context-free grammar, using a right-corner transform to minimize memory usage in incremental processing. This sequence model characterization is attractive as a cognitive model because it does not posit any internal representation of complex phrasal structure beyond the pair of categories in each incomplete constituent resulting from the application of a right-corner transform; and because these incomplete constituents represent contiguous connected chunks of phrase structure, in line with characterizations of chunking in working memory (Miller, 1956). Experiments on large phrase-structure annotated corpora (Marcus et al., 1993) show this model could process the vast majority of sentences in a typical newspaper using only three or four store elements (Schuler et al., 2008; Schuler et al., 2010), in line with recent estimates of human short-term working memory capacity (Cowan, 2001).

This derivation can be applied to efficiently in-crementalize any PCFG model, preserving the probabilistic dependencies in the original model. But, since the model is ultimately defined through transitions on entire working memory stores, it is also possible to relax the independence assumptions from the original PCFG model, and introduce additional dependencies across store elements that do not correspond to context-free dependencies. These additional dependencies might be used approximate dependencies of mildly context-sensitive grammar formalisms like tree adjoining grammars (Joshi, 1985), e.g. to model long-distance dependencies in filler-gap constructions (Kroch and Joshi, 1986), or crossed and nested dependencies in languages like Dutch (Shieber, 1985).

Figure 4 shows a sample store sequence corresponding to a parse of a noun phrase modified by an object relative clause. Here, the affix '-xNP' is used to identify a phrase containing an extracted NP constituent, and the category label 'GCnpS' is used to identify the maximal projection of a gapped clause. If the GC constituent (and only this constituent) is associated with the referent or dependency information of the filler constituent (the bike in this example), this information can be made available during processing from the immediately superior incomplete constituent at the gap position in the relative clause, without passing dependency information down the tree as any kind of feature (Pollard and Sag, 1994), even though this position is not adjacent to the filler in the phrase structure tree (they are separated by the referent or dependency information of the bridge verb 'said'). This is important to

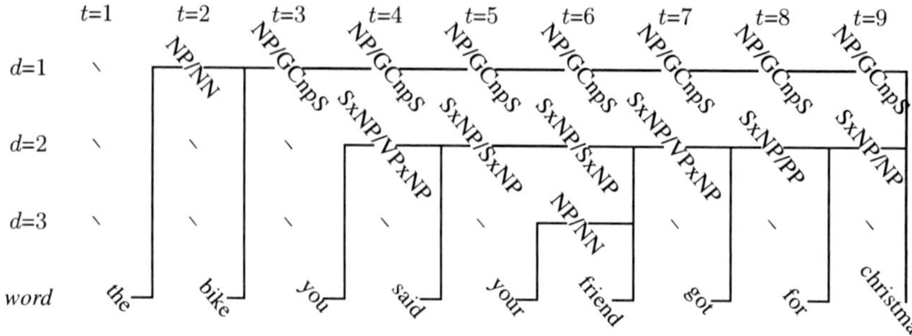

Figure 4: Sample store sequence containing long-distance dependency in a filler-gap construction.

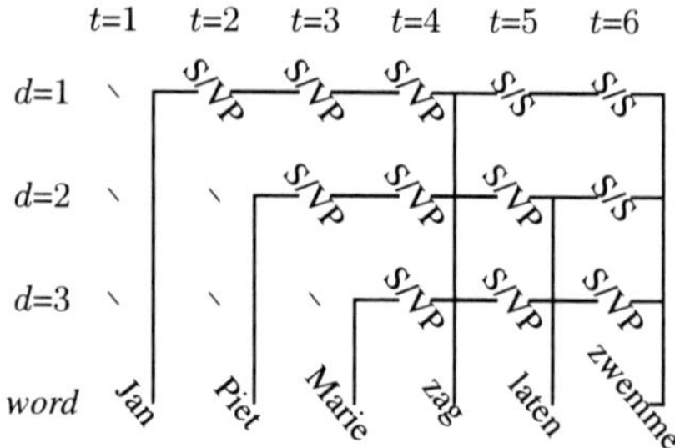

Figure 5: Sample store sequence containing crossed and nested dependencies.

satisfy claims that the model constructs chunks only for contiguous dependency structures (which is not true of propagated 'slash' features.

Figure 5 shows a sample store sequence corresponding to a parse of a Dutch sentence containing crossed and nested dependencies, featuring reductions across non-adjacent depth levels. This requires a more severe relaxation of PCFG independence assumptions, and is beyond the capacity of the HHMM as defined above, but this does preserve the notion of incomplete constituents and general composition established above, and is not beyond the capacity of factored sequence models with human-like memory bounds in general (note that the example sentence can still be parsed with only three store elements). This suggests a promising avenue of generalizing this model to learn parsing transitions that may be broader than those of a strict pushdown automaton.

References

Richard Bellman. 1957. *Dynamic Programming.* Princeton University Press, Princeton, NJ.

Nelson Cowan. 2001. The magical number 4 in short-term memory: A reconsideration of mental storage capacity. *Behavioral and Brain Sciences*, 24:87–185.

Aravind K. Joshi. 1985. How much context sensitivity is necessary for characterizing structural descriptions: Tree adjoining grammars. In L. Karttunen D. Dowty and A. Zwicky, editors, *Natural language parsing: Psychological, computational and theoretical perspectives*, pages 206–250. Cambridge University Press, Cambridge, U.K.

Anthony S. Kroch and Aravind K. Joshi. 1986. The linguistic relevance of tree adjoining grammars. *Linguistics and Philosophy*.

Mitchell P. Marcus, Beatrice Santorini, and Mary Ann Marcinkiewicz. 1993. Building a large annotated corpus of English: the Penn Treebank. *Computational Linguistics*, 19(2):313–330.

George A. Miller. 1956. The magical number seven, plus or minus two: Some limits on our capacity for processing information. *Psychological Review*, 63:81–97.

Kevin P. Murphy and Mark A. Paskin. 2001. Linear time inference in hierarchical HMMs. In *Proc. NIPS*, pages 833–840, Vancouver, BC, Canada.

Carl Pollard and Ivan Sag. 1994. *Head-driven Phrase Structure Grammar*. University of Chicago Press, Chicago.

William Schuler, Samir AbdelRahman, Tim Miller, and Lane Schwartz. 2008. Toward a psycholinguistically-motivated model of language. In *Proceedings of COLING*, pages 785–792, Manchester, UK, August.

William Schuler, Samir AbdelRahman, Tim Miller, and Lane Schwartz. 2010. Broad-coverage incremental parsing using human-like memory constraints. *Computational Linguistics*, 36(1).

William Schuler. 2009. Parsing with a bounded stack using a model-based right-corner transform. In *Proceedings of NAACL*, pages 344–352, Boulder, Colorado.

Stuart Shieber. 1985. Evidence against the context-freeness of natural language. *Linguistics and Philosophy*, 8:333–343.

Non-local Right-Node Raising: an Analysis using Delayed Tree-Local MC-TAG[*]

Chung-hye Han
Department of Linguistics
Simon Fraser University
chunghye@sfu.ca

David Potter
Department of Linguistics
Simon Fraser University
dkp1@sfu.ca

Dennis Ryan Storoshenko
Department of Linguistics
Simon Fraser University
dstorosh@sfu.ca

Abstract

In this paper, we show that the analysis of right-node-raising (RNR) in coordinate structures proposed in Sarkar and Joshi (1996) can be extended to non-local RNR if it is augmented with delayed tree locality (Chiang and Scheffler, 2008), but not with flexible composition (Joshi et al., 2003). In the proposed delayed tree-local analysis, we define multicomponent (MC) elementary tree sets with contraction set specification. We propose that a member of each of the MC sets participates in forming a derivational unit called *contraction path* in the derivation structure, and that contraction paths must be derivationally local to each other for the relevant contraction to be licensed.

1 Introduction

The term right node raising (RNR) was coined by Ross (1967) to describe constructions such as (1), in which an element, here the DP *the theory*, appears to be syntactically and semantically shared at the right periphery of the rightmost conjunct of a coordinate structure.[1] Furthermore, RNR may share an element at unbounded embedding depths (Wexler and Culicover, 1980). In (2)-(5), the shared argument is the object of the verb complement clauses, relative clauses, adjunct clauses and DPs embedded in the coordinating clauses.[2] We can thus characterize examples such as (1) as local RNR and examples such

as (2)-(5) as non-local RNR.[3]

(1) [John likes __] and [Tim dislikes **the theory**].

(2) [John thought you paid __] and [Tim insisted you didn't pay **the rent**].

(3) [John likes the professor who taught __] and [Tim dislikes the student who debunked **the theory**].

(4) [John left before he heard __] and [Mary came after Sue announced **the good news**].

(5) [John likes the big book __] and [Tim likes the small book **of poetry**].

Early transformational analyses, e.g. Ross (1967), explained RNR by extending the standard notion of movement to allow across-the-board (ATB) movement, in which two underlying copies of the shared material are identified during movement, yielding a single overt copy located ex situ, outside of the coordinate structure. This type of analysis implies that, apart from the ATB aspect of the movement, RNR should otherwise behave as typical movement. This prediction is not borne out, however, as RNR is freely able to violate both the island constraints and the right-roof constraint. In example (3), the DP *the theory* is the argument of the verbs in the relative clauses, which are complex noun phrase islands. Under the ex situ analysis, depicted in (6), the shared argument raises out of the coordinate structure, thereby also escaping the complex noun phrase island. Such movement also violates the right-roof constraint, which limits rightward movement to a landing site one bounding node above the source (Sabbagh, 2007). If the relevant bounding nodes are vP and TP and the shared argument is merged under vP, movement outside of the coordinated TP structure would violate this constraint. Such behaviours

---

[*]We thank the anonymous reviewers of TAG+10 for their insightful comments. All remaining errors are ours. This work was partially supported by NSERC RGPIN/341442 to Han.

[1]Subsequently, RNR has been shown to apply to noncoordinate structures as well. These will be discussed in Section 5.

[2]Here we discuss only examples with shared arguments; see Potter (2010) for discussion of shared modifiers in an analysis similar to Sarkar and Joshi (1996).

---

[3]Examples of RNR require stress on the contrasting elements (Hartmann, 2000; Féry and Hartmann, 2005).

are unpredicted if RNR is derived from movement of the shared element to a position outside of the coordinate structure.

(6) $[_{TP}$ John $[_{vP}$ likes the professor who taught t_i $]]$ and $[_{TP}$ Tim $[_{vP}$ dislikes the student who debunked t_i $]]$ **the theory**$_i$.

While some attempt has been made to explain the unpredicted behaviour of RNR in the ex situ analysis, e.g. Sabbagh (2007), an alternative approach to RNR is available which circumvents these complications by locating the shared elements in situ. Sarkar and Joshi (1996) propose such an in situ analysis using Tree Adjoining Grammar (TAG), positing that the shared element is located in the canonical position within the rightmost conjunct. One significant consequence of this analysis is that the contrast between movement and RNR requires no explanation; RNR is not derived from movement, and thus their differences in behaviour are unremarkable.

However, the implementation of Sarkar and Joshi's analysis does make clear predictions for the locality of RNR: it predicts that non-local RNR is illicit. As will be discussed in Section 2, the mechanism proposed by Sarkar and Joshi only permits sharing between two elementary trees that are directly composed. Thus, examples such as (1), in which the shared element *the theory* is an object of the two clauses being coordinated, are permitted. On the other hand, examples such as (2)-(5) are excluded, as the shared arguments in these examples are not objects of the coordinated clauses, but rather objects of clauses embedded within the coordinated clauses. Thus, an unattested contrast in grammaticality is again predicted, in this case between local and non-local RNR.

The remainder of this paper is organized as follows. In Section 2, we first illustrate how local RNR is handled in Sarkar and Joshi (1996), using elementary trees that conform to Frank's (2002) Condition on Elementary Tree Minimality (CETM). We then demonstrate how the mechanisms in Sarkar and Joshi cannot derive instances of non-local RNR with standard TAG. We consider two ways of augmenting the analysis, one with delayed tree locality (Chiang and Scheffler 2008) in Section 3, and the other with flexible composition (Joshi et al. 2003) in Section 4. We show that only the analysis with delayed

tree locality yields well-formed derivation in TAG. In Section 5, we briefly discuss cases of noncoordinate RNR and show that our proposed analysis can be extended to these cases as well.

2 Sarkar and Joshi 1996

Sarkar and Joshi utilize elementary trees with contraction sets and coordinating auxiliary trees. The elementary trees necessary to derive (1) are illustrated in Figure 1. Note that (αthe_theory) is a valid elementary tree conforming to Frank's CETM, as a noun can form an extended projection with a DP, in line with the DP Hypothesis. Also, elementary trees such as (βand_dislikes$_{\{DP\}}$) are in accordance with CETM, as coordinators are functional heads (Potter 2010). In each of (αlikes$_{\{DP\}}$) and (βand_dislikes$_{\{DP\}}$), the object DP node is in the contraction set, notated as a subscript in the tree name and marked in the tree with a circle around it, and represents a shared argument. When (βand_dislikes$_{\{DP\}}$) adjoins to (αlikes$_{\{DP\}}$), the two trees will undergo contraction, sharing the node in the contraction set. Effectively, in the derived tree, the two nodes are identified, merging into one, and in the derivation tree, a DP simultaneously substitutes into the contraction nodes.

The derived and derivation structures are given in Figure 2. In (δ1), (αthe_theory) substitutes into (αlikes$_{\{DP\}}$) and (βand_dislikes$_{\{DP\}}$) simultaneously at the DP node, and in (γ1), the object DPs are merged into one. These are thus directed graphs: a single node is dominated by multiple nodes. Looking at (δ1) again, the elementary trees that are contracted are local to each other derivationally: (αlikes$_{\{DP\}}$) immediately dominates (βand_dislikes$_{\{DP\}}$). It is this local relationship that licenses contraction.

However, in instances of non-local RNR, this local relationship does not obtain. The intended derived structure for (3), for example, is given in Figure 5, using the elementary trees in Figures 1 and 3.[4] But the structure in Figure 5 cannot be generated with the given elementary trees, as it would require an illicit derivation, de-

---

[4]Note that (αlikes) and (βand_dislikes) trees are same as (αlikes$_{\{DP\}}$) and (βand_dislikes$_{\{DP\}}$), except that these do not have contraction nodes.

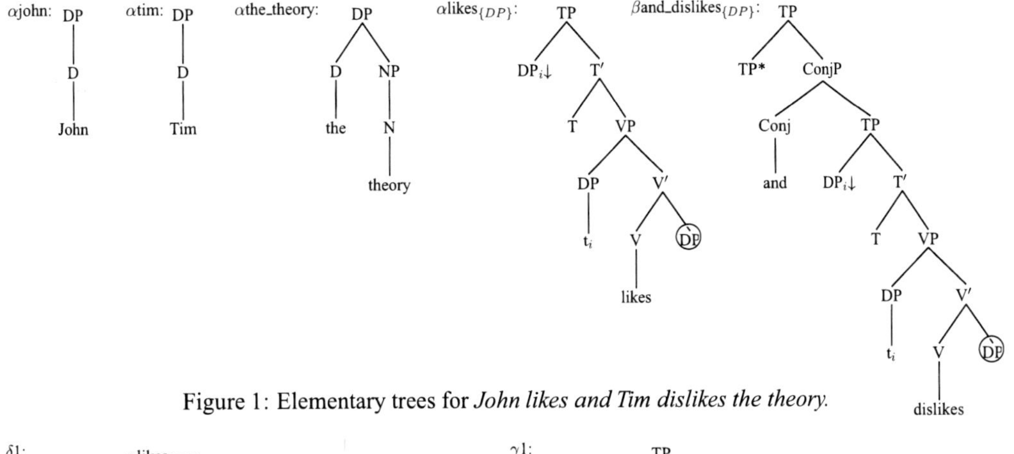

Figure 1: Elementary trees for *John likes and Tim dislikes the theory*.

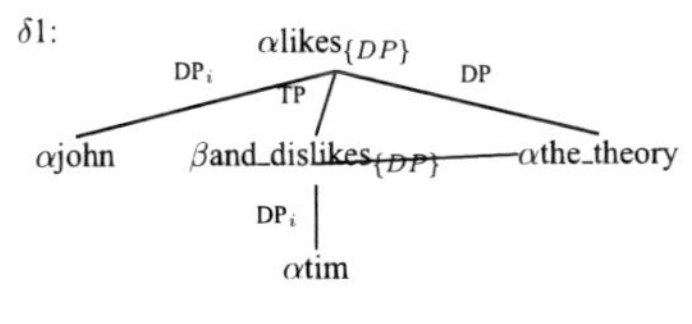

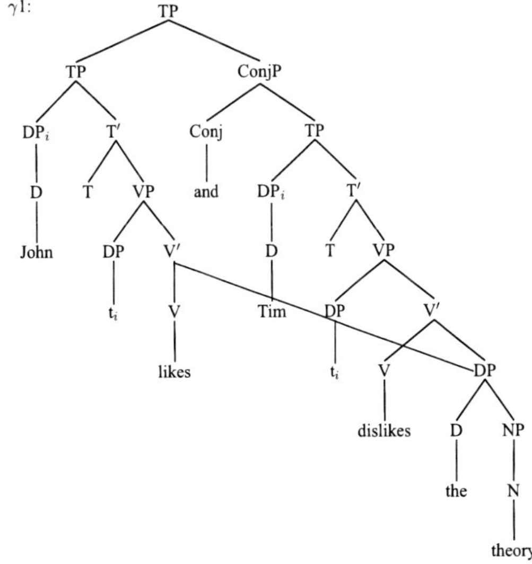

Figure 2: Derivation and derived structures for *John likes and Tim dislikes the theory*.

picted in Figure 4. Here, contraction must occur between the two relative clause elementary trees (βtaught$_{\{DP\}}$) and (βdebunked$_{\{DP\}}$). These relative clause trees though are not derivationally local to each other: they must each adjoin to the DP trees (αthe_professor) and (αthe_student) which in turn must substitute into the object positions of (αlikes) and (βand_dislikes).

3 Derivation using Delayed Tree-Local MC-TAG

To address this problem, we augment Sarkar and Joshi's analysis with delayed tree locality. As defined in Chiang and Scheffler, delayed tree-local multi-component (MC) TAG allows members of an

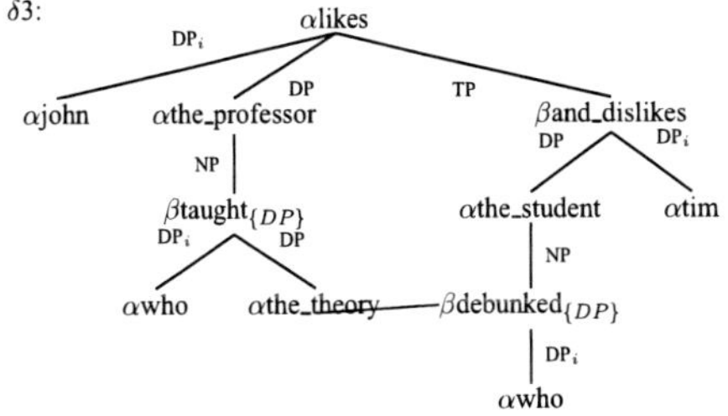

Figure 4: Illegal derivation structure for *John likes the professor who taught and Tim dislikes the student who debunked the theory* using standard TAG

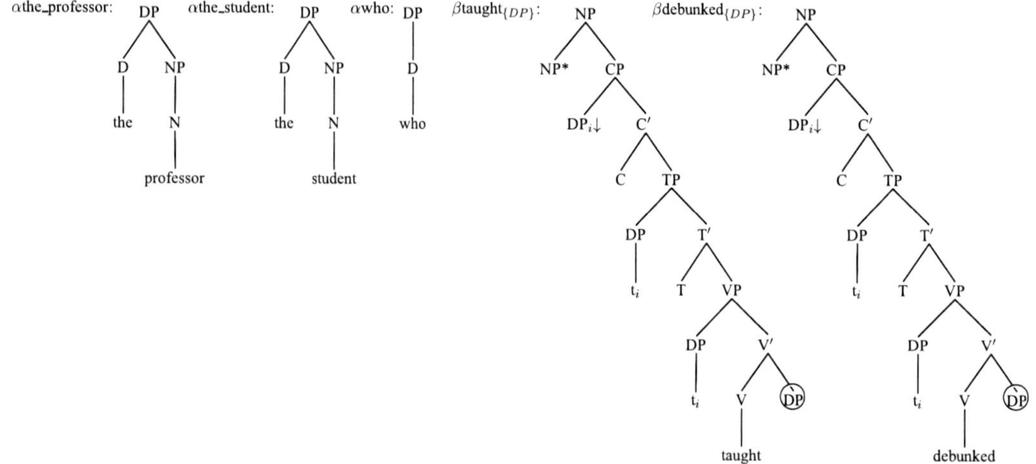

Figure 3: Elementary trees for *John likes the professor who taught and Tim dislikes the student who debunked the theory.*

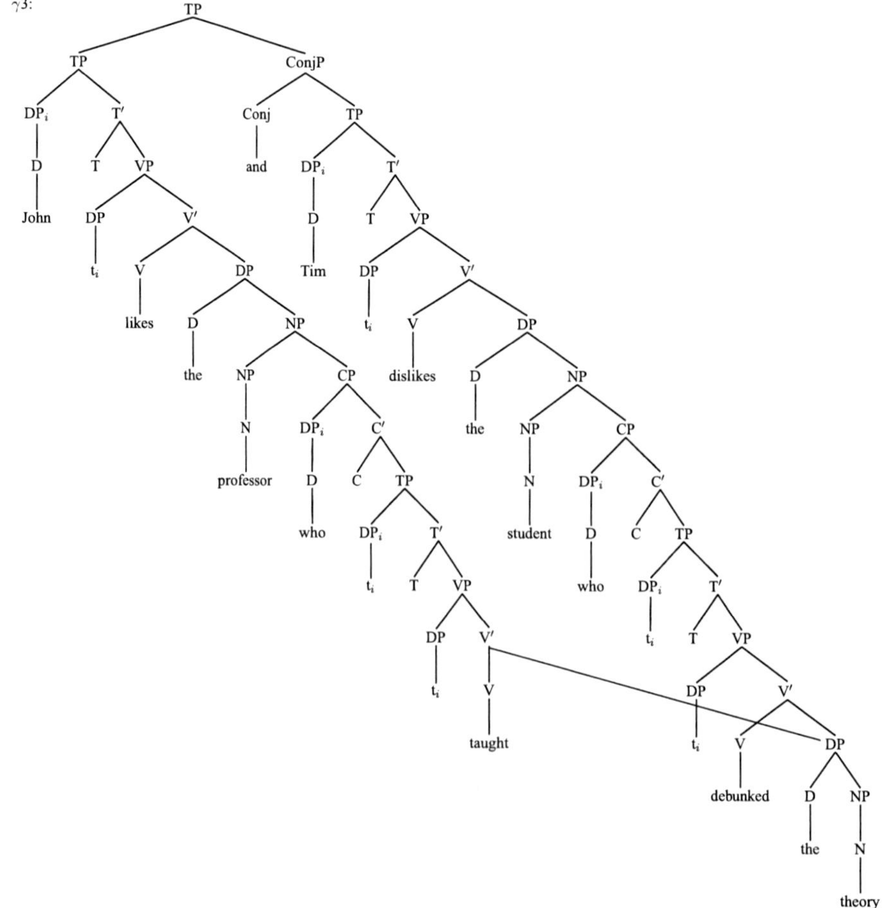

Figure 5: Derived structure for *John likes the professor who taught and Tim dislikes the student who debunked the theory.*

MC set to compose with different elementary trees as long as the members eventually compose into the same elementary tree. In the derivation structure, the members of the MC set do not need to be immediately dominated by a single node, though there must be a node that dominates all the members of the MC set. The lowest such node is called the *destination* of an MC set. The *delay* of an MC set is the union of the paths from the destination to each member of the MC set, excluding the destination itself.

In deriving (3), we propose MC elementary tree sets for relative clauses with shared nodes, as in Figure 6. We postulate a structural constraint between the two trees in the MC set: the degenerate tree component must dominate the relative clause tree component in the derived structure.

In effect, with the addition of the MC tree sets such as those in Figure 6, the specification of contraction sets is now divorced from the elementary trees that compose through coordination. To accommodate this separation, we need to extend the licensing condition for contraction. We take an elementary tree participating in coordination and the immediately dominated degenerate tree with contraction set as a derivational unit, and call it a *contraction path*. We propose that contraction between two MC sets A and B is licensed if A and B have corresponding contraction sets, and the contraction path containing the degenerate tree component of A either immediately dominates or is immediately dominated by the contraction path containing the degenerate tree component of B.

The delayed tree-local derivation for (3) is depicted in the derivation structure in Figure 7, generating the derived structure in Figure 5. (βtaught1$_{\{DP\}}$) adjoins to (αthe_professor), and (βtaught2$_{\{DP\}}$), a degenerate tree, adjoins to the TP node of (αlikes). (βand_dislikes) adjoins to this TP, and (βdebunked2$_{\{DP\}}$) adjoins to the TP of (βand_dislikes). (βdebunked1$_{\{DP\}}$) adjoins to (αthe_student) which substitutes into (βand_dislikes). The delay of the (taught$_{\{DP\}}$) MC set is $\{($\beta$taught1$_{\{DP\}}$), ($\beta$taught2$_{\{DP\}}$), ($\alpha$the_professor)$\}$ and the delay of the (debunked$_{\{DP\}}$) MC set is $\{($\beta$debunked1$_{\{DP\}}$), ($\beta$debunked2$_{\{DP\}}$), ($\alpha$the_student)$\}$. As no derivation node is a member of more than one delay, this is a 1-delayed tree-local MC-TAG derivation. In this

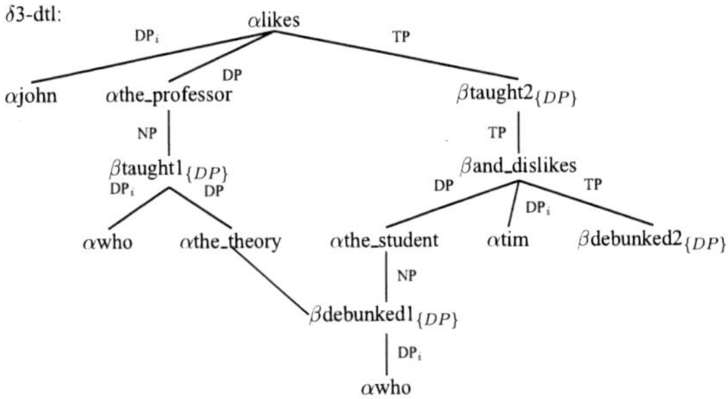

Figure 7: Derivation structure for *John likes the professor who taught and Tim dislikes the student who debunked the theory* with delayed tree locality

derivation, (αlikes) and (βtaught2$_{\{DP\}}$) form a contraction path, which immediately dominates another contraction path, made up of (βand_dislikes), a coordinating auxiliary tree, and (βdebunked2$_{\{DP\}}$), a degenerate tree with a corresponding contraction set specification. As the two paths are local to each other, contraction of the object DPs in the relative clause trees, (βtaught1$_{\{DP\}}$) and (βdebunked1$_{\{DP\}}$), is licensed.

The proposed analysis can rule out (7), where RNR has taken place across a coordinating clause without a shared argument.

(7)   * [John likes the professor who taught _] and [Tim dislikes the student who took the course] and [Sue hates the postdoc who debunked **the theory**].

Due to the domination constraint between the two trees in the MC set, the only plausible derivation is as in Figure 8. But node contraction is not licensed in this derivation, as the two contraction paths, one containing (αlikes) and (βtaught2$_{\{DP\}}$), and the other containing (βand_hates) and (βdebunked2$_{\{DP\}}$), are separated by (βand_dislikes). As the two paths are not derivationally local to each other, contraction between the relative clauses is not licensed.

Local RNR can also be accounted for in terms of the proposed MC set with the contraction set specification, and contraction paths. Returning to (1), its derivation structure can be recast as in Figure 10, using the MC sets in Figure 9. In Chiang and Scheffler's definition of delayed tree-local MC-TAG, one member of an MC set is allowed

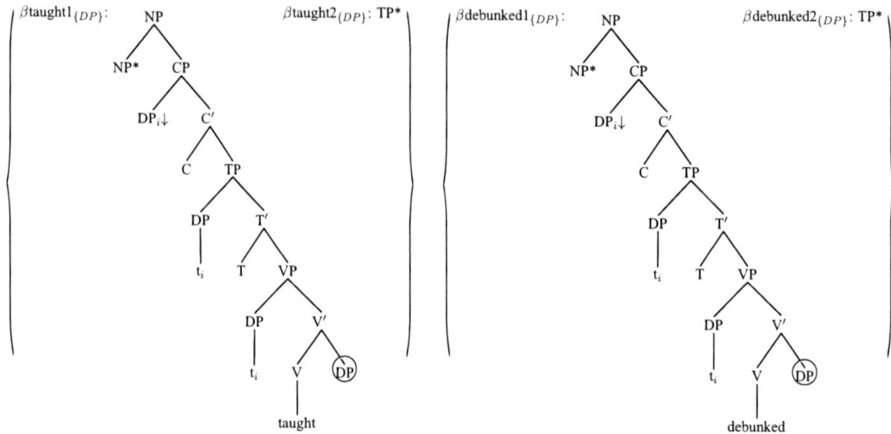

Figure 6: MC sets for relative clauses with contraction sets

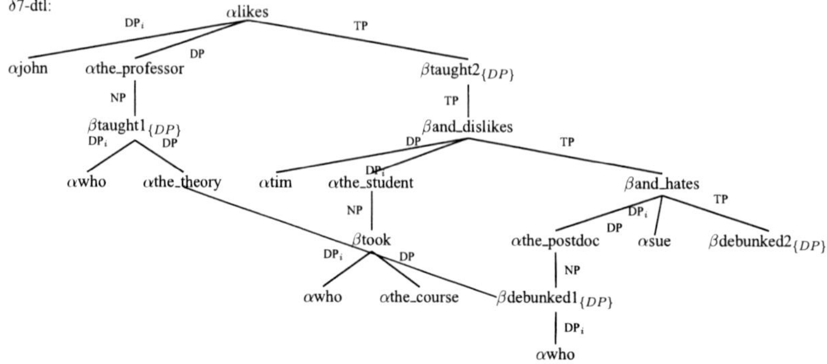

Figure 8: Illegal derivation structure for *John likes the professor who taught and Tim dislikes the student who took the course and Sue hates the postdoc who debunked the theory*

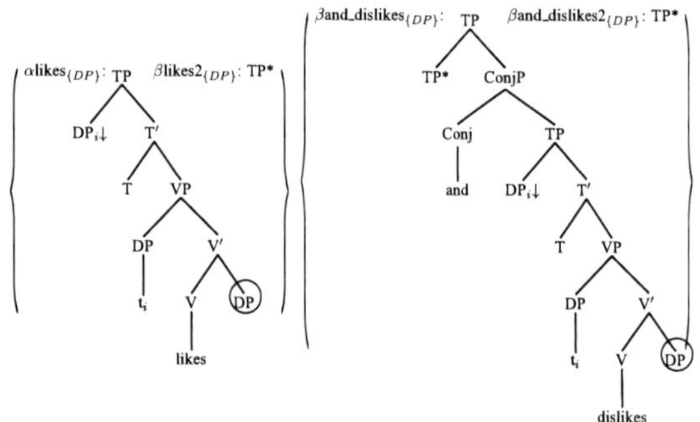

Figure 9: MC sets for *likes* and *and_dislikes* with contraction sets

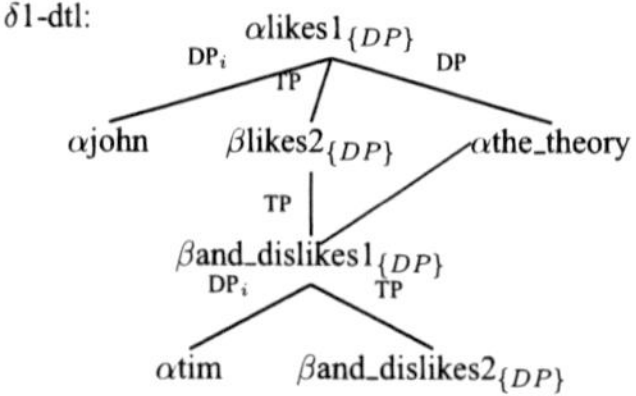

Figure 10: Delayed tree-local derivation for *John likes and Tim dislikes the theory*

4 Derivation using Flexible Composition

to adjoin into another. As such, in Figure 10, (βlikes2$_{\{DP\}}$) adjoins to (αlikes1$_{\{DP\}}$), forming one contraction path, and (βand_dislikes2$_{\{DP\}}$) adjoins to (βand_dislikes1$_{\{DP\}}$), forming another. The two contraction paths are in immediate domination relation, licensing the contraction of the object DPs.

We now attempt to augment Sarkar and Joshi's analysis with tree-local MC-TAG with flexible composition. Flexible composition can be seen as reverse-adjoining: instead of β adjoining onto α at node η, α splits at η and wraps around β. By reversing the adjoining this way, tree-locality can be preserved in an otherwise non-local MC-TAG derivation.

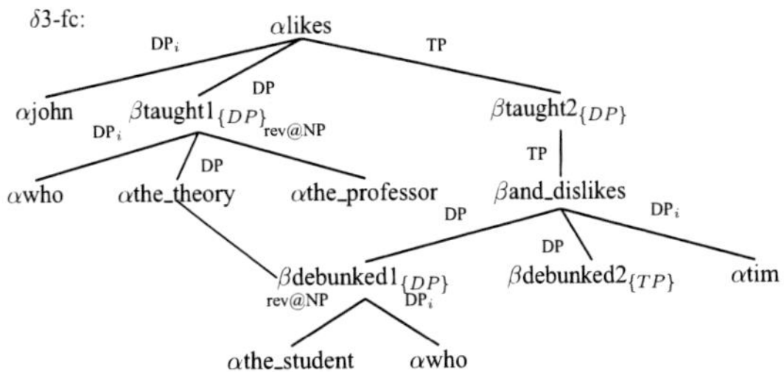

Figure 11: Illegal derivation structure for *John likes the professor who taught and Tim dislikes the student who debunked the theory* with flexible composition

As depicted in the derivation structure in Figure 11, flexible composition seems to keep the derivation tree-local: (αthe_professor) reverse-adjoins to (βtaught1$_{\{DP\}}$) which in turn substitutes into (αlikes), and (βtaught2$_{\{DP\}}$), the other component of the (taught$_{\{DP\}}$) MC set adjoins to (αlikes). And (βand_dislikes) adjoins to (βtaught2$_{\{DP\}}$), (βdebunked2$_{\{DP\}}$) adjoins to (βand_dislikes), and (αthe_student) reverse-adjoins to (βdebunked1$_{\{DP\}}$), which allows (βdebunked1$_{\{DP\}}$) to substitute into (βand_dislikes). The contraction path containing (αlikes) and (βtaught2$_{\{DP\}}$) and the one containing (βand_dislikes) and (βdebunked2$_{\{DP\}}$) are local to each other, and so contraction between the relative clauses should in principle be possible.

But there is a problem with this derivation: it substitutes (βtaught1$_{\{DP\}}$) and (βdebunked1$_{\{DP\}}$) into (αlikes) and (βand_dislikes) respectively. This is problematic because these substitutions are using new DP nodes created by the reverse-adjoining of (αthe_professor) to (βtaught1) and (αthe_student) to (βdebunked1). Though this composition is allowed by the definition in Joshi et al. (2003), it is not allowed by the definition in Chiang and Scheffler (2008), where it is speculated that allowing such derivation may increase the weak generative capacity beyond standard TAG.

This result provides further support for Chiang and Scheffler's (2008) observation that while any derivation using flexible composition can alternatively be expressed in a 2-delayed tree-local MC-TAG, a derivation using a 1-delayed tree-local analysis may not be expressed in an MC-TAG with flexible composition. To verify this observation, Chiang

and Scheffler used ECM construction where there is a binding relationship between the matrix subject and the ECM subject, as in (8).

(8)   John believes himself to be a decent guy. (Ryant and Scheffler, 2006)

They show that though there is a simple derivation using a 1-delayed tree-local MC-TAG, the derivation with flexible composition originally proposed for (8) by Ryant and Scheffler (2006) is actually illegal. There, a reverse-adjoining takes place at a site that is created by a reverse-substitution. We have essentially obtained the same results with the derivation of non-local RNR.

5 Noncoordinate RNR

Following Hudson (1976), Napoli (1983), Goodall (1987), Postal (1994), and Phillips (2003), and as illustrated in (9) and (10), RNR is possible in non-coordinated structures.

(9)   a. [David changed __] while [Angela distracted **the baby**].

        b. [I organize __] more than [I actually run **her life**].

        c. [I organize __] although [I don't really run **her life**].

(10)   a. Of the people questioned, those [who liked __] outnumbered by two to one those [who disliked **the way in which the devaluation of the pound had been handled**]. (Hudson, 1976)

        b. Politicians [who have fought for __] may well snub those [who have fought against **animal rights**]. (Postal, 1994)

        c. The professor [who taught __] dislikes the student [who debunked **the theory**].

Our proposed analysis of coordinate RNR can straightforwardly be extended to the examples in (9). In the derivation of each of the examples, the elementary tree representing the adjunct clause adjoins to the matrix clause, just as the elementary tree representing the coordinated clause did. These elementary trees thus form a natural class with coordinating elementary trees, and as such, they can each form a contraction path with the immediately dominated

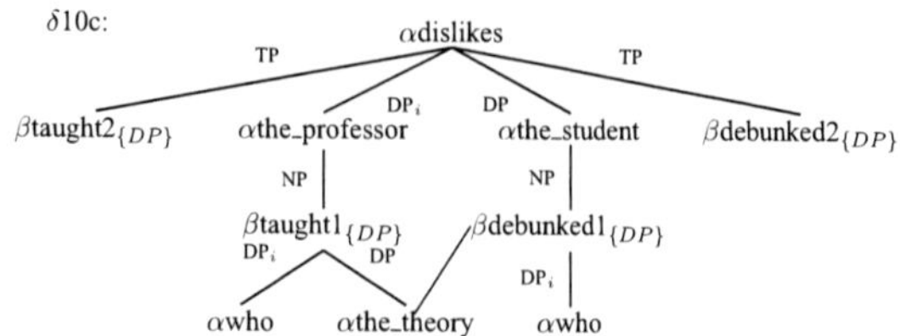

Figure 12: Derivation structure for *The professor who taught dislikes the student who debunked the theory*

degenerate tree. And since the contraction path containing the degenerate tree member representing the matrix clause immediately dominates the one containing the degenerate tree member of the adjunct clause, contraction of the object DPs is licensed.

Unlike the cases of coordinate RNR and the examples in (9), in the examples in (10), the second clause containing the shared argument is not adjoining onto the first clause with the shared argument. Rather, they are relative clauses, each contained in the subject DP and the object DP. (10c), for example, can thus be given a 1-delayed tree-local derivation as in Figure 12, using the elementary tree sets in Figure 6. Here, the degenerate trees, (βtaught2$_{\{DP\}}$) and (βdebunked2$_{\{DP\}}$), both adjoin to (αdislikes), forming two contraction paths, one containing (αdislikes) and (βtaught2$_{\{DP\}}$) and the other containing (αdislikes) and (βdebunked2$_{\{DP\}}$). The two paths are in sister relation, which is arguably as local as immediate domination relation. It thus follows that the contraction of the object DPs in the relative clause trees, (βtaught1$_{\{DP\}}$) and (βdebunked1$_{\{DP\}}$), is licensed.

6   Conclusion

In this paper, we have observed that non-local RNR calls for a TAG derivation that is more descriptively powerful than the one of standard TAG, and applied two such variants of TAG to the problem, tree-local MC-TAG with flexible composition and 1-delayed tree-local MC-TAG. We have shown that the analysis of local RNR proposed in Sarkar and Joshi can be extended to non-local RNR if it is augmented with delayed tree locality but not with flexible composition. We have seen that the proposed analysis is constraining as well, ruling out non-contiguous RNR, and can also be extended to handle cases of noncoordinate RNR.

References

Chiang, David, and Tatjana Scheffler. 2008. Flexible Composition and Delayed Tree-Locality. In *Proceedings of TAG+ 9*. Tübingen, Germany.

Féry, Caroline, and Katharina Hartmann. 2005. Focus and prosodic structures of German Gapping and Right Node Raising. *The Linguistic Review* 22:67–114.

Goodall, Grant. 1987. *Parallel structures in syntax*. Cambridge University Press.

Hartmann, Katharina. 2000. *Right node raising and gapping: Interface conditions on prosodic deletion*. John Benjamins Publishing Company.

Hudson, Richard A. 1976. Conjunction reduction, gapping, and right-node raising. *Language* 52:535–562.

Joshi, Aravind K., Laura Kallmeyer, and Maribel Romero. 2003. Flexible composition in LTAG: Quantifier scope and inverse linking. In *Proceedings of IWCS-5*, eds. Harry Bunt et. al., volume 5, 179–194. Tilburg, The Netherlands.

Napoli, Donna Jo. 1983. Comparative ellipsis: A phrase structure analysis. *Linguistic Inquiry* 14:675–694.

Phillips, Colin. 2003. Linear order and constituency. *Linguistic Inquiry* 34:37–90.

Postal, Paul. 1994. Parasitic and pseudoparasitic gaps. *Linguistic Inquiry* 25:63–117.

Potter, David. 2010. A multiple dominance analysis of sharing coordination constructions using Tree Adjoining Grammar. Master's thesis, Simon Fraser University.

Ross, John Robert. 1967. Constraints on variables in syntax. Doctoral Dissertation, MIT.

Ryant, Neville, and Tatjana Scheffler. 2006. Binding of anaphors in LTAG. In *Proceedings of TAG+ 8*, 65–72. Sydney, Australia.

Sabbagh, Joseph. 2007. Ordering and linearizing rightward movement. *Natural Language and Linguistic Theory* 25:349–401.

Sarkar, Anoop, and Aravind Joshi. 1996. Coordination in Tree Adjoining Grammars: formalization and implementation. In *Proceedings of COLING '96*, 610–615. Copenhagen.

Wexler, Kenneth, and Peter Culicover. 1980. *Formal principles of language acquisition*. Cambridge, MA: MIT Press.

Unifying Adjunct Islands and Freezing Effects in Minimalist Grammars

Tim Hunter
Department of Linguistics
University of Maryland
College Park, MD 20742, USA

Abstract

This paper presents a unified account of two well-known conditions on extraction domains: the "adjunct island" effect and "freezing" effects. Descriptively speaking, extraction is problematic out of adjoined constituents and out of constituents that have moved. I introduce a syntactic framework from which it emerges naturally that adjoined constituents are relevantly like constituents that have moved, unifying the two descriptive generalisations noted above.

1 Overview

Research into the nature of "island constraints" (conditions on domains out of which extraction can occur) is a prominent issue in mainstream syntactic theory. There has been corresponding research into the nature of these constraints in a more mathematically explicit setting within the TAG formalism, aiming to show how island constraints, particularly adjunct islands and wh-islands (eg. Kroch, 1987, 1989; Frank, 1992), might emerge from other independently-motivated properties of the grammar. However within the MG formalism, developed by Stabler (1997) as a precise formulation of the main ideas underlying the most recent incarnation of Chomskyan syntactic theory (Chomsky, 1995), there has been relatively little investigation of the nature of island constraints: to the extent that these phenomena figure in the literature (eg. Gärtner and Michaelis, 2005, 2007), familiar descriptive constraints are simply stipulated individually (eg. no extraction from specifiers, no extraction from adjuncts) for the purpose of investigating not the origin of these constraints but their effects on generative capacity.

In this paper I propose that a particular variant of the MG formalism, motivated by a number of independent considerations, permits a unified account of two well-known island constraints, namely the "adjunct island" effect and "freezing" effects: descriptively speaking, extraction is generally problematic out of adjoined constituents (Cattell, 1976; Huang, 1982) and out of constituents that have moved (Wexler and Culicover, 1981). The crucial ingredients of the formalism are two widely-held intuitions: first, that movement is usefully thought of as "re-merging" (Epstein et al., 1998; Chomsky, 2004), and second, that adjuncts are in some sense more "loosely" attached than arguments are (Chametzky, 1996; Hornstein and Nunes, 2008). A grammatical formalism in which the re-merge conception of movement is fleshed out explicitly makes possible a natural implementation of the idea of adjuncts as loosely attached, which is otherwise difficult to make precise. From this point it emerges that adjoined constituents and moving constituents are, in a certain sense, the same kind of thing; thus by adding a single constraint to our theory we capture at once both adjunct island effects and freezing effects.

The rest of this paper is organised as follows. In §2 I develop the syntactic formalism in which the eventual unification can be stated, starting with the formalism from Stabler (2006) and then introducing two additions/modifications concerning the implementations of movement and adjunction. I begin

§3 by focussing on the prohibition against extraction from adjuncts; having identified the particular constraint that must be imposed on the formalism to enforce this prohibition, I then show that this one constraint also forbids extraction from moved constituents without further stipulation.

2 Syntactic framework

2.1 Insertion and Re-merge: Stabler (2006)

I take as a starting point the variant of the MG formalism presented by Stabler (2006). This system departs from the common conception of movement as an operation which revises or rearranges some existing structure: instead of merging into position A and then moving (perhaps with the help of copying and/or deletion operations) to position B, an element satisfies certain requirements associated with position A while remaining structurally "disconnected" from the rest of the sentence, and then is structurally integrated only into position B. As a result, if we allow new elements to be simply inserted into a derivation with this "disconnected" status, we need only a single feature-checking operation (as opposed to a merging operation which builds structure, and a moving operation which builds structure in addition to dismantling existing structure).[1]

Abstracting away from some details, a derivation of the question 'who did we see' will proceed as shown in Figure 1. Features of the form +f indicate *requirements*, and features of the form -f indicate *properties*. An element bearing -f can discharge another element's corresponding +f requirement, resulting in these two features being "checked" or deleted. Note that when a requirement is discharged, the element bearing -f may be wholly integrated into the structure (via string concatenation), never to be further manipulated, as is case for the subject and question requirements in Figure 1; or it may remain disconnected, as is the case for the object requirement in Figure 1, since 'who' has a remaining property that will discharge the question requirement later.

This conception of syntactic structure-building can be seen as an explicit implementation of the common intuition that movement might be thought

of as merely re-merging: note the parallelism between the discharging of the subject requirement (often thought of as a "merge step") and that of the question requirement (a "move step"). This unification depends on the presence of an insertion operation that adds an element to the derivation without checking any features. In the next subsection I will propose that this insertion operation can also play a role in insightful accounts of adjuncts; more specifically, that adjuncts are elements that are inserted into the derivation but do not thereafter participate in the discharging of any requirements.

This treatment of adjunction is one of two adjustments that I make to the system of Stabler (2006): I describe this first in §2.2, and then the second adjustment, concerning the derivational status of the "disconnected" elements, in §2.3.

2.2 Adjunction as (Only) Insertion

First note that in the derivation in Figure 1, phonological/string composition occurs only upon discharging of requirements (though not conversely). Adjuncts clearly must be phonologically composed with other constituents; to make room for an account where they nonetheless do not participate in any discharging of requirements, these two ideas must be decoupled. The work done at requirement-discharging steps in Figure 1 can be broken into two operations, MRG ("merge") and SPL ("spellout"). The former discharges requirements without phonological composition, and the latter composes a new string from smaller pieces. The string produced by SPL will of course depend on which requirements have been discharged by what, so MRG must leave some record of this for SPL to interpret.

With this division of labour between MRG and SPL, the question arises of "how often" SPL applies in the course of the derivation. If SPL were applied immediately after *every* application of MRG, the result would be effectively the same as in Figure 1. Alternatively, if SPL were applied just once at the end of the derivation, the result would be a system where the abstract structural description of the entire sentence is constructed and only then its string yield computed; this is roughly the position adopted in most works in transformational grammar, including Chomsky (1995) and Stabler (1997). I adopt a position in between these two extremes, incorporat-

---

[1] For further discussion of how this system relates to better-known variants of MGs, see Hunter (2010, ch.1).

$$\langle\ \text{see:: +d+d-V}\ ,\ \{\}\rangle$$
$$\text{insert `who'} \longrightarrow \langle\ \text{see:: +d+d-V}\ ,\ \{\ \text{who:: -d-wh}\ \}\rangle$$
$$\text{discharge object requirement} \longrightarrow \langle\ \text{see:: +d-V}\ ,\ \{\ \text{who:: -wh}\ \}\rangle$$
$$\text{insert `we'} \longrightarrow \langle\ \text{see:: +d-V}\ ,\ \{\ \text{who:: -wh}\ ,\ \text{we:: -d}\ \}\rangle$$
$$\text{discharge subject requirement} \longrightarrow \langle\ \text{we see:: -V}\ ,\ \{\ \text{who:: -wh}\ \}\rangle$$
$$\vdots$$
$$\langle\ \text{did we see:: +wh}\ ,\ \{\ \text{who:: -wh}\ \}\rangle$$
$$\text{discharge question requirement} \longrightarrow \langle\ \text{who did we see}\ ,\ \{\}\rangle$$

Figure 1: Intuitive outline of a derivation in the framework of Stabler (2006).

ing the general idea of the "multiple spellout" proposal from Uriagereka (1999).

Specifically, I propose that SPL applies at the end of each maximal projection. The effect is that the record of discharged requirements left by applications of MRG to be interpreted by SPL (i.e. a partial structural description) can take the simple form of a list: the first element in the list represents the complement of the current maximal projection, the second element the first specifier, and so on.[2] A derivation of the VP constituent of 'we see the man' is shown in Figure 2. Abstracting away from some details which will change shortly: we call a string with an associated list of features a *unit*, and an *expression* consists of a unit, a (possibly empty) sequence of strings, and some additional "disconnected" units (in Figure 2, a set of them, but this will change shortly); MRG and SPL are unary functions on expressions, and INS ("insert") is a binary function on expressions. If SPL applies to an expression of the form $e = \langle u, s, t, \dots \rangle$ where u is a unit and s and t are strings, then this expression is interpreted as encoding a phrase headed by u, with a constituent with yield s in its complement position and a constituent with yield t in its specifier position. Note that SPL applies at the end of each maximal projection: once to "flatten" the DP structure encoded in e_2 to produce 'the man', and once to "flatten" the VP structure encoded in e_7 to produce 'we see the man'. These two steps are illustrated in Figure 3.

For reasons of space I will not be able to justify here the particular choice of a maximal projection as the relevant "phase" or "cycle" of interpretation. The motivation comes in large part from consideration of a distinctive, independently-motivated approach to the semantic composition of neo-Davidsonian logical forms (Parsons, 1990; Pietroski, 2005), according to which complement and specifier positions each take on a particular semantic significance; see Hunter (2010) for extensive discussion. But to illustrate the basic idea, an argument of roughly the same form can be made that maximal projections might constitute a significant phase of interpretation even with respect to phonological/string (rather than semantic) composition: SPL must be sensitive to the distinction between complements and specifiers since (in English) the former are linearised to the right and the latter to the left, and by composing only at the end of each maximal projection we ensure that this distinction is encoded when SPL applies in Figure 2. In a system like the one illustrated in Figure 1 where requirement-discharging and composition are strictly coupled, some other encoding of the complement/specifier distinction must be added instead.[3]

With a VP consisting of just a head, complement and specifier derived as shown in Figure 2, we now have available an interesting analysis of adjunction. I propose that in the derivation of a VP with an additional adjunct, the adjunct is only inserted and

---

[2] I assume for simplicity that a phrase can have multiple specifiers, although the examples in this paper will not make use of any more than one.

[3] Stabler (2006) distinguishes two different "types" of expressions, indicated by ':' and '::', for this purpose.

$$e_1 = \text{INS}(\langle\, \text{the:: +n-d}\, ,\, \{\}\,\rangle\, ,\, \langle\, \text{man:: -n}\, ,\, \{\}\,\rangle) \qquad = \langle\, \text{the:: +n-d}\, ,\, \{\, \text{man:: -n}\, \}\,\rangle$$

$$e_2 = \text{MRG}(e_1) \qquad = \langle\, \text{the:: -d}\, ,\, \text{man}\, ,\, \{\}\,\rangle$$

$$e_3 = \text{SPL}(e_2) \qquad = \langle\, \text{the man:: -d}\, ,\, \{\}\,\rangle$$

$$e_4 = \text{INS}(\langle\, \text{see:: +d+d-V}\, ,\, \{\}\,\rangle\, ,\, e_3) \qquad = \langle\, \text{see:: +d+d-V}\, ,\, \{\, \text{the man:: -d}\, \}\,\rangle$$

$$e_5 = \text{MRG}(e_4) \qquad = \langle\, \text{see:: +d-V}\, ,\, \text{the man}\, ,\, \{\}\,\rangle$$

$$e_6 = \text{INS}(e_5,\, \langle\, \text{we:: -d}\, ,\, \{\}\,\rangle) \qquad = \langle\, \text{see:: +d-V}\, ,\, \text{the man}\, ,\, \{\, \text{we:: -d}\, \}\,\rangle$$

$$e_7 = \text{MRG}(e_6) \qquad = \langle\, \text{see:: -V}\, ,\, \text{the man}\, ,\, \text{we}\, ,\, \{\}\,\rangle$$

$$e_8 = \text{SPL}(e_7) \qquad = \langle\, \text{we see the man:: -V}\, ,\, \{\}\,\rangle$$

Figure 2: A derivation illustrating the division of labour between MRG and SPL.

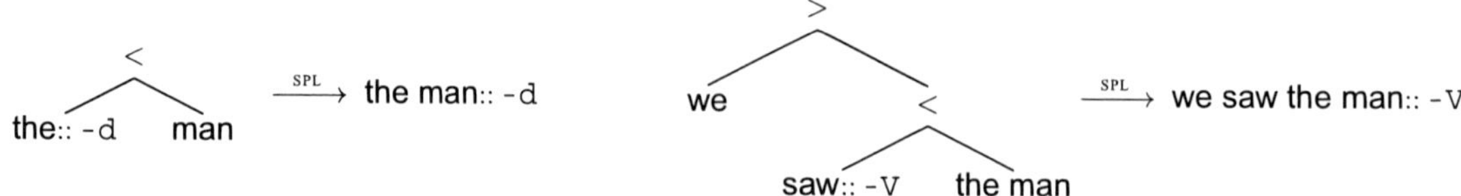

Figure 3: An intuitive illustration of the effects of SPL in Figure 2.

then immediately interpreted by SPL (as opposed to playing a more distinguished role by being affected by MRG). This is particularly plausible on the semantically-motivated understanding of argument positions (Hornstein and Nunes, 2008; Hunter, 2010). A derivation of 'we see the man today' will therefore proceed as in Figure 2 to the point where e_7 is constructed, and then continue as shown in Figure 4. The feature $*$V indicates a constituent that adjoins to a phrase whose head bears -V (i.e. adjoins to a VP).

2.3 Structure Among Disconnected Elements

Intuitively, an expression consists of a central "connected" component — originally a single head unit in Figure 1 and in Stabler (2006), and as of the previous subsection a head unit along with a list of argument-yield strings in Figure 2 and Figure 4 — and some associated "disconnected" units. In an expression $e = \langle C, \{u_1, u_2, \ldots\}\rangle$ let us say that the disconnected units u_i are *subordinate* to the central component C.

Consider now in more detail the derivation sketched in Figure 1. Upon completion of the VP constituent we derive the expression $e_{\text{VP}} = $

$\langle\, \text{we see:: -V}\, ,\, \{\, \text{who:: -wh}\, \}\,\rangle$. Here who is subordinate, in the sense just defined, to we see. Suppose the next maximal projection is a CP, the head of which is pronounced 'did' and which selects a VP complement and attracts a wh-word to its specifier position. Then the derivation will continue by inserting e_{VP} into an expression headed by did:: +V+wh-c .

In the system of Stabler (2006), the disconnected units in an expression are structured simply as a set, so the result of this insertion step will be as follows, *destroying the relationship of subordination between who and we see.*

$$\text{INS}\big(\langle\, \text{did:: +V+wh-c}\, ,\, \{\}\,\rangle\, ,\, e_{\text{VP}}\big)$$
$$= \langle\, \text{did:: +V+wh-c}\, ,\, \{\, \text{we see:: -V}\, ,\, \text{who:: -wh}\, \}\,\rangle$$

In order to maintain this relationship between who and we see when the derivation proceeds beyond construction of the VP (which will be crucial for imposing conditions on extraction domains), we need something more structured than simply a set of units to store an expression's disconnected pieces. Roughly, we might suppose that in place of a set of units we use a set of *expressions*; since this per-

$$e_7 = \qquad\qquad\qquad \langle\, \text{see:: -V} \,,\, \text{the man} \,,\, \text{we} \,,\, \{\} \,\rangle$$

$$e_8 = \text{INS}(e_7, \langle\, \text{today:: } \ast\text{V} \,,\, \{\} \,\rangle) \qquad = \langle\, \text{see:: -V} \,,\, \text{the man} \,,\, \text{we} \,,\, \{\, \text{today:: } \ast\text{V} \,\} \,\rangle$$

$$e_9 = \text{SPL}(e_8) \qquad\qquad\qquad = \langle\, \text{we see the man today:: -V} \,,\, \{\} \,\rangle$$

Figure 4: The end of a derivation showing the adjunction of 'today' to the VP.

mits nesting of expressions, a tree notation is sensible. A tree with C at its root node and $u_1, u_2, \ldots$ as the unordered daughters of this root node will correspond to the expression $\langle C, \{u_1, u_2, \ldots\}\rangle$. The arcs of these trees correspond straightforwardly to subordination relationships. A tree with further levels of embedding encodes the more elaborate internal structure now permitted, not corresponding to any expression of the restricted form $\langle C, \{u_1, u_2, \ldots\}\rangle$

The expression e_{VP} discussed above will therefore correspond to the tree in (1); when this expression is inserted into an expression headed by the complementiser 'did' we keep its internal structure intact, and the result is the tree in (2).

(1)　　we see:: -V　　　(2)　　did:: +V+wh-c
　　　　　　|　　　　　　　　　　　|
　　　who:: -wh　　　　　　we see:: -V
　　　　　　　　　　　　　　　　　|
　　　　　　　　　　　　　　who:: -wh

The effect of inserting one tree τ into another τ' is to add τ as one of the daughters of the root node of τ'. The effect of applying MRG to a tree whose root node has as its first feature a requirement +f, is to "look for" a unit u bearing a property -f somewhere else in the tree, and check these features; if this -f is the only remaining feature on u, then we furthermore record the yield of u at the root node, to be phonologically composed at the next application of SPL, and u is removed from the tree, its daughters inherited by the root node.

The two applications of MRG and the one of SPL that complete the derivation of 'who did we see', starting from the expression in (2), are shown in Figure 5. While all non-root nodes consist of just units, the root node has a unit plus a (possibly empty) list of strings, representing current argument yields as introduced in Figure 2.

Let us say that a unit x is "n-subordinate" to an-

other unit y (in a certain tree τ) iff x can be reached from y by a downward path of length n (in τ). Note that before the first application of MRG in Figure 5, the unit who:: -wh was 2-subordinate to the root of the tree; but when the +V and -V features are checked and we see is established as an argument, its daughter who:: -wh is inherited by the root and is therefore only 1-subordinate to the root.

3　Constraining movement

We can now consider the difference, in our modified syntactic formalism, between licit extraction from a complement and illicit extraction from an adjunct. Having done so we will then see that the property that distinguishes adjuncts from complements also distinguishes in-situ constituents from moved ones. A single constraint can therefore be imposed upon the system that unifies adjunct island effects and freezing effects.

3.1　Prohibiting Extraction from Adjuncts

I take the two sentences in (3) and (4) as representative examples of licit extraction from a complement and illicit extraction from an adjunct.

(3)　　　Who do you think [that John saw ___]?

(4)　　　* Who do you sleep [because John saw ___]?

I assume that the bracketed constituent in (4) is adjoined to VP, though nothing significant hinges on this choice of attachment site. The crucial difference between the two sentences will therefore reside in the construction of their respective matrix VPs: the relevant partial derivations, up to the point where no requirements remain to be discharged and we would expect SPL to apply, are shown in Figure 6.

The two expressions with which the partial derivations in Figure 6 begin represent the two sentences' respective bracketed constituents, extraction from which we are investigating: a CP 'that John

$$\text{did:: +V+wh-c} \xrightarrow{\text{MRG}} \text{did:: +wh-c , we see} \xrightarrow{\text{MRG}} \text{did:: -c , we see, who} \xrightarrow{\text{SPL}} \text{who did we see:: -c}$$
$$|$$
$$\text{we see:: -V}$$
$$|$$
$$\text{who:: -wh} \qquad \text{who:: -wh}$$

Figure 5: Final steps of the derivation of 'who did we see'.

(3)
$$\text{that John saw:: -c} \xrightarrow{\text{INS}} \text{think:: +c-V} \xrightarrow{\text{MRG}} \text{think:: -V , that John saw}$$
$$|$$
$$\text{who:: -wh} \qquad \text{that John saw:: -c} \qquad \text{who:: -wh}$$
$$|$$
$$\text{who:: -wh}$$

(4)
$$\text{because John saw:: } \star V \xrightarrow{\text{INS}} \text{sleep:: -V}$$
$$|$$
$$\text{who:: -wh} \qquad \text{because John saw:: } \star V$$
$$|$$
$$\text{who:: -wh}$$

Figure 6: Comparison of the construction of the matrix VP of the two sentences in (3) and (4).

saw' with a subordinate disconnected 'who' waiting to re-merge and check its -wh feature in the case of (3), and a VP-adjunct 'because John saw', likewise with a disconnected 'who', in the case of (4). Each is inserted into an expression headed by the matrix verb: 'think', which requires a CP complement, in the case of (3), and 'sleep', with no such requirement, in the case of (4).

After this first step the two partial derivations crucially diverge. For (3) a MRG step is required, to check the +c and -c features, before SPL can apply, and as a result who:: -wh is 1-subordinate to the root when the VP is completed and SPL is due to apply. For (4), however, no such MRG step is required: the adjunct is ready to be interpreted as part of the VP in its 1-subordinate position, just as 'today' was in Figure 4, and so SPL is due to apply immediately after the insertion step.

In order to encode the adjunct island constraint we require that the possibility of extracting who is contingent upon the merging of its mother node in these tree representations (here, that John saw), into an argument position. We can do this by stipulating that SPL does not apply to expressions where there exist units 2-subordinate to the root. The partial derivation of (3) in Figure 6 can therefore continue with an application of SPL, producing

$$\text{think that John saw:: -V}$$
$$|$$
$$\text{who:: -wh}$$

but the would-be derivation of (4) cannot.[4]

I should emphasise that I have not said anything insightful so far about the nature of adjunct island effects. This constraint on the expressions to which SPL can apply is simply a restatement of the fact that extraction from adjuncts is prohibited. The attraction of it is that in combination with the implementation of movement that our formalism assumes, the very same constraint simultaneously prohibits extraction from moved constituents. This is what the next subsection will illustrate.

3.2 Freezing effects follow

The adjunct island constraint, we have just seen, amounts to a prohibition on applying SPL to configurations in which a moving unit u is 1-subordinate to a unit u', which is itself adjoined to, and thus 1-subordinate to, the expression's root; in such con-

---

[4]Note that this constraint does not rule out multiple adjuncts independently modifying a single phrase, as long as none of these adjuncts themselves have subordinate parts waiting to re-merge.

figurations u is 2-subordinate to the root. But the general constraint — that SPL may not apply to expressions where some unit is 2-subordinate to the root — also prohibits applying SPL to configurations in which a moving unit u is 1-subordinate to a unit u', which *has not yet reached its final position*, and is thus 1-subordinate to the root. This second kind of configuration is exactly the one that characterises freezing effects.

As a concrete example, I will suppose that (5) is ruled out because 'who' has moved out of a larger constituent which has itself moved: specifically, it has moved out of the subject, which has moved for Case/EPP reasons. I will show that this can be ruled out by the same constraint on SPL that we arrived at above to enforce adjunct islands.

(5)   * Who did [a picture of __] fall (on the floor)?

First consider the derivation of a sentence involving the relevant movement of the subject, but not yet with any additional wh-movement. The relevant part of the derivation of (6) is shown in Figure 7.

(6)   A picture of John fell (on the floor)

The steps in Figure 7 begin at the point where the subject 'a picture of John' has been fully constructed, and it will need to merge into a theta position (-d) and Case position (-k). Note that since its theta position is not its final destination, a unit a picture of John:: -k *remains as a daughter of the root* when the +d and -d features are checked (analogous to 'who' remaining disconnected when the object requirement was discharged in Figure 1). This causes no problem in the derivation of (6) where no movement out of the subject is required: SPL applies to the last expression shown in Figure 7, since we have completed construction of the VP by this point, and the subject 'a picture of John' re-merges into its Case position when the opportunity arises.

Now consider Figure 8, showing the attempted derivation of (5), where 'who' must move out of the subject. After the two steps shown there the +d requirement of 'fall' has been discharged, so SPL is due to apply. However, as observed above, the unit a picture of:: -k remains 1-subordinate to the root fall:: -v , and who:: -wh remains 1-subordinate to a picture of:: -k ; therefore we have

a unit, who:: -wh , which is 2-subordinate to the root fall:: -v and so our constraint from §3.1 prohibits application of SPL.

To see the similarity between adjunct island configurations and freezing configurations, note the similarity between the attempted derivation of (4) in Figure 6, and that of (5) in Figure 8. In each case the constituent out of which who:: -wh needs to move remains 1-subordinate to the root — in the first case, because because John saw:: *v is an adjunct, and in the second case, because a picture of:: -k has not reached its final position. Contrast these in particular with the part of the successful derivation of (3) in Figure 6, where the constituent 'that John saw' out of which who:: -wh needs to move is not subordinate to the expression's root. The proposed constraint therefore makes a natural cut between (i) adjoined constituents and moving constituents, out of which movement is disallowed, and (ii) argument constituents, out of which movement is allowed.

4   Conclusion

In this paper I have argued that two well-known generalisations concerning extraction domains can be reduced to a single constraint: first, the generalisation that extraction from adjuncts is prohibited, and second, the generalisation that extraction from moved constituents is prohibited. I have presented and integrated independently-motivated implementations of movement relations and adjunction, and shown that it emerges from the resulting system that adjoined constituents and moved constituents have a certain shared status. This allows us to add a single constraint to the theory to capture both the existing generalisations.

Acknowledgments

Thanks to Norbert Hornstein, Juan Uriagereka, Amy Weinberg and Alexander Williams for helpful discussion of this work.

References

Cattell, R. (1976). Constraints on movement rules. *Language*, 52(1):18–50.

Chametzky, R. A. (1996). *A Theory of Phrase Markers and the Extended Base*. State University of New York Press, Albany, NY.

a picture of John:: -d -k $\xrightarrow{\text{INS}}$ fall:: +d -V $\xrightarrow{\text{MRG}}$ fall:: -V
| |
a picture of John:: -d -k a picture of John:: -k

Figure 7: Partial derivation illustrating subject movement in (6).

a picture of:: -d -k $\xrightarrow{\text{INS}}$ fall:: +d -V $\xrightarrow{\text{MRG}}$ fall:: -V
| | |
who:: -wh a picture of:: -d -k a picture of:: -k
| |
who:: -wh who:: -wh

Figure 8: Ill-fated attempted derivation of the sentence in (5).

Chomsky, N. (1995). *The Minimalist Program*. MIT Press, Cambridge, MA.

Chomsky, N. (2004). Beyond explanatory adequacy. In Belletti, A., editor, *Structures and Beyond*. Oxford University Press, Oxford.

Epstein, S. D., Groat, E., Kawashima, R., and Kitahara, H. (1998). *A Derivational Approach to Syntactic Relations*. Oxford University Press, Oxford.

Frank, R. (1992). *Syntactic Locality and Tree Adjoining Grammar*. PhD thesis, University of Pennsylvania.

Gärtner, H.-M. and Michaelis, J. (2005). A note on the complexity of constraint interaction: Locality conditions and Minimalist Grammars. In Blache, P., Stabler, E. P., Busquets, J., and Moot, R., editors, *Logical Aspects of Computational Linguistics*, volume 3492 of *Lecture Notes in Computer Science*, pages 114–130. Springer.

Gärtner, H.-M. and Michaelis, J. (2007). Locality conditions and the complexity of Minimalist Grammars: A preliminary survey. In *Model-Theoretic Syntax at 10,* Proceedings of the ESSLLI Workshop (Dublin), pages 87–98.

Hornstein, N. and Nunes, J. (2008). Adjunction, labeling, and bare phrase structure. *Biolinguistics*, 2(1):57–86.

Huang, C. T. J. (1982). *Logical relations in Chinese and the theory of grammar*. PhD thesis, MIT.

Hunter, T. (2010). *Relating Movement and Adjunction in Syntax and Semantics*. PhD thesis, University of Maryland.

Kroch, A. (1987). Unbounded dependencies and subjacency in tree adjoining grammar. In Manaster-Ramer, A., editor, *Mathematics of Language*, pages 143–172. John Benjamins, Amsterdam.

Kroch, A. (1989). Asymmetries in long distance extraction in tree adjoining grammar. In Baltin, M. and Kroch, A., editors, *Alternative conceptions of phrase structure*, pages 66–98. University of Chicago Press, Chicago.

Parsons, T. (1990). *Events in the semantics of English*. MIT Press, Cambridge, MA.

Pietroski, P. M. (2005). *Events and Semantic Architecture*. Oxford University Press, Oxford.

Stabler, E. P. (1997). Derivational minimalism. In Retoré, C., editor, *Logical Aspects of Computational Linguistics*, volume 1328 of *Lecture Notes in Computer Science*, pages 68–95. Springer.

Stabler, E. P. (2006). Sidewards without copying. In Monachesi, P., Penn, G., Satta, G., and Wintner, S., editors, *Proceedings of the 11th Conference on Formal Grammar*.

Uriagereka, J. (1999). Multiple spell-out. In Epstein, S. D. and Hornstein, N., editors, *Working Minimalism*, pages 251–282. MIT Press, Cambridge, MA.

Wexler, K. and Culicover, P. (1981). *Formal Principles of Language Acquisition*. MIT Press, Cambridge, MA.

Reevaluating Gapping in CCG: Evidence from English and Chinese

Nathaniel Little
Yale University
P.O. Box 200209
New Haven, CT 06520
nathaniel.little@aya.yale.edu

Abstract

This paper considers gapping data through the lens of combinatory categorial grammar (CCG) as developed in Steedman (1990, 2000). It analyzes CCG's predictive power in managing a wide variety of cross-clausal gapping data. CCG predicts the typing of the rightmost subject in cross-clausal gapping data as an object; evidence from Case supports this hypothesis. Reflexive binding in cross-clausal structures favors the Szabolcsi (1989) binding proposal, in which binding occurs at the level of the surface structure. Additionally, facts from Chinese buttress the CCG analysis, as its NP category-assignment offers a natural explanation for the ungrammaticality of gapping sentences containing non-quantified NP objects: they are unable to undergo type-shifting.

1 Setting the stage

Ross (1967) gave the name *gapping* to the following phenomenon:

(1) Harry eats beans, and Fred, potatoes.

Since Ross (1967), gapping has received varied accounts; I will center the present discussion on the theoretical problems posed by attempting to describe the data in the context of combinatory categorial grammar (CCG) as developed in Steedman (1990, 2000).

The paper will proceed as follows. First, I review the basic facts for which any theory of gapping must provide an account. Next, I describe the basic mechanics of gapping in CCG. I continue on to discuss data that proves problematic for the CCG account of gapping; I focus on the means by which CCG is able to predict many of the initially problematic data, thereby lending support for an intermediate theory of gapping – one that combines a syntactic and a semantic account. Further support for the CCG analysis comes in the form of apparent instances of gapping in Chinese, as CCG offers a principled account of the alternations between sentences containing quantified and non-quantified NP objects.

2 Gapping: preliminary facts

To begin, let us define gapping as a construction involving (at least) two similar clauses that surface in a contrastive relationship. In (1), we see a contrast between the left conjunct *Harry eats beans* and the right one, *Fred, potatoes*. The two conjuncts are joined through coordination; many theories take coordination to be a foundational property of gapping, but the story is not so simple. English gapping, for example, also occurs in comparatives:

(2) Harry eats more beans than Fred, potatoes.

It is clear from (2) that gapping is not limited to syntactic coordination. Even gapping sentences with coordination need not be marked through the presence of an overt coordinator:

(3) Some ate natto; others, rice.

Cases like (2-3) show that attempts to consider gapping as a uniquely syntactic phenomenon involving the overtly marked coordination of constituents will inevitably fall flat.

Gapping generally involves only one gap, and the item that is "gapped" is at least the main verb, if not additional material:

(4) Harry eats beans, and Fred (eats) potatoes.

The content of the additional material may vary; in many cases, it is part of the verb phrase:

(5) John bought a book at the store, and Bill, online.

The above example shows that not only is the main verb *bought* gapped, but the object *a book* is gapped, as well. In most cases, there may be only one gap – sentences containing multiple gaps are often ungrammatical:

(6) *I gave Mary a flower yesterday, and you, Bill, today.

In the above example, there are two gaps: first, the main verb *gave* is deleted, followed by a second, discontinuous gap in which the object *a flower* is deleted. As shown in (5), it is possible for both a verb and an object to be deleted (or "gapped"), so the problem is not the fact that both items are deleted, but that they are deleted discontinuously. One gap is composed of the main verb *gave*, and the other, discontinuous gap contains the NP *a flower*. The dative NP *Bill* intervenes between the two gaps, which results in ungrammaticality. Yet if the dative object surfaces in a prepositional phrase in a right peripheral position in the clause, the sentence is grammatical, and its meaning is preserved:

(7) I gave a book to Mary yesterday, and
    you, to Bill, three weeks ago.

The contrast between (6) and (7) points to a preference for placing focused material at peripheral positions within the clause. Thus, discontinuous gaps are not generally permitted either because they delete focused elements or they fail to delete non-focused material.

The disparity in grammaticality of (6-7) hints at another general property of gapping: the items in the gapped conjunct must be tied to some material that is sufficiently salient in the discourse to deliver an apparent contrast between the two (or more) conjuncts. This property is represented below (with (1) reprinted as (8a)):

(8) a. Harry eats beans, and Fred, potatoes.
    b. *A* eats *B*, and *C, D*.

Schematically, we see the contrastive relationship set up between the pairs *A,B* and *C,D*, in which the one element of each pair is contrasted with the corresponding element of the other; that is, *A* contrasts with *C*, and *B* with *D*. This relationship must be made clear within the discourse, and sentences uttered in contexts in which such a contrast is absent will be ungrammatical.

These facts are ones that any theory of gapping must be able to explain. What follows is a discussion of CCG's ability to account for this data and for other, similar gapping phenomena.

3 Gapping in CCG

Gapping viewed through the lens of CCG offers an intermediate stage between strongly syntactic and strongly semantic accounts of gapping. The syntactic categories assigned to each lexical item reflect the notion of the gap, and a semantic focus constraint serves to limit gapping to sufficiently salient discourse contexts.

In CCG, there is no underlying syntactic structure, or in fact any deleted structure at all. CCG carries a comparatively free notion of constituency, which allows for surface-level combination between string-adjacent elements into increasingly large, concatenated constituents. In some sense, CCG's idea of constituency, which allows even (traditionally "discontinuous") elements like *Fred, potatoes* to be considered constituents, resembles Ross's (1970) proposal that gapping and VP-ellipsis target and then elide "context variables" that range over strings regardless of constituency. In CCG, the decomposition of elements in the left conjunct allows us to pick out the verb and identify a non-continuous string in the left conjunct, which may then combine with a non-continuous string in the right conjunct to derive a licit sentence. The intuition that gapping targets strings of lexical items that in many cases are either discontinuous or non-standard constituents is one easily captured by CCG; its lexical category assignment, combined with its finite set of combinatory rules, permits the derivation of non-standard constituents without appealing to other levels of structure. Thus, even though Ross's (1970) proposal deals with strings that are deleted – and CCG lacks any notion of underlying structure – the shared intuition is one of non-standard constituency, which may be targeted in instances of VP-ellipsis and (important for present purposes) gapping.

Steedman's (1990, 2000) CCG account of gapping relies on a notion of constituency that is fundamentally different from that of abstract approaches. In CCG, a constituent refers to any entity within the grammar that fulfills two criteria: it must be interpretable, and grammatical rules must be allowed to operate on it (see Steedman 1990 for further discussion). CCG assigns a category to each lexical item; a combinatory rule operates on a pair of string-adjacent lexical items. The derivability of a sentence is determined by the categories of the lexical items and their (in)ability to combine according to CCG's finite set of combinatory rules. One basic rule is function application:

(9) Function Application (> or <)
    a. $X/Y \quad Y \quad \rightarrow \quad X$
    b. $Y \quad X \backslash Y \quad \rightarrow \quad X$

X and Y may be thought of as variables corresponding to categories; directionality of the function is indicated by the direction of the slash (a forward-slash is right-looking, and a backward-slash is left-looking). Function application allows string-adjacent lexical items of the appropriate type to combine. Other rules are necessary for the derivation of sentences containing non-traditional constituents (e.g. *cooked* and *might eat*). Function composition allows such combination:

(10) Forward Composition (>B)

　　a. *X/Y Y/Z* →$_\mathbf{B}$ *X/Z*

Without forward composition, the sentence *I cooked, and might eat, the beans* would be underivable as a complete sentence:

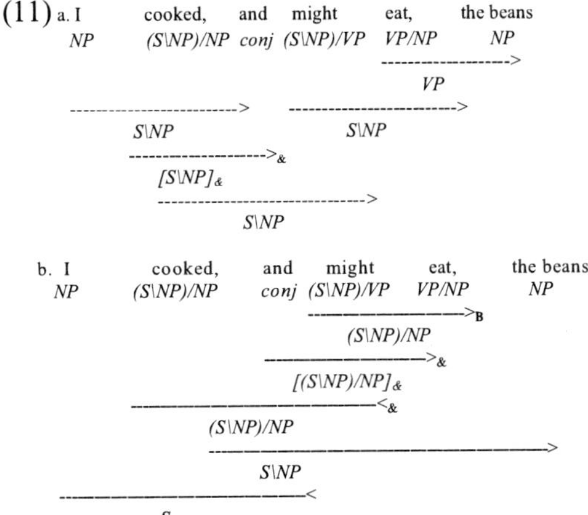

In (11b) above, the non-traditional constituent *might eat* may be derived through forward composition. Similarly, in CCG any item – word, phrase or non-canonical combination of words – may rightly be considered a constituent. Thus, as Steedman notes, a string like *Mary might* is as much a constituent as the predicate *eat the cake* would be in many abstract accounts. This relaxed notion of constituency is articulated in CCG's rules, which allow the concatenation of words into such "non-standard" constituents – including, crucially, the subject/object pairs found in the derivation of gapping sentences (whose analysis is outlined below). Because the second conjunct in gapping sentences is a constituent, coordination may apply to it. Steedman's formulation of CCG thus maintains the idea that gapping respects constituency, by loosening constituency's requirements.

Three additional rules – type-raising, forward mixing composition and decomposition – make possible the derivation of gapping sentences. I will offer a brief treatment of each, though the reader is directed to Steedman (1990, 2000) for a fuller discussion.

Type-raising, along with forward mixing composition, is necessary in order to combine the subject/object remnants in the right conjunct of gapping sentences. Type-raising turns arguments of functions into functions-over-

such-functions-over-arguments (e.g. one normally thinks of nouns as arguments of verbs; in CCG, a type-raised noun becomes a function taking a verb as its argument). A general type-raising schema is shown below:

(12) Type-Raising:

　　A →$_\mathbf{T}$ *B/(B\A) or B\(B/A)*

When applied to subject *NP*s, type-raising is instantiated as follows:

(13) Subject Type-Raising (>T)

　　NP →$_\mathbf{T}$ *S/(S\NP)*

As *NP* objects of a transitive verb, the type-raised category for English objects is that of a function taking a transitive verb as its input and returning a one-argument verb:

(14) Object Type-Raising (<T)

　　NP →$_\mathbf{T}$ *(S\NP)\((S\NP)/NP)*

Type-raising, like other rules in CCG, allows for greater combinatory possibilities and is necessary for the derivation of gapping sentences (among other phenomena). Taking our simple gapping sentence, type-raising gives us the following:

(15) ...Fred,　　　　　potatoes.
　　　　NP　　　　　　　*NP*
　　　--------->T　---------------------<T
　　　S/(S\NP)　*(S\NP)\((S\NP)/NP)*
　　---*

After undergoing type-raising, *Fred* receives the designation *S/(S\NP)* – namely, that of a lexical item looking to its right for a verb seeking a subject to its left. In effect, *Fred* becomes a function over a one-argument verb. Similarly, *potatoes* receives the typing of an object looking to its left for a two-argument verb seeking an object to its right. However, combination of the two items is still blocked without the rule of forward mixing composition, which is shown below:

(16) Forward Mixing Composition (>B$_x$)

　　　[X/Y]$_\&$ Y\Z →$_\mathbf{B}$ [X\Z]$_\&$

　　　where Y = S\NP

Given this rule, the subject and object in the right conjunct may now combine to form a category of the type *S\((S\NP)/NP)*:

(17) Fred,　　　　　potatoes.
　　　NP　　　　　　*NP*
　　--------->T　----------------------<T
　　S/(S\NP)　*(S\NP)\((S\NP)/NP)*
　　------------------------------------>Bx
　　　　S\((S\NP)/NP)

(Note: Marking the subject NP Fred for conjunction, which would have occurred prior to

(17), is not represented in the derivation.[1])
Yet again, however, the derivation is blocked; with the category *S* on one side of the derivation – *Harry eats beans* – and the category *S\((S\NP)/NP)* on the other, there is no means by which the two conjuncts may combine (assuming the right conjunct is marked for coordination). In order to allow such combination, and in order to take into account semantic constraints on gapping, Steedman (1990) posits a rule of decomposition:

 (18) Decomposition (<decompose)
  $X \rightarrow Y\ X\backslash Y$
  where X = S
  and Y = given(X)

Decomposition requires that the category of the decomposed element be *S*, and that the other be provided in the discourse. This semantic discourse-sensitivity helps to limit the *Y* category in (18) to one that is relevant to a particular context. Without the decomposition rule, gapping sentences would be otherwise underivable in CCG; with the rule, we may finally derive the entire gapping sentence:

(19)
```
     Harry eats beans,             and    Fred,        potatoes.
     ------------------            conj    NP             NP
            S                             ------>T ----------------<T
                                          S/(S\NP)  (S\NP)\((S\NP)/NP)
                                          -------------->&
                                          [S/(S\NP)]&
                                          ------------------------------>Bx
                                                    [S\((S\NP)/NP)]&
     ==========================<decompose
     (S\NP)/NP S\((S\NP)/NP)
                     --------------------------------------<&
                              S\((S\NP)/NP)
     ------------------------------------------------------<
                          S
```

When decomposition of the left conjunct occurs, the verb is separated out from the subject and object (or, as I will show, the embedded subject). The decomposition rule applied to the left conjunct of a canonical gapping sentence (e.g. *Harry eats beans*) splits that conjunct into two constituents *(S\NP)/NP* and *S\((S\NP)/NP)*.

---

[1] The rule shown in (17) requires that coordination apply only to the lexical item to its right – and not to the composed *Fred, potatoes* constituent – in order to prevent the derivation of ungrammatical forms like the following, as noted by Steedman (1990):

```
   i. *Eats        Fred,              potatoes.
      ((S\NP)/NP)   NP                   NP
                   --------->T  ----------------------<T
                   S/(S\NP)     (S\NP)\((S\NP)/NP)
                   --------------------------------------->Bx
                              S\((S\NP)/NP)
      --------------------------------------------------<
                          S
```

The second of these constituents can be conjoined with the right conjunct since it is of identical type to produce another constituent of the same type. Finally, the result of coordination serves as the argument to the first of the decomposed constituents. The CCG analysis of gapping thus reflects the intuition that the verb (i.e., the *(S\NP)/NP* derived using decomposition) takes scope over both conjuncts.

4 Cross-clausal gapping

I will now consider data that pose a potential problem for most existing theories of gapping. Most of the data involves instances of what I term cross-clausal gapping, in which a gap ranges across an embedded clause, targeting the matrix and embedded verbs and leaving the subjects of both clauses as remnants. The relation in such gaps is thus one of subject/subject, rather than the typical subject/object relationship found in canonical instances of gapping. Two typical examples are produced below:

 (20) a. John hopes the Bills win, and Fred, the Colts.
   b. Robin knows a lot of reasons why dogs are good pets, and Leslie, cats. (C&J 2005:273)

We see, in both cases, that the sentence-final remnant is a subject – *the Colts* in (20a), and *cats* in (20b) – rather than an object, which causes the CCG derivation to break down. If the phrases in the second conjunct receive the typing of a traditional subject, namely, *NP* or, when type-raised, *S/(S\NP)*, we are left with no means of saving the derivation. If we type both subjects in the right conjunct with nominative Case (i.e. with the typical type-raised subject category), then the derivation fails as shown in (21):

(21)
```
   John hopes the Bills win,   and       Fred,        the Colts.
   ------------------------    conj        NP             NP
              S                          ------>T     -------<T
                                         S/(S\NP)     S/(S\NP)
                                         -------->&
                                         [S/(S\NP)]&
                                         ------------------------*
```

The pair of string-adjacent subjects in the right conjunct cannot combine: even though the subjects have identical typing, and the subject *Fred* is marked for coordination, Steedman's coordination rule cannot save the derivation. As the forward coordination rule has already applied to mark *Fred* for coordination, the left-looking backward coordination rule must then apply; if both subjects in the right conjunct are typed with nominative Case, the derivation fails.

However, CCG's machinery is fully capable of describing the data if we allow one crucial assumption: that the cross-clausal, sentence-final constituent in the second conjunct is typed as an object – just as CCG would predict for the sentence to be derived successfully.

Though this assumption may initially seem somewhat *ad hoc*, evidence from Case lends support for this view. In English gapping sentences, there is a tendency to favor accusative pronominals in the second conjunct. Take the following data:

> (22) a. John thinks (that) Mary will win, and Fred$_i$, him$_j$/*he$_j$/me/*I.[2]
>
> b. I hope (that) Mary wins, and you, him/me.
>
> c. John delivered a speech on why the Giants will win, and Fred, the Bills.

In (22a-b), the rightmost element in the right conjunct may only surface as a pronoun marked for accusative Case – the Case of a traditional object in English. To account for the possibility of subject extraction when *that* is not present in such examples, Steedman suggests that subjects can in some cases be analyzed as objects of the higher predicate. One might be tempted, therefore, to treat (22a) in this fashion, with the embedded subject in the left conjunct *Mary* analyzed as an object of *thinks*. There is reason to doubt this, however: In example (22c) the embedded subject cannot, in fact, be plausibly analyzed as the object of the higher verb. I follow Steedman in assuming that type raising is a reflection of case marking. When one type-raises a subject, for example, the resulting category is an *S/(S\NP)*, which effectively shifts the subject from being the argument of a verb phrase to instead being a function over a function over the argument of a verb phrase – that is, the subject becomes a function that takes a left-looking verb phrase as its own argument.

I posit that the typing of the sentence-final subject as an object points to a requirement that it bear accusative Case. The grammar permits the combination of a type-raised subject and object in CCG; we see quite clearly via empirical gapping data that such an allowance is necessary, both in English and in e.g. German (see Steedman 2000 for further discussion). A sample derivation, parallel to those of canonical English gapping sentences, is shown below:

 Where *him* refers to another discourse-given individual. Example (22b) makes this relationship more apparent.

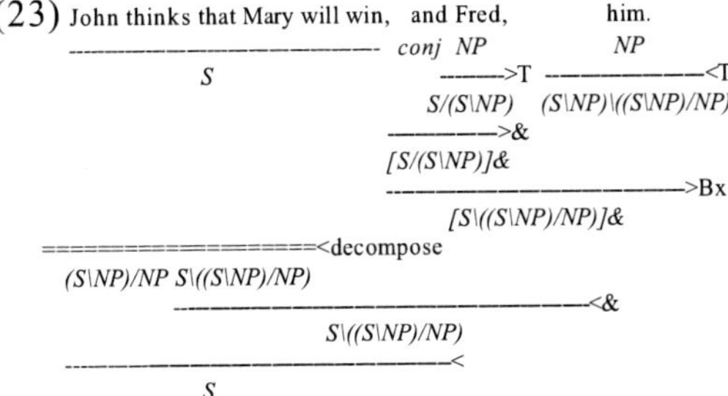

The syntactic apparatus of CCG predicts that the rightmost element in an instance of cross-clausal subject/subject gapping must be typed as an object for the derivation to proceed. Thus, it should not be surprising for us to find the rightmost NP to surface with accusative Case – a surface representation of the fact that the rightmost element should receive object typing.

The account seems more plausible when one considers other, clearly ungrammatical cross-clausal gapping constructions. Oftentimes, the accusative-Case pronoun is required:

> (24) a. John hopes (that) you win, and Fred, me/*I/him/her/*he/*she.
>
> b. John delivered a speech on why Fred resigned, and Bill, me/I*/him/her/*he/she*.

In each of the examples above, the sentence-final remnant – interpreted in (24a) as the subject of the string ____ *win(s)*, and in (24b) as the subject of ____ *resigned* – may only appear in accusative Case.

One might argue that the appearance of accusative Case is simply due to the general unlikelihood of finding sentence-final subjects in English. Much past research (e.g. Schutze 2001) has commented on the status of accusative Case as default Case in English, and some would thereby conclude that this fact renders the analysis moot – that is, that the final subject defaults to accusative Case in the absence of an overt nominative Case assigner.[3] However, I contend that even if the default Case of English is accusative, or even if English favors accusative Case for sentence-final NPs, the analysis still follows: the tendency of English to

---

[3] An additional object of study would be the presence (or lack therof) of cross-clausal gapping in languages that necessarily mark nominative Case overtly, particularly in languages in which default Case is not accusative; if the analysis for English translates crosslinguistically, one would expect that the sentence-final subjects surface in accusative Case, both in instances of pronominals and in non-pronominal NPs.

favor accusative Case sentence-finally receives a surface manifestation via CCG typing.

5 Binding in cross-clausal gapping

Cross-clausal gapping sentences show an interesting property with respect to reflexive binding. Typically, a matrix subject cannot bind an embedded reflexive. However, cross-clausal gapping sentences like (25a-b) demonstrate the necessity of long-distance reflexive binding:

(25) a. *$John_i$ thinks that Mary is in love with himself$_i$.

b. $John_i$ thinks that $Mary_j$ is in love with $Fred_k$, and $Bill_l$, with himself$_{??i/??k/l}$/herself$_{?j}$/him$_{*l}$/her$_{*j}$.

As shown in (25a), in normal (non-gapping) circumstances, the matrix subject cannot bind the embedded reflexive. The most salient reading of sentence (25b) is the one in which Bill thinks that Mary loves him.[4] Under this cross-clausal reading, only the reflexive *himself*, referring to *Bill*, is completely acceptable. The use of *her* to refer to *Mary* is also ungrammatical. In the surface structure, there are no clause boundaries separating *Mary* from *her* – it is a Condition B violation. With CCG, there is no underlying syntactic structure or representation. The CCG notion of surface structure is essentially, 'what you see is what you get,' and the syntax builds up canonically non-standard constituents alongside a corresponding semantic interpretation. Even if the surface structure does not reflect the iteration of *Mary* that one would expect to be present underlyingly in an abstract account (i.e. in the second conjunct, as part of the deleted material), the presence of *Mary* in the first conjunct, together with the lack of a surface-level clause boundary, causes the non-reflexive *her* to be ungrammatical.

Thus, not only is long-distance reflexive binding available, it is in fact a necessity, as the unavailability of co-reference between *Bill* and *him* in (25b) indicates. Additional data provide further support for this picture:

(26) a. Fred thinks (that) Mary will win, and John, himself$_i$/??him$_i$/*he$_i$.

b. Fred believes (that) Mary loves John, and $Bill_i$, himself$_i$/*him$_i$.

c. Mary said (that) the stone had fallen on Sue, and $Bill_i$, on himself$_i$/*him$_i$.

Examples (26a-c) provide a different sort of evidence. As discussed previously, the rightmost element receives accusative case. We see that if this element is interpreted as coreferential with the leftmost element in the gapped constituent, the former must be a reflexive and not a pronoun. This is in contrast to what one would expect if the gapped material were reconstructed. Taking (26c) as an example, if binding occurs at the semantics, then some level of reconstruction of the gapped clause should be possible – and the reflexive should be dispreferred, because of the presence of a clause boundary intervening between *Fred* and *him/himself.* Yet, because the reflexive reading is not only available, but is in fact required, we receive evidence that the binding occurs at the level of the surface syntax, where *Fred* and *him/himself* are string-adjacent and fall within the same binding domain.

In practice, how might one represent binding in the syntax? Steedman (1996) treats binding at the level of predicate-argument structure. He assumes that bound anaphors receive a treatment that is syntactically identical to other NPs; the only difference is that they are marked with a *+ANA* feature. At the level of interpretation, which is built up simultaneously with the syntactic structure, reflexives are interpreted as a function of the type *self'* – the representation of *himself* is shown below:

(27) himself $:= NP_{+ANA,3SM} : self'$

The Steedman approach is similar to the account of reflexives provided by Reinhart and Reuland (1993), in which the reflexive-marking is reflected on the verb. Given the above definition of the *-self* anaphor, the reflexivization of a transitive verb is thus represented with the following rule (from Steedman 1996):

(28) $(S \backslash NP_{agr})/NP : f \rightarrow (S \backslash NP_{agr})/NP_{+ANA,agr} : \lambda g.\lambda y.g\,f\,(ana'y)y$

In such a rule, the resulting predicate-argument structure is the function $gf(ana'y)y$, in which the variable g takes as its range the anaphoric interpretation of *self'*. It should be fairly plain to see how syntactic combination of verb and anaphor occurs derivationally – it proceeds as expected. In the interpretation structure, the semantic construction builds up parallel to its syntactic counterpart. This process restricts anaphoric binding to local domains, but it disallows the application of the λ-calculus to an already-composed constituent.

---

[4] Example (25b) requires some prosodic contrast (in which *John* and *Fred* receive emphasis, then *Bill* and *himself*) to make the cross-clausal reading completely clear, but the same is true for most gapping sentences.

Normally, this would not pose a problem – except in cases like those shown above, in which the cross-clausal gapping sentences demonstrate long-distance reflexive binding. Examples like (26a) require that binding occur at the level of the surface structure, which the Steedman account does not allow. Steedman's rule (28) could account for the cross-clausal cases, if it were able to apply following application of the decomposition rule (18) in the left conjunct; however, the rule (28) is strictly a lexical one and thus cannot apply following decomposition. Counterproposals exist that feature a different sort of reflexive binding – namely, one in which the reflexive is itself marked (rather than the verb) as a λ-operator that turns a two-argument function into a one-argument function, in effect reversing the normal function/argument structure. In such proposals, e.g. Szabolcsi (1989), the reflexive W is essentially a type-raised NP that causes an identity relation between arguments of a verb; this process is shown below (adapted from Szabolcsi 1989):

(29) $W = \lambda f.\lambda x.fxx$

(30) Assuming a transitive verb with interpretation $\lambda y.\lambda z.f\,(yz)$,

$\lambda f.\lambda x.[fxx](\lambda y.\lambda z.g\,[yz]) = \lambda x[gxx]$

This account differs crucially from the Steedman one in that it is the reflexive itself, and not the verb, on which reflexivization is marked. When building up cross-clausal gapping structures that contain long-distance reflexive binding, the Szabolcsi proposal would allow us to derive the proper binding facts for cross-clausal gapping structures; the result of combining the λ-terms for *John, himself* is a function that if given a transitive verb, will return a verb applied to both *John* and *himself* – precisely the intuitive reading of (26a).

Unfortunately, the Szabolcsi proposal runs into problems of its own. Given that it allows for long-distance reflexive binding, the Szabolcsi account overgenerates and permits the derivation of ungrammatical English sentences. If we type reflexives in the same way as other NPs in the syntax, then the proposal derives ungrammatical forms like the following:

(31) *John$_i$ thinks that Mary likes himself$_i$.

The Szabolcsi proposal allows reflexive binding to apply the λ-calculus to composed constituents; without restrictions on the application of binding to composed constituents, examples like (31) are predicted to be grammatical. Thus, although a proposal like the Szabolcsi one is necessary to account for the facts of cross-clausal gapping, it predicts that other long-distance binding will be grammatical, as well. As such, although the Szabolcsi theory is better able to capture the cross-clausal facts than the Steedman one, it fails to earn an unqualified endorsement as a preferred proposal overall.

6 Chinese type-raising

The previous discussion has centered almost exclusively on gapping in English. In the following section, the discussion shifts to a range of data in Chinese that can bring something to bear on the present analysis of gapping.

Wu (2002) adduces a class of gapping-like constructions in Chinese that display interesting behavior. Specifically, Wu shows that instances of gapping in Chinese are restricted to NP objects that carry some form of quantificational force, generally as part of a classifier phrase (a phenomenon also discussed in Li 1988 and Paul 1999). The alternation in grammaticality between quantified NP objects and bare nouns is shown below:

(32) a. Zhangsan chi-le san-ge pingguo, Lisi chi-le si-ge juzi.
    Zhangsan ate three-CL apple   Lisi ate four-CL orange
    'Zhangsan ate three apples and Lisi four oranges.'
                         (Li 1988:41)
b. Zhangsan xihuan pingguo, Lisi *(xihuan) juzi.
    Zhangsan like apple   Lisi like   orange
    'Zhangsan likes apples and Lisi oranges.' (Wu 2002:3)

I take this restriction to demonstrate that type-raising in Chinese is restricted to a specific set of words and phrases, i.e. those carrying quantificational force. Throughout the development of CCG, type-raising has been accepted to occur relatively freely; however, I contend that the alternations in grammaticality in Chinese, and the impermissibility of gapping in sentences where the object lacks quantificational force, support the conclusion that type-raising in Chinese is in fact restricted. Given such a restriction, the facts of gapping in Chinese fall out naturally. Looking to (32a), we see that the object *juzi* "orange" is preceded by *si-ge* "four," also marked as a classifier phrase. The alternation in grammaticality between (32a), with a quantified object, and (32b), which contains the bare NP object *juzi*, is striking, and it provides a minimal pair for the analysis. Simply, when the object is not preceded by a quantificational element – in this case, a classifier phrase – gapping is unavailable.

Representing this fact in CCG is simple. Lexical items are assigned specific categories, and the derivation of gapping sentences requires a highly specific category assignment that allows for the combination of subject and object in the right conjunct via forward crossing composition. In order for the subject and object to combine, each item must be type-shifted from an argument to a function-over-functions-over-arguments. A parametric constraint on the type-shifting of bare NP objects means that in examples like (32b), the subject and object cannot combine, and the derivation crashes. This derivational crash is shown below[5]:

```
(33) *Zhangsan xihuan pingguo,        Lisi       juzi.
     Zhangsan like     apple          Lisi       orange
     ------------------------------ (conj) NP      NP
           S                         --------->T --------*
                                     S/(S\NP)
```

The method for deriving the licit Chinese example (32a) should by now be equally apparent (shown on the next page):

```
(34) Zhangsan chi-le san-ge   pingguo, Lisi  chi-le si-ge      juzi.
     Zhangsan ate    three-CL apple     Lisi  ate   four-CL orange
     ------------------------------ (conj)  NP                   NP
            S                       ------>T  ----------------<T
                                    S/(S\NP)  (S\NP)\((S\NP)/NP)
                                    --------------->&
                                    [S/(S\NP)]&
                                    ---------------------------------->Bx
     ================<decompose   [S\((S\NP)/NP)]&
     (S\NP)/NP  S\((S\NP)/NP)
            ------------------------------------------------<&
            S\((S\NP)/NP)
     --------------------------------------------<
            S
```

Due to the presence of the classifier phrase, the NP object *juzi* may type-shift. It combines with the subject *Lisi* to produce a subject-object constituent, which subsequently combines with the result of the decomposition in the left conjunct. The decomposition separates out the verb from the subject-object constituent, which is then coordinated with the analogous subject-object constituent in the right conjunct. Finally, the coordinated subject-object constituent combines with the transitive verb through function application, and the result is a well-formed sentence. Gapping in Chinese thus depends on the expression of the NP object and its (in)ability to type-shift.

The notion of crosslinguistic variation in the range of NP interpretations is not a new one;

Chierchia (1998) established a system for defining languages in terms of the availability of mass and count nouns, and the expression of each. Chierchia described two features – ±argument and ±predicate – to define the expression of nouns. In some instances, all nouns are arguments (meaning that bare nouns occur freely, as in Chinese); in others, all nouns are predicates (bare nouns are practically, if not totally, excluded, as in French); finally, in still other instances nouns may be either predicates or arguments. This final category (which includes English) allows for greater freedom in type-shifting of phrasal projections. Chierchia applies this expression of type-shifting specifically to mass/count noun distinctions, but the same principle informs our conception of type-shifting in CCG – some languages, like English, do allow type-shifting to occur freely. In others, e.g. Chinese, type-shifting is restricted; simply, bare NPs cannot type-shift.

Chinese allows type-raising only in case there is some quantificational force inherent in the DP; with this single observation, we see that the facts of gapping in Chinese, and the environments in which it is permissible, follow as a natural consequence of the CCG theory.

7 Conclusion

In this paper, I have outlined a number of facts that any theory of gapping must analyze. The CCG proposal of Steedman (1990, 2000), carries a high degree of predictive power in managing the wide variety of cross-clausal gapping data contained herein. CCG predicts the typing of the rightmost subject in cross-clausal gapping data as an object; evidence from Case supports this hypothesis. Reflexive binding in cross-clausal structures favors the Szabolcsi (1989) proposal, in which binding occurs at the level of the surface structure. Additionally, facts from Chinese buttress the CCG analysis, as its NP category-assignment delivers a straightforward explanation for the ungrammaticality of gapping sentences containing non-quantified NP objects: simply, they are unable to undergo type-shifting.

Acknowledgments

Many thanks are due to Robert Frank, Raffaella Zanuttini, fellow linguists in LING 491, friends, family and many others.

---

[5] I assume the presence of coordination on some (perhaps syntactic) level; similar examples, in which a coordinator fails to surface overtly, are also found in English (see example (3)). Such examples have long been noted (see Sag 1976), and I see them as posing no real threat to the CCG analysis of gapping.

References

Chierchia, Gennaro. 1998. Reference to kinds across languages. *Natural Language Semantics* 6:339-405.

Culicover, Peter W., and Ray Jackendoff. 2005. *Simpler Syntax*. Oxford: Oxford University Press.

Li, M.D. (1988) *Anaphoric Structures of Chinese*. Taipei: Student Book Co, Ltd.

Paul, W. 1999. Verb gapping in Chinese: a case of verb raising. *Lingua* 107:207-226.

Reinhart, Tanya, and Eric Reuland. 1993. Reflexivity. *Linguistic Inquiry* 24:657–720.

Ross, John. 1967. Constraints on variables in syntax. Doctoral Dissertation. Massachusetts Institute of Technology.

Ross, John. 1970. Gapping and the order of constituents. In Bierwisch and Heidolph (eds.), *Progress in linguistics*. The Hague: Mouton. 249-259.

Sag, Ivan. 1976. Deletion and logical form. Doctoral Dissertation, Massachusetts Institute of Technology, Cambridge, Massachusetts.

Schütze, Carson. 2001. On the nature of default Case. *Syntax* 4:205-238.

Steedman, Mark. 1990. Gapping as constituent coordination. *Linguistics and Philosophy* 13. 207–263.

Steedman, Mark. 1996. *Surface structure and interpretation*. Cambridge, Mass.: MIT Press.

Steedman, Mark. 2000. *The syntactic process*. Cambridge, MA: MIT Press.

Szabolcsi, A. 1989. Bound variables in syntax (are there any?). In Bartsch, van Benthem, and van Emde Boas (eds.), *Semantics and contextual expression*. Dordrecht: Foris. 295-318.

Wu, Hsiao-hung Iris. 2002. On ellipsis and gapping in Mandarin Chinese. Master thesis. National Tsing Hua University.

Well-Nested Tree Languages and Attributed Tree Transducers

Uwe Mönnich

Theoretische Computerlinguistik
Universität Tübingen
Wilhelmstr. 19
72074 Tübingen
`uwe.moennich@uni-tuebingen.de`

Abstract

Well-nested word languages have been advertised as adequate formalizations of the notion of mild context-sensitivity. The main result of this paper is a characterization of well-nested tree languages in terms of simple attributed tree transducers.

1 Introduction

The intuitive notion of mild context-sensitivity has led to two competing candidates claiming to be an exact formal rendering of the intentions Joshi (1985) was trying to capture when introducing this concept. On the one hand multiple context-free grammars and their equivalents exhibiting a variety of wildly different specifications provide impressive evidence that this precise counterpart of the informal description of mild context-sensitivity constitutes a natural class. On the other hand the well-nested subclass of the multiple context-free grammars has recently been advertised as a formalization more in accordance with Joshi's original intentions ((Kanazawa, 2009), (Kuhlmann, 2007)). Both candidates have counterparts in the realm of tree languages and it is in this context that they are easily recognized as mathematically precise characterizations of two leading linguistic models, minimalist syntax and tree adjoining grammars (cf. (Harkema, 2001), (Michaelis, 2001), (Kepser and Rogers, 2007), (Mönnich, 1997), (Mönnich, 2007)).

The tree languages in question are the multiple regular tree languages ((Raoult, 1997)) and the simple context-free tree languages ((Engelfriet

and Maneth, 2000)). Both language families are proper subfamilies of the tree languages generated by context-free hyperedge-replacement graph grammars and the latter family is identical with the output languages of logical tree-to-tree transductions applied to regular tree languages. The obvious question that poses itself is whether the two restricted rule formats or their corresponding tree transducers, finite-copying top-down tree transducers and simple macro tree transducers (MTT), respectively, can be given an equivalent logical characterization in terms of restrictions on the logical formulae defining the relations in the target structures of logical transductions. This is indeed the case. From results presented in (Bloem and Engelfriet, 2000) and in (Engelfriet and Maneth, 1999) it follows that the tree languages which are the output of finite-copying top-down tree transducers applied to regular tree languages are exactly the output tree languages of logical tree transducers which are direction preserving in the sense that edges in the output trees correspond to directed paths in the input trees. As a preliminary step towards an analogous result for languages generated by simple context-free tree grammars (CFT_{sp}) we'll show in this paper that they are equivalent to the output languages of a highly restricted form of attributed tree transducers (ATT). As emphasized by (Bloem and Engelfriet, 2000), attribute grammars are to be regarded as a specification language and, as such, they are much closer to logical specifications than context-free tree grammars.

In previous work Duske et al. (1977) have characterized the inside-out macro languages due to

(Fischer, 1968) as the output string languages of attribute grammars with one synthesized attribute only. In a nutshell, we lift their result to the tree level and restrict it to the case of well-nested tree languages, which are immune to differences of derivation mode ((Kepser and Mönnich, 2006)) and, a fortiori, are inside-out. In their paper mentioned above Engelfriet and Maneth (2000) point out that well-nested tree grammars can be regarded as a notational variant of simple $MTTs$. Our result could accordingly be interpreted as showing the equivalence between simple $ATTs$ and simple $MTTs$. We believe that our construction that avoids the detour via $MTTs$ has the advantage of establishing a direct link between a procedural and a declarative formalization of well-nestedness.

After these introductory remarks we will recall some basic concepts from the theory of tree languages and the theory of attributed tree transducers. The following section is an attempt at reviewing briefly the notion of mild context-sensitivity from the perspective of context-free graph languages. We will then proceed to prove the equivalence of CFT_{sp} and simple $ATTs$ with one attribute only ($1S - ATT_{ss,si}$). We shall close with some remarks regarding the problems to be solved for a logical characterization of CFT_{sp}.

2 Preliminaries

For any set A, A^* is the set of all strings over A. ε is the empty string, $|w|$ is the length of a string w. N denotes the set $\{0, 1, 2, 3, \ldots\}$ of nonnegative integers.

Let S be a finite set of *sorts*. An S-signature is a set Σ given with two mappings $ar : \Sigma \to S^*$ (the *arity* mapping) and $so : \Sigma \to S$ (the *sort* mapping). The length of $ar(\sigma)$ is called the *rank* of σ, and is denoted by $rank(\sigma)$. The *type* of σ ($\sigma \in \Sigma$) is the pair $\langle ar(\sigma), so(\sigma) \rangle$. The elements of $\Sigma_{\varepsilon,s}$ are also called constants (of sort s).

In case S is a singleton set $\{s\}$, i.e. in case Σ is a *single-sorted* or *ranked alphabet (over sort s)*, we usually write $\Sigma^{(n)}$ to denote the (unique) set of operators of rank $n \in N$; we also write $\sigma^{(n)}$ to indicate that $rank(\sigma) = n$. In this case, which is of particular interest to us, the set of trees T_Σ is defined recursively as follows. Each constant of Σ,

i.e., each symbol of rank 0, is a tree. If σ is of rank k and $t_1, \ldots, t_k$ are trees, then $\sigma(t_1, \ldots, t_k)$ is a tree. A *tree language* $L \subseteq T_\Sigma$ over Σ is a subset of T_Σ. With each tree $t \in T_\Sigma$ we can associate a string $s \in \Sigma_0^*$ by reading the leaves of t from left to right. This string is called the *yield* of t, denoted by $yd(t)$. More formally, $yd(t) = t$ if $t \in \Sigma_0$, and $yd(t) = yd(t_1) \cdots yd(t_k)$ whenever $t = \sigma(t_1, \ldots, t_k)$ with $k \geq 1$. The yield of tree language L is defined straightforwardly as $yd(L) = \{yd(t) | t \in L\}$.

If A is a set (of symbols) disjoint from Σ, then $T_\Sigma(A)$ (alternatively $T(\Sigma, A)$) denotes the set of trees $T_{\Sigma \cup A}$ where all elements of A are taken as constants. Let $X = \{x_1, x_2, x_3, \ldots\}$ be a fixed denumerable set of *input variables* and $Y = \{y_1, y_2, y_3, \ldots\}$ be a fixed denumerable set of *parameters*. Let $X_0 = Y_0 = \emptyset$ and, for $k \geq 1$, $X_k = \{x_1, \ldots, x_k\} \subset X$, and $Y_k = \{y_1, \ldots, y_k\} \subset Y$. For $k \geq 0, m \geq 0, t \in T_\Sigma(X_k)$, and $t_1, \ldots, t_k \in T_\Sigma(X_m)$, we denote by $t[t_1, \ldots, t_k]$ the result of *substituting* t_i for x_i in t. Note that $t[t_1, \ldots, t_k]$ is in $T_\Sigma(X_m)$. Note also that for $k = 0, t[t_1, \ldots, t_k] = t$.

Definition 1 *A context-free tree (CFT) grammar is a tuple $G = (\mathcal{F}, \Omega, S, P)$ where $\mathcal{F}$ and Ω are ranked alphabets of non-terminals and terminals, respectively, $S \in \mathcal{F}^{(0)}$ is the start symbol and P is a finite set of productions of the form*

$$F(y_1, \ldots, y_m) \to \xi$$

where $F \in \mathcal{F}$ and ξ is a tree over $\mathcal{F}$, Ω and Y_m.

If for every $F \in \mathcal{F}^{(m)}$ each $y \in Y_m$ occurs exactly once on the right-hand side of the corresponding rule then the context-free tree grammar is called *simple in the parameters (sp)*. The family of tree languages which is generated by context-free tree grammars which are simple in their parameters is designated as CFT_{sp}.

A grammar $G = \mathcal{F}, \Omega, S, P$ is called a *regular tree (REGT)* grammar if $\mathcal{F} = \mathcal{F}^{(0)}$, i.e., if all non-terminals are of rank 0.

Attributed tree transducers are a variant of attribute grammars in which all attribute values are trees. Besides *meaning names* which transmit information in a top-down manner, attributed tree transducers contain explicit *context names* which allow information to be passed up from a node to its mother. Consequently, arbitrary tree walks can be realized by attributed tree transducers.

Definition 2 *An* attributed tree transducer *(ATT) is a tuple*

$$A = (Syn, Inh, \Sigma, \Omega, \alpha_m, R),$$

where Syn and Inh are disjoint alphabets of synthesized *and* inherited *attributes, respectively, Σ and Ω are ranked alphabets of* input *and* output *symbols, respectively, α_m is a synthesized attribute, and R is a finite set of rules of the following form: For every $\sigma \in \Sigma^{(m)}$, for every $(\gamma, \rho) \in ins_\sigma$ (the set of inside attributes of σ), there is exactly one rule in R_σ:*

$$(\gamma, \rho) \to \xi$$

where $\xi \in T_{\Omega \cup out_\sigma}$ and out_σ is the set of outside attributes of σ.

Definition 3 *For every $\sigma \in \Sigma^{(m)}$, the set of* inside *attributes is the set $ins_\sigma = \{(\alpha, \pi) | \alpha \in Syn\} \cup \{(\beta, \pi i) | \beta \in Inh, i \leq m\}$ and the set of* outside *attributes is the set $out_\sigma = \{(\beta, \pi) | \beta \in Inh\} \cup \{(\alpha, \pi i) | \alpha \in Syn, i \leq m\}$. π and ρ are path variables ranging over node occurrences in the input tree.*

$ATTs$ with rules R_σ at an input symbol σ in which each outside attribute occurs exactly once are called *simple* attributed tree transducers. We denote this class by $ATT_{ss,si}$ on the model of macro tree transducers that are simple, i.e., linear and non-deleting, both in their input variables and in their parameters ($MTT_{si,sp}$).

The *dependencies* between attribute occurrences in an input tree s can be represented with the help of R_σ. An instance of an attribute occurrence (α, π) depends on another occurrence (α', π') if σ labels node u in s, R_σ contains the rule $(\alpha', \pi') \to \xi$ and (α, π) labels one of the leaves in ξ.

The *dependency graph* $D(s)$ of an input tree $s \in T_\Sigma$ consists of the set of attribute occurrences together with the dependencies according to the rules in R. Reversing the direction of these dependencies leads to the notion of a *semantic graph* $S(s)$ of an input tree $s \in T_\Sigma$.

An attributed tree transducer is *noncircular* if the paths of attribute dependencies are noncircular. It is

well known that noncircular $ATTs$ have unique *decorations dec*, functions which assign each attribute occurrence a tree over $\Omega \cup out_\sigma$ in accordance with the productions R_σ.

Definition 4 *The transduction* realized by a noncircular attributed tree transducer A *is the function*

$$\tau_A = \{(s,t) | s \in T_\sigma, t \in T_\Omega, t = dec_s(\alpha_m, \epsilon)\}$$

Remark 1 *$ATTs$ which have synthesized attributes only are very close to top-down tree tranducers. Their rules*

$$(\gamma, \rho) \to \xi \text{ in } R_\sigma$$

correspond to tree transducer rules

$$\alpha(\sigma(x_1, \ldots, x_m)) \to \xi'$$

where $\sigma \in \Sigma^{(m)}$ and ξ' is obtained from ξ by substituting every $(\alpha, \pi i)$ by $\alpha(x_i)$.

3 Mild Context-Sensitivity

Even though the list of characteristic properties Joshi (1985) has suggested as characteristic features of a linguistically adequate extension of context-freeness can hardly be considered as a formally explicit definition it has become accepted as an informal description of a precise counterpart that has turned out to be remarkably stable with respect to a variety of wildly different specifications. This stability provides impressive evidence that the precise counterpart of the informal description of mild context-sensitivity constitutes a natural class. Over the last couple of years the formal characterizations assembled in Tabel 1, which all satisfy the criteria for membership in the class of mildly context-sensitive languages, have turned out to be weakly equivalent.

Besides this group of attempts at providing a formal explication for a framework adapted to the level of complexity found in natural language syntax another proposal for an exact definition of mild context-sensitivity is currently the focus of attention among linguists. We referred above to Kanazawa's claim that the so-called well-nested multiple context-free word grammars constitute a more faithful approximation of Joshi's original ideas than the multiple context-free grammars that were

$$
\begin{aligned}
MCFL \quad &= \text{languages generated by multiple context-free grammars}\\
MCTAL \quad &= \text{languages generated by multi-component tree adjoining grammars}\\
LCFRL \quad &= \text{languages generated by linear context-free rewriting systems}\\
LUSCL \quad &= \text{languages generated by local unordered scattered context grammars}\\
STR(HR) \quad &= \text{languages generated by string generating hyperedge replacement grammars}\\
OUT(DTWT) \quad &= \text{output languages of deterministic tree-walking tree-to-string transducers}\\
ydDT_{fc}(REGT) \quad &= \text{yields of images of regular tree languages}\\
&\quad\ \ \text{under deterministic finite-copying top-down tree transduction}\\
PGRPT \quad &= \text{languages defined by pregroups with tupling}
\end{aligned}
$$

Table 1: Classes of mildly context-sensitive word languages

the most prominent member of the first mathematically precise rendering of the notion of mild context-sensitivity. Well-nested multiple context-free string grammars satisfy the additional condition of a matching-like or well-nested rearrangement of the arguments of non-terminals on the right-hand sides of possible rules allowed by this type of grammar. Furthermore, it is obvious that well-nested multiple context-free languages are included in the multiple context-free languages in general. Besides this formal characterization in terms of well-nested multiple context-free languages, a number of further precise representatives of this second version of mild context-sensitivity have been found. This group assembled in Table 2 may not be as impressive as the long list of equivalent formalizations that was listed in connection with the first proposal for a formal rendering of mild context-sensitivity. Still, the equivalence of such wildly different systems as abstract categorial grammars and (subclasses of) macro tree transducers cannot be a pure coincidence, but has to be accepted as a sign of an underlying conceptual coherence.

The Table 2 contains besides examples of well-nestedness on the level of word languages two specimens of well-nested tree languages. Needless to say, the derived tree structures are well-nested in both alternatives suggested as formal renderings of mild-context-sensitivity. The well-nestedness condition concerns exclusively the rule format. In sharp contrast with the situation on the word level the multiple regular tree languages and the simple context-free languages mentioned in the introduction as candidate formalizations of minimalist syntax and tree adjoining grammars, respectively, are proper subfamilies of the tree languages gen-

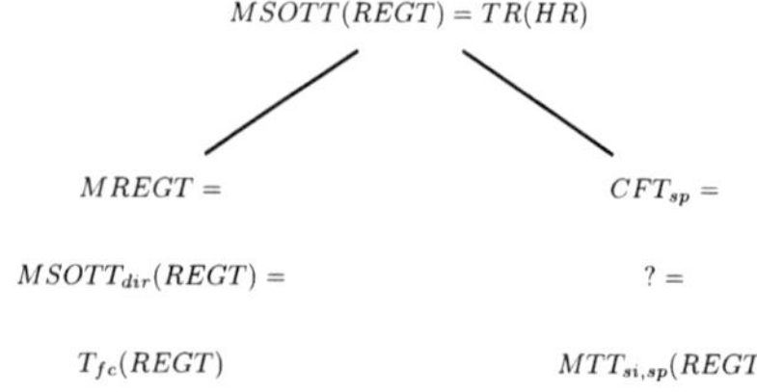

Figure 1: Classes of mildly context-sensitive tree languages

erated by context-free hyperedge-replacement graph grammars $(TR(HR))$ and the latter family is identical with the output languages of logical tree-to-tree transductions applied to regular tree languages $(MSOTT(REGT))$. Both mildly context-sensitive subfamilies of tree languages can be given descriptions in terms of grammatical systems and syntax-directed tree transducers. To repeat their formal characterizations, the multiple regular tree languages are exactly the output tree languages of finite-copying top-down tree transducers (T_{fc}) which, in turn, are the same as the output tree languages of direction preserving logical transductions $(MSOTT_{dir})$. The simple context-free tree languages, analogously, are exactly the output tree languages of simple macro tree transducers which, in turn, are the same as the output tree languages of simple attributed tree transducers with one synthesized attribute only, as shown in this paper. Their logical characterization is still open. Figure 1 summarizes the overview of the previous discussion concerning the inclusion relation among mildly context-sensitive tree languages.

Given the incomparability of the two families of mildly context-sensitive tree languages, the investi-

$$
\begin{aligned}
MCFL_{wn} \quad &= \text{well-nested multiple context-free languages} \\
MAC_{sp} \quad &= \text{simple macro languages} \\
ydCFT_{sp} \quad &= \text{yields of context-free tree languages} \\
ydMTT_{si,sp}(REGT) \quad &= \text{yields of output languages of tree transductions realized} \\
&\quad \text{by simple macro tree transducers taking regular tree languages as input} \\
CFT_{sp} \quad &= \text{simple context-free tree languages} \\
ACG_{(2,3)} \quad &= \text{abstract categorial languages with abstract vocabulary} \\
&\quad \text{of order at most 2 and lexical images of atomic types of order at most 3}
\end{aligned}
$$

Table 2: Classes of well-nested mildly context-sensitive word and tree languages

gation of their formal properties is of obvious interest for the evaluation of the corresponding linguistic frameworks. Should it turn out that ill-nested structures are needed for an adequate representation of structures exemplified in natural syntax the theory of "mildly context-sensitive" graph languages might still be the framework of choice as long as these structures are more tree- than graph-like.

Trees can be uniquely characterised by specifying their hierarchical structure, they can be enumerated by means of a production system and they can be fed into an abstract automaton. For graphs no suitable notion of finite automaton has been proposed. Similarly, Graph grammars, on the other hand, do not generate their output in a way that is patterned by an independently given hierarchical structure which would be intrinsic to this data type.

In spite of this difference of the two data structures, the fact that certain linguistic phenomena are graphs does not as such preclude the possibility of an approach which sees them as the result of a logically defined tree transduction. Bauderon and Courcelle (1987) present an approach to graphs by defining a (generally infinite) set of graph operations such that every finite graph can be constructed by finitely many applications of these graph operations. For the particular licensing theory, head-driven phrase structure grammar ($HPSG$), we have shown ((Kepser and Mönnich, 2003)) that the classes of finite graphs defined by a finite $HPSG$ signature and grammar are indeed such that they cannot be generated by a finite set of graph operations. But this purely meta-theoretic limitation of $HPSG$ in general is not supported by the amount of tree-likeness retained in concrete analysis structures proposed for grammatical phenomena in languages like Serbo-Croatian. It is thus not excluded that the general approach in

terms of syntax-directed morphisms by means of tree-to-tree or tree-to-(tree-like) graph transducers can also be applied to a conceptual framework in which ill-nested derived structures enjoy full citizenship.

4 Main Result

In this section we will present our main result. The proof requires two constructions that reduce simple context-free tree grammars (CFG_{sp}) to simple attributed tree transducers with one synthesized attribute only ($1S - ATT_{ss,si}$) and vice versa.

4.1 From CFT_{sp} to $1S - ATT_{ss,si}$

Before showing that for every $CFG_{sp}\ G$ an $1S - ATT_{ss,si}\ A_G$ can be constructed with the same output language we first regularize G by translating its rules into terms over a new signature that is obtained from the original one by a so-called lifting process (cf. (Maibaum, 1974)). It would have been possible to reduce a given CFG_{sp} directly into an equivalent $1S - ATT_{ss,si}$. We have opted for the indirect approach, because the lifting technique is closely related to a decomposition result for $MTTs$ to the effect that the transformation performed by this family of tree transducers can be split into a symbolic replacement and a second-order substitution (cf. (Engelfriet and Vogler, 1985)). We shall see in the last section that the recourse to context attributes in coping with the second-order substitution cannot be avoided, destroying the prospect of a characterization of well-nestedness by means of straightforward tree homomorphisms.

Definition 5 (LIFT) *Let Σ be a ranked alphabet and X a finite set of variables. The derived N-sorted alphabet Σ' is defined as follows: For each $n \geq 0$,*

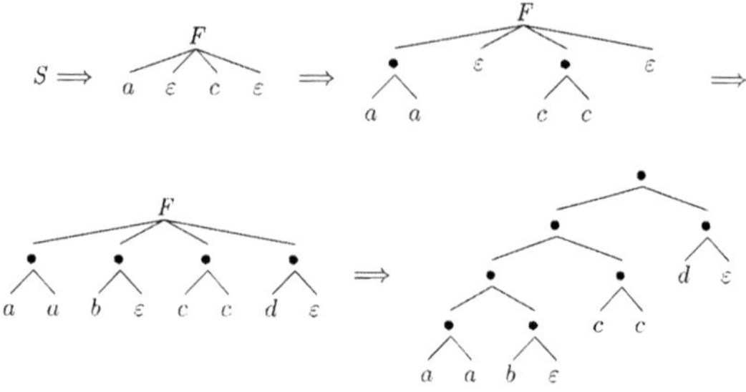

Figure 2: Derivation of $aabccd$.

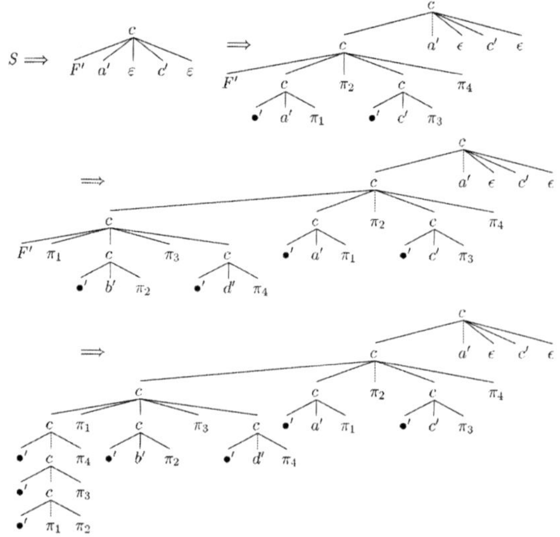

Figure 3: Dervation of lifted $aabccd$.

$\Sigma'_{\varepsilon,n} = \{f' \mid f \in \Sigma_n\}$ *is a new set of symbols of type* $\langle \varepsilon, n \rangle$*; for each* $n \geq 1$ *and each* $i, 1 \leq i \leq n$*,* π_i^n *is a new symbol, the ith* projection symbol *of type* $\langle \varepsilon, n \rangle$*; for each* $n, k \geq 0$ *the new symbol* $c_{(n,k)}$ *is the* (n, k)*th* composition symbol *of type* $\langle nk_1 \cdots k_n, k \rangle$ *with* $k_1 = \ldots = k_n = k$.

For $k \geq 0$*,* $LIFT_k^\Sigma : T(\Sigma, X_k) \to T(\Sigma', k)$ *is defined as follows:*

$$LIFT_k^\Sigma(x_i) = \pi_i^k$$

$$LIFT_k^\Sigma(f) = c_{0,k}(f') \, for \, f \in \Sigma_0$$

$$\mathbf{LIFT}_k^\Sigma(f(t_1, \ldots, t_n)) =$$
$c_{n,k}(f', LIFT_k^\Sigma(t_1), \ldots, LIFT_k^\Sigma(t_n)) \, for \, f \in \Sigma_n$, $n \geq 1$

By way of example, we consider the effect of the lifting transformation on a CFT_{sp} G that generates the language $L(G) = \{a^n b^m c^n d^m\}$, where we have omitted the concatenation symbols. The grammar consists of the terminal alphabet $\Omega = \{\varepsilon^{(0)}, a^{(0)}, b^{(0)}, c^{(0)}, d^{(0)}, \bullet^{(2)}\}$, the non-terminal alphabet $\mathcal{F} = \{S^{(0)}, F^{(4)}\}$ and the following group P of rules:

$$S \to \varepsilon$$
$$S \to F(a, \varepsilon, c, \varepsilon)$$
$$S \to F(\varepsilon, b, \varepsilon, d)$$
$$F(x_1, x_2, x_3, x_4) \to F(\bullet(a, x_1), x_2, \bullet(c, x_3), x_4)$$
$$F(x_1, x_2, x_3, x_4) \to F(x_1, \bullet(b, x_2), x_3, \bullet(d, x_4))$$
$$F(x_1, x_2, x_3, x_4) \to \bullet(\bullet(\bullet(x_1, x_2), x_3), x_4)$$

Figure 2 illustrates a derivation of the string $aabccd$ with explicit concatenation.

The process of applying the lifting transformation to the grammar G given above returns a regular tree grammar G' with the following group of rules P':

$$S' \to \varepsilon$$
$$S' \to c(F', a', \varepsilon, c', \varepsilon)$$
$$S' \to c(F', \varepsilon, b', \varepsilon, d')$$
$$F' \to c(F', c(\bullet', a', \pi_1^4), \pi_2^4, c(\bullet', c', \pi_3^4), \pi_4^4)$$
$$F' \to c(F', \pi_1^4, c(\bullet', b', \pi_2^4), \pi_3^4, c(\bullet', d', \pi_4^4))$$
$$F' \to c(\bullet', c(\bullet', c(\bullet', \pi_1^4, \pi_2^4), \pi_3^4), \pi_4^4)$$

We parallel the derivation of the example string $aabccd$ with the corresponding derivation in the lifted grammar G' in Figure 3.

The terminal tree in Fig 3 over the lifted signature is yet to be translated into the structures generated by the CFT_{sp} G. These latter structures are coded into the lifted trees and are easily retrieved by unraveling the information contained in the projection and composition symbols. Algebraically speaking, the step from the lifted to the intended structures is nothing but the value of the unique homomorphism from the free term algebra into the substitution algebra over the lifted signature. This homomorphism is simulated by the attributed tree transducer which constitutes the core of the proof of the crucial lemma.

Lemma 1 *For every* CFT_{sp} G*, there is an* $1S - ATT_{ss,si}$ A_G *that outputs the same language when applied to the lifted derivation trees of* G'*.*

Proof For a given CFG_{sp} $G = (\mathcal{F}, \Omega, S, P)$ an $1S - ATT_{ss,si} = (Syn, Inh, \Sigma, \Omega, \alpha_m, R)$ A_G that outputs the same language is defined from the components of Gs lifted version in the following way.

- $Syn = \{\alpha\}$ with $\alpha = \alpha_m$ at the root node

- $Inh = \{\beta_j | 1 \leq j \leq m\}$ with m the maximal sort of a lifted non-terminal F'

- Every symbol in the derivation trees is assigned one synthesized attribute.

- Every projection symbol is assigned one inherited attribute

- Every lifted terminal symbol f' of sort n is assigned n inherited attributes.

- The function ass_{inh} assigning inherited symbols to composition symbols c is defined by structural induction on the trees on the rhs of P':

$$ass_{inh}(t) = proj(ass_{inh}(t_1)$$

where $t = c(t_1, \ldots, t_n)$ and where $proj$ deletes all inherited attributes of t_1 that have no counterparts in $ass_{inh}(t_i)$ $(2 \leq i)$.

- Each $R_{\pi_i^n}$ contains the rule

$$\alpha\pi \to \beta_i\pi$$

- Each $R_{f'}$ contains the rule

$$\alpha\pi \to f(\beta_1, \ldots, \beta_n)$$

where n is the sort of f'.

- Each R_c contains the rules

$$\begin{aligned}
\alpha\pi &\to \alpha\pi 1 \\
\beta_i\pi 1 &\to \alpha\pi i + 1 \\
\beta_i\pi j &\to \beta_i\pi
\end{aligned}$$

provided that the inherited attributes belong to the outside attributes of the composition symbol c.

The correctness of the construction follows from an easy rule induction.

Remark 2 *In the proof of Lemma 1 we have slightly departed from the official definition of an ATT by assigning inherited attributes to composition symbols in a context-dependent way. This could be repaired by labeling composition symbols with the non-terminals on the lhs of P.*

By way of example, consider the slightly simplified lifted tree in Figure 4 which is decorated with both the synthesized and inherited attributes and their values. Evaluating the meaning attribute α_m by traveling along the semantic graph results in the output tree $\bullet(\bullet(\bullet(\bullet(a, a), \varepsilon), \bullet(c, c)), \varepsilon)$.

4.2 From $1S - ATT_{ss,si}$ to CFG_{sp}

It was mentioned above that attributed tree transducers are attribute grammars with all their attribute values restricted to trees and their semantic functions to substitution of trees for dependent leaves. Second–order substitution for internal nodes of trees is achieved through the upward information transport that is made possible by the inherited attributes. Integrating this information transfer with the leaf substitution leads to the kind of substitution or adjunction, for that matter, characteristic of context-free grammars.

Lemma 2 *For every $1S - ATT_{ss,si}$ A, there exists an equivalent CFG_{sp} G_A.*

Proof Let $A = (Syn, Inh, \Sigma, \Omega, \alpha_m, R)$ be an attributed tree transducer with one synthesized attribute only such that each outside attribute at an input symbol σ occurs exactly once in R_σ. An equivalent simple context-free tree grammar G_A is defined as follows:

- $\mathcal{F} = \Sigma$ where the arity of non-terminals is given by the number of interited attributes assigned to them in the input tree.

- $\Omega = \Omega$

- $S = \{\sigma^{(0)}\}$ with $\sigma \in \Sigma$ labeling the root of an input tree.

- For every $\sigma \in \Sigma$ we construct a rule

$$\sigma(x_1, \ldots, x_n) \to t$$

where $t = COMP(\xi)$ and ξ is the right-hand side of the only synthesized attribute α in R_σ.

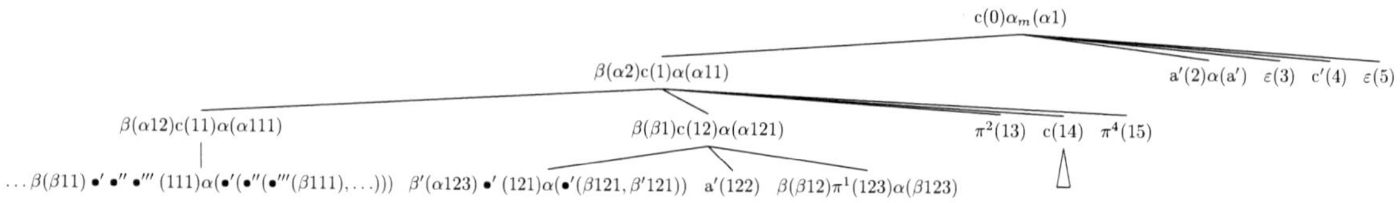

Figure 4: Evaluation of lifted sample tree

The right-hand sides of rules in R_σ are designated by $rhs(\gamma\pi, \sigma)$ in the following:

(i) If $\xi = \alpha\pi i$ then

$$COMP(\xi) = \rho(t_1, \ldots, t_m)$$

where ρ labels the ith daughter of σ, m is the arity of ρ and

$$t_j = COMP(rhs(\beta_j\pi i, \sigma))$$

(ii) If $\xi = \beta_j\pi$ then

$$COMP(\xi) = x_i$$

(iii) If $\xi = f(\xi_1, \ldots, \xi_r)$ for $f \in \Omega^{(r)}$

$$COMP(\xi) = f(COMP(\xi_1), \ldots, COMP(\xi_r))$$

By a routine inspection it is easy to verify that the resulting grammar G_A is indeed simple and that it generates exactly the output language of A.

Remark 3 *The construction in the preceding lemma is inspired by the proofs of Lemma 6.1 in (Engelfriet and Maneth, 1999) and of Lemma 5.11 in (Fülöp and Vogler, 1998). In these references it was shown how to turn an ATT into an equivalent MTT. MTTs can be regarded as tree grammars in which the generation process is controlled by the input trees. In the present case these input structures assume the role of derivation trees. This leads to a certain amount of proliferation in the rule component of the resulting grammar. It is not difficult to prove that this rule proliferation is of no consequence for the derived tree language, i.e., the derived structures.*

By Lemmas 1 and 2 we obtain our main result.

Theorem 1 *The well-nested tree languages are exactly the output languages of simple attributed tree transducers with one synthesized attribute only applied to regular tree languages.*

5 Envoi

Bloem and Engelfriet (2000) have shown that the output language of single use attributed tree transducers applied to regular tree languages are equal to the translations definable by monadic second-order logic. By the result presented in this paper this could be extended to a logical description of simple context-free tree languages. The question, though, of how to give a logical characterization for this family of tree languages is still open. The same question regarding the special case of monadic context-free tree languages was answered in (Mönnich, 2008). The main theorem of that talk states that the edge definitions of a logical characterization with respect to these languages are either direction preserving or direction reversing. This characterization depends crucially on the possibility of proving a Greibach normal form for monadic simple context-free grammars, a result that would require a completely different proof in the case of non-monadic alphabets.

An alternative way out by means of a bimorphic characterization is not open, either. Bimorphisms were introduced by Nivat (1968) for word languages and later extended to trees by Arnold and Dauchet (1982). A bimorphism is a triple $B = (\phi, L, \psi)$ where L is a regular language and ϕ and ψ are homomorphisms. A bimorphism induces a relation B

defined as $B = \{(\phi(t), \psi(t) \mid t \in L\}$. It is interesting to note that the relations specified by tree transducers are captured by bimorphisms in which ψ is unrestricted and ϕ is a relabeling. Shieber (2004) has shown that the relations defined by synchronous tree-substitution grammars correspond exactly to bimorphism relations in which both homomorphisms are linear and non-deleting. An analogous result is not possible for simple context-free tree grammars. Take the familiar example of a simple context-free tree grammar G over a monadic alphabet that generates the language $L = \{a^n(b^n(e))\}$. According to a well-known theorem due to Rounds (1970) every monadic output tree language of a tree transducer applied to a regular language is regular. Consequently, there is no hope of giving a characterization of context-free tree languages without having recourse to context attributes enabling an upward information transport in the controlling input tree.

References

André Arnold and Max Dauchet. 1982. Morphismes et bimorphismes d'arbres. *Theoretical Computer Science*, 20:33–93.

Michel Bauderon and Bruno Courcelle. 1987. Graph expressions and graph rewritings. *Mathematical Systems Theory*, 20:83–127.

Roderick Bloem and Joost Engelfriet. 2000. A Comparison of Tree Transductions Defined by Monadic Second-Order Logic and by Attribute Grammars. *J. Comp. System Sci.*, 61:1–50.

J. Duske, R. Parchmann, M. Sedello, and J. Specht. 1977. Io-macrolanguages and attributed translations. *Information and Control*, 35:87–105.

Joost Engelfriet and Sebastian Maneth. 1999. Macro Tree Transducers, Attribute Grammars, and MSO Definable Tree Translations. *Information and Computation*, 154:34–91.

Joost Engelfriet and Sebastian Maneth. 2000. Tree Languages Generated by Context-Free Graph Grammars. In Hartmut Ehrig et al., editor, *Graph Transformation*, number 1764 in LNCS, pages 15–29. Springer.

Joost Engelfriet and Heiko Vogler. 1985. Macro tree transducers. *Journal of Computer and System Sciences*, 31(1):71–146.

Michael J. Fischer. 1968. Grammars with Macro-Like Productions. In *Proc. 9th IEEE Symp. on Switching and Automata Theory*, pages 131–142.

Zoltán Fülöp and Heiko Vogler. 1998. *Syntax-Directed Semantics - Formal Models Based on Tree Transducers*. Springer, New York and Berlin.

Hendrik Harkema. 2001. *Parsing Minimalist Languages*. Ph.D. thesis, University of California at Los Angeles.

Aravind Joshi. 1985. Tree adjoining grammars: How much context-sensitivity is required to provide reasonable structural descriptions. In David Dowty, Lauri Karttunen, and Arnold Zwicky, editors, *Natural Language Parsing*, pages 206–250. Cambridge University Press.

M. Kanazawa. 2009. The convergence of well-nested mildly context-sensitive grammar formalisms. In *14th Conference on Formal Grammar*. Slides available at http://research.nii.jp/˜kanazawa/.

Stephan Kepser and Uwe Mönnich. 2003. (Un-)Decidability results for head-driven phrase structure grammar. In Giuseppe Scollo and Anton Nijholt, editors, *Proceedings Algebraic Methods in Language Processing (AMiLP-3)*, pages 141–152.

Stephan Kepser and Uwe Mönnich. 2006. Closure properties of linear context-free tree languages with an application to optimality theory. *Theoretical Computer Science*, 354:82–97.

S. Kepser and J. Rogers. 2007. The equivalence of tree adjoining grammars and monadic linear context-free tree grammars. In M. Kracht, G. Penn, and E. Stabler, editors, *Mathematics of Language 10*.

M. Kuhlmann. 2007. *Dependency Structures and and Lexicalized Grammars*. Ph.D. thesis, Saarland University.

Thomas S. E. Maibaum. 1974. A generalized approach to formal languages. *Journal of Computer and System Sciences*, 8(3):409–439.

Jens Michaelis. 2001. *On Formal Properties of Minimalist Grammar*, volume 13 of *Linguistics in Potsdam*. Universität Potsdam.

Uwe Mönnich. 1997. Adjunction as substitution. In G-J. M. Kruijff, G. Morill, and R. Oehrle, editors, *Formal Grammar '97*, pages 169–178.

U. Mönnich. 2007. Minimalist syntax, multiple regular tree grammars and direction preserving tree transductions. In J. Rogers and S. Kepser, editors, *Proceedings Model Theoretic Syntax at 10*.

Uwe Mönnich. 2008. How to Church a Joshi. In *TAG+9*.

Maurice Nivat. 1968. Transductions des langages de chomyky. Thèse d'état, Paris 1968.

Jean-Claude Raoult. 1997. Rational Tree Relations. *Bull. Belg. Math. Soc.*, 4:149–176.

William C. Rounds. 1970. Mappings and grammars on trees. *Mathematical Systems Theory*, 4(3):257–287.

Stuart M. Shieber. 2004. Synchronous grammars as tree transducers. In *Proceedings TAG+7*.

On Calculus of Displacement[*]

Glyn Morrill
Departament de LSI
Universitat Politècnica de Catalunya

Oriol Valentín
Barcelona Media, Centre d'Innovació
Universitat Pompeu Fabra

1   Introduction

The calculus of Lambek (1958) did not make much impact until the 1980s, but for more than twenty years now it has constituted the foundation of type logical categorial grammar. It has occupied such a central position because of its good logical properties, but it has also been clear, even from the start of its renaissance, that the Lambek calculus suffers from fundamental shortcomings, which we shall mention below.

Certainly it seems that the way ahead in logical categorial grammar is to enrich the Lambek calculus with additional connectives. Thus it was proposed to add intersection and union as far back as Lambek (1961), and such extension is what is meant by type logical categorial grammar. Particular inspiration came from linear logic. Propositional linear connectives divide into additives, multiplicatives, and exponentials. Technically, the Lambek connectives are (noncommutative) linear multiplicatives, so it is natural to consider enrichment of Lambek calculus with (noncommutative) additives and exponentials as well. Quantifiers may also be added (Morrill, 1994, ch. 6) and unary modalities (Morrill 1990, 1992; Moortgat 1995).

However, none of these extensions address the essential limitation of the Lambek basis, which is as follows. The Lambek calculus is a sequence logic of concatenation. This is all well and good in that words are arranged sequentially, however natural language exhibits action at a distance: dependencies which are discontinuous. The Lambek calculus can capture some discontinuous dependencies, namely those in which the discontinuous dependency is peripheral. But it cannot capture the same kinds of dependencies when they are nonperipheral, i.e. medial. In this respect the foundation provided by the Lambek calculus is fundamentally imperfect.

A major proposal to refound categorial grammar was made in Moortgat (1997). Observing that the binary Lambek connectives form residuated triples, and unary modalities residuated pairs, Moortgat proposed to multiply such connective families, defining each family with respect to a different primitive mode of composition represented in the metalinguistic sequent punctuation in the inference rules for the connectives of the family. In such multimodal type logical grammar the modes are interrelated by structural rules defining equations and inclusions on the sequent configurations formed by their composition. This constitutes a powerful methodology and has been the inspiration of type logical grammar for a generation, but the addition of structural rules makes derivation laborious to hand and eye, and creates a problematic search space computationally. No single calculus developed according to these design principles particularly stands out for the breadth and elegance of its empirical application. Indeed, it might be remarked that the motto of substructural logic is to drop structural rules, not to introduce more of them.

It is in this context that Morrill and Valentín (2010) offers the displacement calculus. Sure enough this multiplies residuated triple connective families, as in multimodal type logical grammar, but it has a unique primitive mode of composition, concatenation, like the Lambek calculus, and it has a unimodal sequent calculus, like the Lambek calculus. Thus, importantly, it is entirely free of structural rules, and apparently preserves all the other good

[*] The research reported in the present paper was supported by DGICYT project SESAAME-BAR (TIN2008-06582-C03-01).

proof-theoretic properties of the Lambek calculus. Linguistically, and as illustrated in Morrill and Valentín (2010), it is the generalization of the Lambek calculus which has the widest and most economical coverage that we are aware of. The present paper enters into technical consideration of the displacement calculus given this state of affairs. We define this generalization of the Lambek calculus and consider some of the non-context free properties it characterizes.

2 Displacement calculus

The Lambek calculus (Lambek 1958) forms the basis of type logical categorial grammar (Morrill 1994, Moortgat 1997, Morrill forthcoming). It is a sequence logic without structural rules which enjoys Cut-elimination, the subformula property, and decidability. It is intuitionistic, and so supports the standard Curry-Howard type-logical categorial semantics. In this connection it has the finite reading property. But as a logic of concatenation, the Lambek calculus can only analyse displacement when the dependencies happen to be peripheral. As a consequence it cannot account for the syntax and semantics of:

(1)
- Discontinuous idioms (*Mary gave the man the cold shoulder*).
- Quantification (*John gave every book to Mary; Mary thinks someone left; Everyone loves someone*).
- VP ellipsis (*John slept before Mary did; John slept and Mary did too*).
- Medial extraction (*dog that Mary saw today*).
- Pied-piping (*mountain the painting of which by Cezanne John sold for $10,000,000*.
- Appositive relativization (*John, who jogs, sneezed*).
- Parentheticals (*Fortunately, John has perseverance; John, fortunately, has perseverance; John has, fortunately, perseverance; John has perseverance, fortunately*).
- Gapping (*John studies logic, and Charles, phonetics*).
- Comparative subdeletion (*John ate more donuts than Mary bought bagels*).
- Reflexivization (*John sent himself flowers*).

Furthermore, the Lambek calculus is context-free in generative power (Pentus 1992) and so cannot generate cross-serial dependencies as in Dutch and Swiss-German (Sheiber 1985).

The calculus of displacement, like the Lambek calculus, is a sequence logic without structural rules which enjoys Cut-elimination, the subformula property, and decidability (Morrill and Valentín 2010). Moreover, like the Lambek calculus it is intuitionistic, and so supports the standard categorial Curry-Howard type-logical semantics. In this relation it has the finite reading property. It is a logic not only of concatenation but also of intercalation and provides basic analyses of all of the phenomena itemized in (1) (Morrill and Valentín 2010). Furthermore it analyses verb raising and cross-serial dependencies (Morrill, Valentín and Fadda 2009).

The types of the calculus of displacement **D** classify strings over a vocabulary including a distinguished placeholder 1 called the *separator*. The sort $i \in \mathcal{N}$ of a (discontinuous) string is the number of separators it contains and these punctuate it into $i + 1$ continuous substrings. The types of **D** are sorted into types $\mathcal{F}_i$ of sort i as follows:

(2)

$$
\begin{array}{llll}
\mathcal{F}_j & := & \mathcal{F}_i \backslash \mathcal{F}_{i+j} & \text{under} \\
\mathcal{F}_i & := & \mathcal{F}_{i+j} / \mathcal{F}_j & \text{over} \\
\mathcal{F}_{i+j} & := & \mathcal{F}_i \cdot \mathcal{F}_j & \text{product} \\
\mathcal{F}_0 & := & I & \text{product unit} \\
\mathcal{F}_j & := & \mathcal{F}_{i+1} \downarrow_k \mathcal{F}_{i+j}, 1 \leq k \leq i+1 & \text{infix} \\
\mathcal{F}_{i+1} & := & \mathcal{F}_{i+j} \uparrow_k \mathcal{F}_j, 1 \leq k \leq i+1 & \text{extract} \\
\mathcal{F}_{i+j} & := & \mathcal{F}_{i+1} \odot_k \mathcal{F}_j, 1 \leq k \leq i+1 & \text{disc. product} \\
\mathcal{F}_1 & := & J & \text{disc. prod. unit}
\end{array}
$$

Where A is a type we call its sort sA. We present the calculus using a special kind of sequent calculus which we call hypersequent calculus. The set $\mathcal{O}$ of *hyperconfigurations* is defined as follows, where Λ is the empty string and $[]$ is the metalinguistic separator:

(3) $\mathcal{O} ::= \Lambda \mid [] \mid \mathcal{F}_0 \mid \mathcal{F}_{i+1} \{ \underbrace{\mathcal{O} : \ldots : \mathcal{O}}_{i+1 \ \mathcal{O}'s} \} \mid \mathcal{O}, \mathcal{O}$

Note that the hyperconfigurations are of a new kind in which some type formulas, namely the type formulas of sort greater than one, label mother nodes rather than leaves, and have a number of immediate subhyperconfigurations equal to their sort. This signifies a discontinuous type intercalated by these subhyperconfigurations. Thus $A\{\Delta_1 : \ldots : \Delta_n\}$ interpreted syntactically is formed by strings $\alpha_0 + \beta_1 + \alpha_1 + \cdots + \alpha_{n-1} + \beta_n + \alpha_n$ where $\alpha_0 + 1 + \alpha_1 + \cdots + \alpha_{n-1} + 1 + \alpha_n \in A$ and $\beta_1 \in$

$\Delta_1, \ldots, \beta_n \in \Delta_n$. We call these types *hyperleaves* since in multimodal calculus they would be leaves. The sort of a hyperconfiguration is the number of separators it contains. A *hypersequent* $\Gamma \Rightarrow A$ comprises an antecedent hyperconfiguration Γ of sort i and a succedent type A of sort i. The *vector* $\vec{A}$ of a type A is defined by:

$$(4) \quad \vec{A} = \begin{cases} A & \text{if } sA = 0 \\ A\{\underbrace{[] : \ldots : []}_{sA\ []'s}\} & \text{if } sA > 0 \end{cases}$$

Where Γ_1 is a hyperconfiguration of sort at least k and Γ_2 is a hyperconfiguration, $\Gamma_1|_k\Gamma_2$ signifies the hyperconfiguration which is the result of replacing by Γ_2 the kth separator in Γ_1. Where Γ is a hyperconfiguration of sort i and $\Phi_1, \ldots, \Phi_i$ are hyperconfigurations, the generalized wrap $\Gamma \otimes \langle \Phi_1, \ldots, \Phi_i \rangle$ is the result of simultaneously replacing the successive separators in Γ by $\Phi_1, \ldots, \Phi_i$ respectively. In the hypersequent calculus the discontinuous distinguished hyperoccurrence notation $\Delta\langle\Gamma\rangle$ refers to a hyperconfiguration Δ and continuous subhyperconfigurations $\Delta_1, \ldots, \Delta_i$ and a discontinuous subhyperconfiguration Γ of sort i such that $\Gamma \otimes \langle \Delta_1, \ldots, \Delta_i \rangle$ is a continuous subhyperconfiguration. Technically, whereas the usual distinguished occurrence notation $\Delta(\Gamma)$ refers to a context containing a *hole* which is a leaf, in hypersequent calculus the distinguished hyperoccurrence notation $\Delta\langle\Gamma\rangle$ refers to a context containing a hole which may be a hyperleaf, a *hyperhole*. The hypersequent calculus for the calculus of displacement is given in Figure 1.

3 Displacement grammars

We now turn to **D**-grammars and the languages they generate.

Given a vocabulary $V = \Sigma \cup \{1\}$ a lexical assignment $\alpha\colon A$ comprises a type A and a string $\alpha \in V^+ - \{\underbrace{1 + \cdots + 1}_{n} : n > 0\}$ of sort sA. A lexicon is a finite set of lexical assignments.

We define a *labelling* σ of a hyperconfiguration Δ as a mapping sending each type occurrence A in Δ to a string of sort sA. A *labelled hyperconfiguration* Δ^σ comprises a hyperconfiguration Δ and a labelling σ of Δ. We define the *yield* of a labelled hyperconfiguration Δ^σ as follows:

$$\dfrac{}{\vec{A} \Rightarrow A}\ id \qquad \dfrac{\Gamma \Rightarrow A \quad \Delta\langle\vec{A}\rangle \Rightarrow B}{\Delta\langle\Gamma\rangle \Rightarrow B}\ Cut$$

$$\dfrac{\Gamma \Rightarrow A \quad \Delta\langle\vec{C}\rangle \Rightarrow D}{\Delta\langle\Gamma, \overrightarrow{A\backslash C}\rangle \Rightarrow D}\ \backslash L \qquad \dfrac{\vec{A}, \Gamma \Rightarrow C}{\Gamma \Rightarrow A\backslash C}\ \backslash R$$

$$\dfrac{\Gamma \Rightarrow B \quad \Delta\langle\vec{C}\rangle \Rightarrow D}{\Delta\langle\overrightarrow{C/B}, \Gamma\rangle \Rightarrow D}\ /L \qquad \dfrac{\Gamma, \vec{B} \Rightarrow C}{\Gamma \Rightarrow C/B}\ /R$$

$$\dfrac{\Delta\langle\vec{A}, \vec{B}\rangle \Rightarrow D}{\Delta\langle\overrightarrow{A\cdot B}\rangle \Rightarrow D}\ \cdot L \qquad \dfrac{\Gamma_1 \Rightarrow A \quad \Gamma_2 \Rightarrow B}{\Gamma_1, \Gamma_2 \Rightarrow A\cdot B}\ \cdot R$$

$$\dfrac{\Delta\langle\Lambda\rangle \Rightarrow A}{\Delta\langle\vec{I}\rangle \Rightarrow A}\ IL \qquad \dfrac{}{\Lambda \Rightarrow I}\ IR$$

$$\dfrac{\Gamma \Rightarrow A \quad \Delta\langle\vec{C}\rangle \Rightarrow D}{\Delta\langle\Gamma|_k \overrightarrow{A\downarrow_k C}\rangle \Rightarrow D}\ \downarrow_k L \qquad \dfrac{\vec{A}|_k \Gamma \Rightarrow C}{\Gamma \Rightarrow A\downarrow_k C}\ \downarrow_k R$$

$$\dfrac{\Gamma \Rightarrow B \quad \Delta\langle\vec{C}\rangle \Rightarrow D}{\Delta\langle\overrightarrow{C\uparrow_k B}|_k \Gamma\rangle \Rightarrow D}\ \uparrow_k L \qquad \dfrac{\Gamma|_k \vec{B} \Rightarrow C}{\Gamma \Rightarrow C\uparrow_k B}\ \uparrow_k R$$

$$\dfrac{\Delta\langle\vec{A}|_k \vec{B}\rangle \Rightarrow D}{\Delta\langle\overrightarrow{A\odot_k B}\rangle \Rightarrow D}\ \odot_k L \qquad \dfrac{\Gamma_1 \Rightarrow A \quad \Gamma_2 \Rightarrow B}{\Gamma_1|_k \Gamma_2 \Rightarrow A\odot_k B}\ \odot_k R$$

$$\dfrac{\Delta\langle[]\rangle \Rightarrow A}{\Delta\langle\vec{J}\rangle \Rightarrow A}\ JL \qquad \dfrac{}{[] \Rightarrow J}\ JR$$

Figure 1: Calculus of displacement **D**

$$\begin{aligned} (5) \quad & yield(\Lambda^\sigma) = \Lambda \\ & yield([]^\sigma) = 1 \\ & yield((\Delta, \Gamma)^\sigma) = yield(\Delta^\sigma) + yield(\Gamma^\sigma) \\ & yield(A^\sigma) = \sigma(A) \text{ for } A \text{ of sort} 0 \\ & yield((A\{\Delta_1 : \cdots : \Delta_{sA}\})^\sigma) = \\ & a_1 + yield(\Delta_1^\sigma) + a_2 + yield(\Delta_2^\sigma) + \cdots + \\ & a_{sA-1} + yield(\Delta_{sA}^\sigma) + a_{sA} \end{aligned}$$

where in the last line of the definition A is of sort greater than 0 and $\sigma(A)$ is $a_1 + 1 + a_2 + \cdots + a_{sA-1} + 1 + a_{sA}$.

A labelling σ of a hyperconfiguation Δ is *compatible* with a lexicon **Lex** if and only if $\sigma(A)\colon A \in$ **Lex** for every A in Δ. The language $L(\textbf{Lex}, A)$ generated from lexicon **Lex** for type A is defined as follows:

$$(6) \quad L(\textbf{Lex}, A) = \{yield(\Delta^\sigma)|\ \text{such that}$$
$$\Delta \Rightarrow A \text{ is a theorem of } \textbf{D} \text{ and } \sigma \text{ is compatible with } \textbf{Lex}\}$$

Theorem 1 *The problem of recognition in the class of* **D**-*grammars is decidable.*

Proof. Since for every labelling σ compatible with a lexicon for every type A, $\sigma(A)$ contains at least one symbol different from 1, the set of labelled hyperconfigurations such that their yield equals a given α is finite. Now as theoremhood in the **D** is decidable we have then that the problem of recognition is decidable since it reduces to a finite number of tests of theoremhood. $\Box$

A Prolog parser/theorem-prover for the calculus of displacement has been implemented. It operates by Cut-free backward-chaining hypersequent proof search.

4 Some non-context free D-languages

Computer-generated output for the lexicon and analyses of Dutch verb raising and cross-serial dependencies are given in Appendix A. (We abbreviate $\downarrow_1$, $\odot_1$ and $\uparrow_1$ as $\downarrow$, $\odot$ and $\uparrow$; only discontinuities with a single separator are considered in this paper.)

The non-context free language $\{a^n b^n c^n \mid n > 0\}$ is generated by the following assignments where $sA = sB = sC = 1$ and the distinguished type is $A \odot I$.

(7) b: $J\backslash B, J\backslash(A{\downarrow}B)$
  c: $B\backslash C$
  a: A/C

The assignment b: $J\backslash B$ generates $1{+}b$: B. Then combination with the assignment for c generates $1{+}b{+}c$: C and combination of this with the assignment for a gives $a{+}1{+}b{+}c$: A. Wrapping this around the product unit gives $a{+}b{+}c$: $A\odot I$; alternatively b: $J\backslash(A{\downarrow}B)$ which gives $1{+}b$: $A{\downarrow}B$ can infix to form $a{+}1{+}b{+}b{+}c$: B which combines with c and a again, and so on.

The non-context free copy language $\{ww \mid w \in \{a,b\}^+\}$ is generated by the following assignments where $sA = sB = 0$ and $sS = 1$ and the distinguished type is $S\odot I$.

(8) a: $J\backslash(A\backslash S), J\backslash(S{\downarrow}(A\backslash S)), A$
  b: $J\backslash(B\backslash S), J\backslash(S{\downarrow}(B\backslash S)), B$

Let G be a rewrite grammar containing productions of the form $A \to a$ and $B \to cD \mid Dc$. Replacing the former by a: A and the latter by c: $(D{\uparrow}I){\downarrow}B$ gives a displacement grammar which generates the permutation closure of $L(G)$. It follows that there is a displacement grammar for every language Mix_n of strings with equal numbers of symbols $a_1, \ldots, a_n$. In particular, the non context-free language $Mix = \{w \in \{a,b,c\} \mid |w|_a = |w|_b = |w|_c > 0\}$ is generated by the following assignments:

(9) a: $a, (S{\uparrow}I){\downarrow}a$
  b: $(a{\uparrow}I){\downarrow}b$
  c: $(b{\uparrow}I){\downarrow}S$

Here $sA = sB = sC = 0$ and the distinguished type is S. Appendix B contains a sample derivation of this displacement grammar for Mix.

5 A lower bound on the recognizing power of D-grammars

In this section we prove that **D**-grammars recognize the permutation closures of context-free languages.

This result is obtained using a restricted fragment of the calculus. We define the set $T = \{A \mid A \text{ is an atomic type}\} \cup \{(A{\uparrow}I){\downarrow}B \mid A \text{ and } B \text{ are atomic types}\}$. A T-hypersequent is a hypersequent such that the types of the antecedent belong to T and the succedent is an atomic type.

Lemma 2 (Rearrangement lemma) *Let $\Delta \Rightarrow S$ be a provable T-hypersequent. Then, where $\mathcal{D}$ is a derivation of $\Delta \Rightarrow S$, $\mathcal{D}$ can be rearranged into a new derivation $\mathcal{D}^\star$ of $\Delta \Rightarrow S$ in such a way that the height of $\mathcal{D}$ is preserved, and the last rule of $\mathcal{D}^\star$ has an axiom $S \Rightarrow S$ as the right premise, i.e.:*

$$\mathcal{D} \vdash \cfrac{\vdots}{\Delta \Rightarrow S}{\downarrow}L \quad \rightsquigarrow \quad \mathcal{D}^\star \vdash \cfrac{\Gamma([\,]) \Rightarrow {}^\smile A \quad S \Rightarrow S}{\Delta \Rightarrow S}{\downarrow}L$$

where $\Delta = \Gamma({}^\smile A{\downarrow}S)$ for some atomic type A.

Proof.

$$\cfrac{\Gamma([\,]) \Rightarrow {}^\smile P \quad \cfrac{\Delta(Q;[\,]) \Rightarrow {}^\smile R \quad S \Rightarrow S}{\Delta(Q; {}^\smile R{\downarrow}S) \Rightarrow S}{\downarrow}L}{\Delta(\Gamma({}^\smile P{\downarrow}Q); {}^\smile R{\downarrow}S) \Rightarrow S}{\downarrow}L$$

$$\rightsquigarrow$$

$$\cfrac{\cfrac{\Gamma([\,]) \Rightarrow {}^\smile P \quad \Delta(Q;[\,]) \Rightarrow {}^\smile R}{\Delta(\Gamma({}^\smile P{\downarrow}Q);[\,]) \Rightarrow {}^\smile R}{\downarrow}L \quad S \Rightarrow S}{\Delta(\Gamma({}^\smile P{\downarrow}Q); {}^\smile R{\downarrow}S) \Rightarrow S}{\downarrow}L$$

$\Box$

Lemma 3 (Fronting lemma) *Let $\Delta(A) \Rightarrow S$ be a provable T-hypersequent with a distinguished occurrence of type A. Then:*

$$\vdash A, \Delta(\Lambda) \Rightarrow S$$

Proof. We proceed by induction on the length of hypersequents. We shall write $A_1, \cdots, A_j, \cdots, A_n \Rightarrow S$ for $\Delta(A)$ where we consider A_j as the distinguished occurrence we want to be displaced to the left of the antecedent. By the previous lemma, $A_1, \cdots, A_j, \cdots, A_n \Rightarrow S$ has a derivation with last rule:[1]

$$\frac{A_1, \cdots, A_{i-1}, [\,], A_{i+1} \cdots, A_j, \cdots, A_n \Rightarrow R{\uparrow}I \qquad S \Rightarrow S}{A_1, \cdots, A_{i-1}, (R{\uparrow}I){\downarrow}S, A_{i+1} \cdots, A_j, \cdots, A_n \Rightarrow S} {\downarrow}L$$

Two cases are considered:

- Case $A_j \neq (R{\uparrow}I){\downarrow}S$:

We have $(R{\uparrow}I){\odot}I \Rightarrow R$ is provable. By applying the Cut rule to the left premise of the last rule, we derive:

$$A_1, \cdots, A_{i-1}, \Lambda, A_{i+1} \cdots, A_j, \cdots, A_n \Rightarrow R$$

Hence by induction hypothesis:

$$\vdash A_j, A_1, \cdots, A_{i-1}, \Lambda, A_{i+1} \cdots, \Lambda, \cdots, A_n \Rightarrow R$$

We apply now the $\uparrow$ right rule after the introduction of the unit I:

$$\frac{A_j, A_1, \cdots, A_{i-1}, I, A_{i+1} \cdots, \Lambda, \cdots, A_n \Rightarrow R}{A_j, A_1, \cdots, A_{i-1}, [\,], A_{i+1} \cdots, \Lambda, \cdots, A_n \Rightarrow R{\uparrow}I} {\uparrow}R$$

By the $\downarrow$ left rule:

$$\frac{A_j, A_1, \cdots, A_{i-1}, [\,], A_{i+1} \cdots, \Lambda, \cdots, A_n \Rightarrow R{\uparrow}I \qquad S \Rightarrow S}{A_j, A_1, \cdots, A_{i-1}, (R{\uparrow}I){\downarrow}S, A_{i+1} \cdots, \Lambda, \cdots, A_n \Rightarrow S{\uparrow}I} {\downarrow}L$$

In this case, we have proved the fronting lemma.

- Case $A_j = (R{\uparrow}I){\downarrow}S$:

As before we have the following provable hypersequent:

$$A_1, \cdots, A_{i-1}, \Lambda, A_{i+1}, \cdots, A_n \Rightarrow R$$

By the right $\uparrow$ rule after the introduction of I, we derive:

$$[\,], A_1, \cdots, A_{i-1}, \Lambda, A_{i+1} \cdots, A_j, \cdots, A_n \Rightarrow R{\uparrow}I$$

By the left $\downarrow$ rule:

$$\frac{[\,], A_1, \cdots, A_{i-1}, \Lambda, A_{i+1}, \cdots, A_n \Rightarrow R{\uparrow}I \qquad S \Rightarrow S}{(R{\uparrow}I){\downarrow}S, A_1, \cdots, A_{i-1}, \Lambda, A_{i+1}, \cdots, A_n \Rightarrow S} {\downarrow}L$$

We have proved the fronting lemma in case $A_j = (R{\uparrow}I){\downarrow}S$. In both cases then, the lemma is proved. $\square$

---

[1] Without loss of generality we write A_j to the right of $(R{\uparrow}I){\downarrow}S$.

We now show how the permutation closure of any regular language (excluding the empty string) can be recognized by a **D**-grammar. Let $G = (N, \Sigma, P, S)$ be a regular grammar. Suppose G is right-linear. We define a **D**-grammar comprising a lexicon **Lex$_G$** with atomic types the nonterminals N of G. The vocabulary of **Lex$_G$** is $\Sigma \cup \{1\}$. For every production of the form $A \to c$ with A nonterminal and $c \in \Sigma$, we stipulate that $c\colon A \in$ **Lex$_G$**. And for every production of the form $B \to cA$ (with $A, B \in N$ and $c \in \Sigma$), we stipulate $c\colon (A{\uparrow}I){\downarrow}B \in$ **Lex$_G$**. We want to prove that the language recognized by **Lex$_G$** with distinguished symbol S is the permutation closure of the language generated by G: $L(\mathbf{Lex_G}, S) = Perm(L(G, S))$. The following lemmas prove the equation.

Lemma 4 $L(G, S) \subseteq L(\mathbf{Lex_G}, S)$.

The proof of this lemma proceeds by a simple induction on the length of the derivations of G. The base case is obvious. For the inductive case, suppose we have the derivation whose rewritten string is $a_1 \cdots a_n A$ such that $A \to cB \in P$. Then by induction hypothesis $a_1 + \cdots + a_n \in L(G, B) \subseteq L(\mathbf{Lex_G}, B)$. Hence there exists a labeled hyperconfiguration Δ^σ whose types belong to the types of $\mathbf{L_G}$, $\vdash \Delta \Rightarrow B$ and the yield of Δ^σ is $a_1 + \cdots + a_n$; after the introduction of the unit:

$$\frac{\dfrac{I, \Delta \Rightarrow B}{[\,], \Delta \Rightarrow B{\uparrow}I} {\uparrow}R \qquad A \Rightarrow A}{(B{\uparrow}I){\downarrow}A, \Delta \Rightarrow A} {\downarrow}L$$

Now, $c\colon (B{\uparrow}I){\downarrow}A \in \mathbf{Lex_G}$. Hence $c + a_1 + \cdots + a_n \in L(\mathbf{Lex_G}, \mathbf{A})$.

Lemma 5 $Perm(L(G, S)) \subseteq L(\mathbf{Lex_G}, S)$

Proof. Let $\Delta \Rightarrow S$ be a provable hypersequent with a compatible labelling such that the yield of Δ is $w \in L(G, S)$ and the types occurring in Δ belong to the set of types of **Lex$_G$**:

$$a_1 : A_1, \cdots, a_n : A_n \Rightarrow S, \ w = a_1 + \cdots + a_n$$

By the fronting lemma, any type A_i can be fronted, i.e.: $\vdash a_i : A_i, a_1 : A_1, \cdots, a_{i-1} : A_{i-1}, \Lambda, a_{i+1} : A_{i+1}, \cdots, a_n : A_n \Rightarrow S$. By repeating this process via the fronting lemma, any permutation of the initial w can be obtained. $\square$

Lemma 6 $L(\mathbf{Lex_G}, S) \subseteq Perm(L(G, S))$

Proof. We prove that for every atomic type $A \in N$, $L(\mathbf{Lex_G}, A) \subseteq Perm(L(G, A))$. This entails in particular $L(\mathbf{Lex_G}, S) \subseteq Perm(L(G, S))$ where $S \in N$ is the distinguished nonterminal symbol. The proof goes by induction on the height of derivations of hypersequents $\Delta \Rightarrow A$ such that the types of Δ belong to the types of $\mathbf{Lex_G}$. Case that the height is 0: let $A \in N$ be such that $A \to a$ is a production of G and $a \in V$. Then $a : A \in \mathbf{Lex}$. Case that the height is greater than 0: suppose we have a $\mathbf{Lex_G}$-derivation of $\Delta \Rightarrow A$ with height $n+1$. By the rearrangement lemma, the derivation of $\Delta \Rightarrow A$ can modified in such a way that the height of the derivation is preserved and one of the premises is an axiom:

$$\frac{\Delta([\,]) \Rightarrow A{\uparrow}I \quad S \Rightarrow S}{\Delta((A{\uparrow}I){\downarrow}S) \Rightarrow S} \ {\downarrow}L$$

By a simple reasoning we have $\Delta(\Lambda) \Rightarrow A$ with height lesser or equal than the height of $\Delta([\,]) \Rightarrow A{\uparrow}I$. Since the types of $\Delta(\Lambda)$ belong to the types of $\mathbf{Lex_G}$ we can apply the induction hypothesis, and then we have that $L(\mathbf{Lex_G}, A) \subseteq Perm(L(G, A))$. Now, every $w \in L(\mathbf{Lex_G}, A)$ is the permutation of some $\widetilde{w} \in L(G, A)$. If we apply the rule $S \to cA$ we get $c + \widetilde{w} \in L(G, S)$. But $c : (A{\uparrow}I){\downarrow}S$. Hence, if we insert c in w we get a permutation of $c + \widetilde{w}$. $\square$

Theorem 7 *For every regular grammar G we have $L(\mathbf{Lex_G}, S) = Perm(L(G, S))$*

Corollary 8 *For every context-free language L, the permutation closure of L $Perm(L)$ is recognized by a $\mathbf{D}$-grammar.*

Proof. By an argument invoking properties of semi-linear sets,[2] we know that any permutation closure of a context-free language is equal to the permutation closure of some regular language. This reduces the proof of this corollary to the class of regular languages. The previous theorem proves it. $\square$

---

[2] See van Benthem (1991).

Appendix A. Computer-generated output for Dutch verb raising and cross-serial dependencies

boeken : N : *books*
cecilia : N : c
de : N/CN : ι
jan : N : j
helpen : $J\backslash((N\backslash Si){\downarrow}(N\backslash(N\backslash Si)))$: $\lambda A\lambda B\lambda C\lambda D((help\ D)\ (B\ C))$
henk : N : h
kan : $(N\backslash Si){\downarrow}(N\backslash S)$: $\lambda A\lambda B((isable\ B)\ (A\ B))$
kunnen : $J\backslash((N\backslash Si){\downarrow}(N\backslash Si))$: $\lambda A\lambda B\lambda C((beable\ C)\ (B\ C))$
las : $N\backslash(N\backslash S)$: *reads*
lezen : $J\backslash(N\backslash(N\backslash Si))$: $\lambda Aread$
nijlpaarden : CN : *hippos*
voeren : $J\backslash(N\backslash(N\backslash Si))$: $\lambda Afeed$
wil : $(N\backslash Si){\downarrow}(N\backslash S)$: $\lambda A\lambda B((wants\ B)\ (A\ B))$
zag : $(N\backslash Si){\downarrow}(N\backslash(N\backslash S))$: $\lambda A\lambda B\lambda C((saw\ C)\ (A\ B))$

(1) **jan+boeken+las** : S

$N : j, N : books, N\backslash(N\backslash S) : reads \ \Rightarrow \ S$

$$\frac{\quad N \Rightarrow N \quad \dfrac{N \Rightarrow N \quad S \Rightarrow S}{N, N\backslash S \Rightarrow S} \ \backslash L}{N, N, N\backslash(N\backslash S) \ \Rightarrow \ S} \ \backslash L$$

$((reads\ books)\ j)$

(2) **jan+boeken+kan+lezen** : S

$N : j, N : books, (N\backslash Si){\downarrow}(N\backslash S) : \lambda A\lambda B((isable\ B)\ (A\ B)), J\backslash(N\backslash(N\backslash Si)) : \lambda Aread \ \Rightarrow \ S$

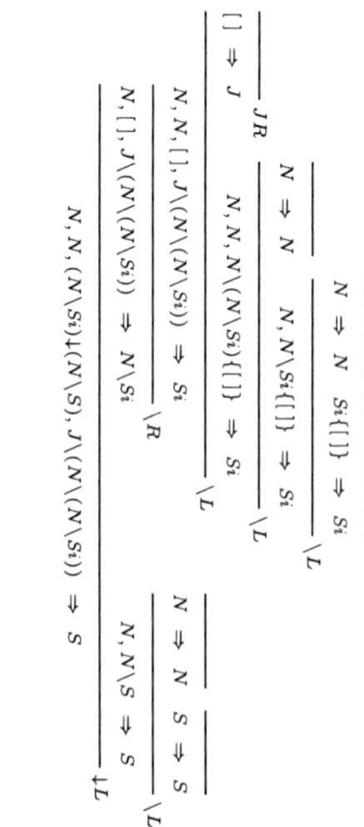

$((isable\ j)\ ((read\ books)\ j))$

(3) **jan+boeken+wil+kunnen+lezen** : S

$N : j, N : books, (N\backslash Si){\downarrow}(N\backslash S) : \lambda A\lambda B((wants\ B)\ (A\ B)), J\backslash((N\backslash Si){\downarrow}(N\backslash Si)) : \lambda A\lambda B\lambda C((beable\ C)\ (B\ C)), J\backslash(N\backslash(N\backslash Si)) : \lambda Aread \ \Rightarrow \ S$

$$\dfrac{[\,] \Rightarrow J \text{ (JR)} \quad \dfrac{\dfrac{[\,] \Rightarrow J \text{ (JR)} \quad \dfrac{\dfrac{N \Rightarrow N \quad \dfrac{N \Rightarrow N \quad \dfrac{\overline{N \Rightarrow N} \quad \overline{Si\{[\,]\} \Rightarrow Si}}{N, N\backslash Si\{[\,]\} \Rightarrow Si}\backslash L}{N, N, N\backslash(N\backslash Si)\{[\,]\} \Rightarrow Si}\backslash L}{N, N, [\,], J\backslash(N\backslash(N\backslash Si)) \Rightarrow Si}\backslash L}{N, [\,], J\backslash(N\backslash(N\backslash Si)) \Rightarrow N\backslash Si}\backslash R \quad \dfrac{\overline{N \Rightarrow N} \quad \overline{Si\{[\,]\} \Rightarrow Si}}{N, N\backslash Si\{[\,]\} \Rightarrow Si}\backslash L}{N, N, (N\backslash Si)\downarrow(N\backslash Si)\{[\,]\}, J\backslash(N\backslash(N\backslash Si)) \Rightarrow Si}\downarrow L}{N, N, [\,], J\backslash((N\backslash Si)\downarrow(N\backslash Si)), J\backslash(N\backslash(N\backslash Si)) \Rightarrow Si}\backslash L}{N, [\,], J\backslash((N\backslash Si)\downarrow(N\backslash Si)), J\backslash(N\backslash(N\backslash Si)) \Rightarrow N\backslash Si}\backslash R \quad \dfrac{\overline{N \Rightarrow N} \quad \overline{S \Rightarrow S}}{N, N\backslash S \Rightarrow S}\backslash L}{N, N, (N\backslash Si)\downarrow(N\backslash S), J\backslash((N\backslash Si)\downarrow(N\backslash Si)), J\backslash(N\backslash(N\backslash Si)) \Rightarrow S}\downarrow L$$

$((wants\ j)\ ((beable\ j)\ ((read\ books)\ j)))$

(4) **jan+cecilia+henk+de+nijlpaarden+zag+helpen+voeren** $: S$

$N : j, N : c, N : h, N/CN : \iota, CN : hippos, (N\backslash Si)\downarrow(N\backslash(N\backslash S)) : \lambda A\lambda B\lambda C((saw\ C)\ (A\ B)), J\backslash((N\backslash Si)\downarrow(N\backslash(N\backslash Si))) : \lambda A\lambda B\lambda C\lambda D((help\ D)\ (B\ C)), J\backslash(N\backslash(N\backslash Si)) : \lambda A feed \Rightarrow S$

$$\dfrac{CN \Rightarrow CN \quad \dfrac{[\,] \Rightarrow J \text{ (JR)} \quad \dfrac{\dfrac{[\,] \Rightarrow J \text{ (JR)} \quad \dfrac{\dfrac{N \Rightarrow N \quad \dfrac{N \Rightarrow N \quad \dfrac{\overline{N \Rightarrow N} \quad \overline{Si\{[\,]\} \Rightarrow Si}}{N, N\backslash Si\{[\,]\} \Rightarrow Si}\backslash L}{N, N, N\backslash(N\backslash Si)\{[\,]\} \Rightarrow Si}\backslash L}{N, N, [\,], J\backslash(N\backslash(N\backslash Si)) \Rightarrow Si}\backslash L}{N, [\,], J\backslash(N\backslash(N\backslash Si)) \Rightarrow N\backslash Si}\backslash R \quad \dfrac{N \Rightarrow N \quad \dfrac{\overline{N \Rightarrow N} \quad \overline{Si\{[\,]\} \Rightarrow Si}}{N, N\backslash Si\{[\,]\} \Rightarrow Si}\backslash L}{N, N, N\backslash(N\backslash Si)\{[\,]\} \Rightarrow Si}\backslash L}{N, N, N, (N\backslash Si)\downarrow(N\backslash(N\backslash Si))\{[\,]\}, J\backslash(N\backslash(N\backslash Si)) \Rightarrow Si}\downarrow L}{N, N, N, [\,], J\backslash((N\backslash Si)\downarrow(N\backslash(N\backslash Si))), J\backslash(N\backslash(N\backslash Si)) \Rightarrow Si}\backslash L}{N, N, N/CN, CN, [\,], J\backslash((N\backslash Si)\downarrow(N\backslash(N\backslash Si))), J\backslash(N\backslash(N\backslash Si)) \Rightarrow Si}/L}{N, N, N/CN, CN, [\,], J\backslash((N\backslash Si)\downarrow(N\backslash(N\backslash Si))), J\backslash(N\backslash(N\backslash Si)) \Rightarrow N\backslash Si}\backslash R \quad \dfrac{N \Rightarrow N \quad \dfrac{\overline{N \Rightarrow N} \quad \overline{S \Rightarrow S}}{N, N\backslash S \Rightarrow S}\backslash L}{N, N, N\backslash(N\backslash S) \Rightarrow S}\backslash L}{N, N, N, N/CN, CN, (N\backslash Si)\downarrow(N\backslash(N\backslash S)), J\backslash((N\backslash Si)\downarrow(N\backslash(N\backslash Si))), J\backslash(N\backslash(N\backslash Si)) \Rightarrow S}\downarrow L$$

$((saw\ j)\ ((help\ c)\ ((feed\ (\iota\ hippos))\ h)))$

Appendix B. Computer generated derivation of $accbab$ in Mix

$$\dfrac{\dfrac{\dfrac{\dfrac{\dfrac{\dfrac{\dfrac{\overline{a \Rightarrow a}}{a, I \Rightarrow a}IL}{a, I, I \Rightarrow a}IL}{a, I, I, I \Rightarrow a}IL}{a, I, I, [\,] \Rightarrow a{\uparrow}I}{\uparrow}R \quad b \Rightarrow b}{a, I, I, (a{\uparrow}I)\downarrow b \Rightarrow b}\downarrow L}{a, I, [\,], (a{\uparrow}I)\downarrow b \Rightarrow b{\uparrow}I}{\uparrow}R \quad \dfrac{\dfrac{\dfrac{S \Rightarrow S}{S, I \Rightarrow S}IL}{S, [\,] \Rightarrow S{\uparrow}I}{\uparrow}R \quad \dfrac{\dfrac{\dfrac{\overline{a \Rightarrow a}}{a, I \Rightarrow a}IL}{a, [\,] \Rightarrow a{\uparrow}I}{\uparrow}R \quad b \Rightarrow b}{a, (a{\uparrow}I)\downarrow b \Rightarrow b}\downarrow L}{S, (S{\uparrow}I)\downarrow a, (a{\uparrow}I)\downarrow b \Rightarrow b}\downarrow L}{\dfrac{a, I, (b{\uparrow}I)\downarrow S, (a{\uparrow}I)\downarrow b, (S{\uparrow}I)\downarrow a, (a{\uparrow}I)\downarrow b \Rightarrow b}{a, [\,], (b{\uparrow}I)\downarrow S, (a{\uparrow}I)\downarrow b, (S{\uparrow}I)\downarrow a, (a{\uparrow}I)\downarrow b \Rightarrow b{\uparrow}I}{\uparrow}R \quad S \Rightarrow S}}{a, (b{\uparrow}I)\downarrow S, (b{\uparrow}I)\downarrow S, (a{\uparrow}I)\downarrow b, (S{\uparrow}I)\downarrow a, (a{\uparrow}I)\downarrow b \Rightarrow S}\downarrow L$$

References

Joachim Lambek. 1958. The mathematics of sentence structure. *American Mathematical Monthly*, 65:154–170. Reprinted in Buszkowski, Wojciech, Wojciech Marciszewski, and Johan van Benthem, editors, 1988, *Categorial Grammar*, Linguistic & Literary Studies in Eastern Europe volume 25, John Benjamins, Amsterdam, 153–172.

J. Lambek. 1961. On the Calculus of Syntactic Types. In Roman Jakobson, editor, *Structure of Language and its Mathematical Aspects, Proceedings of the Symposia in Applied Mathematics XII*, pages 166–178. American Mathematical Society, Providence, Rhode Island.

Michael Moortgat. 1995. Multimodal linguistic inference. *Journal of Logic, Language and Information*, 5:349–385. Also in *Bulletin of the IGPL*, 3(2,3):371–401, 1995.

Michael Moortgat. 1997. Categorial Type Logics. In Johan van Benthem and Alice ter Meulen, editors, *Handbook of Logic and Language*, pages 93–177. Elsevier Science B.V. and The MIT Press, Amsterdam and Cambridge, Massachusetts.

Glyn Morrill and Oriol Valentín. 2010. Displacement Calculus. To appear in the Lambek Festschrift, special issue of *Linguistic Analysis*. http://arxiv.org/abs/1004.4181.

Glyn Morrill, Oriol Valentín, and Mario Fadda. 2009. Dutch Grammar and Processing: A Case Study in TLG. In Peter Bosch, David Gabelaia, and Jérôme Lang, editors, *Logic, Language, and Computation: 7th International Tbilisi Symposium, Revised Selected Papers*, number 5422 in Lecture Notes in Artificial Intelligence, pages 272–286, Berlin. Springer.

Glyn Morrill. 1990. Intensionality and Boundedness. *Linguistics and Philosophy*, 13(6):699–726.

Glyn Morrill. 1992. Categorial Formalisation of Relativisation: Pied Piping, Islands, and Extraction Sites. Technical Report LSI-92-23-R, Departament de Llenguatges i Sistemes Informàtics, Universitat Politècnica de Catalunya.

Glyn V. Morrill. 1994. *Type Logical Grammar: Categorial Logic of Signs*. Kluwer Academic Press, Dordrecht.

Glyn V. Morrill. forthcoming. *Categorial Grammar: Logical Syntax, Semantics, and Processing*. Oxford University Press.

M. Pentus. 1992. Lambek grammars are context-free. Technical report, Dept. Math. Logic, Steklov Math. Institute, Moskow. Also published as ILLC Report, University of Amsterdam, 1993, and in *Proceedings Eighth Annual IEEE Symposium on Logic in Computer Science*, Montreal, 1993.

Stuart Shieber. 1985. Evidence Against the Context-Freeness of Natural Language. *Linguistics and Philosophy*, 8:333–343. Reprinted in Walter J. Savitch, Emmon Bach, William Marsh and Gila Safran-Naveh, editors, 1987, *The Formal Complexity of Natural Language*, D. Reidel, Dordrecht, 320–334.

J. van Benthem. 1991. *Language in Action: Categories, Lambdas, and Dynamic Logic*. Number 130 in Studies in Logic and the Foundations of Mathematics. North-Holland, Amsterdam. Revised student edition printed in 1995 by MIT Press.

Unavoidable Ill-nestedness in Natural Language and the Adequacy of Tree Local-MCTAG Induced Dependency Structures

Joan Chen-Main* and Aravind K. Joshi*[+]
*Institute for Research in Cognitive Science, and [+]Department of Computer and Information Science
3401 Walnut Street, Suite 400A
University of Pennsylvania
Philadelphia, PA 19104-6228, USA
`{chenmain, joshi}@seas.upenn.edu`

Abstract

Within generative approaches to grammar, characterizing the complexity of natural language has traditionally been couched in terms of formal language theory. Recently, Kuhlmann (2007) and collaborators have shown how derivations of generative grammars can be alternately represented as dependency graphs. The properties of such structures provide a new perspective of grammar formalisms and different metric of complexity. The question of complexity of natural language can be recast in dependency structure terms. Ill-nested structures have been assigned to some examples in the literature (Boston et al, 2009, Maier and Lichte, 2009), but the availability of well-nested alternatives prevents the use of these examples to claim that ill-nestedness is an unavoidable linguistic reality. This paper claims that two examples, one German and one Czech, are unavoidably ill-nested, indicating that ill-nestedness is indeed unavoidable in natural language. We conclude that formalisms that generate only well-nested structures, such as TAGs, are not quite powerful enough. However, the tree-local multi-component extension to TAG does generate ill-nested structures, providing just the appropriate amount of complexity in dependency structure terms for characterizing natural language.

1 Introduction

Within generative approaches to human grammar, characterizing the complexity of natural language has traditionally been couched in terms of formal language theory. For some time, it appeared that the weak generative capacity of context free grammars might be adequate for capturing natural language. After the linguistic patterns reported by Shieber (1985) and Culy (1985) indicated that this was not so, Joshi (1985) proposed that a grammar that adequately described natural languages should have four particular properties, dubbing the class of such grammars as mildly context-sensitive. A number of independently developed grammar formalisms not only had these properties but turned out to be weakly equivalent (Joshi et al., 1991).

Recently, Kuhlmann (2007) and collaborators have connected the generative grammar approach with the dependency grammar approach, where linguistic analysis is based on word-to-word relationships. In particular, two properties that are naturally defined over dependency structures, *gap degree* (a measure of discontinuity) and *well-* vs. *ill-nestedness* (whether interleaving substructures are permitted) carve out classes of structures that are systematically related to the derivations of generative grammars. For example, derivations in CFGs correspond to well-nested, gap degree zero dependency structures while derivations in lexicalized Tree Adjoining Grammars (LTAGs) correspond to well-nested, gap degree ≤ 1 dependency structures (Bodirsky et al., 2005).

These properties of associated dependency structures provide a new perspective of generative grammars and a different metric of complexity. The question of the complexity of natural language can be recast in dependency structure terms. It turns out that more than 99.5% of the structures in both the Prague Dependency Treebank (PDT) (Hajič et al., 2001) and Danish Dependency Treebank (DDT) (Kromann. 2003) are well-nested and gap degree ≤ 1 (Kuhlmann and Nivre, 2006). However, it is not obvious what to conclude regarding the gap degree and ill/well-nestedness of natural language from the small number of remaining data. While ill-nested structures have been assigned to some examples in the literature (Boston et al, 2009, Maier and Lichte, 2009), a closer look at these examples shows that reasonable alternative analyses result in structures that are no longer ill-nested. Specifically, when the auxiliary is assumed to be a dependent of the main verb instead of vice versa, the examples become well-nested. This precludes us from using these examples to make the kind of strong claim we would like to: that ill-nestedness is an unavoidable linguistic reality. Our first contribution is the articulation of two empirically verifiable questions of theoretical interest: Does natural language include structures that are unavoidably ill-nested and/or gap degree > 1? Our second contribution is the submission of two examples, a German construction that involves both extraposition and a split quantifier, and a Czech comparative, which we claim are unavoidably ill-nested. Based on these, we conclude that ill-nestedness is indeed unavoidable in natural language and grammars that generate only well-nested structures (such as LTAG) are not quite powerful enough.

Unlike LTAG, its Tree Local Multi-component extension (TL-MCTAG) does have the capacity to induce structures that are ill-nested (Kuhlmann and Möhl, 2006) and also to accommodate the two examples we present. This aligns well with what we know about TAG and TL-MCTAG in traditional terms: Although TL-MCTAGs are weakly equivalent to TAGs, they are more powerful than TAGs in terms of strong generative capacity, i.e., they permit the derivation of structures not derivable in TAGs, and thus have been argued to be a necessary extension to TAGs on linguistic grounds.

The paper is structured as follows. Section 2 reviews the notions of gap degree and well-/ill-nestedness. Section 3 uses LTAG to illustrate how a derivation of a generative grammar can be alternately represented as a dependency graph and reviews how the class of LTAG derivations corresponds to the class of well-nested and gap degree ≤ 1 dependency structures. Section 4 turns to linguis-

tic data. We show how plausible alternate reanalyses can lead to well-nestedness for some previous examples, and discuss the two examples for which we argue that ill-nestedness is unavoidable. Section 5 shows how an analysis for our German example is available in the TL-MCTAG extension, which permits derivations associated with ill-nested dependency structures. Section 6 compares and contrasts dependency structures induced by TAGs with those induced by Combinatorial Categorial Grammars (Koller and Kuhlmann, 2009) and Minimalist Grammars (Boston et al, 2009). Section 7 summarizes and concludes the paper.

2 Discontinuity in Dependency Structures

The dependency structures we refer to in this paper are 3-tuples: a set of nodes, a dominance relation, and a (total) precedence relation. Dominance is encoded via a directed edge and precedence is encoded via left to right position on the page. Here, we review two measures of discontinuity defined on dependency structures. Expanded explanation can be found in (Kuhlmann and Nivre, 2006).

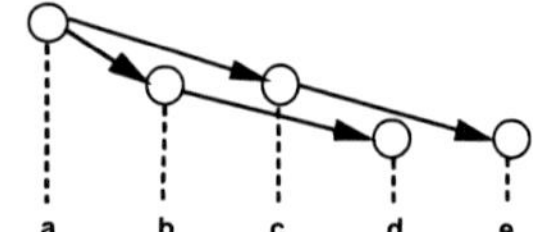

Figure 1. An example dependency structure

2.1 Gap Degree

It will be useful to first define the term *projection*.
Definition: The projection of a node x is the set of nodes dominated by x (including x).
Definition: A *gap* is a discontinuity with respect to precedence in the projection of a node in the dependency structure. (E.g. in Figure (1), the node *c* is the gap preventing *b* and *d* from forming a contiguous interval.)
Definition: The *gap degree of a node* is the number of gaps in its projection.
Definition: The *gap degree of a dependency structure* is the max among the gap degrees of its nodes.

2.2 Well-/Ill-nestedness

Definition: If the roots of two subtrees in the dependency structure are not in a dominance relation, then the trees are *disjoint*.
Definition: If nodes x_1, x_2 belong to tree X, nodes y_1, y_2 belong to tree Y, precedence orders these

nodes: $x_1 > y_1 > x_2 > y_2$, and X and Y are disjoint, then trees X and Y *interleave*. (E.g, in Figure (1), b and d belong to the subtree rooted in b, while c and e belong to the subtree rooted in c. These two subtrees are disjoint. Since the nodes are ordered $b > c > d > e$, the two trees interleave.)

A dependency graph with interleaving subtrees is *ill-nested*, as in (1). A dependency graph with no interleaving is *well-nested*, (e.g Fig. (2d)).

3 LTAG Derivations as Dependency Structures

The LTAG induced dependency structures detailed by Bodirsky et al. (2005) provide an example of how a derivation of a generative grammar can be translated into a dependency graph, retaining information from both the derivation itself and its final phrase structure. We illustrate using a derivation based on the cross-serial dependencies seen in Dutch subordinate clauses, shown in Figure 2. (2a) shows a set of four LTAG elementary trees. (2c) is the derivation structure showing how these four trees combine to yield the derived phrase structure in (2b). (2d) shows the dependency structure that corresponds to this derivation.

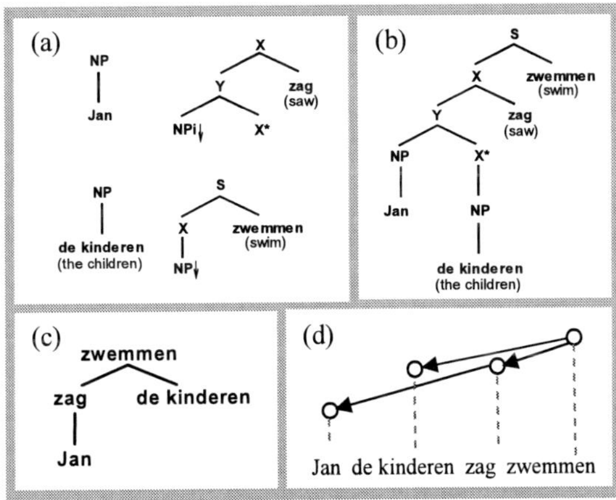

Figure 2. Grammar, phrase structure, and derivation for *Jan de kinderen zag zwemmen* and corresponding graph drawing

First, the set of nodes in the dependency structure corresponds to the set of lexical anchors of the elementary trees. For example, *Jan* anchors an NP tree in (2a). Thus, *Jan* will be a node label in any dependency structure induced by an LTAG derivation involving this tree. Second, the directed edges between the nodes in the dependency structure

mirror the immediate dominance relation in the derivation tree.[1] E.g. Just as the *zwemmen* node has the *zag* and *de kinderen* nodes as its two children in (2c), so does the *zwemmen* node have *zag* and *de kinderen* as dependents in (2d). Lastly, the ordering of the nodes in the dependency structure is exactly the ordering of the terminals in the derived phrase structure.

3.1 The Source of Gaps in LTAG

In TAG-induced dependency structures, a gap arises from an interruption of the dependencies in an auxiliary tree. The lexical anchor of an auxiliary tree and the pronounced material that is combined into that tree will be part of the same projection in the induced dependency structure. Pronounced material below the foot of the auxiliary tree, however, will belong to the tree "hosting" the auxiliary tree, and will not be part of the same projection.[2] If Tree B is adjoined into Tree A, the gap is the material in A that is below the foot node of B. E.g. in the derivation in Figure 2, *de kinderen* is substituted into the *zwemmen* tree below the node into which the *zag* tree adjoins into the *zwemmen* tree. Thus, *de kinderen* interrupts the pronounced material on the left of the *zag* tree's foot node, *Jan*, from the pronounced material on the right of the foot node, *zag*. Since standard TAG auxiliary trees have only one foot, each projection in a TAG-induced dependency structures can have at most one gap.

3.2 Well-nestedness in LTAG

LTAG-induced dependency structures are all well-nested. Recall that the sole source for gaps is pronounced material in the "host" tree below the foot of an auxiliary tree. Suppose an LTAG derivation did have a corresponding ill-nested dependency structure. I.e. suppose Tree A and Tree B are disjoint subtrees in the dependency structure, nodes from Tree A interrupt nodes from Tree B, and nodes from Tree B interrupt nodes from Tree A. If the nodes of Tree A interrupt the nodes of Tree B, this implies that in the derivation, Tree B is an aux-

---

[1] Whereas in standard dependency graphs, adjunction of t2 to t1 generally corresponds to a dependency directed from t2 to t1, in a TAG-induced dependency graph, adjoining t2 to t1 corresponds to the reverse dependency.

[2] Since each node of an LTAG-induced dependency structure is associated with the lexical anchor of an LTAG tree, we have assumed dependency structure nodes to be associated only with pronounced material.

iliary tree that adjoins into Tree A. However, if the nodes of Tree B likewise interrupt the nodes of Tree A, this implies that Tree A is also an auxiliary tree and that it adjoins into Tree B. It is not possible that an LTAG derivation should include Tree A and Tree B adjoining into one another.

4 Linguistic Examples of Ill-nestedness

4.1 Nestedness and Alternative Analyses

It is clear that a linguistic example that requires ill-nestedness will involve at least two discontinuous constituents. However, this is a necessary condition, not a sufficient one. Apparent ill-nestedness can sometimes be avoided via a plausible alternate reanalysis. For example, a number of ill-nested German examples from a dependency version of the TIGER (a phrase structure based treebank to which a conversion algorithm has been applied) are ill-nested only when the auxiliary is assumed to be the root and the main verb and subject are daughters of the auxiliary. When the main verb is assumed to be the root instead, and the subject and auxiliary verb are assumed to be dependents of the main verb, the dependency structure becomes well-nested.[3] This is the case with examples in Maier and Lichte (2009) (examples from converted dependency treebanks) and also the double extraposition example in English in Boston et al (2009) (authors' original example). Because the ill-nestedness depends on choosing the auxiliary verb as the root, we cannot use these examples to make the kind of strong claim we would like to: that ill-nestedness is an unavoidable linguistic reality.

4.2 Ill-nestedness in German

Our example from German involves two discontinuities, extraposition from an NP and a split quantifier. In example (1b) below, the relative clause *der am meisten Geld hatt* 'who had the most money' has been extraposed away from the NP *der Student* 'the student,' and the NP *Bücher* 'books' is separated from its quantifier *drei* 'three.' The canonical order is given in (1a).[4]

---

[3] Thanks to Marco Kuhlmann for making the TIGER examples available and to Tatjana Scheffler for this observation.
[4] Appropriate context and intonation will, of course, make this reading easier. The example has contrastive stress and a contrastive reading and is felicitous in a context such as the one below. Tatjana Scheffler is gratefully acknowledged for providing this example and context.

(1) a. [*Der Student* [*der am meisten Geld*
    the student, who the most   money
    hatte]] *hat* [*drei* [*Bücher*]] *gekauft.*
    had   has   three books   bought
  b. Bücher hat DER Student drei gekauft,
    Books has that student three bought
    der am MEIsten Geld   hatte.
    who the most   money had

The ill-nested part of the structure involves the sub-structures rooted in *Bücher* 'books' and *hatte* 'had.' Note that these two root nodes are not in any dominance relation and are therefore disjoint. The projection of the former includes *Bücher* and *drei* 'three.' The projection of the latter includes *der Student, der, am moisten Geld*, and *hatte*. As the figure shows, the projection of *Bücher* is interrupted by *der Student*, and the projection of *hatte* is interrupted by *drei*.

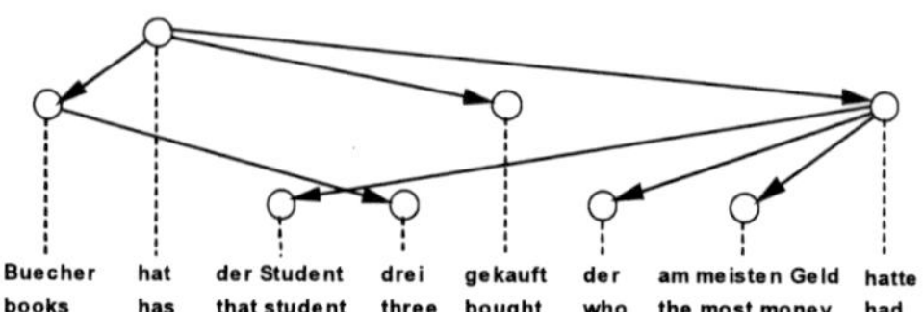

Figure 3. Dependency structure 1 for (1b): aux dominates main verb

Interestingly, this German construction remains ill-nested when we suppose instead that the main verb is the root, reversing the dependency between the main verb and the auxiliary. As can be seen in the dependency structure in Fig. 4, the ill-nested substructures are unaffected. This alternate analysis lends itself well to a TAG based analysis, which would typically assume the main verb to be the root (allowing verbs and substitution nodes for their arguments to be elementary tree local).

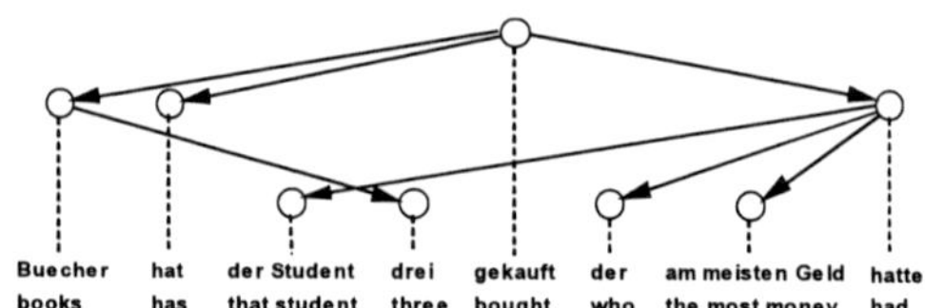

Figure 4. Dependency structure 2 for (1b): main verb dominates aux

---

A: Every student bought multiple items in the store. Some bought three magazines, some bought two calendars, some bought two books, and the oldest student bought three books.
B: No, hat DER Student drei gekauft, der am meisten Geld hatte.

4.3 Ill-nestedness in Czech

Boston et al. (2009) note that ill-nested structures have been assigned to Czech comparatives. Their example, sentence number Ln94209_45.a/18 from the PDT 2.0, can be glossed as "A strong individual will obviously withstand a high risk better than a weak individual" and is given in Fig. 5. It is of particular interest because, like our German example, the ill-nestedness here involves two constituents between which it would be difficult to justify a dependency. This suggests that the substructures corresponding to the two constituents will remain disjoint under reasonable analyses, and thus, the dependency structures will remain ill-nested.

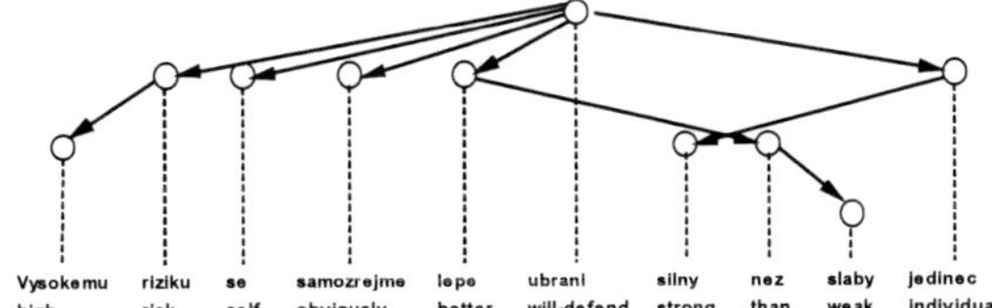

Figure 5. Ill-nested Czech comparative from PDT[5]

5 TL-MCTAG Induced Dependency Structures

MCTAG (Weir 1988) is one of the most widely used extensions for handling linguistic cases that are difficult for classic TAG. Whereas TAG takes the basic unit to be a single elementary tree, MCTAGs extend the domain of locality to encompass a set of trees. The tree-local MC-extension, in which all members of an multi-component set must combine into the same "host" tree, allows for linguistically satisfying accounts for a number of attested phenomena, such as: English extraposition (Kroch and Joshi 1990), subj-aux inversion in combination with raising verbs (Frank 2002), anaphoric binding (Ryant and Scheffler 2006), quantifier scope ambiguity (Joshi et al. 2003).

We have assumed here that each MC-set is lexicalized and that the set of nodes in MCTAG-induced dependency structures corresponds to the set of lexical anchors, just as we assumed for LTAG-induced dependency structures. Silent elements, such as traces, do not anchor an elementary tree, and so do not correspond to a node in the de-

pendency structure. Kuhlmann and Möhl (2006) show that dependency structures induced from tree-local MCTAG derivations in this way include structures that are ill-nested and/or gap degree > 1.

5.1 Additional Source of Gaps in MC-TAGs

In 3.1, we noted that the source of every gap in an LTAG induced dependency structures is an interruption of the dependencies of an auxiliary tree. Thus, a MC-set comprised of two auxiliary trees allows the potential for at least two gaps in MCTAG induced dependency structures, one associated with each foot. There is a second source of gaps in MCTAG: a gap may arise as a result of any pronounced material between two components. Thus, the maximum gap degree $= 2n - 1$, where n is the maximum number of components in any elementary tree set.

5.2 Ill-nestedness in MC-TAG

Because material between the nodes where two components of a MC-set compose into a host tree can also create a gap, even a tree-local MCTAG that allows only substitution can induce an ill-nested dependency structure. Ill-nestedness arises when two MC-sets combine into the same host tree and the nodes into which each set combines interleave. This will be illustrated below by the TL-MCTAG derivation for our German example.

5.3 The Adequacy of TL-MCTAG

The MC-TAG derivation for (1b) will require a tree headed by *gekauft* 'bought' (shown in 6h) into which two MC-sets combine, one for *Bücher* 'books' and its trace (shown in 6b) and a second for *hatte* (and the rest of the relative clause) and its trace (shown in 6a). The singleton sets involved are also shown in Fig 6c-6h. To derive (1b), *drei* (6f) adjoins into the β component of (6b), which substitutes into the lower NP of the *gekauft* tree, (6h). The α component of (6b) adjoins to the root of (6h). To accomplish extraposition, we make use of *flexible composition*, the mirror operation of adjoining: If tree A adjoins into tree B, the combination can be alternatively viewed as tree B "flexibly" composing with tree A (Joshi et al. 2003, Kallmeyer and Joshi 2003).[6] By enriching MCTAG

---

[5] The non-lexical root node and punctuation node are removed for simplicity. Thanks is due to Marisa Ferrara Boston for making this PDT structure available.

[6] A TL-MCTAG with flexible composition can also be viewed as an MCTAG allowing *delayed tree-locality* (Chiang and Scheffler, 2008).

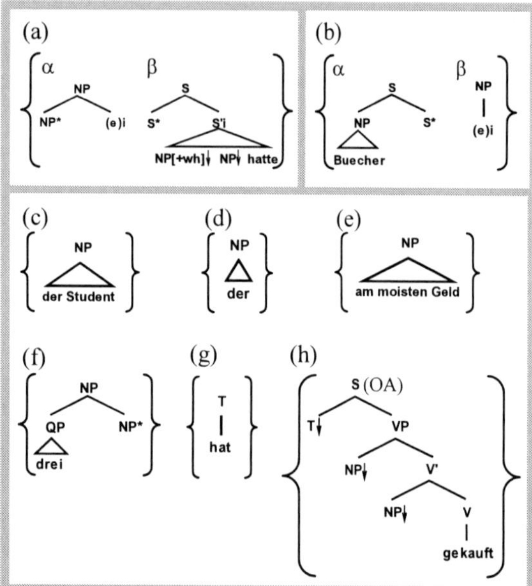

Figure 6. MC-set for extraposition of a relative clause, MC-set for split quantifier, and singleton sets for deriving example (1b)[7]

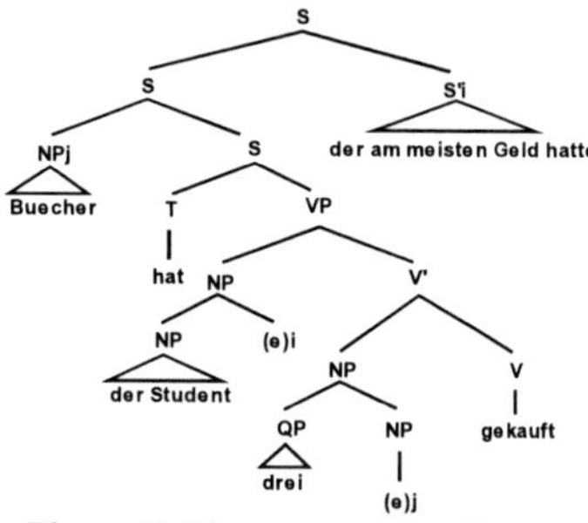

Figure 7. Phrase structure for example (1b)

with this perspective of adjoining, some derivational steps which appear to permit components from the same MC-set to combine into different-trees can be recast as abiding by tree-locality. *Der Student*, (6c), flexibly composes into the αcomponent of the set in (6a), while *der*, (6d), and *am meisten Geld*, (6e), substitute into the β component. The (derived) α component of (6a) adjoins into the highest NP node in (6h), while β, the extraposed relative, adjoins into the root of (6h). Additionally, (6g), the auxiliary verb, substitutes

---

[7] The V2 requirement in German can be handled with an *obligatory adjoining* constraint (denoted OA) on the S node of the tree for the main verb. The particular implementation of the V2 requirement is not relevant to our main argument. See (Kinyon et. al. 2006) for a TAG approach to V2.

into the T node of (6h) the *gekauft* tree. This derivation yields the phrase structure in Fig. 7 and corresponds to the dependency structure in Fig. 4. We have not fully committed to the direction of the dependency for flexible composition. If flexible composition is to be truly viewed as an alternate conception of adjoining, then perhaps the direction of the dependency when A flexibly composes into B should be identical to that of the dependency when B adjoins into A. Whatever the outcome, the ill-nestedness of our German example remains, as can be seen in the alternate dependency structure in Fig. 8. The ill-nestedness involves the same nodes, but the roots of the disjoint substructures are now *Bücher* and *der Student*.[8]

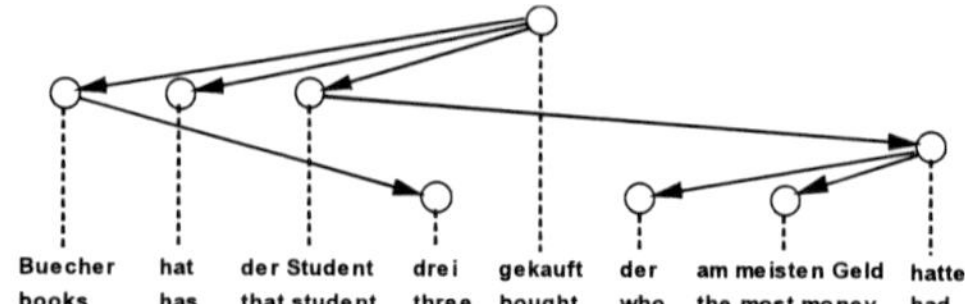

Figure 8. Dependency structure 3 for (1b): *Der student* governs *hatte*

6 Dependency Structures Across Generative Frameworks

6.1 CCGs and Dependency Structures

Koller and Kuhlmann (2009) show how derivations in (a fragment of) Combinatory Categorial Grammars (CCG) (Steedman, 2001) can be viewed as dependency structures. The source of gaps appears to correspond to alternating application of the CCG operations forward and backwards composition, making it difficult to state a bound on gap degree. As the authors show, it follows that TAG (which induces gap degree ≤ 1 structures) does not generate the same class of dependency structures as CCG. It is unclear, however, whether or not ill-nested structures are permitted.

6.2 MGs and Dependency Structures

Boston et al (2009) approach Minimalist Grammars (MG) (Stabler, 1997) from a dependency

---

[8] Thus, there is some room to accommodate Candito and Kahane's (1998) arguments that the direction of the dependency for adjoining is the reverse of that for substitution. Note further that in the MCTAG case, a non-uniform interpretation of derivation tree arcs raises the issue of the direction of the dependency in the case where one component adjoins into a host tree while a second component combines via substitution.

structure perspective, showing that ill-nested structures are derivable and showing how gaps arise. In MG induced dependency structures, every gap is associated with movement (although not every movement corresponds to a gap). In MGs, every movement involves a liscensor and licensee pair, both of which are lexical entries. At first blush, it appears that the unlimited number of movements (i.e. uses of these entries) permitted during an MG derivation also permits an unbounded number of gaps. It turns out, however, that the gap degree for the class of dependency structures associated with a particular MG is bound by the number of licensees in that MG's lexicon due to two linguistic considerations. First, each licensee features depends on a linguistically motivated functional category. Thus, the number of features permitting movement is finite. Second, the ShortestMovementConstraint, which has been incorporated into the MG definition, prohibits subsequent uses of the same licensee feature from interacting with the first use. The subderivations are, in the relevant sense, independent, generating substructures whose gap degree is bound by the number of licensee features. The result is that even as an MG derivation grows, the gap degree does not increase beyond the number of licensee features. (Boston, Hale, p.c.)

6.3   Comparison with TL-MCTAG

The most obvious difference across formalisms is the source of gaps and, consequently, the ease with which a bound on gap degree can be stated. For TL-MCTAG, a bound is straightforwardly stated via the maximum number of components permitted in an elementary set. Though TL-MCTAG as a formal system allows any number of components in an MC-set, TL-MCTAG as used in linguistic analyses typically uses only two components (Chen-Main and Joshi, 2007). In a sense, TL-MCTAG with two components arises naturally from standard TAG, particularly when adjoining is viewed as reversible. In the case where tree A adjoins into a tree internal node x in B, reversing the composition can be recast as follows: B is split into a two-component set at node x with one component adjoining into the root of tree A and the second component substituting into the foot of A. Motivating three-component sets is more difficult.

A question that remains is whether or not there constructions that are unavoidably gap degree 2 or more. We are aware of one gap degree 2 example

from a Hindi dependency treebank that is being developed with the annotation scheme detailed in (Begum et al, 2008) (Mannem, p.c.), though we have not yet investigated whether other plausible analyses will retain the gap degree 2 property.

7   Summary

This paper raises the question of whether or not natural language includes structures that are unavoidably ill-nested and/or gap degree > 1, and motivates this issue as part of understanding the complexity of natural language in dependency structure terms. Based on one German linguistic example and one Czech example from the PDT, we conclude that the answer to the first question is affirmative and that a grammar formalism on the right track for characterizing human language should be able to induce ill-nested structures. TL-MCTAG's ability to cover ill-nested structures bolsters its candidacy as a good model of natural language, but, as yet, it is unclear whether its ability to also induce dependency structures that are gap degree > 1 is linguistically useful or not. The next step is to find examples that are unavoidably gap degree >1.

These issues are relevant not only for TL-MCTAG but also for other generative approaches that induce ill-nested, gap degree > 1 dependency structures, such as Minimalist Grammars (Boston et. al. 2009). Moreover, we predict that other formalisms which are equivalent in traditional terms will also induce such structures, mirroring the convergence noted in (Joshi et al., 1991). However, because these formalisms employ different formal objects and operations, we also expect more nuanced differences, such as the source of gaps, or the ease with which one can state a bound on gap degree in each framework.

Acknowledgments

Special thanks is due to Marisa Ferrara Boston, Lucas Champollion, John Hale, Marco Kuhlmann, Prashanth Mannem, Beatrice Santorini, and Tatjana Scheffler for helpful discussion and especially assistance with data.

References

Rafiya Begum, Samar Husain, Arun Dhwaj, Dipti Misra Sharma, Lakshmi Bai and Rajeev Sangal. 2008. Dependency Annotation Scheme for Indian Languages. In *Proceedings of The Third International Joint Conference on Natural Language Processing*, Hyderabad, India.

Manuel Bodirsky, Marco Kuhlmann, and Mathias Möhl. 2005. Well-nested drawings as models of syntactic structure. In *10th Conference of Formal Grammar and 9th Meeting on Mathematics of Language*, Edinburgh, UK.

Marisa Ferrara Boston, John T. Hale, and Marco Kuhlmann. 2009. Dependency structures derived from Minimalist Grammars. In *Proceedings of Mathematics of Language 11*, 11-22.

Marie-Hélène Candito and Sylvain Kahane. 1998. Can the TAG derivation tree represent a semantic graph? An answer in the light of Meaning-Text Theory. In *Proceedings of TAG+4*, Philadelphia, USA.

Joan Chen-Main and Aravind K. Joshi. 2007. Multicomponent Tree Adjoining Grammars, dependency graph models, and linguistic analyses. In *Proceedings of the ACL 2007 Workshop on Deep Linguistic Processing*, Prague, 1-8.

David Chiang and Tatjana Scheffler. 2008. Flexible Composition and Delayed Tree-Locality. In *Proceedings of TAG+9*, Tübingen, Germany.

Christopher Culy. 1985. The complexity of the vocabulary of Bambara. *Linguistics and Philosophy*, 8:345-351.

Robert Frank. 2002. Phrase Structure Composition and Syntactic Dependencies. MIT Press.

Jan Hajič, Barbora Vidova Hladka, Jarmila Panevová, Eva Hajičová, Petr Sgall, and Petr Pajas. 2001. Prague Dependency Treebank 1.0. LDC, 2001T10.

Aravind K. Joshi. 1985. How much context-sensitivity is required to provide reasonable structural descriptions: Tree adjoining grammars. In David Dowty, Lauri Karttunen, and Arnold Zwicky (eds.), *Natural Language Parsing: Psychological, Computational, and Theoretical Perspectives*, 206-250. Cambridge University Press.

Aravind K. Joshi, K. Vijay-Shanker, David Weir. 1991. The convergence of mildly context-sensitive grammar formalisms. In Peter Sells, Stuart Shieber, Thomas Wasow (eds.), *Foundational Issues in Natural Language Processing*, 31–81. MIT Press.

Aravind K. Joshi, Laura Kallmeyer, and Maribel Romero. 2003. Flexible composition in LTAG: quantifier scope and inverse linking. In H. Bunt and R. Muskens (eds.), *Computing Meaning 3*. Kluwer.

Laura Kallmeyer and Aravind K. Joshi. 2003. Factoring predicate argument and scope semantics: underspecified semantics with LTAG. *Research on Language and Computation* 1(1-2), 3-58.

Alexandra Kinyon, Owen Rambow, Tatjana Scheffler, Sinwon Yoon, and Aravind K. Joshi. 2006. The Metagrammar Goes Multilingual: A Crosslinguistic Look at the V2-Phenomenon. In *Proceedings of TAG+8*, Sydney, Australia, 17-24.

Alexander Koller and Marco Kuhlmann. 2009. Dependency trees and the strong generative capacity of CCG. In *Proceedings of the 12th Conference of the EACL*, 460-468, Athens, Greece.

Anthony Kroch and Aravind K. Joshi. 1990. Extraposition in a Tree Adjoining Grammar. In G. Huck and A. Ojeda, eds., *Syntax and Semantics: Discontinuous Constituents*, 107-149.Matthias Trautner Kromann. 2003. The Danish Dependency Treebank and the DTAG treebank tool. In *2nd Workshop on Treebanks and Linguistic Theories (TLT)*, 217-220.

Marco Kuhlmann. 2007. Dependency Structures and Lexicalized Grammars. PhD thesis, Saarland University, Saarbrücken, Germany.

Marco Kuhlmann and Mathias Möhl. 2006. Extended cross-serial dependencies in Tree Adjoining Grammars. In *Proceedings of TAG+8*, Sydney, Australia, 121-126.

Marco Kuhlmann and Joakim Nivre. 2006. Mildly nonprojective dependency structures. In 21st International Conference on Computational Linguistics and 44th Annual Meeting of the ACL (COLING-ACL), Companion Volume, Sydney, Australia.

Wolfgang Maier and Timm Lichte. 2009. Characterizing Discontinuity in Constituent Treebanks. In *Proceedings of the 14th Conference on Formal Grammar*, Bordeaux, France.

Neville Ryant and Tatjana Scheffler. 2006. Binding of anaphors in LTAG. In *Proceedings of TAG+8*, Sydney, Australia, 65-72.

Stuart Shieber. 1985. Evidence against the contextfreeness of natural language. *Linguistics and Philosophy* 8:333–343.

Stabler, Edward P. 1997. Derivational minimalism. In *Proceedings of Logical Aspects of Computational Linguistics*, 68-95.

Mark Steedman. 2001. *The Syntactic Process*. MIT Press.

David Weir. 1988. *Characterizing mildly context-sensitive grammar formalisms*. PhD dissertation, University of Pennsylvania, Philadelphia, USA.

Generating LTAG grammars from a lexicon-ontology interface

Christina Unger   **Felix Hieber**   **Philipp Cimiano**

Semantic Computing Group
Cognitive Interaction Technology – Center of Excellence (CITEC)
University of Bielefeld, Germany
`{cunger,fhieber,cimiano}@cit-ec.uni-bielefeld.de`

Abstract

This paper shows how domain-specific grammars can be automatically generated from a declarative model of the lexicon-ontology interface and how those grammars can be used for question answering. We show a specific implementation of the approach using Lexicalized Tree Adjoining Grammars. The main characteristic of the generated elementary trees is that they constitute domains of locality that span lexicalizations of ontological concepts rather than being based on requirements of single lexical heads.

1 Introduction

Many approaches to the interpretation of natural language represent meanings as generic logical forms. However, some domain-specific applications require semantic representations that are aligned to a specific ontology and thus cannot be provided by a generic, ontology-independent semantic construction. To illustrate this, consider the example of a geographical ontology that contains a data property[1] *population* relating states to their number of inhabitants. When constructing a natural language interface to this ontology, it has to be taken into account that *population* can be expressed in different ways – directly as in 1, or with related vocabulary as in 2 and 3.

1. The <u>population of</u> Hawaii is 1 300 000.

---

[1]Ontologies distinguish two kinds of relations: *object properties*, that link individuals to individuals, and *data properties*, that link individuals to data values (e.g. strings or integers).

2. Hawaii <u>has</u> 1 300 000 <u>inhabitants</u>.

3. 1 300 000 <u>people live in</u> Hawaii.

For these sentences, Boxer (Bos, 2008) generates generic Discourse Representation Structures (DRSs) that can roughly be represented as in 4 (for the sentence in 1) and 5 (for the sentences in 2 and 3).

4.

$$\begin{array}{|l|}
\hline
x_0\ x_1 \\
\hline
hawaii(x_0) \\
population(x_1) \\
of(x_1, x_0) \\
\mid x_1 \mid\ \geq 74\,000\,000 \\
\hline
\end{array}$$

5.

$$\begin{array}{|l|}
\hline
x_0\ x_1\ x_2 \\
\hline
hawaii(x_0) \\
inhabitant(x_1) \\
have(x_2) \\
agent(x_2, x_0) \\
patient(x_2, x_1) \\
\mid x_1 \mid\ \geq 74\,000\,000 \\
\hline
\end{array}
\qquad
\begin{array}{|l|}
\hline
x_0\ x_1\ x_2 \\
\hline
hawaii(x_0) \\
people(x_1) \\
live(x_2) \\
agent(x_2, x_1) \\
in(x_2, x_0) \\
\mid x_1 \mid\ \geq 74\,000\,000 \\
\hline
\end{array}$$

Note that while the predicate *population* can be taken to directly correspond to the concept *population* in the ontology, the predicates *live* and *inhabitant*, for example, would yield an empty extension if evaluated with respect to the ontology. We would need additional meaning postulates that relate these predicates to *population*, or, alternatively, some postprocessing that transforms generic forms like in 5 into a more specific form equivalent to 4.

An arguably more elegant and useful solution is to let the semantic vocabulary follow the vocabulary of the ontology in the first place, i.e. to right away construct the specifc logical form 4 also for the sentences in 2 and 3. This, however, raises another problem. In order to arrive at the meaning in 4, the semantic contributions of the lexical items have to be adjusted. In the case of 3, for example, the predicate *population* can be assumed to be the semantic contribution of the noun phrase inhabitants, while the verb have is semantically empty. In 2, on the other hand, the predicate *population* might be contributed by the verb live, while the noun people is semantically empty. Although this does not seem problematic in this case, there might not exist a general way to assign meanings to lexical items consistently. Imagine, for example, the ontology also contains a concept *people*, which plays a role in a different context. Then the noun people needs a non-empty semantic interpretation – possibly one which clashes with its use in 3.

The challenging goal thus is to construct an interpretation for sentences that uses the vocabulary of the ontology and therefore might deviate from the surface structure of the sentence. We propose to meet this challenge by determining basic semantic units with respect to an ontology. Assuming a tight connection between syntactic and semantic units, then also basic syntactic units turn out to depend on a particular ontology, and hence the whole syntax-semantics interface becomes ontology-specific.

We show an implementation of this approach using Lexicalized Tree Adjoining Grammars. They are particularly well-suited for the task of compositional ontology-specific interpretation due to their extended domain of locality and their tight connection between syntax and semantics. The general procedure we follow consists of two steps. First, the ontology is connected to a lexicon model that specifies how concepts in the ontology can be realized (e.g. the concept *borders* can be realized as the transitive verb *to border* or as a noun with a prepositional phrase, *border of*). And second, this lexicon model is used to automatically construct grammar entries that are aligned to the underlying ontology. Both steps will be described in the next section.

2 Generating ontology-specific grammars

We assume a grammar to be composed of two parts: an ontology-specific part and an ontology-independent part. The ontology-specific part contains lexical entries that refer to individuals, concepts and properties in the underlying ontology. It is generated automatically from an ontology-lexicon interface model, as described below. The ontology-independent part comprises domain-independent expressions like determiners and auxiliary verbs. It needs to be specified by hand, but can be reused across domains.

We assume grammar entries to be pairs of a syntactic and a semantic representation. As syntactic representation we take trees from Lexicalized Tree Adjoining Grammar (Schabes 1990), LTAG for short. LTAG is very well-suited for ontology-based grammar generation, mainly because it allows for flexible basic units; we will demonstrate the importance of this below. As semantic representations we take DUDEs (Cimiano, 2009) – representations similar to Underspecified Discourse Representation Structures (UDRSs) (Reyle, 1993) augmented with information that facilitate a flexible semantic composition. This semantic flexibility nicely matches the syntactic flexibility provided by LTAG.

The first step in generating the domain-specific part of a grammar is to enrich the underlying ontology with linguistic information. The framework we use for this is LexInfo (Buitelaar et al., 2009). LexInfo offers a general frame for creating a declarative specification of the lexicon-ontology interface by connecting concepts of the ontology to information about their linguistic realization, in particular word forms, morphological information, subcategorization frames and mappings between syntactic and semantic arguments. For example, the LexInfo entry for the verb *to border* looks as depicted in Figure 1. It comprises the verb's lemma together with other written forms (in principle all inflected forms, generated by a separate morphology module), and its syntactic behaviour. The syntactic behaviour specifies the syntactic arguments on the one hand, here simply called subject and object, and the semantic arguments on the other hand. The semantic arguments correspond to domain and range of a predicate that refers to the concept *borders* in the ontology (in our case a relation between two states). The predicative representation also specifies mappings between the syntactic and semantic arguments, more specifically between the subject of the verb and the domain of

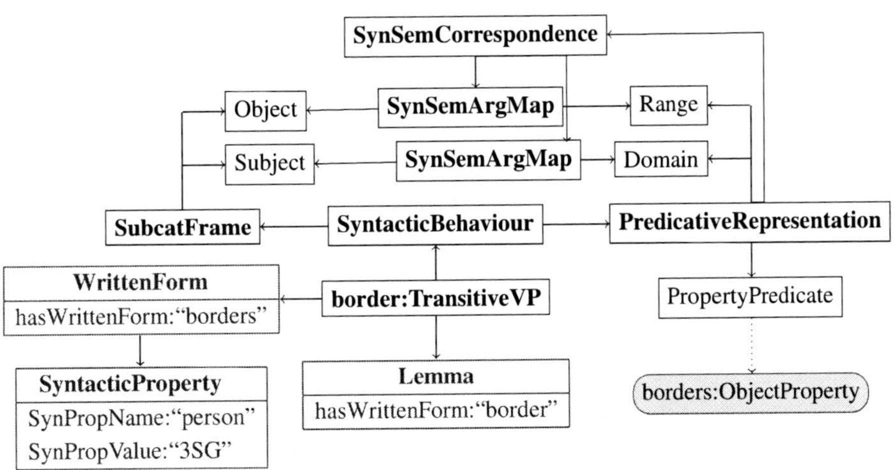

Figure 1: LexInfo entry for *to border*

the denoted relation, as well as the object of the verb and the range of the relation.

Analogously, LexInfo provides general structures for specifying the syntactic and semantic properties of other categories such as intransitive verbs, noun phrases, nouns with prepositional arguments, and so on. An example of a noun with a prepositional argument is *border of*; the according LexInfo entry is given in Figure 2. Its structure is very similar to the transitive verb entry, the main difference being the additional specification of the preposition required by the noun.

Associating concepts of the ontology with such LexInfo structures is a one-to-many mapping, since most concepts can have different lexicalizations. For the relation *borders*, for example, we would specify the TransitiveVP entry in Figure 1 as well as the NounPP entry in Figure 2. Note that both denote a predicate that is related to the same relation *borders* in the ontology.

The process of specifying all possible lexicalization alternatives is, up to now, done by hand. However it can in principle be automatized if the ontology labels are chosen in a way such that they can be processed by a part-of-speech tagger and related to possible realizations, e.g. with the help of a corpus.

Once a LexInfo model of the ontology is specified, the next step is to generate grammar entries from it. To this end, the lexical entries specified in the LexInfo model are input to a general mechanism

that automatically generates corresponding pairs of syntactic and semantic representations. For the transitive verb entry of *to border* in Figure 1, for example, a number of elementary LTAG trees are generated – two of them are given in 6 and 7. Both trees are paired with the DUDE in 8.

6.

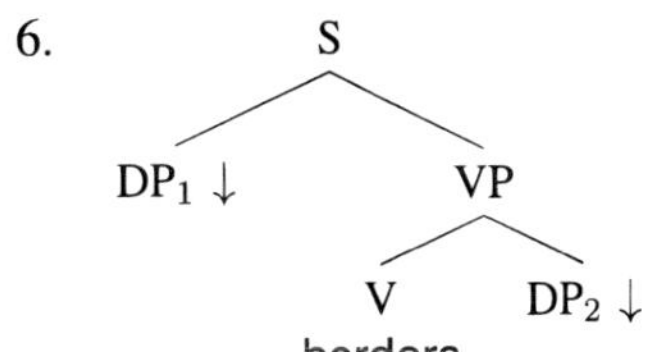

7.

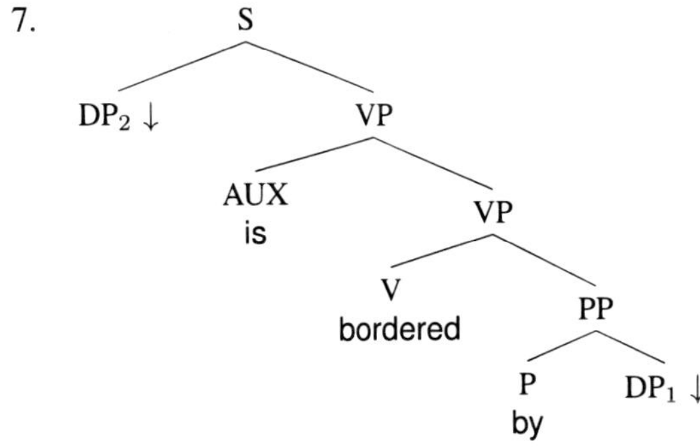

8.

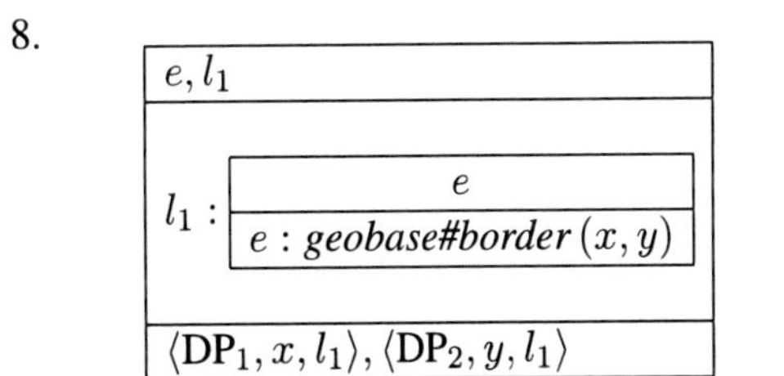

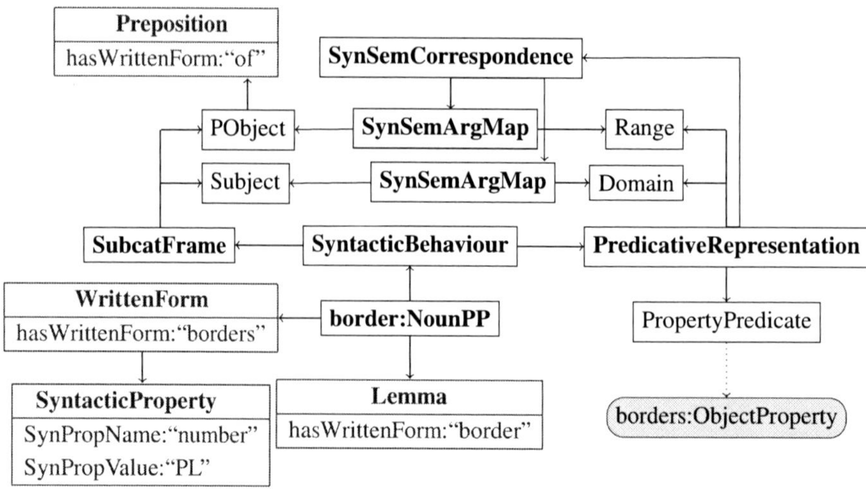

Figure 2: LexInfo entry for *border of*

This semantic representation contains a DRS labeled l_1, which provides the predicate *geobase#border* corresponding to the intended concept in the ontology. This correspondence is ensured by using the vocabulary of the ontology, i.e. by using the URI of the concept instead of a more generic predicate. The prefix *geobase#* is short for `http://www.geobase.org/` and specifies the namespace of the *Geobase* ontology, which we use (more on this in the next section). Furthermore, the semantic representation contains information about which substitution nodes in the syntactic structure provide the semantic arguments x and y. That is, the semantic referent provided by the meaning of the tree substituted for DP_1 corresponds to the domain of the semantic predicate, while the semantic referent provided by the meaning of the tree substituted for DP_2 corresponds to the predicate's range. Note that the order of the substitution nodes is reversed in the passive tree structure in 7.

Additional grammar entries generated from the LexInfo model in Figure 1 are adjunction trees for relative clauses and the gerund *bordering*, together with a semantic representation similar to 8. In all these cases the syntactic structure encoded in the elementary trees captures the lexical material that is needed for verbalizing the concept *borders*. This is the reason why the generated syntactic structures slightly differ from what one would expect from an LTAG elementary tree. Elementary trees are commonly assumed to constitute extended projections of lexical items, comprising their syntactic and semantic arguments, cf. (Frank, 1992). In our generated grammar, however, elementary trees do not build around lexical items but rather around lexicalizations of concepts from the ontology. That is, not only the semantic primitives but also the syntactic domain of locality are imposed by the underlying ontology. In many cases, this domain does not extend beyond the familiar lexical projections (recall the tree in 6), however it might contain more lexical material. For example, for the *population* example from the beginning we would need a tree like in 9.

9.

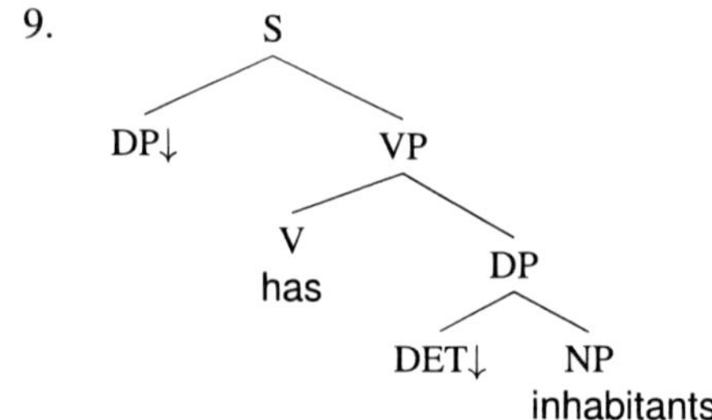

Also, for a concept such as *highest point*, that relates states and locations, we would want to generate a tree like in 10.

10.

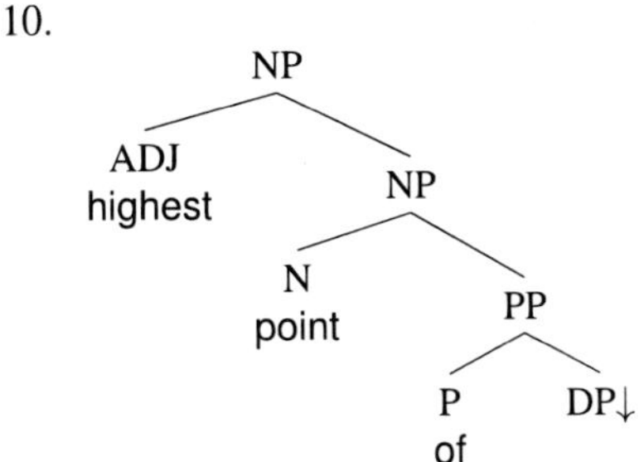

As one of the reviewers points out, an alternative approach to dealing with such cases would be to generate derivation trees that are composed of a more conventional set of elementary trees. Although this is doubtlessly a reasonable and elegant idea, we confined ourselves to generating grammar entries solely from the ontology, i.e. without reference to an additional, given set of basic structures.

Yet another example worth considering is the case of adjectives. Figure 3 shows the LexInfo entry for the adjective *high* in its attributive use. Semantically, it refers to a data property *height* in the ontology, that maps mountains to integers. The domain of this property corresponds to the syntactic argument which the adjective requires (namely the noun that it modifies), and it is also linked to the ontology via a selectional restriction that specifies to which class the domain must belong, in this case *mountain*. When building a grammar entry, this selectional restriction is encoded in the DUDE's argument requirements. Additionally, the PredicativePresentation contains information about the polarity of *high* (which provides the $\geq$ in the adjective's semantics) and the value from which on something counts as high. So a generated grammar entry for *high* would contain the following LTAG tree and DUDE:

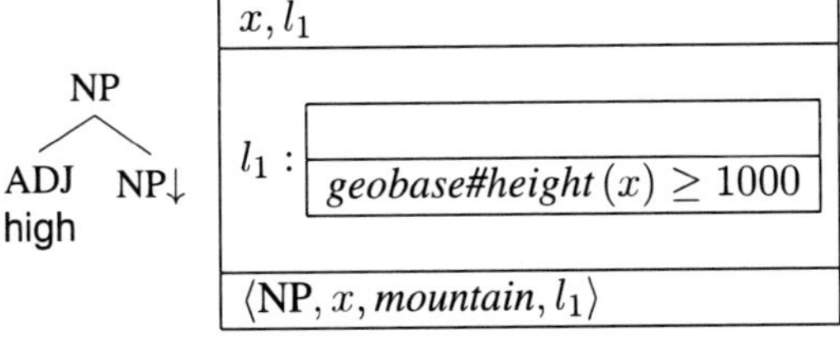

From the same LexInfo model, grammar entries for the comparative and the superlative case are generated. The written form of the adjective in these cases is determined by the morphology module ac-cording to the MorphologicalPattern.[2]

The methods for generating grammar entries from the LexInfo model run automatically. They build on templates that are defined for every LexInfo type (or syntactic category, if you want), i.e. for intransitive and transitive verbs, for nouns with prepositional complements, for adjectives, and so on. They use the subcategorization frame of a lexical entry in LexInfo in order to build an appropriate LTAG tree, and they use the mapping between syntactic and semantic arguments to connect substitution nodes in the tree with argument requirements in the semantic representation.

Although the templates that guide the generation of grammar entries have to be specified by hand for each language one wants to cover, they are completely general in the sense that they are not tied to a particular LexInfo model. Therefore they need to be built only once and can be reused when other LexInfo models are built for other ontologies. Up to now we provide extensive templates for English and basic ones for German. However there is no principled restriction to certain languages since LexInfo is designed in a largely language-independent way.

In the following section we demonstrate our approach with a particular application, a question answering system, and point out the amount of work that is needed for lexicalizing an ontology.

3 Applying the approach to question answering on Geobase

We deployed the approach sketched in the previous section in the context of a question answering system on Raymond Mooney's *Geobase* dataset, which comprises geographical information about the US. Our OWL version of it contains 10 classes (such as *city, state, river, mountain*), 692 individuals instantiating them, 9 object properties (such as *borders, capital, flows through*) and another 9 data properties (such as *population* and *height*).

The LexInfo model constructed for this ontology contains 762 lexical entries. 692 of them correspond to common nouns representing individuals, which are constructed automatically. The remaining 70 entries were built by hand, using the API that LexInfo

---

[2]For more details on adjectives in LexInfo see (Buitelaar et al., 2009).

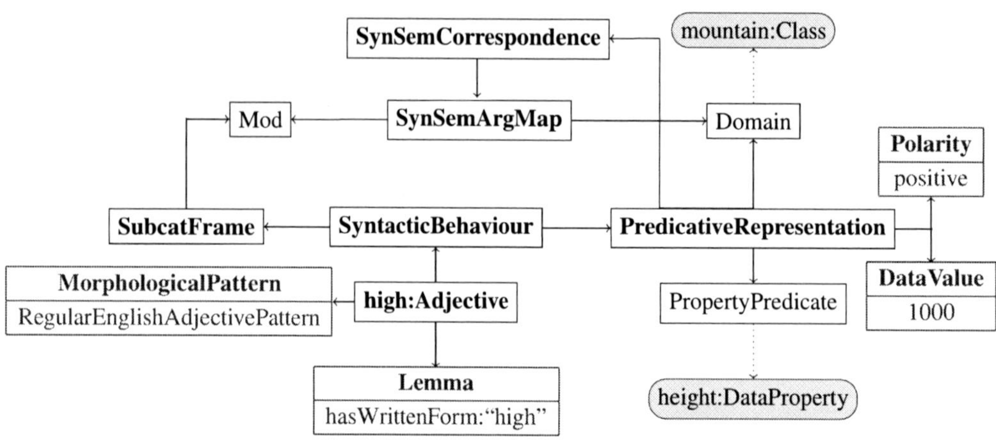

Figure 3: LexInfo entry for *high*

provides. If we generously assume an effort of 5 minutes for building one such entry, the amount of work needed for lexicalizing the ontology amounts to approximately 6 hours. Then from those Lex-Info entries, 2785 grammar entries (i.e. pairs of LTAG trees and DUDEs) were automatically generated according to the templates we specified. In addition, we manually specified 149 grammar entries for domain-independent elements such as determiners, wh-words, auxiliary verbs, and so on.

The complete set of grammar entries finally constitutes a domain-specific grammar that can be used for parsing and interpretation. We demonstrate this by feeding it into our question answering system *Pythia*. (For the Geobase dataset, the LexInfo model, the grammar files and a demo check `http://sc.cit-ec.uni-bielefeld/pythia`). Its architecture is depicted in Figure 4. First, the input is handed to a parser that works along the lines of the Earley-type parser devised by Schabes & Joshi (Schabes & Joshi, 1988). It constructs an LTAG derivation tree, considering only the syntactic components of the lexical entries involved. Next, syntactic and semantic composition rules apply in tandem in order to construct a derived tree together with an according DUDE. The syntactic composition rules are TAG's familiar substitution and adjoin operation, and the semantic composition rules are parallel operations on DUDEs: an argument saturating operation (much like function application) that interprets substitution, and a union

operation that interprets adjoin. Once all argument slots are filled, the constructed DUDE corresponds to an equivalent UDRS, which is then subject to scope resolution, resulting in a set of disambiguated Discourse Representation Structures. Those can subsequently be translated into a query language.

As an example, consider the input question **Which states border Hawaii?**. The parser produces the following derivation tree:

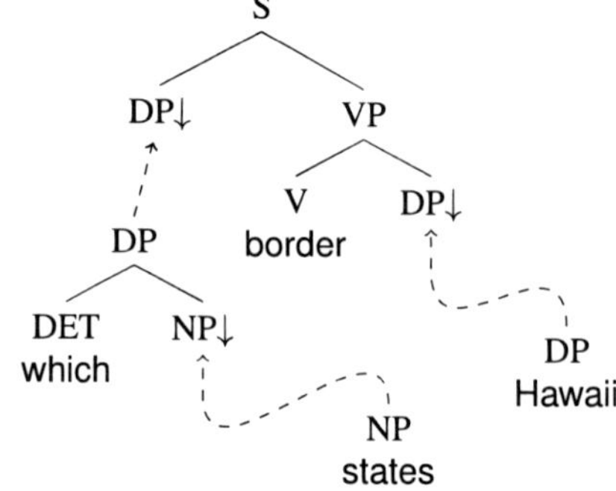

Applying all substitutions yields the derived tree:

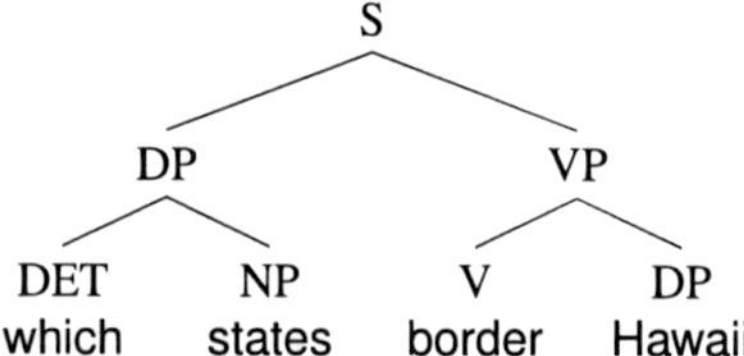

Parallel to this, a semantic representation is built which resolves to the following DRS:

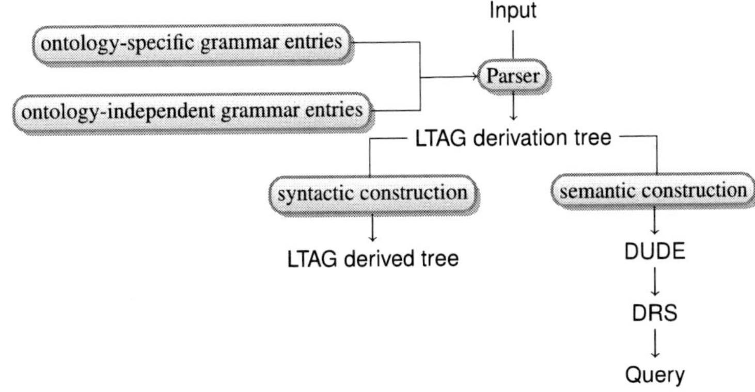

Figure 4: Architecture of *Pythia*

$?x\ y$
$geobase\#state(x)$
$y = geobase\#hawaii$
$geobase\#border(x, y)$

Subsequently, this DRS is translated into the following FLogic query (Kifer & Lausen, 1989):

```
FORALL X Y <- X:geobase#state
  AND equal(Y,geobase#hawaii)
  AND X[geobase#border -> Y].
orderedby X
```

The query is then evaluated with respect to the ontology using the OntoBroker Engine (Decker et al., 1999). Since there are no states bordering Hawaii, the returned result is empty.

4   Related work

Our work bears strong resemblance to semantic grammars (Burton, 1976; Hendrix, 1977), for their motivation was very similar to ours: Since some syntactic constituents contribute little or nothing to meaning, and since meaning components may be distributed across parse trees, grammar rules should not be syntax-driven but tailored to a particular semantic domain. Burton and Hendrix therefore specified phrase-structure grammars that rely on semantic classes instead of syntactic categories. The main disadvantage, however, are its limited possibilities for reuse. A semantic grammar is tailored to one specific domain and cannot easily be ported to another one. Although our approach also yields a grammar which is aligned to a given ontology, it builds on a principled syntactic and semantic theory and therefore bears enough linguistic generality to be easily portable to new domains.

Our approach is also related to the *Ontological Semantics* framework of Nirenburg & Raskin (Nirenburg & Raskin, 2004), which attempts to construct ontological representations as well. However, in their case the ontology is assumed to be fixed and cannot be exchanged. The strength of our approach is that it can be adapted to different domains by the fact that the grammar is directly generated from an abstract specification of the lexicon-ontology interface.

Our approach is also close to recent work by Bobrow and others (Bobrow et al., 2009). The main difference, however, is that they rely on rewriting steps while we directly construct an ontology-specific underspecified semantic representation. Thus, in our case the syntax-semantics interface itself is ontology-specific. This is an advantage, in our view, as the ontology can be used at construction time for disambiguation, for example. But it is still up to future research to show whether rewriting or direct mapping approaches are more suitable to ontology-specific interpretation.

5   Conclusion

A range of applications, such as question answering with respect to a particular domain, require a domain-specific interpretation of natural language expressions. We argued that building generic logical forms is often not suitable for this task. We therefore proposed an approach that relies on generating grammars from an underlying ontology. We took grammar entries to consist of semantic representations with a vocabulary that is aligned to that of the ontology, and syntactic representations that comprise all lexical material needed for verbalizing the ontology concepts.

We demonstrated that Tree Adjoining Grammars fit such an approach very nicely, mainly because of their extended domain of locality, the resulting flexibility regarding basic syntactic units, and due to their tight syntax-semantics interface.

Although the grammars we generate are aligned to one specific ontology, the mechanism that generates them is completely general and works independent of the underlying ontology. This is because it does not generate grammar entries from the ontology itself but rather relies on a mediating lexicon model that contains all relevant linguistic information. Whenever we want to port our question answering system, for example, to a different domain, only the lexicon model would need to be replaced.

We illustrated that the lexicalization of an ontology requires only a reasonable amount of manual engineering. However, it does not easily scale to very large ontologies. It will therefore be subject of future research to automatize this process.

Another area for further work is the amount of LTAG trees that are generated. Up to now, they comprise all possible alternations; for example, for a transitive verb, the basic transitive structure is generated, together with corresponding wh-movement trees, passive trees, relative clause trees, and so on. This leads to redundancies in the grammar generation mechanism and misses important linguistic generalizations. A more principled approach would involve general rules that derive those additional trees from the basic transitive structure.

Acknowledgments

We would like to thank the reviewers for their helpful comments and John McCrae for all LexInfo-related work and discussions.

References

Daniel G. Bobrow and Cleo Condoravdi and Lauri Karttunen and Annie Zaenen. 2009. *Learning by reading: normalizing complex linguistic structures onto a knowledge representation.* AAAI Symposium 2009: Learning by Reading and Learning to Read.

Johan Bos. 2008. *Wide-Coverage Semantic Analysis with Boxer.* Proceedings of Semantics in Text Processing (STEP 2008), pages 277–286. Research in Computational Semantics, College Publications.

Paul Buitelaar and Philipp Cimiano and Peter Haase and Michael Sintek. 2009. *Towards Linguistically Grounded Ontologies.* Proceedings of the 6th Annual European Semantic Web Conference (ESWC).

Richard R. Burton. 1976. *Semantic Grammar: An Engineering Technique for Constructing Natural Language Understanding Systems.* Tech. Report 3453, Bolt, Beranak and Newman Inc., Cambridge, MA.

Philipp Cimiano. 2009. *Flexible Composition with DUDES.* Proceedings of the 8th International Conference on Computational Semantics (IWCS'09).

Stefan Decker and Michael Erdmann and Dieter Fensel and Rudi Studer. 1999. *Ontobroker: Ontology Based Access to Distributed and Semi-Structured Information.* Database Semantics: Semantic Issues in Multimedia Systems, Kluwer. Pages 351–369.

Robert Frank. 1992. *Syntactic Locality and Tree Adjoining Grammar: Grammatical, Acquisition and Processing Perspectives.* Ph.D. thesis, University of Pennsylvania.

Gary G. Hendrix. 1977. *Human engineering for applied natural language processing.* Proceedings of the Fifth International Joint Conference on Artificial Intelligence, pages 183–191.

Michael Kifer and Georg Lausen. 1989. *F-Logic: A Higher-Order language for Reasoning about Objects, Inheritance, and Scheme.* SIGMOD Record 18(2): 134–146. ACM, New York.

Sergei Nirenburg and Victor Raskin. 2004. *Ontological Semantics.* MIT Press.

Uwe Reyle 1993. *Dealing with ambiguities by underspecification: construction, representation and deduction.* Journal of Semantics 10: 123–179.

Yves Schabes and Aravind K. Joshi 1988. *An Earley-type parsing algorithm for Tree Adjoining Grammars.* Proceedings of the 26th annual meeting on Association for Computational Linguistics (ACL), pages 258–269.

Restricting Inverse Scope in Synchronous Tree-Adjoining Grammar

Michael Freedman
Yale University
370 Temple Street, Rm 210
New Haven, CT 06511, USA
michael.freedman@yale.edu

Robert Frank
Yale University
370 Temple Street, Rm 312
New Haven, CT 06511, USA
bob.frank@yale.edu

Abstract

This paper provides an account for inverse scope restrictions with nominal quantifiers using synchronous tree adjoining grammar. It aims to provide an alternative account to Beghelli & Stowell's (1997) work on similar data.

1 Introduction

Recent work in the study of the syntax-semantics interface [Nesson and Shieber, 2006, 2007, 2008] using *s*ynchronous tree-adjoining grammars (STAGs) has attempted to cover a broad range of empirical issues with respect to scopal interactions (control verbs, relative clauses, inverse linking). The majority of this work has attempted to relax the locality restrictions enough to be able to derive possible interpretations while remaining as restricted as possible.

These analyses however are unable to account for asymmetries in the scopal interaction of nominal quantifiers (see §2). This paper aims to explain these asymmetries through two novel mechanisms: (1) Operations on an elementary tree must proceed in the opposite order of the prominence ordering of the nodes on the tree (to be explained in §3). (2) Different classes of quantifiers, represented as multi-component sets, differ in their derivation procedure, where some classes must combine simultaneously in an elementary tree while other classes' scopal tree is able to adjoin later in the derivation.

This paper gives an alternative analysis to Beghelli and Stowell's (henceforth B&S) (1997)

analysis of quantifier scope in English. In particular this paper examines the restriction on inverse scope readings in English when the object quantifier is a count quantifier as compared to the the ability to have inverse scope readings when the quantifier is a universal quantifier. Additionally, these same restrictions will be shown to hold in the double object constructions in English.

This paper will then extend this analysis to quantifier scope puzzles in Mandarin Chinese and Hungarian. Quantifier scope in both Mandarin and Hungarian is said to correspond to the hierarchical positions of the nominal quantifiers, allowing no scopal ambiguities. Yet it has been observed that there are certain constructions in both languages where there are scopal ambiguities. Mandarin "passive" sentences and Hungarian sentences where both quantifiers follow the verb are known to allow inverse scope readings as well as surface scope readings. Previous analyses of these phenomena in conjunction with the constraints proposed in this paper derive the ambiguity in these constructions while keeping the other constructions unambiguous in their scope readings.

The organization of the paper will be as follows: §2 will describe the restrictions on inverse scope reading in English sentences with two nominal quantifiers. §3 will explain the derivational constraints utilized for the English analysis. §4 will show how these constraints derive the right scope readings in the examples described in §2. §5 will describe and analyze the Mandarin and Hungarian extensions to the analysis. §6 will conclude the paper, offering some further areas for exploration.

2 Data

2.1 English Nominal Quantifiers

As discussed in Beghelli and Stowell [1997], certain classes of nominal quantifiers are able to scope over quantificational subjects when in object position, while other classes may not. This is exemplified in (1) and (2).

(1) Every student read 2 papers. ($\forall > 2, 2 > \forall$)

(2) Every student read more than 2 papers.
    ($\forall > 2+, 2+ \not> \forall$)

The examples in (1) and (2) show that quantifiers like *2* (called group-denoting quantifier phrases (GQPs) by B&S) can take wide scope while in object position while quantifiers like *more than 2* (called count quantifier phrases (CQPs) by B&S) cannot. Universal quantifiers (DQPs) also pattern with GQPs by being able to scope over the denotation of the subject NP, as shown in (3).

(3) 2 students read every book. ($\forall > 2, 2 > \forall$)

2.2 English Double Object Construction

Double object constructions in English also seem to follow the same pattern where DQPs seem to be able to take scope over other quantifiers when in a hierarchically lower position, while CQPs are unable to (as in (4)[1]. The pattern of scope rigidity versus scope ambiguity is exhibited in both double object and prepositional dative constructions in (4) and (5).

(4) a. John assigned more than 2 students every paper on the syllabus. ($\forall > 2+, 2+ > \forall$)

   b. John assigned every student more than 2 papers on the syllabus. ($\forall > 2+$)

(5) a. John assigned more than 2 papers on the syllabus to every student. ($\forall > 2+, 2+ > \forall$)

   b. John assigned every paper on the syllabus to more than 2 students. ($\forall > 2+$)

---

[1]Some speakers consider this construction to be unambiguous. An analysis of this dialectal difference is outside the scope of this paper and awaits future work.

3 Restricting Inverse Scope

3.1 Inverse Scope in STAG

Common to many STAG analyses is the use of *multiple adjunction* [Schabes and Shieber, 1994] to get inverse scope. With multiple adjunction, the scopal part of all QPs are able to adjoin at the same node in the course of the derivation. A further convention states that the later combined tree adjoins above the earlier combined tree. Inverse scope is derived because either quantifier is able to adjoin first. This type of analysis runs into problems accounting for the data in §2 because the only restriction on scopal parts of two clausemate quantifiers is that they both appear within the semantic tree associated with the verb of which they are both arguments. As a result, it fails to distinguish among different classes of quantifiers and also between the scopal possibilities when the quantifiers are in subject and object position.

3.2 Beghelli & Stowell

B&S obtain the differences in scope possibilities (developed within the minimalist framework) by positing a series of functional projections above VP. They argue that different sets of quantifiers have different features that need to be checked and this leads to movement at LF where the QPs move to a functional projection that satisfies some feature. They categorize quantifier phrases into five groups: Interrogative QPs, Negative QPs, Group-denoting QPs, Distributive QPs, and Count QPs. Each group is denoted by a shared semantic feature: WhQPs introduce questions, NQPs negate, GQPs denote groups (and plural individuals), DQPs distribute over sets and are universally quantified, and CQPs count individuals with a certain property. The different scope possibilities are constrained by the positions each class of quantifier can move to. The different functional projects (hierarchically ordered) with the associated QP class that moves to the specifier position of the functional projection are in (6).

(6) RefP(GQP) > CP(WhQP) > AgrSP(CQP) > DistP(DQP) > ShareP(GQP) > NegP(NQP) > AgrOP(CQP)

B&S's solution to why CQPs can't scope over the subject quantifier while in object position is that a CQP in object position is only able to move to the specifier of AgrOP while GQPs and DQPs move to a position higher in the structure. The c-command relationship then determines the scope relation.

Although this style of analysis may be available in a STAG, this paper aims to provide an alternative account. An alternative account is preferable because (a) this type of analysis seems to go against the spirit of STAG where syntactic and semantic elements combine synchronously; and (b) it is worth while to see if this approach can be simplified within STAG. Complexities that arise in the B&S analysis include the notion that quantifiers must be ambiguous as to their feature specifications, and that a large number of functional projections are necessary for any verbal tree. For instance they analyze 'every' as a DQP or a GQP, this would entail three different possible landing spots for 'every' and thus three different lexical items.

3.3 Current Proposal

Our proposed analysis assumes a synchronous derivation [Shieber and Schabes, 1990], multi-component trees (MCTAG) [Joshi, 1987], and multiple adjunction. Also following the literature on multiple adjunction, I will assume that the tree that is adjoined later in the derivation scopes over the previously adjoined structure [Schabes and Shieber, 1994].

The analysis aims to capture the intuition that the derivation of the sentence reflects the sentence structure and that a different structure stems at least partially from a different derivation. For the present data this assumes that there is a structural difference between the two different scope readings. In the present analysis this will manifest itself in the semantic trees.

3.4 Hierarchy in Derivation Order

Traditionally, TAGs do not specify the order of derivation among the substitution and adjoining operations that target a given elementary tree. One way in which to limit the inverse scope possibilities is to restrict the ordering of such operations in the following fashion: The order of operations on an elementary tree must proceed in the opposite order of the asymmetrical c-command (ACC) and irreflexive dominance (DOM) ordering of the nodes of the tree. More formally we define a relation PROM in (7) and

then impose the following restriction in (8).

(7) $\mathrm{PROM}_{def} = \{(x,y)|(x,y) \in \mathrm{DOM}_{irr} \cup \mathrm{ACC}\}$

(8) PROMINENCE RESTRICTION ON DERIVATION (PROD)
If node a in syntactic tree T is targeted (by substitution or adjoining) prior to node b in T, then (a,b) must not be in PROM

This constraint ensures that a hierarchically lower node is targeted before a higher one. The dominance relation applies in sentences like (9) where the adverb that adjoins to S scopes over the adverb that scope over VP.

(9) a. Intentionally, John knocked twice.

   b. Twice, John knocked intentionally

The c-command relation applies in the cases of nominal quantifiers discussed in §2. Since the subject of a transitive sentence c-commands its object, the object quantifier must combine into the elementary tree first in the derivation. Since the combination of the syntactic and semantic trees is synchronous, this restriction does not allow scope ambiguity in these cases.

3.5 Relaxing Derivation Order

Different applications of MCTAG have assumed that the properties of all instances of multicomponent adjoining in a grammar behave in a uniform fashion, whether restricted to being tree-local, set-local, or non-local. In particular MCTAG [Joshi, 1987] assumes that all members of a tree set combine with a target tree simultaneously and VTAG [Rambow, 1994, Nesson and Shieber, 2008] assumes that that there is no simultaneity constraint on members of a tree set. I propose instead that a tree set can specify derivational restrictions on its use during a derivation. In particular, I will consider two possibilities for a given set, which interact with my proposal concerning derivational order:

1. Simultaneous combination (SC): the integration of the trees within a tree-set must take a single point in a derivation.

2. Delayed combination (DC): the integration of the trees within a tree-set may take place at different points during the derivation.

Only the variable-trees must be derived following the hierarchical order (as in vector-TAG [Rambow, 1994, Nesson and Shieber, 2008]). I argue that the different classes of quantifiers differ along the SC/DC dimension. Specifically, the tree-set of CQPs is SC, while the other QP classes are DC. For present purposes, it will suffice for me to assume that all quantifier trees are constrained to adjoin in a tree-local fashion. Note that non-local derivation in combination with SC will be equivalent to non-local MC-TAG and is NP-hard to parse[Rambow and Satta, 1992, Champollion, 2007].[2]

3.6 English Nominal Quantifiers

With these preliminaries in place, we can now turn to the analysis of the scopal asymmetries in (1) and (2). Since the object QP in (1) is DC, two possible derivations are available (using the trees in Figure 1). In the first of these, the object quantifier *2 papers* is combined first, following the PROMINENCE RESTRICTION ON DERIVATION order. On the semantic side, this means that the variable tree must be substituted into the *read* tree. At this point, the scopal component is also free to adjoin to the t* root of the *read* tree. If it does this, the subsequent integration of the subject quantifier *every student* will result in the scope of the universal being outside of the numeral (as in figure 1). In the other derivation, the DC property of the universal quantifier tree is exploited. The scope portion of the numeral quantifier is not adjoined immediately. Instead, the derivation proceeds through the integration of the subject quantifier, including its scope, and then the scope of the object quantifier is finally adjoined. This yields wide scope for the object quantifier (as in figure 1).

For example (2), in which the object quantifier, in virtue of being a CQP, is SC, only the first of these derivations is possible: the scope of *more than 2 books* must adjoin to t* at the point that the variable is substituted, resulting in obligatory narrow scope for the object quantifier.

Note that when CQPs are in subject position, they nonetheless show scope ambiguity with respect to

object quantifiers, as in (10).

(10) More than 2 students read every book.
$(2+ > \forall)$

This possibility is predicted by the current analysis: the flexibility of the object quantifier to adjoin at t* either before or after the subject quantifier will permit the generation of either scope, even in the face of a SC requirement on the subject quantifier.

The double object construction described in §2 also can be explained using the c-command constraint and delayed combination. Adopting the Larsonion VP-shell analysis [Larson, 1988] as in figure 2, the node that is targeted by the goal object c-commands the node that is targeted by the theme object. Theme object quantifiers that have the DC property are able to take scope over the theme object quantifier, while ones that have the SC property are unable to. The prepositional dative case works analogously, where only when the lower goal object has the DC property does inverse scope take place.

4 Extending the Analysis

The behavior of nominal quantifiers in various other languages differs from the English case described above. Both Mandarin and Hungarian are purported to have their scope ordering match surface structure very closely. "Active" Mandarin sentences and Hungarian sentences where both quantifiers are in the pre-verbal field only have surface scope readings. This corresponds with all the quantifiers in both languages having the SC feature. Yet there are constructions in both languages where scope ambiguity does arise. This section aims to show how the constraints in this analysis are able to account for the varying scopal behavior in these languages without DC.

4.1 Data

4.1.1 Mandarin Chinese Passives

Aoun and Li [1993] observes that there is a distinction in the scope possibilities between (11) and (12). In (11), the subject QP must scope over the object QP. This contrasts with the sentence in (12) where the inverse scope reading is possible. Traditionally (11) has been categorized as an active sentence and (12) as the passive with BEI being alter-

---

[2]Thanks to an anonymous reviewer for pointing this out.

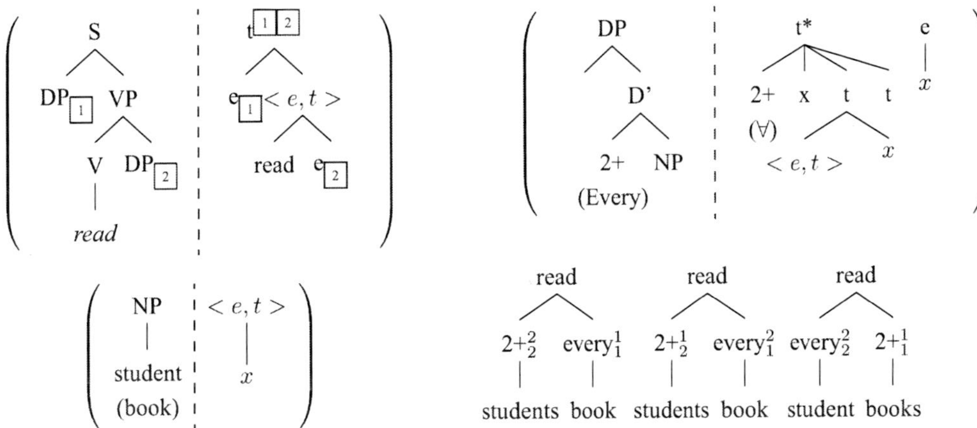

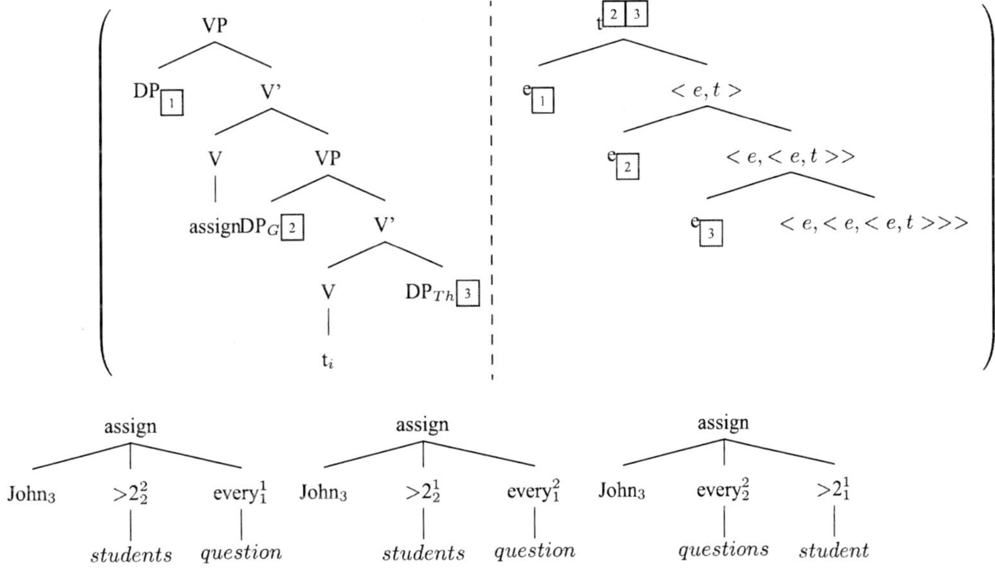

Figure 1: This figure shows elementary trees for the verb, quantifiers, and NPs. Derivation trees for examples (2) and (3) are provided: the leftmost and middle derivation trees show the two ordering options when a DQP is in object position and the rightmost one shows the one option when a CQP is in object position. The subscripted numbering represents the order of syntactic derivation the superscripted numbering represents the order of semantic derivation of the scopal-trees with delayed combination.

Figure 2: This figure shows elementary trees for the ditransitive verb *assign*; all other trees needed for this derivation are in figure 1. Derivation trees for (4) are provided: the leftmost and middle show the two ordering options when a DQP is in the lower object position and the one option when a CQP is in the lower object position. The subscripted numbering represents the order of syntactic derivation the superscripted numbering represents the order of semantic derivation of the scopal trees with delayed combination.

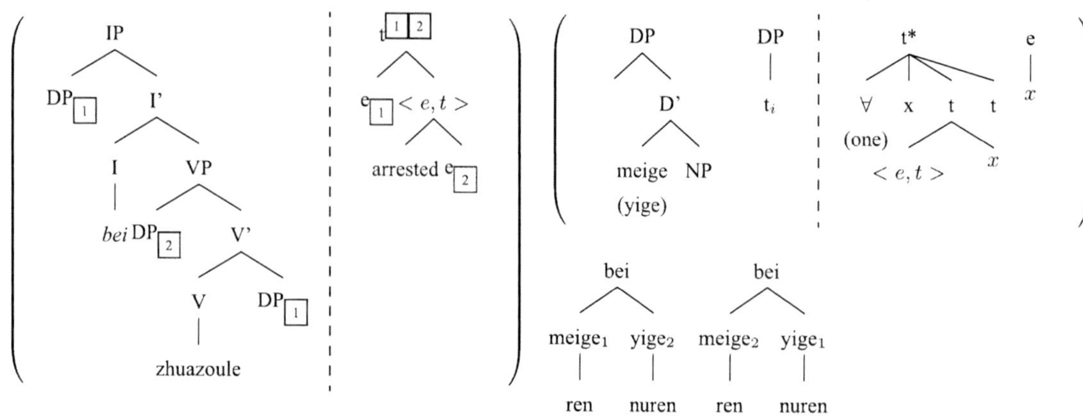

Figure 3: This figure shows (1) an elementary tree containing BEI and a main verb. It has three positions for DP substitutions. (2) A multi-component tree for *m*eige, and (3)derivation trees for the BEI sentence. The leftmost derivation tree has *meige* adjoin first making *yige* take wide scope. The rightmost derivation tree has *yige* adjoin first making *meige* take wide scope. The numbering on these trees represents the ordering on the derivation where either of the quantifiers is able to combine first. Not pictured are trees corresponding to the NPs and the other quantifier; these trees are identical to the trees for the same type lexical items in figure 1.

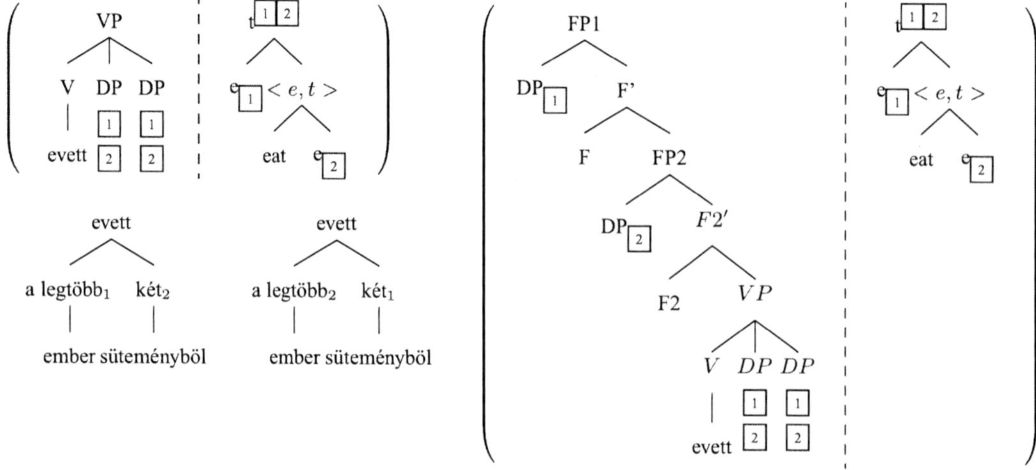

Figure 4: This figure shows (1) an elementary tree for the verb *evett* with a flat structure for the arguments. (2) an elementary tree for *evett* where there are functional projections above VP where multi-component QP sets combine both in the FP and under VP, and (3)derivation trees for the sentence. The leftmost tree is for the sentences (13) or (14). The rightmost derivation tree is for example (13) and is only available when the tree with functional projections is the verbal tree. Not pictured are trees corresponding to the NPs and the quantifiers; these trees are identical to the trees for the same type lexical items in figures 1 and 3.

natively a passive marker or preposition-like lexical item.

(11) Meigeren dou xihuan yige nuren
     everyone all like   one woman
     'Everyone loves a woman' $(\forall > 1)$

(12) Meige ren dou bei yige nuren zhuazou le
     every man all BEI one woman arrested
     'Everyone was arrested by a woman
     $(\forall > 1, 1 > \forall)$

4.1.2 Hungarian Scope

In Hungarian, transitive sentences with two quantifiers can be in a number of different word orders. When both quantifiers precede the verb the scope ordering is strict and no inverse scope reading is possible, as in (13). When both quantifiers are unstressed and follow the verb inverse scope readings are possible, as in (14).

(13) tegnap   a   legtöbb ember két
     yesterday the most   person two
     süteményböl evett
     cakes-from ate
     'Yesterday most people ate from two cakes'
     (most > 2)

(14) tegnap   evett a   legtöbb ember
     yesterday ate the most   person
     két süteményböl
     two cakes-from
     'Yesterday most people ate from two cakes'
     (most $> 2, 2 >$ most)

4.2 Extending the Analysis

The syntactic trees chosen for the Mandarin and Hungarian data in figures 3 and 4 are chosen based on previous analyses of this data. Aoun and Li [1993] argue that the trace allows either scope reading because each quantifier c-commands the other. Kiss [2002] argues that the structure of Hungarian has a hierarchical preverbal field and a flat structure in the VP field. Ambiguous scope is available when the quantifiers are in the VP field because neither c-commands the other, yet while they are above VP

there is surface scope because one quantifier will c-command the other. Both of these analyses base their analysis off of the idea that c-command relations derive scope relations [May, 1977].

These cases force us to complicate the analysis given in §3. In both the Hungarian and Mandarin cases quantifiers are represented by MC-sets. As such, there are cases where a MC-set both commands and is c-commanded by some other tree (set). The current definition of PROM when utilized by PRoD leads to paradox as two different nodes cannot be be targeted until the other one has been targeted. The definition of PROM needs to be refined by accounting for this configuration. To do this a new relation PROM' will be defined in (7).

(15) PROM'$_{def}$ = $\{(x,y)|(x,y) \in$ PROM, no z such that (1) $(y,z) \in$ PROM, (x,z) is targeted by a MC-set or (2) $(z,x) \in$ PROM, (z,y) is targeted by a MC-set.$\}$

The definition of PROM' eliminates from PROM pairs (a,b),(b,c) where a and b are targeted by different MC-sets (a,c) and (b); and (a,b) and (b,c) are in PROM. In these cases there is no possible ordering between the two sets based on their hierarchical position. PROM' then replaces PROM in the PRoD.

The Mandarin data falls out from this revised PRoD. First, the restriction against inverse scope in the "active" sentences can be explained if Mandarin quantifiers all obey simultaneous combination. The interaction of the quantifiers in the syntactic tree explains the scope ambiguity in the "passive" sentences. The higher surface quantifier is analyzed as a multi-component set. The lexical tree substitutes into the higher DP and the trace tree substitutes into the lower DP. In transformational terms the trace-tree occupies the base position and the lexical tree occupies the surface (moved-to) position. Between these two positions is the other quantifier. It is represented by a singleton tree set. The asymmetrical c-command relations between the three nodes that the quantifiers occupy are the following: The lexical-tree of the higher quantifier c-commands the lower quantifier and the lower quantifier c-commands the trace-tree. Since both quantifiers c-command each other they are not in PROM' and there is no restriction in their derivation because neither derivation order violates the PRoD. This allows either quantifier to take wide scope during the derivation of the semantic tree. This produces the scope ambiguity, and does so without delayed combination. Thus, both the strict scope behaviour and ambiguous scope behaviour can be derived.

The Hungarian data also can be derived given the revised PROD. The ambiguous scope cases are derived because the nodes the quantifiers substitute into are not in a PROM relation with respect to one another. Thus either DP is able to combine first and on the semantic side either scopal tree is able to then adjoin first. The unambiguous case is derived because the highest DP node is in a PROM' relation with a DP under VP. Thus the tree-set that targets the DP under FP2 must combine first with the elementary tree. On the semantics side the scopal tree must attach before the scopal tree for the other quantifier. This produces the surface scope reading only.

5 Conclusions and Further Ideas

5.1 Summary

This paper has explored one method of restricting scope relations in S-TAG. The two mechanisms discussed in the paper have been shown to predict the correct scope possibilities in English sentences with subject and object quantifiers (and object quantifiers in the double object construction), in Mandarin Chinese "active" and "passive" constructions, and the different Hungarian configurations. The former utilized both the PROM constraint on derivation and delayed combination while the latter two utilized only a revised PROM constraint.

5.2 Further Work

Further work on this topic involves a more indepth look at the scopal possibilities in the English, Mandarin, and Hungarian. Notably a comparison to Szabolcsi [1997] for Hungarian would be advantageous. Further work on this analysis involves seeing how the constraints proposed in this paper interact with other scopal elements. For instance how does this paper's analysis affect the scopal possibilities between negative markers, questions, or intentional operators, and nominal quantifiers. Phenomena from other languages should also be explored: It might prove interesting to see what languages utilize DC and which don't and whether DC varies cross-

linguistically in what lexical items possess it. Evidence for this type of analysis may be borne out of a coherent typology. Another avenue of exploration would be to seek out an alternative to the PROM' relation that is less complex and independently motivated.

References

J. Aoun and Y.A. Li. *Syntax of scope*. The MIT Press, 1993.

F. Beghelli and T. Stowell. The Syntax of Each and Every. *Ways of scope taking*, pages 71–107, 1997.

L. Champollion. Lexicalized non-local MCTAG with dominance links is NP-complete. In Gerald Penn and Ed Stabler, editors, *Proceedings of Mathematics of Language (MOL) 10*, CSLI On-Line Publications, 2007.

A. Joshi. An Introduction to Tree Adjoining Grammar. *Mathematics of Language*, 1987.

K.É. Kiss. *The syntax of Hungarian*. Cambridge Univ Pr, 2002.

R.K. Larson. On the double object construction. *Linguistic inquiry*, 19(3):335–391, 1988.

R. May. *The Grammar of Quantification*. PhD thesis, MIT, 1977.

R. Nesson and S. Shieber. Simpler TAG semantics through synchronization. In *Proceedings of the 11th Conference on Formal Grammar, Malaga, Spain*, pages 29–30, 2006.

R. Nesson and S. Shieber. Extraction phenomena in synchronous TAG syntax and semantics. In *Proceedings of the NAACL-HLT 2007/AMTA Workshop on Syntax and Structure in Statistical Translation*, pages 9–16. Association for Computational Linguistics, 2007.

R. Nesson and S. Shieber. Synchronous vector tree adjoining grammars for syntax and semantics: Control verbs, relative clauses, and inverse linking. In *Proceedings of the Ninth International Workshop on Tree Adjoining Grammars and Related Formalisms*, pages 73–80, 2008.

O. Rambow. *Formal and Computational Aspects of Natural Language Syntax*. PhD thesis, University of Pennsylvania, Philadelphia, PA, 1994.

O. Rambow and G. Satta. Formal properties of non-locality. In *Proceedings of 1st International Workshop on Tree Adjoining Grammars*, 1992.

Y. Schabes and S. Shieber. An alternative conception of tree adjoining derivation. *Computational Linguistics*, 20:91–124, 1994.

S. Shieber and Y. Schabes. Synchronous tree-adjoining grammars. In *Proceedings of the 13th conference on Computational linguistics-Volume 3*, pages 253–258. Association for Computational Linguistics Morristown, NJ, USA, 1990.

A. Szabolcsi. *Ways of scope taking*. Springer, 1997.

Surprisal Derives the Recent Filler Heuristic in Mildly Context Sensitive Grammars

Kyle Grove
Linguistics
Cornell University
211 Morrill Hall
Ithaca, NY 14853, USA
`kwg33@cornell.edu`

Abstract

This paper provides a new account for why online processing of filler-gap relative clause dependencies is more difficult in cases where filler-gap interacts with object control than in cases involving subject control, as reported by Frazier et al. (1983). Frazier et al. (1983) argued for a Recent Filler heuristic in which the parser expects to discharge the most recent filler at every gap site. We observe that statistical subcategorization preferences on the control verb and the embedded verb 'sing' interact, favoring subject control disambiguation.

We employ surprisal (Hale, 2001) as a complexity metric on filler-gap structures by construing control as a Movement operation in Minimalist Grammars (Stabler, 1997). We obtain greater surprisals for the Distant Filler condition, deriving the prediction that the Recent Filler heuristic falls out from statistical subcategorization preferences.

1 Introduction

In filler-gap constructions, [1] the parser must map a non-local dependency between an extraposed element (the 'filler' nominal element) and a position in the subcategorization frame (the 'gap') of a verb to-be-determined. When filler-gap sentences contain complex verb structure such as control verbs, ambiguity can result because there are multiple potential gap sites the filler could conceivably have been extraposed from. The complexity of this task

---

[1] Many thanks are due to John Hale, Julie Balazs, David Lutz and Effi Georgala for advice and critique of this paper. Any errata and shortcomings in this work are surely mine, and not theirs.

is demonstrated in 1, where a single prefix (1a. and 1b.) can be disambiguated in two quite different ways.

(1) a. Everyone liked the woman the little child begged to sing those stupid French songs.

  b. Everyone liked the woman the little child begged to sing those stupid French songs for.

(Frazier et al., 1983, 203)

(2) a. The child$_1$ begged the woman$_2$ to t$_2$ sing those songs.

  b. The child$_1$ begged to t$_1$ sing those songs for the woman.

With object control (OC) verbs (1a and 2a), the subject of the infinitival 'sing' is the object of the transitive control verb 'begged', but with subject control (SC) verbs (1b and 2b), the subject of the infinitival is the subject of an intransitive control verb. While these conditions can generally be disambiguated at the control verb in non-relativized contexts (2), relativization of the control verb's object removes the disambiguating cue in object control cases. Thus, the prefix 'Everyone loved the woman the child begged to sing those ...' is locally ambiguous, and is disambiguated by either the continuation (... *for.*), in the subject control case, or the sentence abruptly ending (.), in the object control case.

Frazier et al. (1983) argued that the lesser difficulty of SC filler-gap supports an account where a strictly serial parsing strategy is guided by a Recent Filler heuristic. The Recent Filler heuristic holds that in cases where the parser is presented with multiple fillers for a single gap, it expects to map the most recent filler to that gap. When this expectation is defeated by new sentential material, the parser must backtrack until it can recover to an analysis congruent with this material.

The Recent Filler heuristic was disconfirmed in Boland et al. (1990). Boland et al. (1990) employed a semantic mismatch paradigm for object control verbs in which the raiser-to-object is potentially an implausible subject of the embedded infinitival. This effect is seen in 3, where 3b is semantically anomalous due only to the infinitival verb; horses and outlaws both make excellent receivers of signals, but horses lack the ability to surrender weapons.

(3)   a. The cowboy signaled the outlaw to surrender his weapons quietly.

        b. The cowboy signaled the horse to surrender his weapons quietly.

        (Boland et al., 1990, 416)

By applying semantic mismatch to filler-gap dependencies, an extraposed element could be manipulated for semantic plausibility as a potential filler for a gap site. Boland et al. (1990) developed Distant Filler sentences which featured such plausability mismatches, using wh-questions. In these sentences, the recent filler matched the gap-site verb for plausability, but the distant filler did not.

(4)   a. Which outlaw did the cowboy signal to surrender his weapons quietly?

        b. Which horse did the cowboy signal to surrender his weapons quietly?

        (Boland et al., 1990, 417)

Boland et al. (1990) used an online plausability monitoring task in which participants where asked to incrementally indicate whether the sentence was plausible. If participants employed the Recent Filler heuristic, then they should be unaware of plausability mismatches which obtain only on the Distant Filler structural analysis. Participants detected implausibility immediately, suggesting that they do not rely on a Recent Filler heuristic.

2 Hypothesis

We argue contra Frazier et al. (1983) that the Recent Filler effect arises from the parser's statistical knowledge of verb subcategorization. We observe (in Fig. 14, Appendix) that the Recent Filler analysis requires a prepositional attachment for the verb 'sing' and a subject control frame for the control verb, while the Distant Filler analysis requires there to be no PP attachment on 'sing', and an object control frame for the control verb. We anticipate the verb 'sing', used throughout the materials in Frazier et al. (1983), to exhibit frequent prepositional phrase attachment. We hypothesize that corpus-derived probabilistic weightings on PP-attachment and control verb subcategorization frames are incorporated in a probabilistic grammar that biases towards the Recent Filler analysis. As sentences are parsed, the probabilities in this grammar represent degrees of belief which are prone to revision as evidence is collected; dramatic revisions of belief suggest that the parse has been particularly difficult. We employ surprisal (Hale, 2001) as a psycholinguistic linking theory which characterizes the severity of this belief update. We predict that object control Distant Filler continuations will have greater surprisal at the disambiguating continuation than subject control Recent Filler continuations.

3 Background

3.1 Grammar

How best to represent the argument sharing that control and raising verbs exhibit has generated debate among syntacticians and semanticists (Jacobson, 1992; Chomsky and Lasnik, 1993; Steedman, 1994; Hornstein, 2000). Chomsky and Lasnik (1993) represents the external argument of the infinitival verb as being satisfied by a phonetically unrealized pronominal, PRO, which is to be mapped thematically to the corresponding argument in the control verb by a structural construal operation external to the core grammar. Hornstein (2000) argues instead that the Movement operation available to the core grammar is responsible for this mapping. Jacobson (1992) focuses more on the subcategorization frames of the verbs than the arguments themselves. On an approach such as in Jacobson (1992), a control or raising verb acts as a functor on the infinitival verb, mapping the arguments of the infinitival onto the matrix verb.

We constructed a mildly context sensitive Minimalist Grammar (MG) (Stabler, 1997) that implements a non-pronominal theory of control (Jacobson, 1992; Pollard and Sag, 1994; Steedman, 1994; Hornstein, 2000) as a type of Movement operation between the subject position of the embedded verb and an object or subject position in the control verb. We leave as an empirical question whether other approaches to control would yield the same human sentence processing prediction. Rendering control as Move in MG is advantageous in several ways. First, properties of the Minimalist Grammars formalism have been studied in depth: sentences in an MG language can be parsed efficiently and parses in MG possess a context-free backbone which can be leveraged with PCFG methods. Second, since relative clause extraposition is also treated as Move in our grammar, we can model the complexity of the interaction between filler-gap and control more easily than we could if control were handled in some other component of the grammar.

In MGs, a lexical item has a distinct set of syntactic (SYN) features, which uniquely determine a movement chain that the lexical item can participate in (Hale and Stabler, 2005). Thus, we model lexical subcategorization frames in MGs by a one-to-many encoding between phonetic (PHON) features and SYN features: an ambiguous control verb such as 'wanted' is modeled in an MG lexicon with redundant lexical entries, as shown in Fig. 1.

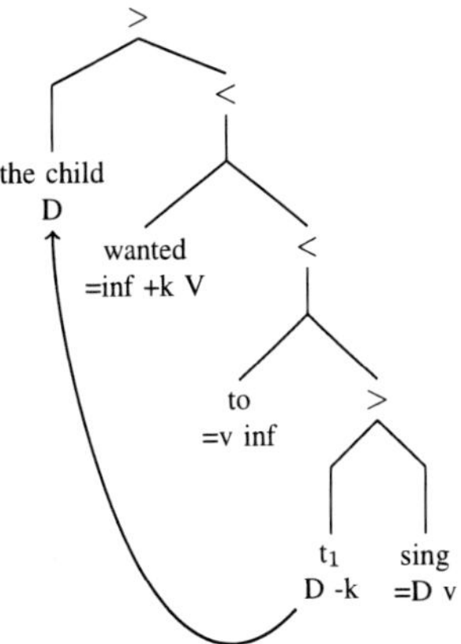

Figure 2: Derived Tree for Subject Control

::=>V =D v   to :: =v inf
wanted :: =inf +k v   wanted :: =inf +k V
the :: =N D -k   the :: =N D
woman :: N   child :: N

Figure 1: MG Fragment for Control

Derived Trees for Subject and Object Control are depicted in Figs. 2 and 3.

In both subject and object control verbs, the control dependency is triggered by the Merge of a nominal category whose SYN is D -k in the specifier of

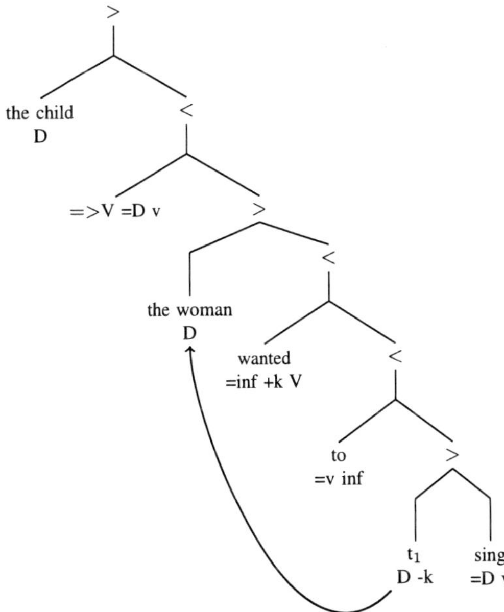

Figure 3: Derived Tree for Object Control

the infinitival verb. The landing site of this nominal category is determined by the location of the corresponding +k attractor feature. When the control verb has SYN =inf +k v as in Fig. 2, the nominal with -k feature will move to the specifier of 'little v', the subject position of the control verb. Subject-to-subject movement derives the semantic intuition that in 'The child asked to sing', the child has two semantic roles: it is both an asker and a (potential) singer. However, when the control verb has SYN =inf +k V, such in Fig. 2, the subject of the embedded verb raises to the object position of the matrix verb, specifier of V. Raising-to-object derives the semantic intuition that in 'The child asked the woman to sing', the woman is a potential singer but the recipient of the request; the child is the asker.

The object of an object control verb could undergo further extraposition via relativization. The interaction of an ambiguous control verb and relativization renders thematic assignment difficult because the extraposed object could either have moved from the object of the control verb or from another position in the structure. In Figs. 4 and 5, we demonstrate a promotion analysis of relative clauses following Kayne (1994) and Bianchi (2004). On this analysis, the relative pronoun and relativized nominal are a constituent underlyingly. As seen in Fig. 5, the =N feature on relative pronoun 'who' triggers Merge with the N category feature on woman, yielding a category whose PHON is 'who woman' and syntactic feature inventory is D -arel. This D is Merged into an argument position as the embedded verb's argument structure is composed with Merge operations up to the head '=T +arel Crel'. The Merge of '=T +arel Crel' with the derived category 'T -arel' establishes an embedded clause with syntactic features '+arel Crel -arel'. The '+arel/-arel' feature pair cancels by triggering Movement of the -arel feature, extracting 'who woman' out of the embedded clause as indicated by the lower arrow in Fig. 5. Merge of '=Crel +nom agrD' ultimately results in the remnant movement of 'woman', as indicated by the higher arrow in Fig. 5. This series of movement correctly derives the ordering of subject and object relative clauses in English. This strategy treats reduced relative clauses by substituting the null relative pronoun '::=N D -arel' in Fig. 4 for its non-null counterpart 'who :: = N D -arel'.

<pre>
the :: =>agrD D   :: =Crel +nom agrD
:: =T +arel Crel   =v T
who :: =N D -arel   :: =N D -arel
woman :: N   sing :: =D v
</pre>

Figure 4: MG Fragment for Relative Clause

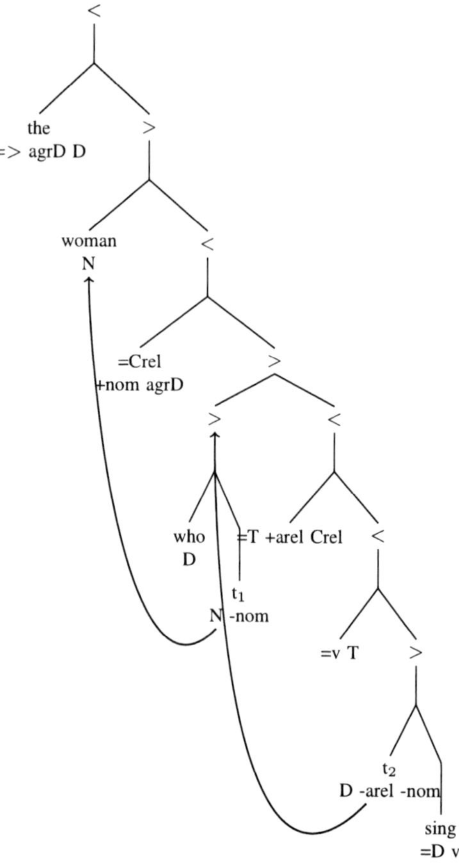

Figure 5: Derived Tree for Relative Clause

3.2 Surprisal

Following Hale (2001), we employ information theory to model the strangeness of parser actions. This study pursues the hypothesis that information about verbal subcategorization frequencies biases the human sentence processor against object control (Distant Filler) filler-gap resolutions of the ambiguous prefix. We predict that a parser with this stochastic grammatical knowledge will model this expectancy by exhibiting greater surprisal on object control/Distant Filler continuations than on subject control/Recent Filler continuations.

Surprisal (Hale, 2001) hypothesizes that perceived difficulty of human sentence processing at a token of interest is associated with the unexpectedness of the new token. On a given string, the surprisal of a token situated between positions *n-1* and *n* is the logarithm of the ratio of the probabilities of prefixes starting at 0 and ending at *n-1* and *n*.

$$\text{surprisal} = \log_2 \frac{\alpha_{n-1}}{\alpha_n}$$

Figure 6: Surprisal of a word given a PCFG

Surprisal formalizes the intuition that some words are syntactically costly to incorporate, by measuring the rate at which those words reduce the total probability allocated to all incrementally viable analyses. Surprisal predicts garden pathing when new tokens rule out much probability mass.

4   Methodology

We used Tregex (Levy and Andrew, 2006) on Penn Treebank (Marcus et al., 1994) to obtain counts for object control and subject control for each control verb used in Experiment 2 of Frazier et al. (1983), using the queries indicated in Fig. 7. We considered a verb frame as an instance of subject control when the verb node was sister to an S node which dominated a null pronominal subject (NP-SBJ) whose annotation was either PRO or -NONE-. We considered a verb frame as an instance of object control when the verb frame was sister to an S-node whose NP-SBJ had non-null string yield. We excluded instances of passivized object control, which structurally resemble cases of subject control.

Subject Control
VP<(/VB.?/<(/expect.[s|ed|ing]/) $+NP $(S<(NP-SBJ<-NONE-$(VP<TO))))
VP < (/VB.?/ < (/expect.[s|ed|ing]/) $+NP $(S<(NP-SBJ<PRO$(VP<TO))))
Object Control
VP < (/VB.?/ < (/expect.[s|ed|ing/]) $(S<(NP-SBJ<!-NONE-$(VP<TO))))

Figure 7: Tregex Queries for Control Verbs

We obtained the following counts in Fig. 8 for the four verbs in Experiment 2 of Frazier et al. (1983), verifying that subject control is prevalent in the Penn Treebank.

Verb	Subject Control	Object Control
want	344	47
expect	509	200
choose	23	1
ask	16	35

Figure 8: Corpus Counts for Control Verbs

We also obtained counts for prepositional phrase attachment preferences for the verb 'sing', as shown in Fig. 9, also verifying that PP-attachment is particularly frequent for the verb 'sing'.

Verb	PP	¬ PP
sing	7	6

Figure 9: Corpus Counts for PP Attachment

We also obtained counts for reduced relative constructions and main clause constructions, as well as counts for the transitivity of 'sing'. These factors were common across all conditions. For each of the factors, we constructed a parameter by converting the count into a ratio, through dividing the individual outcome's count by the summed count of all possible outcomes. We built a representative minitreebank of $4 * 2^4 = 64$ sentences, where each sentence contained: either a subject or object control verb; in either a main clause or reduced relative clause usage; with or without a prepositional phrase attachment to the verb; and with either a transitive or intransitive use of the verb 'sing', for each of the four control verbs. Each sentence was weighted with the product of the parameters particular to that condition.

An MG statistical prefix parsing system was used to obtain surprisals for the ambiguous prefix common to 1a and 1b and the subject and object control continuations. For each prefix, a parse forest is built; this parse forest is equivalent to a context-free grammar (Billot and Lang, 1989), which can be augmented with probabilities to obtain a probabilistic context free grammar. At training time, the parser uses Weighted Relative Frequency Estimation (Chi, 1999) to estimate a PCFG model of the minitreebank. At testing time, the parser constructs a probabilistic model at each prefix; these prefixes are represented as straightline finite state automata whose suffixes are self loops. The parser estimates for each

$$_0 v_6 \rightarrow {}_0 D_2 \; {}_2 {=} D \; v_6$$

Figure 10: A situated MG rule.

prefix automaton a weighted intersection PCFG using the renormalization technique in Nederhof and Satta (2006). In this intersection PCFG, each category is 'situated' with indices, i.e. the situated category is the product of grammatical categories and automaton transitions used in its derivation.

5 Results

We found greater surprisals on distant filler continuations for three of the four verbs.

Verb	Recent Filler	Distant Filler
wanted	1.448 bits	2.978 bits
expected	1.819 bits	2.176 bits
asked	2.392 bits	1.608 bits
chose	1.213 bits	4.241 bits

Figure 11: Surprisal Results

These compare to the Frazier et al. (1983) results, presented below.

Verb	Recent Filler	Distant Filler
wanted	980 msec.	1168 msec.
expected	997 msec.	1082 msec.
asked	969 msec.	1132 msec.
chose	915 msec.	1050 msec.

Figure 12: Frazier Mean Reaction Times

The surprisal data suggest that no special heuristic is required to explain the Recent Filler expectation in Frazier et al. (1983); the expectation arises naturally on a probabilistic grammar which has knowledge of subcategorization frequencies for verbs. The Recent Filler analysis of the ambiguous prefix requires that 1) the verb 'sing' exhibit PP-attachment; 2) the control verb be a subject control verb. The Distant Filler analysis requires the conjunction of two lower probability events: 1) that the verb 'sing' exhibit no PP-attachment; 2) that the control verb be an object control verb. The Distant Filler continuations yield greater surprisals because the parser

must segue rapidly from a highly probable parse forest which is uncommitted to verb information to a much less probable parse forest which is committed to generally unlikely beliefs about the matrix and embedded verb.

6 Discussion

Our claim that the surprisal results reflect rapid shifts in parser beliefs about control and PP-attachment is borne out by examining the parse forest conditioned on each prefix. We examined the parse forest conditioned on the ambiguous prefix (of the 'want' condition) and found an MG category which was parent of two different MG rules; one which reflected the Recent Filler/Subject Control strategy and one which reflected the Distant Filler/Object Control strategy. We depict these rules in Fig. 13.

0.766(: v -arel -nom)→(: +k v -arel -nom -k)
0.234(: v -arel -nom)→(: =D v -arel -nom) (:D)

Figure 13: Probabilistic MG Rules for Recent and Distant Filler

The derived MG category (v -arel -nom) is simply a verbal category with features that license relative clause extraction. In the Recent Filler rewrite, this category is formed from a unary Move application which moves 'the child' to derive Subject Control via the (+k,-k) case feature pair. In the Distant Filler rewrite, (v -arel -nom) is formed from the binary Merge application where 'the child' is merged as the subject of the control verb; 'woman' has already moved for Object Control. The probabilities [2] attached to these rules show that the Recent Filler bias falls out from statistical verb subcategorization information; the parser predicts that the Recent Filler continuation is three times as likely as the Distant Filler continuation.

We built a Minimalist Grammar which treats Control as Move so that we could easily model the interactions of control and filler-gap. Future work would look to explore whether other approaches to control verbs would yield similar surprisal results. We could

---

[2]Importantly, all the categories below this production in the 'branch' have deterministic rewrites with probability 1.

for instance operationalize Jacobson (1992) syntactically with MG adjunction; we would allow the control verb to incorporate the infinitival verb directly, rather than using Move to share nominal arguments between them. Alternatively, we could develop a system that treats control using a null pronominal utilizing Conjunctive Grammars (Okhotin, 2001) to simulate the seperate Base and Control modules of a Government and Binding style grammar.

We derived Frazier et al. (1983)'s Recent Filler preference as an epiphenomenon of a statistical parser's knowledge of verb subcategorizations. The embedded verb 'sing' exhibits an affinity for PP-attachment which together with knowledge of subcategorization rates of control verbs directly gives rise to the effect in Frazier et al. (1983). Our model showed that the Recent Filler effect is more likely due to the rapid integration of verbal subcategorization frames which provide rich information about the structural environment.

References

Valentina Bianchi. 2004. Resumptive relatives and lf chains. In Luigi Rizzi, editor, The Structure of CP and IP, pages 76–114. Oxford University Press, Oxford.

Sylvie Billot and Bernard Lang. 1989. The structure of shared forests in ambiguous parsing. In Proceedings of the 27th annual meeting on Association for Computational Linguistics, pages 143–151. Association for Computational Linguistics Morristown, NJ, USA.

Julie E. Boland, Michael K. Tanenhaus, and Susan M. Garnsey. 1990. Evidence for the immediate use of verb control information in sentence processing. Journal of Memory and Language, 29(4):413–432.

Zhiyi Chi. 1999. Statistical properties of probabilistic context-free grammars. Computational Linguistics, 25(1):131–160.

Noam Chomsky and Howard Lasnik. 1993. The theory of principles and parameters. Syntax: An international handbook of contemporary research, 1:506–569.

Lyn Frazier, Charles Clifton, and Janet Randall. 1983. Filling gaps: Decision principles and structure in sentence comprehension. Cognition, 13(2):187–222.

John T. Hale and Edward P. Stabler. 2005. Strict deterministic aspects of minimalist grammars. Logical aspects of computational linguistics, pages 162–176.

John T. Hale. 2001. A probabilistic Earley parser as a psycholinguistic model. In Proceedings of NAACL, volume 2, pages 159–166.

Norbert Hornstein. 2000. Move! A Minimalist Theory of Construal. Blackwell, Oxford.

Pauline Jacobson. 1992. Raising without movement. 48:149–194.

Richard S. Kayne. 1994. The Antisymmetry of Syntax. MIT Press.

Roger Levy and Galen Andrew. 2006. Tregex and Tsurgeon: tools for querying and manipulating tree data structures. In Proceedings of the Fifth International Conference on Language Resources and Evaluation. Citeseer.

Mitchell P. Marcus, Beatrice Santorini, and Mary Ann Marcinkiewicz. 1994. Building a large annotated corpus of English: The Penn Treebank. Computational linguistics, 19(2):313–330.

Mark-Jan Nederhof and Giorgio Satta. 2006. Estimation of consistent probabilistic context-free grammars. In Proceedings of the main conference on Human Language Technology Conference of the North American Chapter of the Association of Computational Linguistics, pages 343–350. Association for Computational Linguistics Morristown, NJ, USA.

A. Okhotin. 2001. Conjunctive grammars. Journal of Automata, Languages and Combinatorics, 6(4):519–535.

Carl J. Pollard and Ivan A. Sag. 1994. Head-driven phrase structure grammar. University of Chicago Press.

Edward P. Stabler. 1997. Derivational minimalism. In Logical Aspects of Computational Linguistics., pages 68–95. Springer.

Mark Steedman. 1994. Binding and Control in CCG and its Relatives. IRCS Technical Reports Series, page 161.

7 Appendix

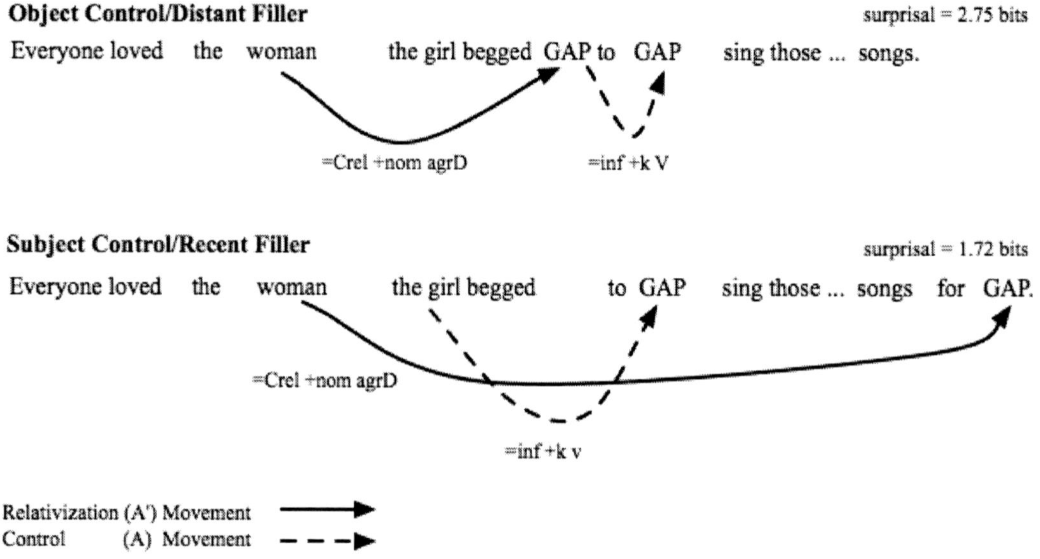

Figure 14: Online Processing of Control and Relativization with Mean Surprisals

From Partial VP Fronting towards Spinal TT-MCTAG*

Timm Lichte
Emmy Noether Research Group
Collaborative Research Center 833
University of Tübingen
`timm.lichte@uni-tuebingen.de`

Abstract

In the face of partial fronting phenomena in German, we introduce *spinal TT-MCTAG*, a new MCTAG variant that integrates features of LTAG-spinal and TT-MCTAG. Using spinal TT-MCTAG we arrive at flat syntactic structures which make available a consistent account for the data.

1 Introduction

While the examination of coherent constructions in German has resulted in the design of TAG-extensions such as V-TAG (Rambow, 1994) and TT-MCTAG (Lichte, 2007), which can cope with a good deal of critical data, a remaining desideratum for both accounts is the analysis of embedded partial fronting of verbal heads, exemplified in (1).

(1) Zu reparieren versprochen hat ihn Peter.
    to repair   promised   has it Peter
    'Peter has promised to repair it.'

Here, the fronted material *zu reparieren versprochen* embeds the non-finite verb *zu reparieren*, whose remote complement *ihn* is on the other side of the finite verb *hat*.

To see the problem, consider the slightly simpler instance of partial VP fronting in (2), where no additional embedding of a verbal head takes place.

(2) Zu reparieren versprach ihn Peter.
    to repair   promised it Peter
    'Peter promised to repair it.'

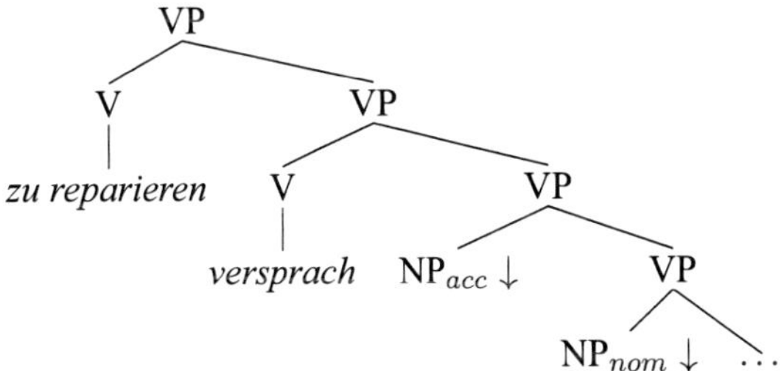

Figure 1: Right-branching derived tree for (2).

The intended derived tree for (2) would be the one in Fig. 1. In terms of TT-MCTAG, this would be derivable with the tree tuples in Fig. 2. A tree tuple consists of two components, namely a single elementary tree, called the *head tree*, and a set of auxiliary trees, called the *argument trees*. The usage of tree tuples is constrained in the following way: each argument tree either adjoins directly at the head tree, or indirectly under *node sharing*, i.e. in the derivation tree the head tree dominates an auxiliary tree γ and γ dominates the argument tree through a path of adjunctions at the root node.[1] Crucially, the tree tuples in Fig. 2 do not contain lexically anchored heads, which can be regarded as a downside, since it dissolves the encoding of the dependency relation. We refer to this desirable, yet dismissed property as the *head tree constraint*.

The schema of the tree tuples in Fig. 2 is reminiscent of the elementary tree sets that are used in the V-TAG approach in (Rambow, 1994), depicted in Fig. 3. Note that V-TAG basically is a non-local

---

*I am indebted to Laura Kallmeyer for helpful comments.

[1]See (Kallmeyer, 2009) for a formal explication.

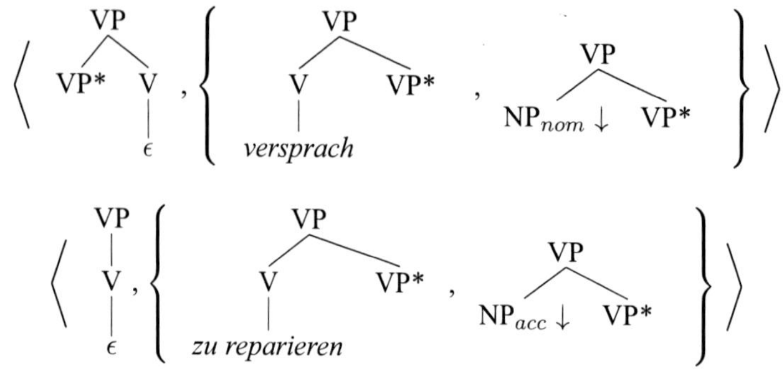

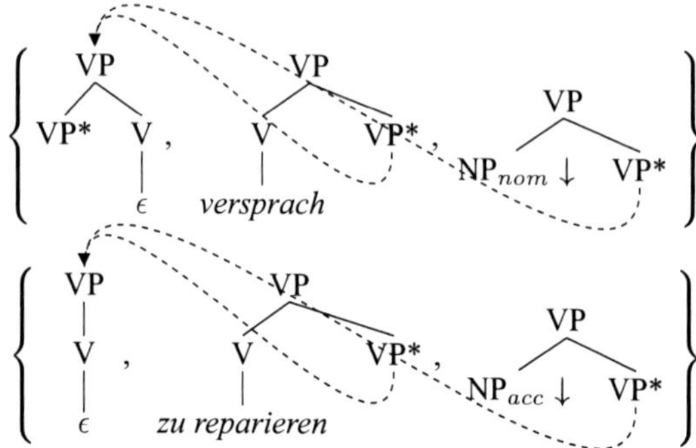

Figure 2: Tree tuples for the derived tree in Fig. 1.

Figure 3: The corresponding V-TAG tree sets of the tree tuples in Fig. 2. Dominance links are expressed by dashed arrows.

MCTAG, where locality is recovered by dominance links (indicated as dashed arrows) and integrity constraints, that refer to the derived tree.

Both approaches essentially rely on the existence of a dominance relation between the elementary trees of the respective multicomponent structures, be it in the derivation tree for TT-MCTAG, or in the derived tree for V-TAG. While such a dominance relation can be found in Fig. 1, the intended derived structure for (1) essentially is the one in Fig. 4, which has a complex prefield constituent[2]. Here, no dominance relation of the embedded verbal head *zu reparieren* and its argument *ihn* can be established, and therefore, this structure cannot be derived in a linguistically appealing way no matter whether we choose TT-MCTAG or V-TAG.

____

[2]The prefield in German immediately precedes the finite verb in verb second configurations. In general, it is occupied by one single constituent.

As mentioned in (Lichte, 2007), the extension of node sharing to tree sharing could solve this dilemma in the case of TT-MCTAG. However, the exact complexity class being unknown, tree sharing seems to extend complexity somewhat in practice. Moreover, it is unclear, how such an extension would transfer to V-TAG. Note that, other than (Gerdes, 2004), we aim at an analysis which restricts itself immediately through the formalism that derives the syntactic structure.

2 Adapting the derived structures

Our strategy is to adapt the derived syntactic structure such that we obtain a dominance relation between the head and its argument both in the derivation tree and the derived tree. It has been already mentioned in (Lichte, 2007) that fronting phenomena no more pose a problem if the derived structure is left branching, such as in in Fig. 5. Both

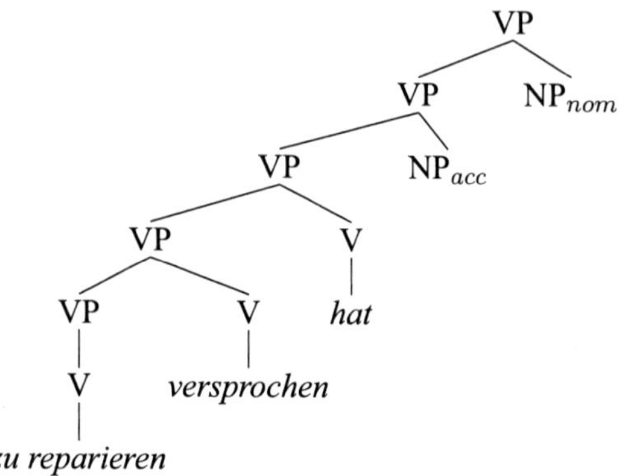

Figure 5: Left branching derived tree for (1).

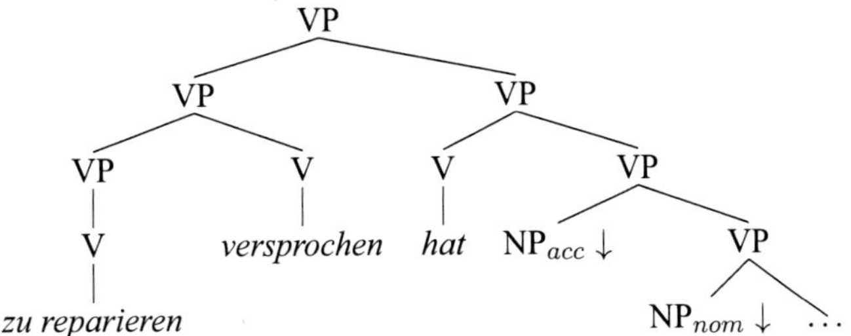

Figure 4: Left- and right-branching derived structure of the embedded partial VP fronting datum in (1).

the TT-MCTAG approach and the V-TAG approach then would suffice. This adaptation, however, is not desirable since, amongst others, the argument trees would also be required to be left-branching, leading to massive ambiguity in the lexicon due to the availability of right-branching and left-branching solutions.

Instead, we propose a flat derived structure for the complex partial fronting case, as sketched in Fig. 6, in which the NP-arguments are immediate daughters of the VP-root. Doing this allows for a unified account of fronting cases and cases of canonical word order.

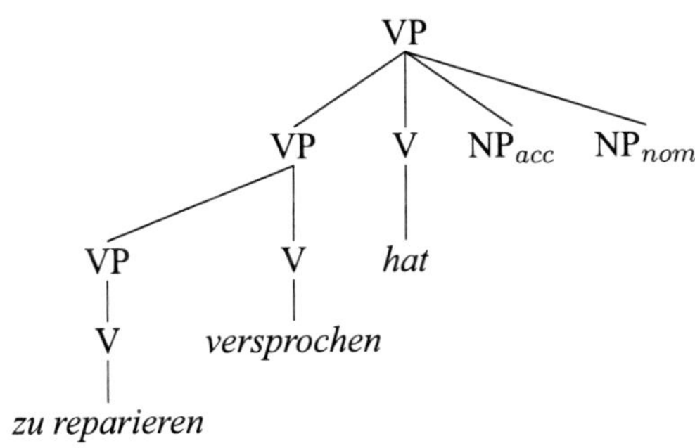

Figure 6: Flat derived tree for (1).

3   Spinal TT-MCTAG

Aiming at a flat derived structure such as in Fig. 6, we introduce a new TT-MCTAG variant that ties in with ideas recently laid out under the name LTAG-spinal in (Shen, 2006). In place of substitution, LTAG-spinal uses a rewriting operation called attachment, which is congruent with sister adjunction (Rambow et al., 1995; Chiang, 2003). Combining two trees γ_i and γ_j via attachment means that in the

resulting tree one inner node v_i of γ_i dominates the root node v_j of γ_j, such that γ_j immediately precedes or follows the subtree dominated by v_i in γ_i. See Fig. 7 for an example from (Shen, 2006). Both arguments and modifiers are integrated by attachment, and thus elementary trees receive a "spinal" shape.

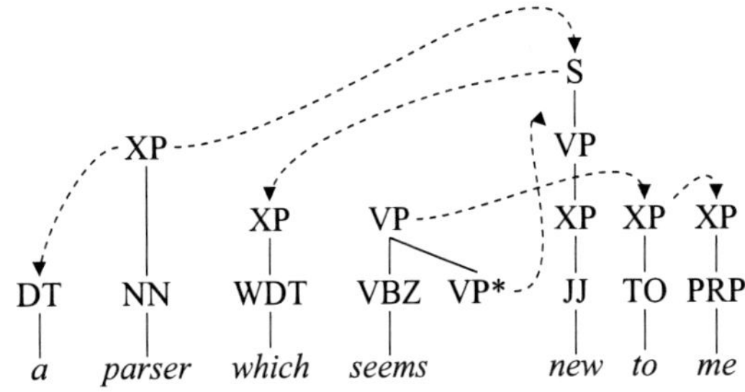

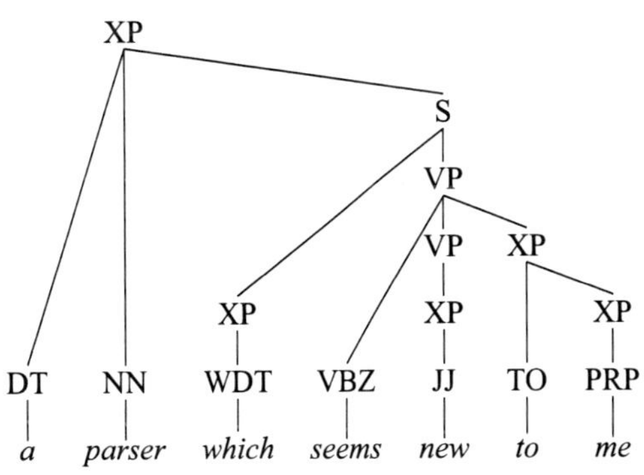

Figure 7: LTAG-spinal derivation example.

Spinal TT-MCTAG with attachment

If we supply TT-MCTAG with attachment analogously to LTAG-spinal, the result provides sufficient means to account for (1), as shown in Fig. 8. Other than with regular TT-MCTAG, arguments are realized by auxiliary trees with a single node. Furthermore, attachment takes over the role of substitution in that it defines islands for argument head dislocations, while node sharing still relies on root node adjunction.

Lexical partition of the derived tree:

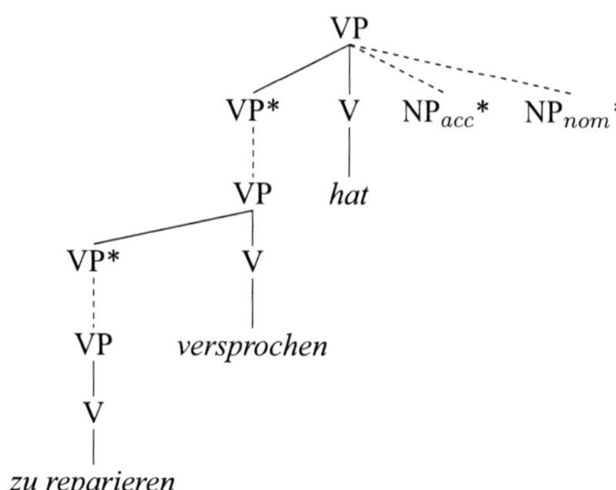

zu reparieren

Lexical entries:

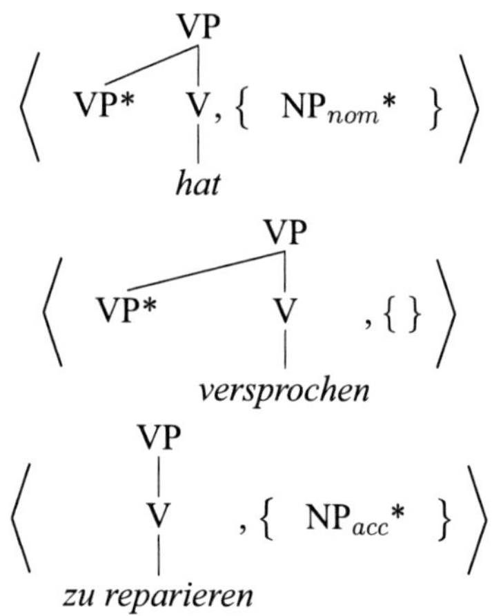

zu reparieren

Figure 8: Derivation and lexical entries according to TT-MCTAG with attachment.

However, spinal TT-MCTAG with attachment is not without severe drawbacks. Since NPs can get attached to the head tree as unrestrictedly as modifiers, nothing so far prevents nominative NPs from attaching to the head tree in any number and any order. The way of licensing of nominal arguments by ad-

joining auxiliary trees from the argument set only requires the existence of proper NPs. One could apply some kind of downstream semantic filter, but we will explore a syntactic solution in the second version of spinal TT-MCTAG. More importantly, while embedded partial VP-fronting can be accounted for now, new gaps open concerning the coverage of other partial VP-fronting phenomena, such as in (3).

(3) Zu reparieren hat er ihn versprochen.
    to repair   has he it   promised
    'He has promised to repair it.'

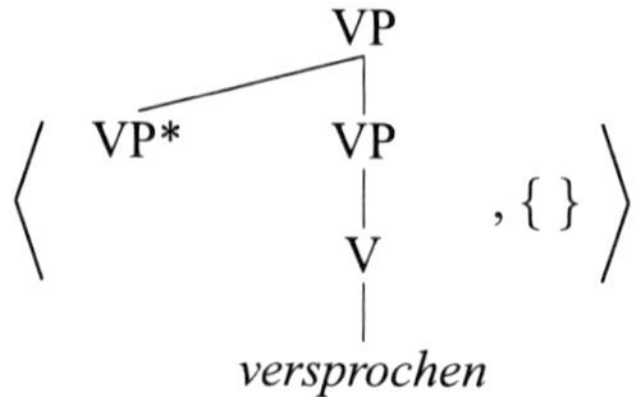

versprochen

Figure 9: Tree tuple for *versprochen* in (3).

Other than in (1) and (2), the verb *versprochen* and the head of its verbal argument *zu reparieren* are not adjacent, but separated by the finite auxiliary *hat* and one argument from each of the full verbs. Since the tree of *versprochen* would still have to adjoin to the tree of *zu reparieren* in order to allow for the dislocation of its argument *ihn*, the tree tuple for *versprochen* would look as in Fig. 9, including an additional lower VP-node. This lower VP-node would be essential for providing a landing site for the wrapped material, i.e. *hat, er* and *ihn*. The result would be, however, that the argument tree of *zu reparieren* (that adjoins into the tree of *ihn*) would not be able to attach at the root node of the tree of *versprochen* and the node sharing relation between *zu reparieren* and its argument would be lost.

This problem is not at all new, but echos the situation of the original TT-MCTAG account as described above. And again, neglecting the head tree constraint would help. Alternatively, one could think of modifying the current version of spinal TT-MCTAG with attachment (e.g., by reactivating substitution). But instead of this, I will introduce a second version of spinal TT-MCTAG, that successfully circumvents this concession.

Spinal TT-MCTAG with fusion

Instead of attachment, we make use of a similar but novel rewriting operation that we refer to as *fusion*. The fusion operation is the amalgamation of single nodes rather than the drawing of a new edge. More formally spoken: If two nodes v_i, v_j of trees γ_i, γ_j are fused, in the resulting tree (i) they are replaced by a node v', for which it holds that all in-going edges of v_i, v_j now point to v' and (ii) the subtrees dominated by v_i and v_j are immediately adjacent and dominated by v' in the resulting tree. We restrict fusion to pairs of nodes, of which at least one node is the root node of the respective tree, in order to maintain the tree shape of the derived tree. Furthermore, it holds that the categorial labels of the fused nodes must be identical.

An important split then is between fusion of root nodes and fusion of a root and a non-root node: the former one, but not the latter one, is non-embedding in that the affected trees are equivalent in the derivation process. In that respect, fusion at inner nodes bears more similarity to attachement and multiple adjunction (Schabes and Shieber, 1994). Fusion in general, however, integrates both arguments and modifiers. The derived tree in Fig. 6 is then the result of the derivation and the lexical entries in Fig. 10. Note that adjunction only applies to the root node of target trees. The division of labor is the following: adjunction extends locality, while fusion at an inner node parallels substitution and defines islands of locality. Hence, the argument set of tree tuples consists of spinal trees that have non-terminal leaves (i.e. the argument slots) and that either are initial or auxiliary trees. To give an example, the NP-slots in the argument sets of the tuples in Fig. 10 constitute islands, whereas the VP-slots do not. The derivational meaning of tree tuples is then the following: The argument trees are (directly or indirectly) fused with the head tree, otherwise the argument trees stand in a node sharing relation to the head tree based on the derivation tree.

Other than the proposal with attachment, it is now possible to underspecify the relative position of the head anchor and the verbal complement. The derivation of the partial fronting case in (3), therefore, does not require concessions such as the violation against the head tree constraint. In fact, it does not even

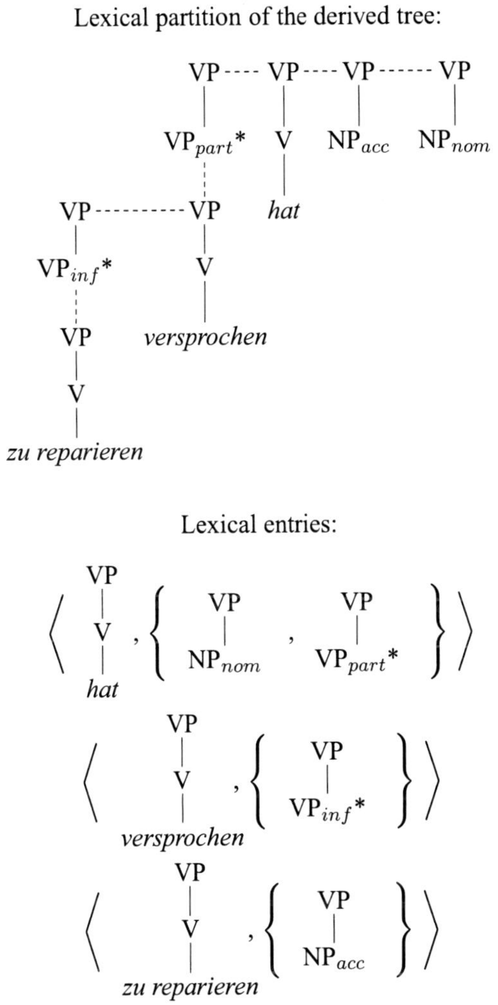

Lexical partition of the derived tree:

Lexical entries:

Figure 10: Derivation and lexical entries according to spinal TT-MCTAG with fusion.

require further lexical variation such that the tree tuples in Fig. 10 suffice also to this end.

This shift to the fusion operation, however, has significant effects on the nature of the derivation tree and thus on the notion of node sharing. Moreover, it is necessary to define a regulation method for fusion which differs from usual feature-unification-based approaches. Both issues are covered separately in the next two sections.

4   The new face of the derivation tree

Since fusion at the root node is understood as being inherently non-embedding, it is indicated with chains as nodes in the derivation tree. Edges are then used for the representation of fusion to some non-root node, and for the representation of adjunction. In other words, edges are dominance relations, whereas nodes represent precedence relations. Hence, the derivation in Fig. 10 receives the derivation tree in Fig. 11. Note that the edge label indicates adjunction (A) or fusion (F) followed by the tree label of the embedding tree. Fusion labels furthermore contain the Gorn address of the embedding tree.[3] Other than in TAG derivation trees, auxiliary trees dominate their target since adjunction is only necessary at the root node.

Such derivation trees can be defined in the following way: A **spinal TT-MCTAG derivation tree** is a tuple $D = \langle C, V, E \rangle$ with labelling functions $l_E : E \to L_E$ and $l_V : V \to L_V$, where V is the set of nodes, C is the set of chains[4] with $C = V \times 2^{V \times V}$ and E is the set of edges with $E = C \times C$. It holds that E is a tree over C. For each $v \in V$ there is exactly one $\zeta \in C$ with $\zeta = \langle V_\zeta, E_\zeta \rangle$, such that $v \in V_\zeta$.

The idea of node sharing is to constrain the path between the head and its argument in a derivation tree. Elementary trees, however, now correspond to nodes of chains. This can be accounted for in the following way: Given a spinal TT-MCTAG derivation tree $D = \langle C, V, E \rangle$, a **path** P between nodes v_i, v_j in chains $\zeta_i, \zeta_j \in C$ is a subset of E, such that $\zeta_i \overset{*}{\to}_P \zeta_j$.

Therefore, the path from the argument NP_{acc} to its head zu_reparieren in Fig. 11 is the edge label sequence $A.VP_{part}$, $A.VP_{inf}$.

5 Adapting the node sharing relation

Having explained paths in such derivation trees, we can now specify the node sharing relation that is essential for the derivational meaning of tree tuples: Given two nodes $v_i, v_j \in V$ in a spinal TT-MCTAG derivation tree D, v_i is in the node sharing relation to v_j , iff all edges in the path P from v_i to v_j according to D have the label A.TID, with TID being a tree label. This excludes edges with label F.TID.p,

$p > 0$. A node sharing relation of this kind holds for the nodes with label NP_{acc} and zu_reparieren in the derivation tree in Fig. 11. Note that, contrary to the original definition of node sharing, the argument now dominates the head in the derivation tree.

Finally, we can explicate, what a well-formed derivation tree for a spinal TT-MCTAG G is: Given a spinal TT-MCTAG derivation tree $D = \langle C, V, E \rangle$, if $v_1, \ldots, v_n \in V$ are pairwise different nodes for which it holds that $l_V(v_i) = \gamma$ for $1 \leq i \leq n$ with γ being the head tree of a tree tuple $\langle \gamma, A \rangle$ in G, then for each $\gamma' \in A$, there are pairwise different nodes $u_1, \ldots, u_n \in V$ with $l_V(u_i) = \gamma'$ for $1 \leq i \leq n$. Furthermore, u_i and v_i are members of a chain $\zeta \in C$, or u_i is a member of $\zeta_u \in C$ and v_i is a member of $\zeta_v \in C$ and $\zeta_v \to \zeta_u$, or u_i is in a node sharing relation to v_i.

This also holds for the derivation tree in Fig. 11.

6 The regulation of fusion

Substitution and adjunction is usually regulated by using some kind of feature unification, also referred to as top-bottom unification. This has to be adapted in the case of attachment, since attachment, other than substitution and adjunction, needs to be regulated also with respect to the direction of attachment.[5] Fusion, on the other side, does not seem to be compatible with a feature unification account due to its non-embedding nature. Instead, we propose and briefly sketch a novel regulation method, where node labels refer to recursive transition networks (RTN,(Woods, 1970)). RTNs are named finite state automata where transitions may additionally depend on successful calls of further RTNs. Other than regular finite state automata, RTNs are weakly equivalent with CFGs. We use RTNs in the following way: a categorial label of a node in a elementary tree, say VP_{fin}, does not stand for a set of features, but maps onto an RTN as depicted in Fig. 12, such that fusion effects state transitions rather than feature unifications. This implies a strict order on the application of fusion from the left to the right. While the non-terminals AP, NP and VP point to respective RTNs, the POS-labels V_{fin} and PART(ICLE) can

---

[3]The Gorn address of the root node is ε while the Gorn address of the ith daughter of a node with Gorn address p is $p \cdot i$.

[4]Chains are trees where the nodes have out-degree and in-degree of at most 1.

[5]C.f. sister adjunction constraints (SAC) from (Rambow et al., 1995).

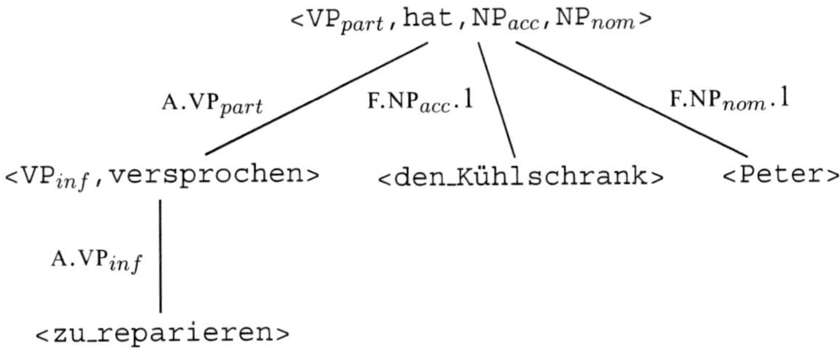

Figure 11: Derivation tree for (1) according to the spinal TT-MCTAG in Fig. 10.

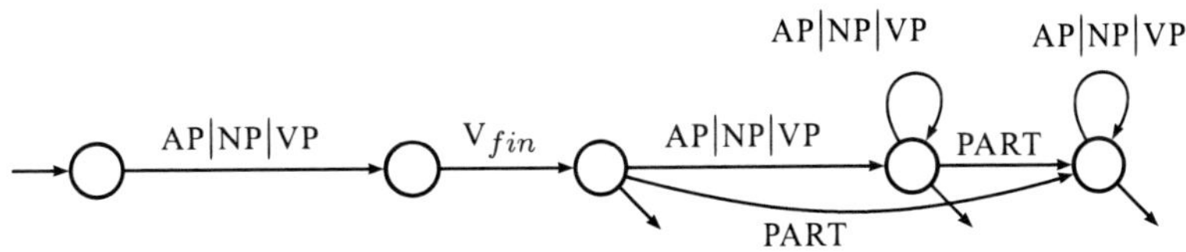

Figure 12: A recursive transition network for the label VP_{fin}, i.e. a finite clause.

be regarded as terminal symbols. Note that the provided prototype of a VP_{fin}-RTN straightforwardly accounts for the prefield conditions for German - the conditions being that the prefield, i.e. the preverbal position, must be occupied and there is exactly one constituent that occupies it.

7 The generative power of spinal TT-MCTAG

From a linguistic point of view, one central ingredient of mild context-sensitivity certainly is the potential for the analysis of cross-serial dependencies. While German usually serves as an exemplar of a center embedding language, it also allows for cross-serial dependencies (to some degree) due to the flexible order of the nominal arguments. This can be observed, e.g., in (4).

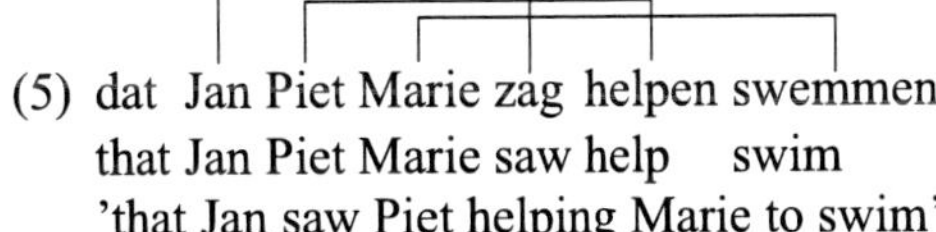

(4) dass den Kühlschrank ihm Peter reparieren half
    that the fridge   him Peter repair   helped
    'that Peter helped him to repair the fridge'

This kind of cross-serial dependency guided by case is derivable in both versions of a spinal TT-MCTAG. The order of the NP sequence and the verbal complex is basically independent. In Dutch, however,

where the mapping of verbs and arguments depends on their relative order, this does not suffice. The assumed generalization is that the ith noun can be only the subject of the ith verb, but counting so far is not supported by spinal TT-MCTAG.

(5) dat Jan Piet Marie zag helpen swemmen
    that Jan Piet Marie saw help   swim
    'that Jan saw Piet helping Marie to swim'

8 Conclusion

Certain partial VP fronting phenomena in German seem to pose an intractable problem for currently available MCTAG variants for German, i.e. V-TAG and TT-MCTAG. This paper therefore proposed to aim at flatter derived structures and investigated ways to modify TT-MCTAG, in order to generate them. Ideas for two novel variants of TT-MCTAG, spinal TT-MCTAG with attachment and spinal TT-MCTAG with fusion, were sketched, which both offer means to account for the data in question. It turned out that spinal TT-MCTAG with fusion performs better, since it is straightforwardly applicable to other phenomena of flexible word order without violating the head tree constraint, contrary to spinal TT-MCTAG with attachment. Another major advantage is that the number of lexical entries considerably reduces due to the spinal shape of the head tree. In return, the shape of the derivation tree had to be modified, replacing atomic node labels by chains, which correspond to the non-embedding nature of the fusion operation. For the regulation of fusion, we proposed to use recursive transition networks instead of feature unification. These modifications due to fusion certainly are far-reaching, but we think that they are far from being mere technical repairs. RTNs, for example, offer interesting means to express syntactic generalizations.

Certainly, the current paper does not present a complete picture of the proposal, and there are many aspects, e.g. complexity issues and the regulation by RTNs, that have to be worked out in further research.

References

Manuel Bodirsky, Marco Kuhlmann, and Mathias Möhl. 2005. Well-nested drawings as models of syntactic structure. In *In 10th Conference on Formal Grammar and 9th Meeting on Mathematics of Language (FG-MOL05)*, Edinburgh.

David Chiang. 2003. Statistical parsing with an automatically extracted tree adjoining grammar. In Rens Bod, Remko Scha, and Khalil Sima'an, editors, *Data Oriented Parsing*, pages 299–316. CSLI Publications.

Kim Gerdes. 2004. Tree Unification Grammar. In Lawrence S. Moss and Richard T. Oehrle, editors, *Electronic Notes in Theoretical Computer Science*, volume 53. Elsevier. Proceedings of the joint meeting of the 6th Conference on Formal Grammar and the 7th Conference on Mathematics of Language.

Laura Kallmeyer. 2009. A declarative characterization of different types of multicomponent tree adjoining grammar. *Research on Language and Computation*, 7:55–99.

Marco Kuhlmann and Mathias Möhl. 2006. Extended cross-serial dependencies in Tree Adjoining Grammars. In *Proceedings of the 8th International Workshop on Tree Adjoining Grammar and Related Formalisms*, pages 121–126, Sydney.

Timm Lichte. 2007. An MCTAG with tuples for coherent constructions in German. In *Proceedings of the 12th Conference on Formal Grammar*. Dublin, Ireland, 4-5 August 2007.

Owen Rambow, K. Vijay-Shanker, and David Weir. 1995. D-tree grammars. In *Proceedings of the 33rd Annual Conference of the Association for Computational Linguistics*, Cambridge, MA.

Owen Rambow. 1994. *Formal and Computational Aspects of Natural Language Syntax*. Ph.D. thesis, University of Pennsylvania, Philadelphia. IRCS Report 94-08.

Yves Schabes and Stuart Shieber. 1994. An alternative conception of tree-adjoining derivation. *Computational Linguistic*, 20(1):91–124.

Libin Shen. 2006. *Statistical LTAG Parsing*. Ph.D. thesis, University of Pennsylvania.

William A. Woods. 1970. Transition network grammars for natural language analysis. *Commun. ACM*, 13:591–606, October.

Gapping through TAG Derivation Trees[*]

Timm Lichte and **Laura Kallmeyer**
Emmy Noether Research Group, SFB 833, University of Tübingen
`timm.lichte@uni-tuebingen.de, lk@sfs.uni-tuebingen.de`

Abstract

This work provides a TAG account of gapping in English, based on a novel deletion-like operation that is referred to as *de-anchoring*. De-anchoring applies onto elementary trees, but it is licensed by the derivation tree in two ways. Firstly, de-anchored trees must be linked to the root of the derivation tree by a chain of adjunctions, and the sub-graph of de-anchored nodes in a derivation tree must satisfy certain internal constraints. Secondly, de-anchoring must be licensed by the presence of a homomorphic antecedent derivation tree.

1 Introduction

Existing TAG-accounts of gapping propose the contraction of nodes (Sarkar and Joshi, 1997) or adopt elementary trees with a gap that lack the verbal anchor (Babko-Malaya, 2006) or combine the gapped elementary tree with its antecedent site into a tree set within an MCTAG-account (Seddah, 2008). This work breaks new ground in that it uses *de-anchoring*, a deletion-like operation, for the modelling of gapping, which applies to elementary trees while being licensed by the derivation tree of licit TAG-derivations. De-anchoring removes the anchors of an elementary tree and can be seen to parallel PF-deletion in generative grammar (Hartmann, 2000; Merchant, 2001).

Our work is inspired by recent ideas from (Osborne, 2008; Kobele, 2009). Working in minimalist grammar, (Kobele, 2009) states the following Derivational Identity Hypothesis (DIH): "If a syntactic object SO_1 is elided under identity with SO_2, then SO_1 and SO_2 have been derived in exactly the same way." A strict reading of the DIH then leads to the prediction that subtrees of the derivational structure can be a target of a deletion-like operation that yields gapped structures only if an isomorphic antecedent subtree of the derivation structure exists.

(Osborne, 2008), on the other side, transfers the notion of major constituent, that is seen as being central to the licensing of gapping (Hankamer, 1973; Neijt, 1979; Chao, 1987), from generative grammar to a dependency-based description of gapping. A major constituent is then "a constituent the head [i.e. the governor] of which is, but the root of which is not, a link in the predicate chain". The predicate chain is made of the verbal complex. Gapping then complies to the *Restriction on Internal Sharing* (RIS): "The gap of conjunct-internal sharing may not cut into a major constituent."

We combine these approaches by describing gapping in TAG as a de-anchoring operation restricted by the derivation tree.

The paper is structured as follows: In the next section, we introduce the operation of de-anchoring. Then, in Sections 3 and 4, we develop relevant constraints for de-anchoring, based on the derivation tree. Section 5 points out some potential problems of our approach while Section 6 discusses its relation to the aforementioned proposals. Finally, Section 7 briefly mentions some aspects of implementation.

---

[*]We are grateful to Maribel Romero and Andreas Konietzko; the paper has benefitted a lot from discussions with them. Furthermore, we would like to thank three anonymous reviewers for their valuable comments.

2 The Idea of De-Anchoring

In our TAG derivation trees, the edge label S, followed by the Gorn address of the substitution node, indicates substitution, whereas A indicates adjunction, again followed by the Gorn address of the adjunction site.[1] As an example, Fig. 1 shows the derivation of (1-a).

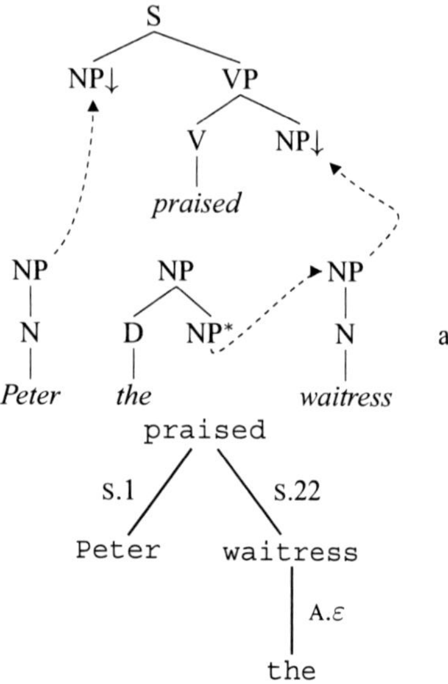

Figure 1: Derivation and derivation tree for "Peter praised the waitress".

(1) a. Peter praised the waitress.
    b. Adam praised Mary, and Peter ~~praised~~ the waitress.

We write derivation trees as graphs $\langle V, E, r \rangle$ where V is the set of *vertices* or *nodes*, $E \subset V \times V$ the set of *edges* and there is a *labeling function* l that assigns a label $l(v)$ to each node $v \in V$ and a label $l(e)$ to each edge $e \in E$. $r \in V$ is the *root node*, i.e., the node with in-degree 0. E^* represents the reflexive transitive closure of E, i.e., the dominance relation in the tree.

We say that an elementary tree γ is *de-anchored* if the terminals of γ are deleted (i.e., replaced with a label ε), while the other parts of γ are retained, thus preserving, e.g., case marking and semantics.

An example is the gapping correlate of (1-a) in (1-b) and its derivation tree in Fig. 2, in which the root node is de-anchored, indicated by crossing out the node label.

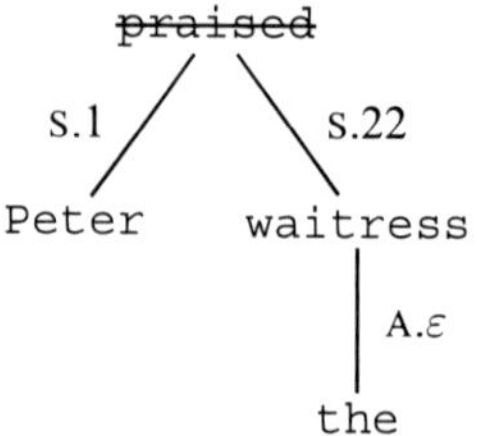

Figure 2: Derivation tree for "Peter ~~praised~~ the waitress".

Interesting questions are now, what kind of elementary trees can be de-anchored ("internal conditions on de-anchoring"), and what types of configurations allow for de-anchoring ("external conditions on de-anchoring"). We will formulate both types of conditions depending on the TAG derivation tree.

3 Internal Conditions on De-Anchoring

Based on Fig. 2, a preliminary formulation of the internal condition would be that only root nodes of derivation trees can be de-anchored while complete subtrees of the root node are major constituents. This explains the unavailability of (2).

(2) *Adam praised Mary and Peter ~~praised the~~ waitress.

However, there are cases where not only the root is part of the gap. Examples are (3) and (4).

(3) a. John gives Mary a book and Peter ~~gives Mary~~ a disk.
    b. John gives Mary a book and ~~John gives~~ Peter a disk.

(4) a. John is fond of Mary and Mary ~~is fond~~ of Sue.
    b. John is a reader in linguistics and Mary ~~is a reader~~ in philosophy.

In (3), in addition to the deleted verb, one of its substituted arguments is deleted as well. The derivation trees for the parts containing the gaps are shown in Fig. 3. This suggests that, if an element is de-anchored, each of its S-daughters can be de-anchored as well.

---

[1] The Gorn address of the root node is ε while the Gorn address of the *i*th daughter of a node with Gorn address p is $p \cdot i$.

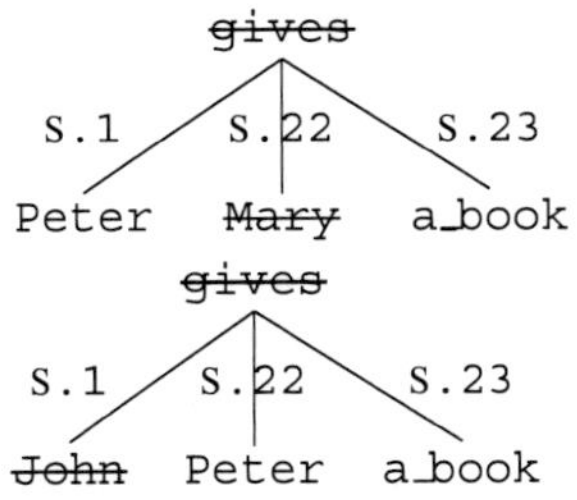

Figure 3: Derivation trees for (3).

In (4) , the deleted part includes a copula and a predicate. In XTAG (XTAG Research Group, 2001), copula as in (4) receive a small clause analysis. We adapt this idea, differing from the XTAG-analysis, however, in treating prepositions not as co-anchors of the predicate (see Fig. 4). In this analysis the predicate *fond* is the root of the derivation tree, and it dominates the copula verb.

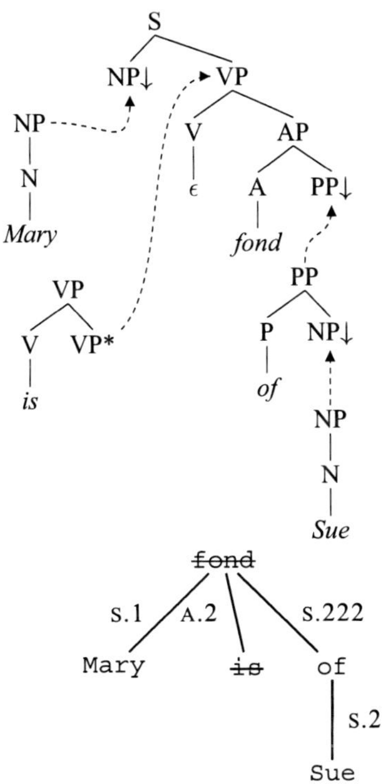

Figure 4: Derivation for "Mary ~~is fond~~ of Sue".

In order to account for (4) and (3), we revise our internal condition as follows: The gap constitutes a single A-branch in the derivation tree. An A-branch is a path of nodes connected by A-edges. Furthermore, if a node in the derivation tree is de-anchored,

its S-daughters can be de-anchored as well.

The gap may also contain a chain of control verbs, as has been noted already in (Ross, 1970), exemplified in (5).

(5)   I want to try to begin to write a novel, and

    a.   Mary ~~wants to try to begin to write~~ a play.
    b.   Mary ~~wants to try to begin~~ to write a play.
    c.   Mary ~~wants to try~~ to begin to write a play.
    d.   Mary ~~wants~~ to try to begin to write a play.

XTAG adopts an analysis of control verbs that adjoins the control verb at the embedded infinitive and that uses an empty category PRO that substitutes into the subject NP slot. Such infinitives allow only PRO as subjects; this constraint is achieved via corresponding features on the substitution node. The elementary trees are shown in Fig. 5.

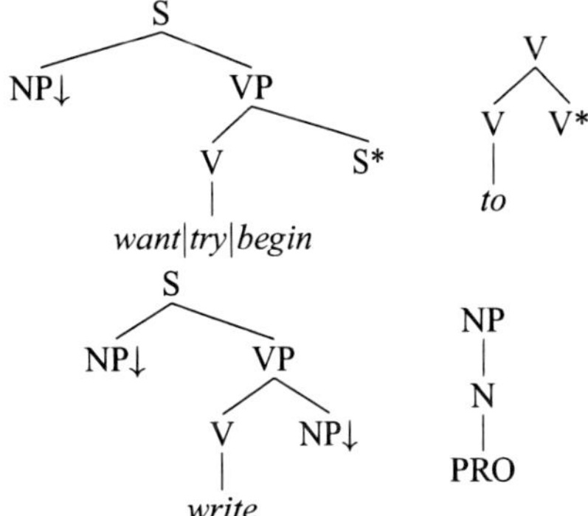

Figure 5: Elementary trees for control verbs in the spirit of XTAG.

The derivation tree for (5-a) is shown in Fig. 6. Three observations are striking: (i) the remnants *Mary* and *a play* are complements of different verbs; (ii) the gaps are variable in size; (iii) the gaps constitute A-subtrees rather than just A-branches.

The first observation contradicts the here proposed conception of major constituency, since the first remnant *Mary* is not an immediate daughter of the root. Instead, it is the immediate S-daughter of a node on a A-subtree.

The second observation suggests that a partial de-anchoring of the A-subtree is possible: the maximal gap in (5-a) corresponds to the A-branch, which is de-anchorable from the edge towards and including the root, as the other gap options in (5-b)-(5-d) show.

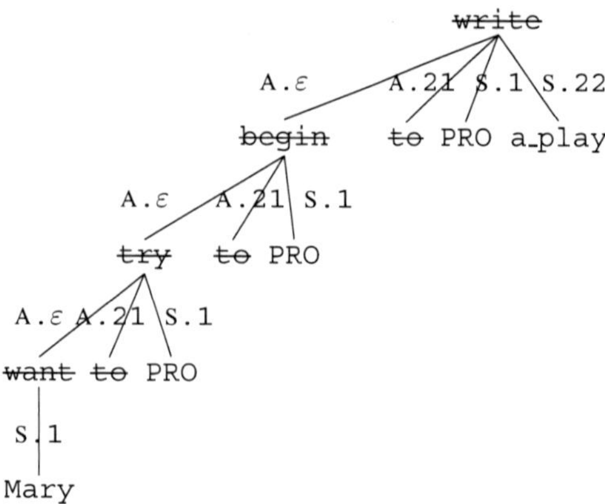

Figure 6: Derivation for (5-a).

Finally, we learn from the third observation that we have to either disallow the infinitive marker *to* to adjoin to the verbal stem and rather give it a lexical analysis, or we have to allow the de-anchoring of sister nodes, hence of A-subtrees of the derivation tree. When the mother is not de-anchored, however, it moreover holds that only the node adjoining highest can be de-anchored. This captures the unavailability of a sole de-anchoring of the infinitive marker:

(6) *... and I want ~~to~~ try to begin to write a novel.

In order to formulate our internal condition, we need the following notions: Given a derivation tree $\delta = \langle V, E, r \rangle$, we call the sub-graph γ of de-anchored nodes a *gap*. Given a node $v \in V$ with A-daughters $v_1, \ldots, v_k$, we call $\langle v, v_i \rangle$ a maximally high adjunction if its label is A.p and all edges $\langle v, v_j \rangle$, $j \neq i$, $1 \leq j \leq k$, are labeled A.pq with $q \neq \varepsilon$.

Gaps must satisfy the following **Internal Condition on De-Anchoring**:

1. γ must be a tree $\gamma = \langle V_g, E_g, r_g \rangle$ with $V_g \subset V, E_g \subset E$;

2. there must be an A-branch (possibly empty) from the root of δ to the root of γ such that all edges on this path are maximally high adjunctions;

3. for every node $v_g \in V_g$, it holds that all A-daughters of v_g in δ are also part of γ. I.e., for all $v_g \in V_g$ and all $v \in V$, if $\langle v_g, v \rangle \in E$ and

$l(\langle v_g, v \rangle) = $ A.p for some Gorn address p, then $v \in V_g$;

4. for every node $v_g \in V_g$, it holds that an S-daughter v_s of v_g in δ can be part of γ; if so, all nodes dominated by v_s in δ must also be part of γ. I.e., for all $v_g \in V_g$ and all $v \in V$ such that $\langle v_g, v \rangle \in E$ and $l(\langle v_g, v \rangle) = $ S.p for some Gorn address p, if $v \in V_g$, then it holds for all v' with $\langle v, v' \rangle \in E^*$ that $v' \in V_g$.

It follows that in our model **major constituents** correspond to S-daughters of nodes of the A-subtree below the root node. It is not permitted to delete only parts of them. This use, however, is not extensionally congruent with Osborne's use of the term, since he also applies it to modifiers.

4   External Conditions on De-Anchoring

Gapping is further constrained by a certain parallelism of the ellipsis site and the antecedent site. We assume here that an antecedent derivation tree represents the first conjunct of a coordinative construction whose second conjunct includes the ellipsis. We call this aspect the *external conditions* on de-anchoring, and we will be mainly dealing with homomorphism properties of the derivation trees of the ellipsis site and the antecedent site. A strict formulation of the external condition would be that de-anchored nodes must have a corresponding node in the antecedent derivation tree, such that both have (i) an identical position in their derivation trees (i.e. an identical path to the respective root nodes) and (ii) an identical node label, given that the node label always identifies an elementary tree unambiguously.

This is however too restrictive: Gapping is known to allow number mismatch between elided material and its antecedent, see (7) and also (5) above.

(7)   I am flying to Europe, and you ~~are flying~~ to Asia.   (Osborne, 2008)

We hence need complex node labels that help to abstract away from number information, as is depicted in Fig. 7. Then, instead of requiring the identity of the entire feature structure, we require only the identity of specific features. In particular, we require the LEMMA feature to be identical for the two nodes while the ANCHOR and NUM features can be different.

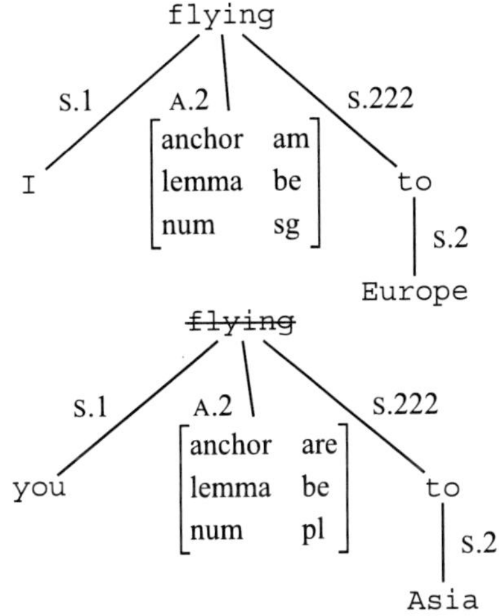

Figure 7: Derivation trees of the first and second conjunct of (7) with complex nodes.

Furthermore, dissimilarities of other properties of ellipsis and antecedent could be permissible, though not as easily as number mismatch. For example, the gapped verb could be differing from the antecedent verb wrt. word order, such as in (8), and subcategorization properties, as shown in (9).

(8) ?This guy she likes, and Mary ~~likes~~ Peter.

(9)   a. ?Peter was looking for the Olympic games and Mary ~~was looking~~ after the children.
   b. ?Peter ate and Mary ~~ate~~ a whole chicken.

These kinds of mismatch would also be handled in terms of partial identity of complex node labels in the derivation tree.

On the other side, certain properties of the nodes in question must be identical, most prominently their position within the derivation tree: In (10), the antecedent verb *ordered* is embedded in a fronted adverbial clause, whereas the elided correspondent is the matrix verb and hence in the root position of the second conjunct.

(10) *Since Peter ordered a beer, the waitress instantly reached for the fridge and Mary ~~ordered~~ a whole chicken.

Likewise, we claim that mismatches of voice and tense are not acceptable (see (11)).

(11) a. *Peter was informed by the young police officer, and the older one ~~was informing~~ Mary.
   b.? *Peter had to clean the floor last week, and Mary ~~has to clean~~ the kitchen this week

The **External Condition on De-Anchoring** is then as follows: A derivation tree δ containing a gap $\gamma = \langle V_g, E_g \rangle$ is licensed if the following holds: There are two subtree $\delta_1 = \langle V_1, E_1, r_1 \rangle$, $\delta_2 = \langle V_2, E_2, r_2 \rangle$ of δ such that δ represents the conjunction of δ_1 and δ_2, γ is a subtree of δ_2 and there is a homomorphism $h : V_g \to V_1$ such that:

1. Identity of paths to root nodes: for all $v \in V_g$: There are $v_1^{(2)}, \ldots, v_k^{(2)} \in V_2$ for some $k \geq 1$ with $v_1^{(2)} = r_2$, $v_k^{(2)} = v$ and $\langle v_i^{(2)}, v_{i+1}^{(2)} \rangle \in E_2$ and $l(\langle v_i^{(2)}, v_{i+1}^{(2)} \rangle) = l_i$ for $1 \leq i < k$ iff there are $v_1^{(1)}, \ldots, v_k^{(1)} \in V_1$ with $v_1^{(1)} = r_1$, $v_k^{(1)} = h(v)$ and $\langle v_i^{(1)}, v_{i+1}^{(1)} \rangle \in E_1$ and $l(\langle v_i^{(1)}, v_{i+1}^{(1)} \rangle) = l_i$ for $1 \leq i < k$.

2. Identity of specific features: for all $v \in V_g$: Certain feature values are identical for v and $h(v)$ in δ. These include at least LEMMA, TENSE and VOICE.

5   Problems

The internal condition on de-anchoring correctly allows for the de-anchoring of S-nodes, accounting for examples such as (12).

(12) John gave a book to Mary and
   a. Peter ~~gave a book~~ to Sue.
   b. Peter ~~gave~~ a report ~~to Mary~~.

This, however, is too permissive. It needs to be carefully constrained, in order to rule out instances of bare argument ellipsis such as in (13), which are traditionally judged ungrammatical (see, e.g., (Jackendoff, 1971, (27-a)), (Johnson, 2004, p.3)).

(13) *John gave a book to Mary and
   Peter ~~gave a book to Mary~~.

Interestingly enough, Osborne's proposal is also too permissive in this respect, and this also holds for the proposals of, e.g., (Neijt, 1979) and (Hartmann, 2000, p.144).

The internal condition, moreover, turns out to be too restrictive when it comes to adverbial remnants. Consider the gapping instance in (14) and its derivation tree in Fig. 8.[2]

(14) Mary always finishes her homework, but Peter ~~finishes his homework~~ only sometimes.

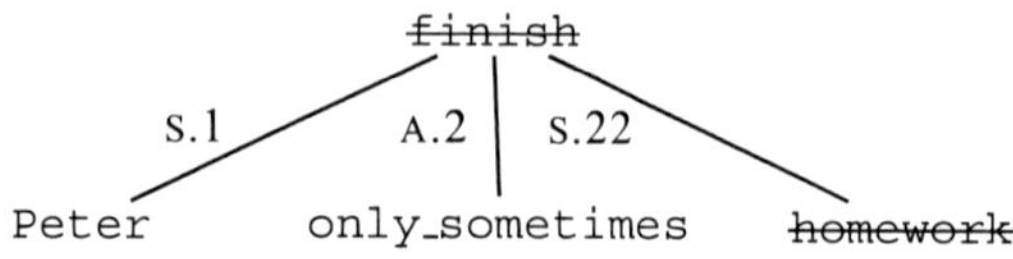

Figure 8: Derivation tree of (14).

We must observe that the adverb remains overt while its dominating A-node is de-anchored. This contradicts the internal condition according to which A-daughters of de-anchored nodes must be de-anchored as well. A solution could be to enable the optionality of the de-anchoring of adverbs. This would make it necessary to have access to a distinctive feature of adverbs and verbs in the process of de-anchoring, e.g., by having access to the feature structure used for implementing the external condition below. The distinction could be a distinction between *modifier auxiliary trees* (adverbs, adjectives, etc.) and *predicative auxiliary trees* (verbs selecting for a sentential complement). This distinction already has been used in (Schabes and Shieber, 1994).

A further example of an adverb that is not de-anchored is (15). The derivation tree is shown in Fig. 9.

(15) Mary is always fond of cheese cake, but Peter ~~is~~ only sometimes ~~fond of cheese cake~~.

Here, the adverb remains overt while not only its dominating A-node but also its dominated A-node are de-anchored. Hence, the A-branch is de-anchored with a hole. This clearly contradicts the internal condition on de-anchoring. Making use of concepts such as sister adjunction, one

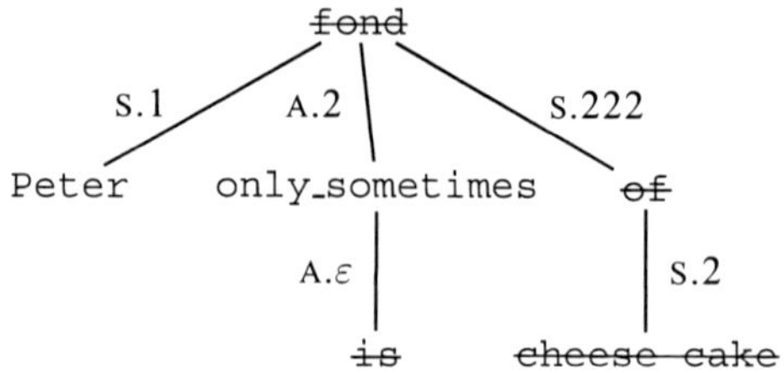

Figure 9: Derivation tree of (15).

could rearrange the derivation tree such that is and only_sometimes are siblings, directly dominated by fond. This would reduce the example to an example of the type of (14).

Finally, the internal condition on de-anchoring proves too permissive in cases, where the A-tree does not correspond to a small clause or a control chain, but rather to , e.g., a bridge verb construction. Consider the derivation tree in Fig. 10 resulting from the XTAG analysis for (16):

(16) Larry thinks Sue is nice.

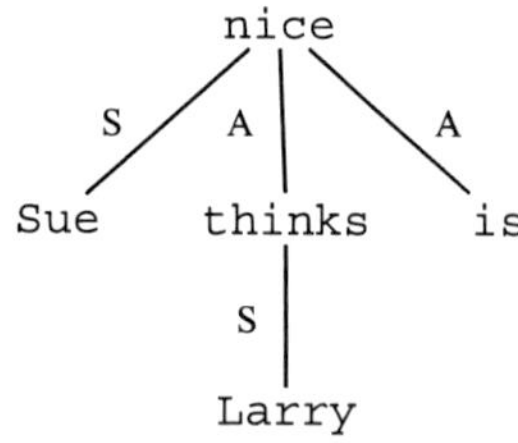

Figure 10: Derivation trees for "Larry thinks Sue is nice".

Since both the bridging verb *thinks* and the embedded finite auxiliary verb *is* directly adjoin to the small clause anchored by *nice*, the derivation tree contains exactly two A-branches. Taken the internal condition for granted, the acceptability of the following gaps is predicted:

(17) Larry thinks Sue is nice and

    a. *Sue ~~thinks~~ Larry is funny.

    b. *Sue ~~thinks~~ Larry ~~is nice~~.

(17-a) and (17-b) are claimed to be unacceptable (see, e.g., (Sag, 1976, p.198)), (Johnson, 2004, p.18), (Osborne, 2008, (106))).[3] The internal con-

---

[2] Note that the alternative gapping instance "Peter ~~always finishes his homework~~ only sometimes" is not ruled out by the syntax.

[3] (17-a) can be improved by adding a that-complementizer, i.e. "Larry thinks that Sue is nice and Sue ~~thinks~~ that Larry is

dition might thus be too permissive.

One could argue that the verb *thinks* in (16) is no bridge verb, but receives an analysis, where the clausal complement is substituted into the elementary tree of *thinks*. Gapping into the clausal complement would thus be blocked since a de-anchoring of *nice* would also require a de-anchoring of the entire complement clause. This move, however, would explain only such simple cases. Where the bridge verb analysis with adjunction is inevitable, it would still predict the availability of the following, highly awkward gapping instance:

(18) ?*Who does Mary think Bill likes and
     who ~~does~~ Sue ~~think~~ Joe ~~likes~~.

Note however that the available literature on gapped bridge verb constructions seems to be very slim. Furthermore, the dependency analysis in (Osborne, 2008) can correctly predict the unacceptability of (17-b) only by the cost of stipulating two separate predicate chains. The syntactic characterization of those predicate chains and their separation is again obscure.

6   Related Work

Previous TAG-accounts of gapping consider only a very limited set of data. Furthermore, complex gaps such as (4) and (5) pose a serious challenge for those accounts that model the ellipsis-antecedent relations syntactically, such as (Sarkar and Joshi, 1997) and (Seddah, 2008). In the simple cases of gapping, (Sarkar and Joshi, 1997) let the preterminal nodes contract such that anchoring (i.e. lexicalization) happens at the same time as substitution and adjunction during the parse. When gaps are complex, however, not yet anchored derived trees have to be contracted instead of not yet anchored elementary trees. In other words, contraction would then also operate on non-immediate daughters of the conjunctor in the derivation tree. Unfortunately, Sarkar and Joshi do not elaborate on the details of this powerful extension, in particular on how to constrain it.

(Seddah, 2008) also analyzes simple cases of gapping. In his approach, he combines the elementary trees of the antecedent verb and the elided verb

into a single tree set. The resulting MCTAG is constrained to be tree-local. To process complex gaps in this vein, however, requires more expressive power: since, e.g., the control verbs and their elided counterpart adjoin into different trees from different elementary trees belonging to the same tree set, we need at least set-locality. This illustrates the so far unnoticed complication due to complex gaps.

It remains to say that the semantic account in (Babko-Malaya, 2006) is not affected in this respect.

Even though we share with (Kobele, 2009) the interest in derivational structures along the Derivational Identity Hypothesis (DIH), his account (within the minimalist grammar framework) differs considerably from ours. The main reason for this contrast is the fundamentally differing nature of the respective derivational structures. In minimalist grammar, the non-terminal nodes of the derivation tree indicate combinatorial operations, i.e., merge and move. Most importantly, the predicate-argument relation is opaque, which also follows from the fact that minimalist grammar does not dispose of an extended domain of locality. Since the DIH suggests that only common subderivations are subject to deletion, Kobele's account seems to run into difficulties when applied even to simple cases of gapping. In fact, Kobele does not flesh out a theory of gapping in his paper. He is more concerned with voice mismatches in sluicing constructions, where his account is particularly fruitful.

Compared to (Kobele, 2009), our account bears more similarity to the theory of gapping in terms of dependency structures as presented in (Osborne, 2008). This follows from the fact that TAG-derivation trees and dependency structures share crucial commonalities, even though complementation in some cases (e.g. with control verbs) receives an inverted dominance relation. Hence, the empirical predictions for gapping should overlap for the most part, if not completely. Crucial differences, however, can be found in the technical specification: while Osborne remains vague about the syntactic nature of a "predicate chain", which constitutes a gap, and refers to its semantic contribution instead, we propose an intrinsically syntactic delimitation of gaps based on A-subtrees. Osborne's proposal, furthermore, does not account for the variability of gaps within control chains. This is maybe

---

funny". (c.f. (Sag, 1976, p.198)),(Osborne, 2008, (5))

due to the fact that Osborne aims at rephrasing major constituency in terms of dependency, and control chains are considered not to involve major constituents. Finally, our account includes an explication of the antecedent-ellipsis relation in terms of a homomorphism on derivation trees, which Osborne's proposal lacks completely.

The problems of our account concerning the role of adverbs reflect the ambivalence of adjunction with respect to complementation and modification. This work would, thus, benefit from a convergence with dependency representations in this regard.

7   Implementation Issues

As we have seen when formulating the external condition, de-anchoring is licensed only if we can find a homomorphic antecedent node in the derivation tree of the first conjunct. This could be exploited for parsing. The idea is to allow some kind of *multiple use under de-anchoring* for selected elementary trees. Whenever a de-anchored tree is used during parsing, we check the internal and external conditions for de-anchoring on the part of the derivation tree that is already available.

8   Conclusion

This paper has provided an account of gapping in English within LTAG. We have exploited the fact that LTAG provides an extended domain of locality and, besides the derived trees, generates also derivation trees that abstract away from details of the constituency structure and that are close to dependency trees. We claim that LTAG derivation trees are an appropriate structure for restricting the availability of gapping constructions.

In our approach, gapping is achieved via an operation of de-anchoring that deletes lexical anchors from elementary trees. Inspired by recent research on gapping and relations to the derivation structure in the context of minimalist grammar, we have formulated a list of licensing conditions on the derivation tree that allow for de-anchoring within gapping constructions. Even though there are cases that remain problematic, our approach covers a large part of the gapping phenomena discussed in the literature.

References

Olga Babko-Malaya. 2006. Semantic interpretation of unrealized syntactic material in LTAG. In *Proceedings of the Eighth International Workshop on Tree Adjoining Grammar and Related Formalisms*, pages 91–96, Sydney, Australia, July. Association for Computational Linguistics.

Wynn Chao. 1987. *On ellipsis*. Ph.D. thesis, University of Massachusetts, Amherst, Massachusetts.

Jorge Hankamer. 1973. Unacceptable ambiguity. *Linguistic Inquiry*, 4(1):17–68.

Katharina Hartmann. 2000. *Right Node Raising and Gapping*. John Benjamins, Amsterdam.

Ray S. Jackendoff. 1971. Gapping and related rules. *Linguistic Inquiry*, 2(1):21–35.

Kyle Johnson. 2004. In search of the English middle field. Unpublished manuscript. University of Massachusetts at Amherst.

Gregory M. Kobele. 2009. Syntactic identity in survive-minimalism. Ellipsis and the derivational identity hypothesis. In *Towards a Derivational Syntax: Survive-Minimalism*. John Benjamins.

Jason Merchant. 2001. *The Syntax of Silence*. Oxford Univ. Press.

Anna H. Neijt. 1979. *Gapping: A Contribution to Sentence Grammar*. Ph.D. thesis, Utrecht University.

Thomas Osborne. 2008. Major constituents and two dependency grammar constraints on sharing in coordination. *Linguistics*, 46:1109–1165.

John Robert Ross. 1970. Gapping and the order of constituents. In Manfred Bierwisch and Karl Erich Heidolph, editors, *Progress in Linguistics*, pages 249–259. Mouton, The Hague.

Ivan A. Sag. 1976. *Deletion and logical form*. Ph.D. thesis, MIT.

Anoop Sarkar and Aravind Joshi. 1997. Handling coordination in a tree adjoining grammar. Longer version of paper in Proceedings of COLING 1996. Draft of August 19, 1997.

Yves Schabes and Stuart M. Shieber. 1994. An Alternative Conception of Tree-Adjoining Derivation. *Computational Linguistics*, 20(1):91–124, March.

Djamé Seddah. 2008. The use of MCTAG to process elliptic coordination. In *Proceedings of The Ninth International Workshop on Tree Adjoining Grammars and Related Formalisms (TAG+9)*.

XTAG Research Group. 2001. A Lexicalized Tree Adjoining Grammar for English. Technical report, Institute for Research in Cognitive Science, University of Pennsylvania, Philadelphia, PA.

Control Verbs, Argument Cluster Coordination and MCTAG

Djamé Seddah
Alpage & Univ. Paris-Sorbonne
Paris, France
djame.seddah@paris-sorbonne.fr

Benoit Sagot
Alpage, Inria
Paris, France
benoit.sagot@inria.fr

Laurence Danlos
Alpage & Univ. Paris 7
Paris, France
laurence.danlos@linguist.jussieu.fr

Abstract

In this paper[1] we present an extension of MC-TAGs with Local Shared Derivation (Seddah, 2008) which can handle non local elliptic co-ordinations. Based on a model for control verbs that makes use of so-called *ghost trees*, we show how this extension leads to an analysis of argument cluster coordinations that provides an adequate derivation graph. This is made possible by an original interpretation of the MCTAG derivation tree mixing the views of Kallmeyer (2005) and Weir (1988).

1 Introduction

Elliptic coordinate structures are a challenge for most constituent-based syntactic theories. To model such complex phenomena, many works have argued in favor of factorized syntactic structures (Maxwell and Manning, 1996), while others have argued for distributive structures that include a certain amount of non-lexically realized elements (Beavers and Sag, 2004). Of course, the boundary between those two approaches is not sharp since one can decide to first build a factorized syntactic analysis and then construct a more distributive structure (*e.g.,* logical or functional).

So far, the Combinatorial Categorial Grammar (CCG) framework (Steedman, 2001) is considered as one of the most elegant theories in accounting for coordination. Indeed, the CCG syntactic layer, which is closely tied to an syntax-semantic interface handled in a lexicalized way, permits the coordination of nonstandard constituents that cause a non-trivial challenge for other frameworks. On the other hand, some phenomena such as coordination of un-like categories are still a challenge for theories based on strict atomic category coordination.

In the broader context of ellipsis resolution, Dalrymple et al. (1991) propose to consider elided elements as free logical variables resolved using Higher Order Unification as the solving operation. Inspired by this approach and assuming that non-constituent coordination can be analyzed with ellipsis (Beavers and Sag, 2004),[2] we consider elliptic coordination as involving parallel structures where all non lexically realized syntactic elements must be represented in a derivation structure. This path was also followed by Seddah (2008) who proposed to use the ability of Multi Component TAGs (MCTAGs) (Weir, 1988) to model such a parallelism by including conjunct trees in a same tree set. This simple proposal allows for a straightforward analysis of gapping constructions. The coverage of this account is then extended by introducing links called *local shared derivations* which, by allowing derivations to be shared across trees of a same set, permit to handle various elliptic coordinate structures in an efficient way. This work showed that, assuming the use of regular operators to handle n-ary coordinations, a broad range of coordinate structures could be processed using a Tree-Local MCTAG-based formalism named Tree Local MCTAG with Local Shared Derivations. Nevertheless, being tied to the domain of locality of a tree set, the very nature of this mechanism forbids the sharing of derivations between different tree sets, thus preventing it from analyzing non-local elliptic coordinations.

In this paper, we introduce an extension of this model that can handle non-local elliptic coordination — close to unbounded ellipsis (Milward, 1994) —, which can be found in structures involving

---

[1]The first and second authors gratefully acknowledge the support of the ANR SEQUOIA (ANR-08-EMER-013). We thank Pierre Boullier, Éric de La Clergerie, Timm Lichte, Grzegorz Chrupala and our anonymous reviewers for their comments. All remaining errors would be ours.

---

[2]See (Abeillé, 2006; Mouret, 2006) for discussions about this assumption.

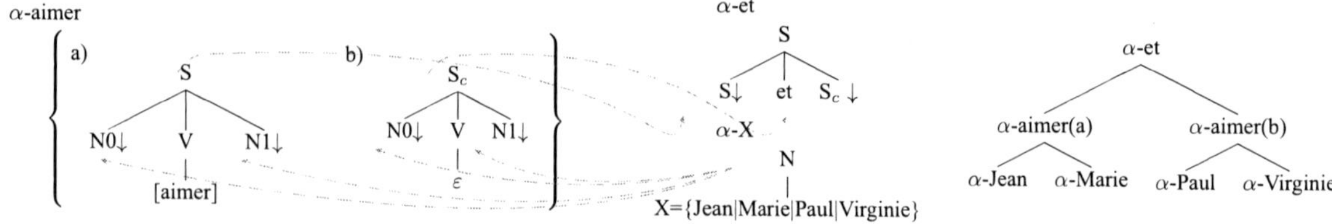

Figure 1: Sketch of an analysis for "Jean aime Marie et Paul Virignie"
The root label of α-aimer(b) is subscripted in order to avoid overgeneration cases such as *"Paul ε Virginia and John loves$_i$ Mary".
The same procedure is applied for the remaining analysis although the marks are not displayed.

control verbs and elliptic coordinations.
We also show how our model can cope with argument cluster coordination and why an interpretation of the derivation tree mixing David Weir's (1988) original view of MCTAG derivation tree, where each MC set is interpreted as a unique node, and the one introduced by Laura Kallmeyer (2005), where the derivations are the ones from the underlying TAG grammar, is required to yield a derivation tree as close as possible to a proper predicate-argument structure.

2 Standard elliptic coordinate structures

An MCTAG account of many coordinate structures involving ellipsis has been proposed by Seddah (2008). The core idea is to use the extended MC-TAG's domain of locality to enforce a somewhat strict parallelism between coordinate structures.

For example, gapping, as in (1) can be modeled, without any specific operation, by including in a same MC-Set two trees that are identical except for one thing: one is fully lexicalized whereas the other one is anchored by an empty element.

(1) Jean aime$_i$ Marie et Paul ε_i Virginie
    John loves$_i$ Mary and Paul ε_i Virginia

Calling this second lexically unrealized tree a *ghost tree*, the missing anchor can be retrieved simply because the tree it anchors is in the same MC-Set as its *ghost tree*. In other words, the label of the MC-Set includes the anchor of its fully lexicalized tree. The application of this model to (1) is shown in Figure 1.
Note that this account only requires the expressivity of Tree-Local MCTAGs and that unlike other approaches for gapping in the LTAG framework

(Sarkar and Joshi, 1996; Seddah and Sagot, 2006; Lichte and Kallmeyer, 2010), this proposal for gapping does not require any special device or modification of the formalism itself.

In order to model derivations that involve the elision of one syntactic verbal argument as in right node raising cases (RNR) or right subject elision coordinations, the formalism is extended with oriented links, called *local shared derivation (local SD)*, between mandatory derivation site nodes: whenever a derivation is not realized on a given node and assuming that a local SD has been defined between this node and one possible antecedent, a derivation between those nodes is inserted in the derivation structure.[3]
Furthermore, if the constraint of having identical tree schema in a tree set (one being fully lexicalized and the other anchored by an empty element) is relaxed, one gets the possibility to give more flexibility to the structure parallelism enforced by this model of gapping. This is what is needed to handle coordination of unlike categories and zeugma constructions (Seddah, 2008).
In the same spirit, by viewing the anchoring process as a regular derivation[4], and hence allowing local SDs to occur on anchoring derivations as well, one can get a very flexible model allowing for trees, sharing the same tree schema but with different anchors, to be coordinated. Thus, RNRs are simply analyzed in this framework by having two identical tree schema anchored by two different verbs and with one local shared derivation occurring from the $N1$ node of the right conjunct tree to the $N1$ of its

---

[3]Note that a real derivation always has precedence over a local shared one.

[4]Represented, for simplicity, as a special case of substitution labeled $V_{anchor} \downarrow$ in the relevant figure.

left counterpart. Such an analysis of RNR for (2) is shown on Figure 2.

(2) Jean fabrique ε_i et Marie vend [des crêpes]$_i$
    John makes ε_i and Mary sells pancakes$_i$

3 MCTAG with Local Shared Derivations

Following Kallmeyer (2005), we define an MCTAG as a tuple $G_{MCTAG} = \langle I, A, N, T, S \rangle$, where I (resp. A) is the set of initial (resp. auxiliary) trees, N (resp. T) the set of nonterminal (resp. terminal) labels and S the set of elementary MC-Sets. A *MC-TAG with Local Shared Derivations (MCTAG-LSD)* G whose underlying MCTAG is G_{MCTAG} is defined as $G = \langle I, A, N, T, S, L \rangle$, where L is the set of oriented links between two leaf nodes of two trees in a same MC-Set in S.

MCTAG-LSD derivations extend derivations of the underlying MCTAG by allowing for *local shared derivations*, that we shall now define.

Let $\Gamma = \{\gamma_0, \ldots, \gamma_n\}$ be an MC-Set in S. Let L_Γ be the set of (oriented) links in Γ, i.e. pairs of the form $\langle N_L, N_R \rangle$ where N_L and N_R are nodes in two different trees in Γ. Let us suppose that:

- a tree γ' is substituted on a node N_L in a tree γ_i

- there exists a node N_R in another tree $\gamma_j \in \Gamma$ such that $\langle N_L, N_R \rangle$ is in L_Γ

Then, a local shared derivation can be created as follows:

- a substitution link between γ' and γ_j is added in the derivation structure; thus, γ' has at least two ancestors (γ_i and γ_j) in the derivation structure, which becomes a DAG instead of a tree;

- an initial tree anchored by an empty element is substituted on the node N_R.[5]

Note that this also applies for mandatory adjunctions, besides substitutions.

Any MCTAG derivation is a valid MCTAG-LSD derivation. However, local shared derivations allow for performing additional derivation operations.

Therefore, the language generated by G strictly contains the language generated by G_{MCTAG}. However, these additional derivations can be simulated in a pure MCTAG fashion, as follows. For a given MCTAG-LSD MC-Set that contains a unique local shared derivation link, we can generate two MCTAG MC-Sets, one that would enforce the substitution by lexicalized trees at both ends of the link, and one that would enforce the substitution of a lexicalized tree at the starting node of the link and the substitution of a *ghost tree* at the other end of the link. This mechanism can be generalized to MC-Sets with more than one local shared derivation. This sketeches the proof that the set of languages generated by MCTAG-LSDs is the same as that generated by MCTAGs. Therefore, MCTAG-LSDs and MCTAGs have the same weak generative capacity. Moreover, these considerations still hold while restricting G_{MCTAG} to be TL-MCTAG. Therefore, TL-MCTAG-LSDs and TL-MCTAGs have the same weak generative power.

In order to cope with very large grammar size, the use of regular operators to factorize out TAG trees has been proposed by (Villemonte de La Clergerie, 2005), and has lead to a drastic reduction of the number of trees in the grammar. The resulting formalism is called *factorized TAGs* and was adapted by Seddah (2008) to the MCTAG-LSD framework in order to handle n-ary coordinations. The idea is to factorize MCTAG-LSD sets that have the same underlying MCTAG set (i.e. they are identical if links are ignored). Indeed, all such MC sets can be merged into one unique tree set associated with the union of all corresponding link sets. However, as with factorized TAGs, we need to add to the resulting tree set a list of constraints, R, on the construction of local shared derivations. The result is an extended formalism, called *factorized MCTAG-LSD*, which does not extend the expressive power of *MCTAG-LSD* but allows for more compact descriptions. Our resulting coordination scheme is shown on Figures 3 and Figure 4.

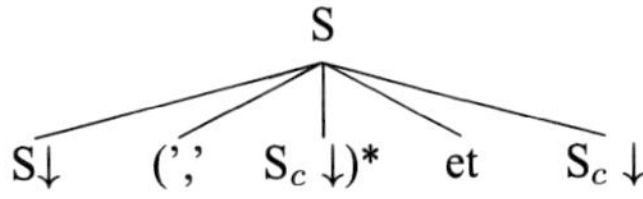

Figure 3: Factorized α-et with n conjuncts

---

[5] Another possibility would be to merge N_R with N_L, as for example in (Sarkar and Joshi, 1996). However, this leads to derived DAGs instead of trees.

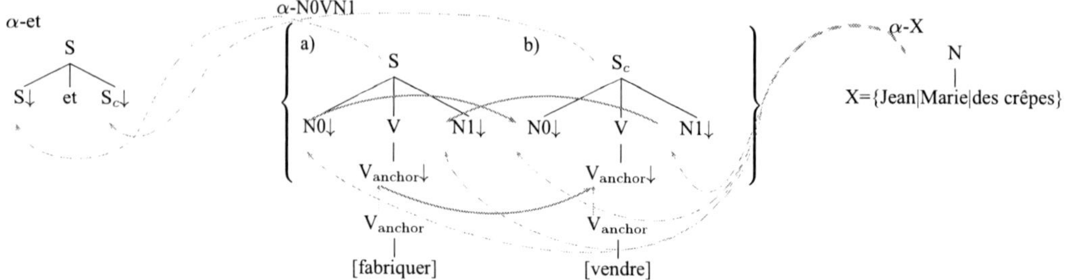

Figure 2: Sketch of a right node raising derivation for: *Jean vend ε_i et Marie fabrique [des crepes]$_i$* (*John makes ε_i and Mary sells pancakes$_i$*) (Seddah, 2008). *Note that the tree set $\alpha N0VN1$ includes all possible Local Shared Derivation links, even though only the link between the two N0 nodes is used here.*

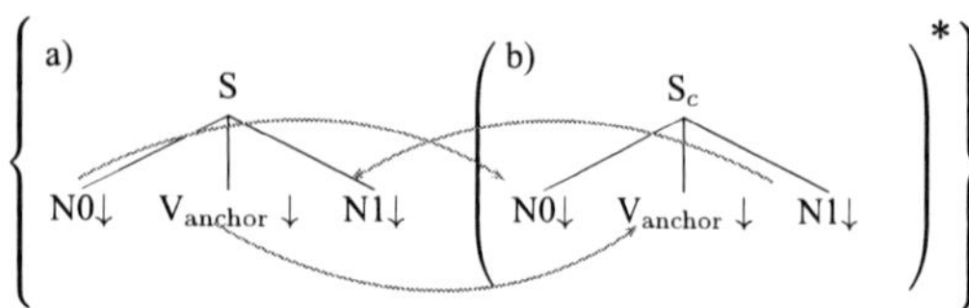

Figure 4: Factorized MC-Set with Local SDs. *Constraints are not displayed.*

4   The case for Unbounded Ellipsis

The problem with this model is its heavy dependence on the domain of locality of a tree set. In fact, if creating a link between two derivation site nodes inside the same tree set is straightforward, things become complicated if the derivations that must be shared involve two nodes from different tree sets. For example, in cases involving a control verb and right-subject ellipsis such as in (3), the subject is shared among the three verbs, although the control verb elementary tree (see Figure 6) cannot be in the same tree set as the others.[6]

(3) Jean$_i$ ronfle et ε_i espère ε_i dormir
   John$_i$ snores and ε_i hopes ε_i to sleep

4.1   Control Verb and MCTAG

Regarding the control verb phenomenon, an LTAG analysis was proposed by Seddah and Gaiffe (2005)[7] involving a complex parsing device, the so-called *argumental fusion*, and a lexicon based information structure, the *control canvas*, stating which argument is controlled by the verb (*e.g.* subject for *to*

hope and object for *to forbid*). The idea there was to view control verbs as capable of transferring their controlled argument to the trees in which they adjoin by the means of partial derivations, allowing for the creation of a *pseudo-derivation* between the argument of the control verb tree (i.e. Control Tree) and the embedded verb. This *pseudo-derivation* accounts for the fact that a syntactic argument of the embedded verb is not realized whereas its morphological features are actually transfered from the Control Tree substitution node through percolation of its feature structure,[8] thus making the underlying unrealized derivation explicit.[9] Figure 6 gives an overview of the process leading to a derivation graph.

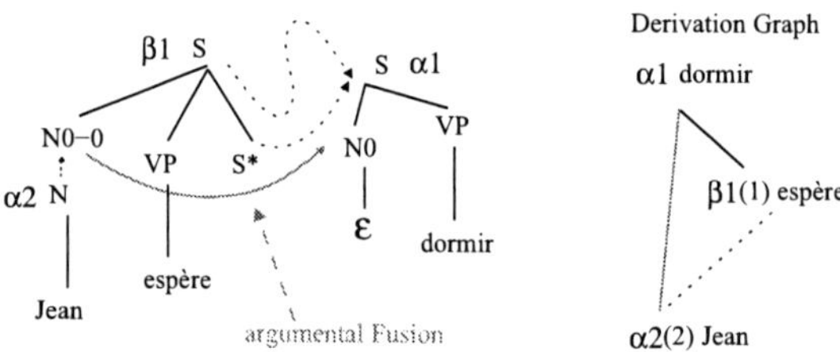

Figure 6: Overview of control verb analysis, (Seddah and Gaiffe, 2005)

This analysis can be rephrased in our framework by associating the control tree with a single node sharing a derivation with the node controlled by the verb, as illustrated in Figure 7.

---

[6]We assume a non-VP coordination analysis of (3).

[7]The *pure* LTAG analysis of French control verbs was initially proposed by Abeillé (1998).

[8]See this example of feature transfer in French:

Marie$_i$ espère ε_i être   belle.
Mary-FEM-SG$_i$ hopes ε_i to be   pretty-FEM-SG.

[9]This mismatch between the derivations underlying a derived structure and the *real* derivation structure is also noted by Kallmeyer (2002) for quantifier and verb interrelations.

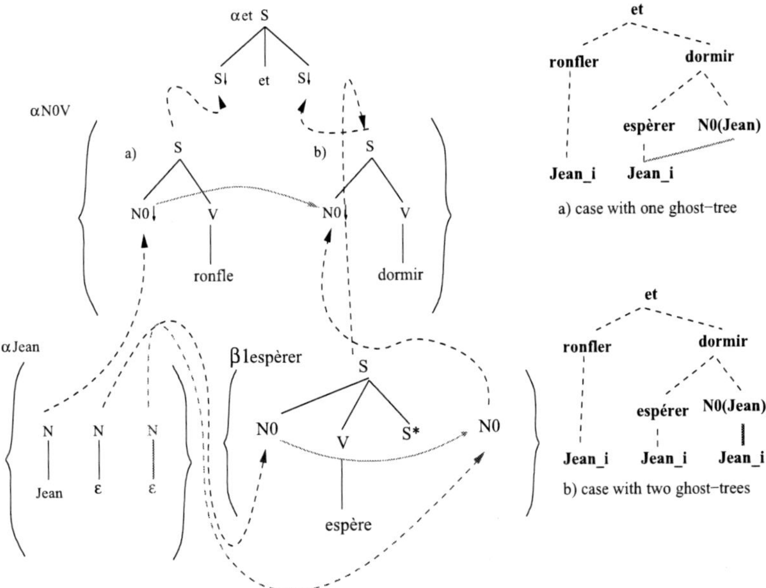

Figure 5: MCTAG-LSD derivation for *"Jean ronfle et espère dormir"* (*John snores and hopes to sleep*)
For the sake of legibility, anchoring derivations of verbal trees are not displayed in this figure.

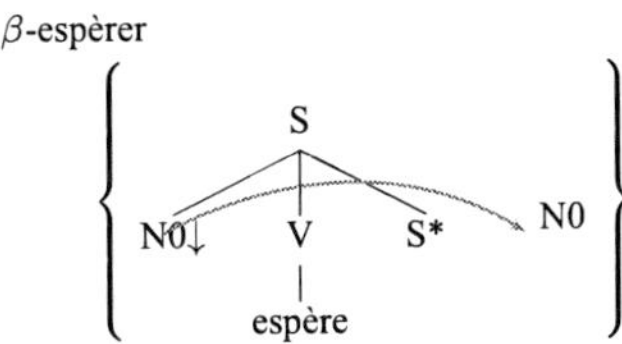

Figure 7: MC-Set for control verb *espérer* (*to hope*) and derivation tree for 3.

Note that similarly to the initial LTAG implementation discussed above, where the *argumental fusion* could only occur on the node of a tree where the control tree was to adjoin, it is necessary to restrict the substitution of the control verb MC set's *single* node in the same way. In other words, to avoid overgeneration, in the case of chain of controls (e.g., *John hopes to forbid Mary to sleep*), the derivations of a control verb MC set's trees must be tree local.[10]

4.2 Control Verb and Coordination

Until now, we have assumed that only initial trees anchored by verbs could be described in an MC-Set together with their *ghost trees*. Therefore, there is no way to create derivation links between different MC-Sets for providing an elegant analysis of (3) while re-

maining in TL-MCTAG-LSD. Nevertheless, nothing prevents us from allowing nominal trees to be characterized in the same way. This allows a (lexically) anchored tree to substitute into a tree of a given MC-Set while one of its *ghost trees* substitutes into another tree from a different tree set. Thus, it becomes possible to substitute a tree anchored by *Jean* into the tree anchored by *dormir*, while its unrealized counterpart will substitute into the argument node of the control verb, therefore allowing the derivation tree displayed in Figure 5a. As one tree is derived into one MC-Set and its *ghost tree* into another, this analysis falls beyond TL-MCTAG, and benefits from the larger expressivity of NL-MCTAGs.

It shall be noted that having an unrestricted potential number of unrealized *ghost trees* inside a nominal MC-Set means that a substitution of such a *ghost tree* can occur in lieu of a shared derivation, thus allowing coindexations of derivation nodes instead of sharing (cf. Figure 5b).

This potential source of ambiguity could be circumvented by stating precedence rules between shared derivations and *ghost* derivations (i.e. derivation of *ghost trees*). Nevertheless, such an ambiguity is precisely what is needed to provide an analysis of argument cluster coordination in our framework, as we shall now demonstrate.

---

[10]Thanks to Timm Lichte for bringing this case to our attention.

5 Argument cluster coordination

Assuming an ellipsis analysis for argument cluster coordination (ACC; (Beavers and Sag, 2004)), sentences such as (4) can be simply analyzed as a case of gapping plus a right subject elision in our framework. This requires an MC-Set α-donner which includes a tree anchored by *donner/give* and its *ghost tree*, as depicted in Figure 8.

(4) Jean_i donne_j une fleur à Marie et ε_i ε_j une bague à Paul
John gives Mary a flower and Paul, a ring

However, let us assume an analysis involving a right subject elision and a gapping of the main verb. Then, using the extension of our framework that we defined for handling unbounded ellipsis (section 4), the subject of ε_j can be obtained in two different ways: (i) via a local shared derivation as sketched in the previous sections (no *ghost tree* is needed in the MC-Set α-Jean, which contains one unique tree); or (ii) as a *ghost tree* that belongs to the MC-Set α-Jean.

Note that if we follow Weir's (1988) original definition of MCTAG derivation, both ways to obtain the subject lead to the same derivation structure. Our own model implies that derivation steps with LSD or involving *ghost trees* will lead to different structures. This comes from the fact that our model is based on Kallmeyer's per-tree interpretation of MC-TAG derivation.

More precisely, Weir's definition of MCTAG derivation always implies a sharing, whereas Kallmeyer's own definition leads to two different, possibly co-indexed, nodes. These two possible interpretations of derivation can handle the difference between (i) an elided anchor that refers to the same individual or event as the anchor of the lexicalized tree in the same MC-Set (as *Jean* in (4)) and (ii) an elided anchor that refers to another (co-indexed) instance of the same class of individuals, or events, (as *fleur/flower* in (5)).

(5)
Jean_i donne_j une fleur_k bleue à Marie et
John_i gives_j a blue flower_k to Mary and
ε_i ε_j une ε_k rouge à Paul
ε_i ε_j a red (one)_k to Paul

Therefore, what we need is a mechanism that can determine whether a given MC-Set denotes a unique event or individual, the latter corresponding to the sharing case or a list of events or individuals that are instances of the same class of events or individuals. Such a mechanism requires more than just syntactic information, typically it needs to rely on an adequate type system.

Let us consider again example (5). Whatever the interpretation of the derivation operations, the derivation runs as follows. Nominal MC-sets α-fleur and α-Jean include *ghost trees*, whereas the auxiliary trees β-bleu and β-rouge have no *ghost trees*.[11] The auxiliary tree in β-bleu adjoins to the non-ghost tree in α-fleur while the one in β-rouge adjoins to the *ghost tree* in α-fleur. The determiners are treated in the same way. Next, the tree based on the non-ghost tree in α-fleur substitutes in the non-ghost tree in α-donner, whereas the other tree substitutes in the ghost tree in α-donner.[12] The gapping and right subject elision are then handled as in Section 2.

Now, let us suppose that we associate the MC-Set α-Jean with a type $<e>$ and the MC-Set α-fleur with type $<e,t>$. Let us postulate that we use Kallmeyer's per-tree interpretation for MC-Sets with type $<e,t>$ and Weir's interpretation for MC-Sets with type $<e>$, the resulting derivation structure would be exactly the expected predicate-argument structure as shown in Figure 9b and will only require the expressive power of Set Local MC-TAGs.

To show how such a structure could be generated, we assumed a rather naive syntax-semantics interface where all elements of a nominal MC-set have the same scope, regardless of their semantic types. That is, as pointed out by an anonymous reviewer, if an NP is right-node-raised, or undergoes a right-subject elision,[13] we can have an NP with type $<e,t>$ that leads to a wide scope reading which would imply a single node in the derivation tree. In fact, should we want to distinguish between narrow

---

[11] Allowing unlimited adjunction of *ghost* auxiliary trees would lead to many spurious ambiguities, whereas having modal verbs or adverbs together with their *ghost trees* in a MC set would certainly be a step toward an elegant treatment of elided modifiers.

[12] To avoid spurious ambiguities when *ghost trees* are substituted, Local Shared Derivations could be used to check that the right *ghost tree* has been derived wrt to its antecedent.

[13] e.g., *[Someone from NY]$_i$ seems to have won the cup and ε_i is likely to win the lottery.*

α-donner

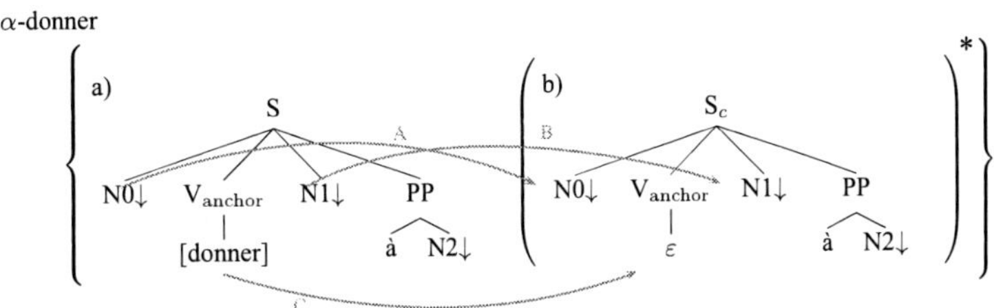

Figure 8: MC-Set α-donner *(Constraints on links are defined as follows: $\{(A, \{B|C\})\}$)*

and wide scope readings, we would need a richer model that could infer scope information from all trees of a MC-set. It would be very interesting to see how a model *à la* Kallmeyer and Joshi (2003) could be integrated in our framework. In fact, the idea of adding another type of node carrying scope information through the derivation structure seems natural considering the nature of our proposal.

6 Discussion

If syntactic and semantic structures were tied by a strict isomorphism, the TAG derivation tree, with its strict encoding of subcategorized arguments, could have been considered as a proper predicate-argument structure. Unfortunately, due to a lack of expressive power, most of the complicated cases of mismatch between syntax and semantics cannot be formalized without breaking the elegance of TAGs' main property, namely that dealing with elementary trees means dealing with partial dependency structures. Over the last fifteen years, solving this problem has mobilized many teams, and, as noted by (Nesson and Shieber, 2006), led to the emergence of two schools. One focusing on giving more expressive power to the formalism in order to ease either a tight integration between the logical and the syntactic layers (Kallmeyer and Joshi, 1999; Gardent and Kallmeyer, 2003) or a capacity to handle, for instance, free word order languages (Lichte, 2007). The other school focuses either on keeping the syntactic TAG backbone as pure as possible, by designing a new derivation operation to handle coordination (Sarkar and Joshi, 1996) or on carefully designing a syntax-semantic interface built upon TAG derivations (Shieber and Schabes, 1990; Shieber and Nesson, 2007). Our proposal stands in between as we acknowledge that pure TAGs are not powerful

enough to carry on simple analysis of complex phenomena while bringing the derivation tree closer to a predicate-argument structure. Recent proposals in the synchronous TAG framework share the same concern. In fact, Shieber and Nesson (2007) use Vector MCTAG (Rambow, 1994), for its ability to underspecify dominance relations and provide the synchronized logical layer with a derivation structure suitable for the analysis of control verbs. However, as we have shown, our solution for control requires a generalization of the mechanism designed for handling elliptic coordination that needs the expressive power of Non Local MCTAGs and tight integration of our proposal with a syntax-semantic interface. This raises two open questions: What generative power do we really need to build appropriate derivation structures? More importantly, where do we want syntax to stop?

7 Conclusion

We have shown how to extend an MCTAG account of coordination with a simple mechanism added on top of its extended domain of locality and which enables the handling of more complex constructions involving control verbs and elliptic coordinations. We have also shown how argument cluster coordinations could be treated in our framework without any special treatment besides the inclusion of a small type inference system if one wants to provide a proper dependency structure. Our work also shows that our treatment of such coordinate constructions needs the expressive power of Non Local MCTAGs to cope with unbounded ellipsis and Set Local MC-TAGs for ACC.

References

Anne Abeillé. 1998. Verbes "à monté" et auxiliaires dans

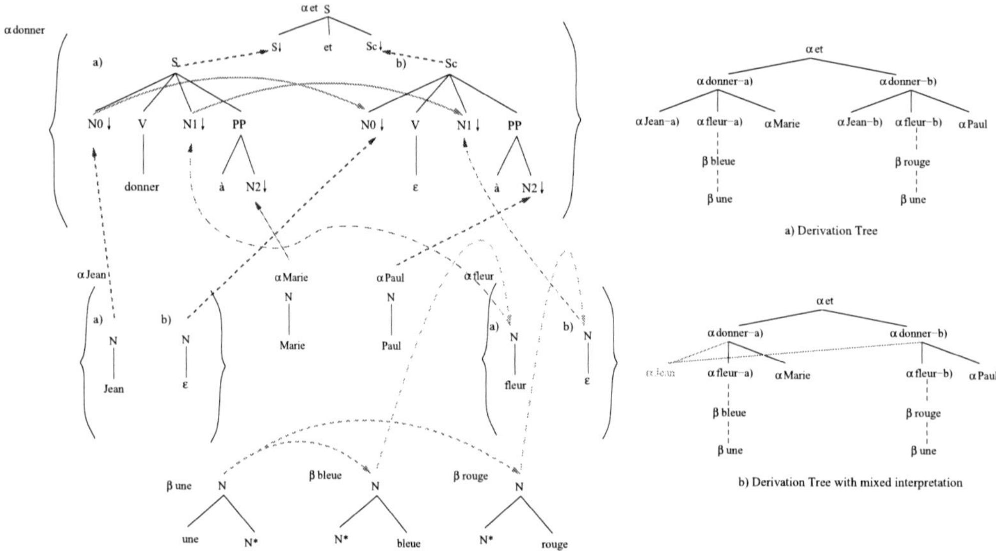

Figure 9: Sketch of derivations for Argument Cluster Coordination of sentence 5 (John$_i$ gives$_j$ a blue flower$_k$ to Mary and $\varepsilon_i\ \varepsilon_j$ a red (one)$_k$ to Paul)

For the sake of readability, local shared derivations (from (a)N0 to (b)N0 and (b)N1 to (a)N1) are not displayed in this figure.

une grammaire d'arbres adjoints. *LINX*, (39):119–158.

Anne Abeillé. 2006. In defense of lexical coordination. In P.Cabredo O.Bonami, editor, *Empirical Issues in Formal Syntax and Semantics 6*. CSSP online Proceedings.

John Beavers and Ivan A. Sag. 2004. Coordinate ellipsis and apparent non-constituent coordination. In *Proceedings of the HPSG04 Conference*, pages 48–69.

Mary Dalrymple, Stuart M. Shieber, and Fernando C. N. Pereira. 1991. Ellipsis and higher-order unification. *Linguistics and Philosophy*, 14(4):399–452.

Claire Gardent and Laura Kallmeyer. 2003. Semantic construction in feature-based tag. In *EACL '03: Proceedings of the tenth conference on European chapter of the Association for Computational Linguistics*, pages 123–130, Budapest, Hungary. Association for Computational Linguistics.

Laura Kallmeyer and Aravind Joshi. 1999. Factoring predicate argument and scope semantics: Underspecified semantics with LTAG. In *Proceedings of the 12th Amsterdam Colloquium, December*.

L. Kallmeyer and A. Joshi. 2003. Factoring Predicate Argument and Scope Semantics: Underspecified Semantics with LTAG. *Research on Language & Computation*, 1(1):3–58.

Laura Kallmeyer. 2002. Enriching the tag derivation tree for semantics. *Proceedings of KONVENS 2002*, pages 67–74.

Laura Kallmeyer. 2005. A declarative characterization of a declarative characterization of multicomponent tree adjoining grammars. In *Proceedings of Traitement automatique des langues Naturelles - TALN'05*, Dourdan, France.

Timm Lichte and Laura Kallmeyer. 2010. Gapping through TAG derivation trees. In *Proceedings of The 10th International Conference on Tree Adjoining Grammars and Related Formalisms (TAG+10)*, Yale, USA, June.

Timm Lichte. 2007. An MCTAG with Tuples for Coherent Constructions in German. In *Proceedings of the 12th Conference on Formal Grammar 2007.*, Dublin, Ireland.

John T. Maxwell, III and Christopher D. Manning. 1996. A theory of non-constituent coordination based on finite-state rules. In Miriam Butt and Tracy Holloway King, editors, *On-line Proceedings of the LFG96 Conference*.

David Milward. 1994. Non-constituent coordination: Theory and practice. In *Proceedings of the 15th international conference on Computational linguistics (COLING94)*, volume 2, pages 935–941.

François Mouret. 2006. A phrase structure approach to argument cluster coordination. In Stefan Müller, editor, *Proceedings of the 13th International Conference on Head-Driven Phrase Structure Grammar*, pages 247–267, Stanford. CSLI Publications.

Rebecca Nesson and Stuart M. Shieber. 2006. Simpler tag semantics through synchronization. In *Proceedings of the 11th Conference on Formal Grammar, Malaga, Spain*, pages 29–30.

Owen Rambow. 1994. *Formal and Computational Aspects of Natural Language Syntax*. Ph.D. thesis, University of Pennsylvania.

Anook Sarkar and Aravind K. Joshi. 1996. Handling coordination in a tree adjoining grammar. Technical report, Dept. of Computer and Info. Sc., Univ. of Pennsylvania, Philadelphia, PA.

Djamé Seddah and Bertrand Gaiffe. 2005. How to build argumental graphs using TAG shared forest: a view from control verbs problematic. In *Proceedings of the 5th International Conference on the Logical Aspect of Computional Linguistic - LACL'05, Bordeaux, France*, Apr.

Djamé Seddah and Benoît Sagot. 2006. Modeling and analysis of elliptic coordination by dynamic exploitation of derivation forests in LTAG parsing. In *Proceedings of TAG+8*, Sydney, Australia.

Djamé Seddah. 2008. The use of MCTAG to Process Elliptic Coordination. In *Proceeding of the Ninth International Workshop on Tree Adjoining Grammars and Related Formalisms (TAG+9)*, Tuebingen, Germany, June.

Stuart M. Shieber and Rebecca Nesson. 2007. Extraction phenomena in synchronous tag syntax and semantics. In *Proceedings of the Workshop on Syntax and Structure in Statistical Translation, Rochester, New York*, volume 26.

Stuart Shieber and Yves Schabes. 1990. Synchronous Tree Adjoining Grammars. In *COLING*, volume 3, pages 253–260, Helsinki.

Mark J. Steedman. 2001. *The Syntactic Process*. The MIT Press, Cambridge, MA.

Éric Villemonte de La Clergerie. 2005. From meta-grammars to factorized TAG/TIG parsers. In *Proceedings of the Fifth International Workshop on Parsing Technology (IWPT'05)*, pages 190–191, Vancouver, Canada, October.

David J. Weir. 1988. *Characterizing mildly context-sensitive grammar formalisms*. Ph.D. thesis, Philadelphia, PA, USA. Supervisor-Aravind K. Joshi.

Building factorized TAGs with meta-grammars

Éric Villemonte de la Clergerie
INRIA - Rocquencourt - B.P. 105
78153 Le Chesnay Cedex, FRANCE
`Eric.De_La_Clergerie@inria.fr`

Abstract

Highly compacted TAGs may be built by allowing subtree factorization operators within the elementary trees. While hand-crafting such trees remains possible, a better option arises from a coupling with meta-grammar descriptions. The approach has been validated by the development of FRMG, a wide-coverage French TAG of only 207 trees.

1 Introduction

Tree Adjoining Grammars (TAG – (Joshi, 1987)), plus feature decorations, provide a powerful and elegant formalism to capture many syntactic phenomena, due to the adjoining mechanism, tree lexicalization, and extended domain of locality of trees. However, it is well-known that the two last properties easily lead to a combinatorial explosion in term of trees, with large coverage grammars of several thousand trees (or even more) (Crabbé, 2005; Abeillé, 2002). This explosion induces problems of development and maintenance of the grammars, but also of efficiency during parsing. Several approaches have been proposed to remedy to the situation, either on the maintenance side or on the efficiency side. On the maintenance side, besides the notion of families present in the XTAG architecture (Doran et al., 1994), one may cite the use of metarules (Prolo, 2002) to derive trees from the "canonical" versions, and meta-grammars (Candito, 1999; Duchier et al., 2004) where the grammars are derived from a constraint-based modular level of syntactic descriptions organized as an inheritance hierarchy of elementary classes. On the efficiency side, besides more or less clever lexicalization-based

filtering techniques (such as *suppertagging*), one may cite the factorization of common sub-trees using automata (Carroll et al., 1998) or the possibility to attach, modulo regular expressions, several possible tree traversals to a tree (Harbusch and Woch, 2004). However, no approach cover both side of the problem, namely maintenance and efficiency. In particular, finding common sub-trees in a large TAG (with decorated nodes) is a difficult task (from an algorithmic point of view) and attaching tree traversals requires some efforts from the grammar writer. We propose a more modular approach based on the use of local subtree factorization operators that be expressed locally and easily in the elementary classes of a metagrammar. The generation of complete minimal trees by a meta-grammar compiler combines all these local factorizations to produce highly factorized trees that couldn't easily have been written by hand. These ideas have been validated during the development of FRMG, a large coverage French meta-grammar producing only 207 trees.

Some background about Meta-Grammars is provided in Section 2. Tree factoring through MG descriptions is illustrated by a few syntactic phenomena in Section 3. In Section 4, we present FRMG. Because a grammar is only useful with a parser, Section 5 precises some aspects of this parser, focusing on those that ensure its efficiency. Finally, Section 6 presents some results.

2 Meta-Grammars

Meta-Grammars favor the modular development of grammars by grouping small sets of elementary constraints in *classes* related to micro syntactic phenomena. Elementary constraints include node equality (A=B), node dominance (immediate with A $>>$ B or not with A $>>$+ B) and node precedence (A $<$ B). Decoration constraints as feature structures may also be attached to nodes (node v: [person: 1|3, mood :~imperative|gerundive]) or to a whole class (desc :[extraction : —]), allowing, as values, constants, recursive feature structures, (possibly negated) finite set values, and variables. Path-based equations may also be used to unify decorations (node(Det). top.number = node(N).top.number or desc. diathesis = node(V).top. diathesis).

Classes are organized in a multiple inheritance hierarchy (using the $<:$ operator), allowing to progressively refine and enrich syntactic notions (for instance the notion of subject to get extracted subjects, impersonal subjects, French post-verbal subject, ...), a class inheriting its ancestors' constraints.

A crossing mechanism is used to combine the terminal classes (e.g. the classes with no children, wrt the inheritance hierarchy). The existing MG formalisms implement various flavors of crossing mechanisms, the general idea being to accumulate the constraints of the parent classes while checking that they remain satisfiable. Close from the original MGs (Candito, 1999) but constrained to be monotonic, we use a resource-based crossing mechanism: a class C^- may require some resource R (− subject) while another class C^+ may provide this resource R (+ subject). In that case, we try to combine C^- and C^+, neutralizing the resource R. The basic resource-based mechanism has been extended with the notion of namespace, allowing a class C^- to require the same resource R several times but in distinct namespaces N_i (for instance, requiring two instances of agreement constraints on distinct nodes with — det :: agr and —root :: agr). The constraints from the R-provider class C^+ are renamed with namespace N to avoid names clashes for nodes, variables, and resources, as shown by the following equation:

$$C^-[-N::R \cup \mathcal{K}^-] \oplus C^+[+R \cup \mathcal{K}^+] =$$
$$(C^- \oplus N::C^+)[=N::R \cup \mathcal{K}^- \cup N::\mathcal{K}^+]$$

The surviving neutral classes (i.e. those requiring or providing no resources) are used to generate a minimal set of minimal trees, given their constraints. Again, the notion of tree minimality depends on the

flavor of MGs and also on the target syntactic formalism (for instance MC-TAGs for (Kallmeyer et al., 2008)). In general, a minimal tree does not introduce nodes not mentioned in the constraints and replaces non immediate dominance constraints by parent relations. In our case, we also try also to preserve tree factoring as much as possible.

3 From MGs to factorized trees

Tree factoring relies on regexp-like operators working on nodes, or more precisely on the subtrees rooted by these nodes. The (informal) notation $T[(t_1 \mathrm{op}\ t_2)]$ denotes the application of the operator op on subtrees t_1 and t_2 in the context of tree T.

3.1 Disjunction

The first operator concerns disjunction over nodes, with $T[(t_1; t_2)]$ straightforwardly equivalent to the set of trees $T[t_1]$ and $T[t_2]$. At the level of MGs, disjunction is explicitly introduced with special nodes carrying the information type: alternative . The alternatives nodes are largely used, for instance to represent all possible realizations for a subject as sketched in the following class:[1]

```
class collect_real_subject {
  node SAlt: [type: alternative ];
  SAlt >> S_Cl;
  node S_Cl: [type: coanchor, cat: cl ];
  SAlt >> S_NP;
  node S_NP: [type: subst, cat: np ];
  SAlt >> S_Sent;
  node S_Sent: [type: subst, cat: S ]; ...}
```

3.2 Optionality and guards

From disjunction immediately derives the optionality operator with $T[t?] \equiv T[(\epsilon; t)]$. At MG level, a node may be marked as optional using the optional feature. Note that even a special alternative node may be made optional, for instance the previous SAlt node.

However, most of the times, a node is made optional with conditions: positive (resp. negative) guards[2] may be used to control the presence (resp. absence) of a node. A guard G is a Boolean disjunctive and conjunctive formula over path equa-

---

[1] The examples are simplified versions of classes in FRMG.

[2] The term *guard* comes from the Constraint Programming community.

tions. For instance, the presence of a subject may be (naively) controlled by the verb mood, with:

```
SAlt =>
    node(V).top.mood = ~imperative;
~ SAlt =>
    node(V).top.mood = imperative;
```

More formally, a guard G is equivalent to a finite set Σ_G of substitution, implying that $T[(G_+, t; G_-)]$ may be replaced by the finite set of trees $\{T[t]\sigma \| \sigma \in \Sigma_{G_+}\} \cup \{T[\epsilon]\sigma \| \sigma \in \Sigma_G\}$.

More than one guard may be progressively attached to a node while crossing classes. The positive guards from one part and the negative ones from the other part are separately combined using conjunction, which may finally lead to complex guards. However, for neutral classes, a set of rewriting rules is used to reduce the guards by removing the parts that are trivially true or false[3]. Obviously, if a guard is of the form $G = G_1 \wedge G_2$ and G_1 is shown to be trivially true (resp. false) then G may be reduced to G_2 (resp. to false).

Guards are heavily used in FRMG. Actually, positive guards are also used on non optional nodes to attach disjunctive constraints to a node, or constraints to a node under a disjunctive node, for instance to state that a sentential subject should be in subjunctive mood:

```
S_Sent +
    node(V).top.mood=value(~subjunctive)
```

3.3 Repetition

The Kleene star operator provides subtree repetition, with $T[t*] \equiv \{T[\epsilon], T[t], T[(t, t)], \ldots\}$. More formally, the Kleene operator may be removed by introducing an extra node category X_{t*} used as a substitution node in $T[X_{t*}]$, and two extra trees $X_{t*}(\epsilon)$ and $X_{t*}(t, X_{t*})$.[4]

At MG level, a (possibly special) node may be repeated using the `star` feature. Concretely, in FRMG, the Kleene star operator have only been used to represent repetition of coordinated components in coordination.

```
class coord {
```

```
node Seq: [type: sequence, star: *];
Seq < SeqLast;
Seq >> Punct_Comma;
Seq >> coord2
SeqLast >> coo;
SeqLast >> coord3;
coo < coord3; }
```

3.4 Shuffling

Less known but well motivated in (Nederhof et al., 2003) to handle free word ordering, the *shuffling* (or interleaving) of two sequences $(a_i)_{i=1\cdots n} \#\#(b_j)_{j=1\cdots m}$ returns all sequences containing all a_i and b_j in any order that preserves the original orderings (i.e. $a_i < a_{i+1}$ and $b_j < b_{j+1}$). For instance, the shuffling of a, b with c, d returns the sequences "a, b, c, d", "a, c, b, d", "a, c, d, b", "c, a, b, d", "c, a, d, b", and "c, d, a, b". In our case, the shuffle operator $\#\#$ is used on sequences of subtrees, with in particular $T[(t_1\#\#t_2)] \equiv \{T[(t_1, t_2)], T[(t_2, t_1)]\}$.

At MG level, shuffling naturally arises from underspecification of the ordering between sibling nodes. For instance, the constraints "N >> N_1, N>> N_2, N >> N_3, and N_1 < N_2" produce the (minimal) tree fragment $N((N_1, N_2)\#\#N_3)$, stating that N_3 may occur anywhere (before, between, after) relatively to the sequence N_1, N_2. In FRMG, free node ordering is, in particular, present between verb arguments, including inverted subject, such as in

le livre que donne (à Paul) (son ami   ...)
the book that gives (to Paul) (his friend ...)

To block free node ordering, one has to explicit the precedence constraints or use the special rank feature with the first or last values to force the position of a node wrt its siblings.[5] Finally, the shuffle operator is systematically expanded when covering a foot node, in order to ease the detection of TIG auxiliary trees (Section 5).

3.5 Some complements

The above-presented operators are first generic, being adaptable for many grammatical formalisms and not just for TAGs. Secondly, they do not change the expressive power of TAGs. As sketched, they may indeed be progressively removed to get a finite set of

---

[3]An equation is trivially true (resp. false) if true (resp. false) without further instantiation of the decorations.

[4]This scheme only applies if t does not cover a foot node, and therefore Kleene stars are not allowed over such subtrees.

[5]of course, it is an error to have several sibling nodes carrying the first (or the last) value.

standard TAG trees, possibly by adding some extra new non-terminals. However, the number of extra trees may be exponential in the number of operators in a tree. Concretely, these operators provide a way to factorize a large number of trees into a single tree. Such a compact tree S may be understood as representing a large set of potential traversals through the non-terminals occurring in S, similar in some aspects to (Harbusch and Woch, 2004).

Of course, it is important that these operators may be used at parsing time with none or low overhead (as shown in Section 6), in particular for the complex shuffle and Kleene star operators. In our case, very informally, the implementation of these two operators relies on the capacity to create and manage continuations. For the Kleene star operator, at some point one may choose between two continuations: *"exit the loop"* or *"reenter the loop"*. For the shuffle operators, at each step, one may choose between the continuations *"advance in sequence 1"* and *"advance in sequence 2"*.

4 A French Meta-Grammar

Based on the potentialities of the MG formalism and its coupling with factoring operators, FRMG was developed for French in 2004 and maintained since then. The generated grammar turned out to be a very compact grammar with only 207 trees (in May 2010), produced from 279 classes, 197 of them being terminal. This compactness does not hinder coverage or efficiency as we will see.

It may look surprising to get less trees than classes. There are two reasons for this situation, both of them resulting from the modularity of meta-grammars. First, the trees are generated from the terminal classes, some of these classes inheriting from many ancestor simple classes. Secondly, some trees result from the crossing of many terminal classes.

Actually, the compactness is even more severe than it looks with only 21 trees used to cover all verbal constructions with up to 3 arguments (including subjects), covering "canonical" constructions, passive ones, extraction ones (for relatives, interrogatives, clefted, topicalizations), impersonal ones, causative ones (partially), subject inversions, support verbs (such as *faire attention à / take care of*), ... Two extra trees are available for auxiliary verbs.

20 trees are anchored by adjectives, providing elementary subcategorization for sentential arguments (*il est évident qu'il doit partir – it is obvious that he should leave*) and 40 for adverbs, a rather non-homogeneous syntactic category (Table 1(a)). It is difficult to describe the coverage of the grammar. Let us say that besides the verbal constructions, the grammar partially covers most punctuations, coordinations, superlatives, comparatives, floating incises (adverbs, time modifiers, ...), ...

Table 1(a) shows that 65 trees are not anchored, which does not mean they have no lexical component. It rather reflects the idea that their underlying semantic is not related to a lexical form. For instance, we use a non-anchored tree roughly equivalent to $NP(*NP, S)$ to attach relative sentences on nouns, this tree being used both when the relative pronoun in S is an extracted argument or a modifier

Table 1(b) shows that compactness really arises from the factoring operators, and more specifically from guards. However, the use of these operators is not evenly distributed among all trees. Only a small set of complex trees (the verbal and adjectival ones) are concerned, as shown for tree #198 corresponding to the verbal canonical construction for most subcategorization frames. This tree results from the crossing of 36 terminal classes and is formed of 63 nodes, not including the special nodes listed in Table 1(b). It would be very difficult to craft and maintain this tree by hand. The Figure 1 shows a simplified representation of tree #198, not showing the content of the guards (for the nodes with a green background) and also not showing some nodes. The diamond-shaped nodes represent the alternative (|) and shuffle (##) nodes. In particular, we have a disjunction node (left side) over the possible realizations (nominative clitic, nominal group, sentences, prepositional group) for the subject in canonical position, and a shuffle operator (right side) over 2 possible arguments groups and a postverbal subject (which is also usable with a preposition for causative constructions).

Still, several questions arises in presence of such trees. The first one concerns the level of factorization squeezed in this tree. The unfolding of a previous version of the grammar (February 2007) produced almost 2 millions trees, 99.98% of them being generated by the verbal trees. The equivalent of

anchored	v	coo	adv	adj	csu	prep	aux	prop. n.	com. n.	det	pro	Not anchored
142	21	26	40	20	6	5	2	3	1	1	5	65

(a) Distribution by anchors

	Guards	Disjunctions	Interleaving	Kleene Stars
all trees	2609	152	22	27
tree #198	106	6	1	0

(b) Distribution by factorization operators

Table 1: Grammar anatomy

tree #198 was the most productive one with around 700000 unfolded trees.[6]

Given these figures, one may wonder about the potential overgenerativity of the grammar and its overhead at parsing time. Practically, overgeneration seems to be adequately controlled through the guards, with no obvious overhead. Another reason explaining this behaviour may come from the constraints provided by the forms of the input string. Indeed, tree #198 covers many subcategorization frames, much more than the number of frames usually attached to a given verb. The notion of family attached to a frame as defined in the XTAG model (Doran et al., 1994) is therefore no longer pertinent. Instead, we use a more flexible mechanism based on the notion of *hypertags* (Kinyon, 2000). A hypertag is a feature structure, issued from the class decorations, providing information on the linguistic phenomena covered by a tree or allowed by a word. The anchoring of a tree by a word is only possible if their hypertags do unify, as illustrated by Fig. 2. The verb "promettre/ `to promise`" may anchor tree #198, only selecting (after unification) the presence of an optional object (`arg1.kind`) and of an optional prepositional object (`arg2.kind`) introduced by "à/*to*" (`arg2.pcas`). The link between an hypertag $\mathcal{H}$ and the allowed syntactic constructions is done through the variables occurring in $\mathcal{H}$ and in the guards and node decorations. A partial anchoring is done at load time to select the potential trees, given the input sentence, and a full anchoring is then performed, on demand, during parsing. Anchoring through hypertags offers a powerful way to restrict the generative power of the factorized trees.

---

[6]It should be noted that while it is easy to naively unfold the operators, it is much more difficult and costly to get a minimal set of unfolded trees.

5 Building efficient parsers

The French TAG grammar is compiled offline into a chart parser, able to take profit of the factoring operators. Actually, several optimizations, developed for TAGs (and not related to MGs), are also applied to improve the efficiency of the parser.

The first optimisation is a static analysis of the grammar to identify the auxiliary trees that behave as left or right auxiliary trees as defined in Tree Insertion Grammars (TIG – (Schabes and Waters, 1995)), a variant of TAGs that may be parsed in cubic time rather than $O(n^6)$ for TAGs. Roughly speaking, TIG auxiliary trees adjoin material either on the left side or the right side of the adjoined node, which actually corresponds to the behavior of most auxiliary trees. TIG and TAG auxiliary trees may be used simultaneously leading to a hybrid TAG/TIG parser (Alonso and Díaz, 2003).

Another static analysis of the grammar is used to identify the node features that are left unmodified through adjoining, greatly reducing the amount of information to be stored in items, and potentially increasing computation sharing. A third static analysis is used to compute a left-corner relation to be used at parsing time.

When parsing starts, besides the non-lexicalized trees that are always loaded, the parser selects only the trees that may be anchored by a form of the input sentence, using the hypertag information of both forms and trees. Other lexical information are also used. During parsing, the parser uses a left-to-right top-down parsing strategy with bottom-up propagation of the node decorations. The left-corner relation controls the selection of syntactic categories and of trees at a given position in the input sentence.

Several experiments on test suites and corpora have shown the strong gains resulting from these op-

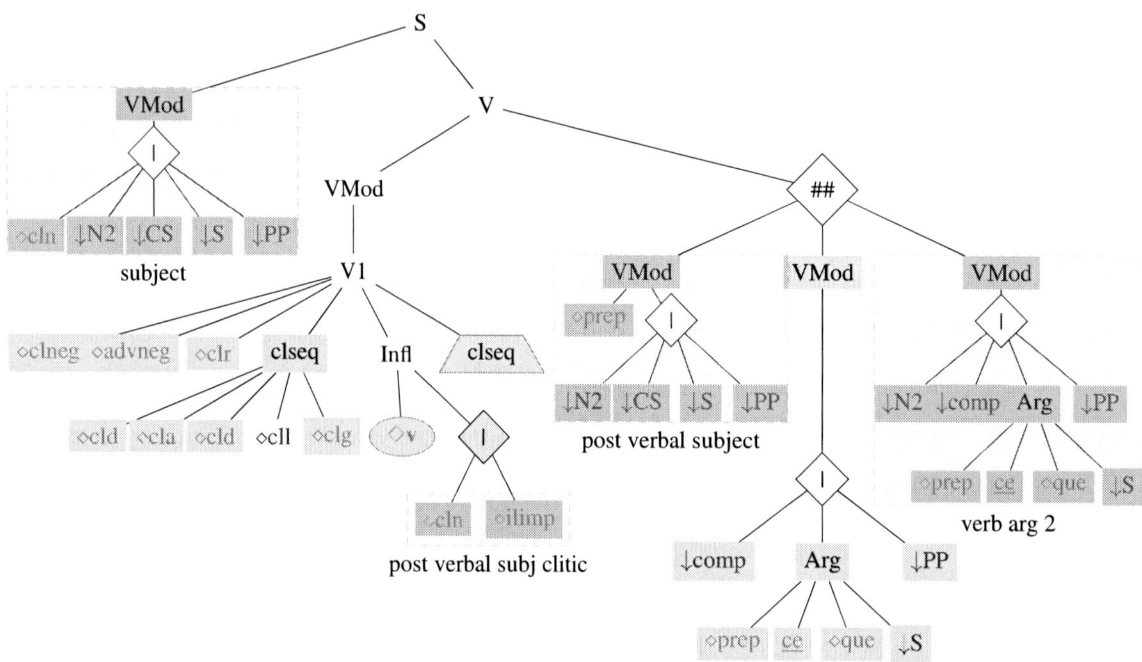

Figure 1: Tree #198 (simplified)

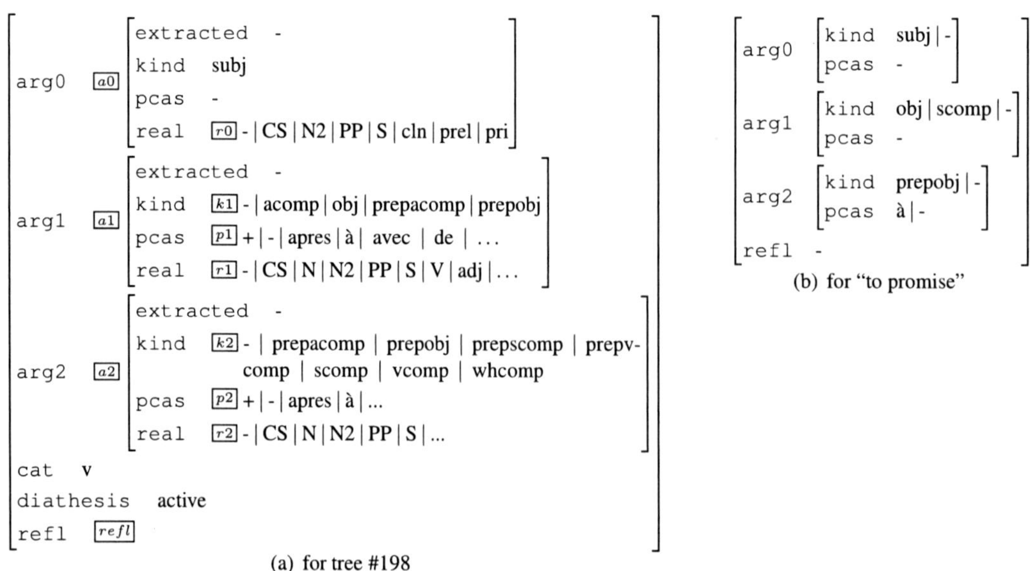

(a) for tree #198

(b) for "to promise"

Figure 2: Grammar and lexicon hypertags

timisations, in particular for the left-corner relation (Table 1(b)).

While it would possible to parse tagged sentences, the parser rather takes word lattices as input and returns the shared forest of all possible derivations. When no full parses are found, the parser switches to a robust mode used to return a set of partial parses trying to cover to input sentence in some best way. In post-parsing phases, the derivation forests may be converted to dependency shared forests, which may then be disambiguated.

6 Some results

Many efforts have been devoted to improve the meta-grammar and the parser, in terms of accuracy, coverage (in terms of full parses), efficiency and level of ambiguity.

Accuracy has been tested by participating to 3 parsing evaluation campaigns for French, in the context of the French actions EASy and Passage (Paroubek et al., 2008). Table 2 shows the F-measures for 6 kinds of chunks (such as GN, GV, PP, ...) and 14 kinds of dependencies (such as SUBJ-V, OBJ-V, CPL-V, ...) for the two first campaigns[7]. The evolution between the 2 campaigns is clear, with a 3rd position on relations in 2007. The corpus **EasyDev** of the first campaign (almost 4000 sentences) has been used to steadily improve the grammar (and the disambiguation process).

Campaign	f-measure Chunks	f-measure Relations
2004	69%	41%
2007	89%	63%

Table 2: Results for the French evaluation campaigns

The other parameters (coverage, efficiency and ambiguity) are controlled by regularly parsing several corpora, including the EASy development corpus, as shown in Table 3. The time figures should be taken with some caution, having been computed over various kinds of environments, including laptops, desktops and grid computers[8]. For instance,

---

[7]The results of the last campaign, run over a 100 million word corpus, are not yet available.

[8]including the Grid'5000 experimental testbed, being developed under the **INRIA ALADDIN** development action with support from CNRS, RENATER and several Universi-

recent figures computed after porting to 64bit architectures have shown a preliminary speedup by 2.

Corpus	#sentence	Cov.	time (s)	amb.
EUROTRA	334	100%	0.15	0.63
TSNLP	1161	95.07%	0.07	0.46
EasyDev	3879	64.73%	0.93	1.04
JRCacquis	1.1M	51.26%	1.41	1.1
Europarl	0.8M	70.19%	1.69	1.36
EstRep.	1.6M	67.05%	0.69	0.92
Wikipedia	2.2M	69.11%	0.49	0.87
Wikisource	1.5M	61.08%	0.71	0.89
AFP news	1.6M	52.15%	0.51	1.06

Table 3: Coverage, avg time, and avg ambiguity

To test the impact of factorization on parsing time, we have partially unfactorized FRMG, keeping all trees but #198. For #198, we have expanded the guards and the shuffle operators (but kept the disjunctions) and then intersected with the 195 verbal subcategoriztion frames present in our LEFFF lexicon. We got a version of FRMG with 5934 trees, 5729 being derived from #198. This grammar was already too large to be able to compile the left-corner relation in reasonable time and space, so Table 4 compares the evaluation times (in seconds) on the 3879 sentences of EasyDev for the unfactorized version and for the factorized version with no left corner. We see that the factorized version (with no left-corner) is slightly faster than the unfactorized one, which a contrario confirms that factorization induces no overhead. Table 4 also shows that FRMG with left-corner is around twice faster than the version with no left-corner. The fact that the left-corner relation can be computed for the factorized version but not easily for the (partially) unfolded one highlights another advantage of the factorization.

parser	avg	median	90%	99%
factorized	0.64	0.16	1.14	6.22
fact. -lc	1.33	0.46	2.63	12.24
-fact -lc	1.43	0.44	2.89	14.94

Table 4: Factorized vs non-factorized (in seconds)

---

ties as well as other funding bodies (see https://www.grid5000.fr).

7 Conclusion

The modularity of MGs combined with tree factoring offers an elegant methodology to design maintainable grammars that remain small in size, opening the way to more efficient parsers, as shown for a large coverage French MG. It should also be noted that the modularity of MGs makes easier the port of a MG for a close language.

The trees that are generated may be very complex but should rather seen as a side-product of simpler linguistic descriptions that are MGs. In other words, the TAGs tend to become an operational target formalism for MGs and the focus is now about improving the MG formalisms to get simpler notations for some constraints (such as node exclusion) and also to incorporate more powerful constraints.

Actually, TAGs as a target formalism are not powerful enough to capture some important syntactic phenomena, for instance deep genitive extractions. A natural evolution would be to use (local) Multi-Components TAGs instead of TAGs, as initiated by (Kallmeyer et al., 2008) for a German grammar. At MG level, the shift is relatively simple, mostly concerning the way the minimal trees are generated.

However, even with MGs, hand-crafting a large coverage grammar remains a complicated and long-standing task. In particular, while the modularity of MGs is a clear advantage for maintenance, tracking the cause of a non-analysis and of some overgeneration may be very difficult because hidden in the interactions of several constraints coming from many classes. Besides large regression test suites, there is a need for a sophisticated debugging environment, allowing us to track, at parsing time, the origin of all constraints.

References

A. Abeillé. 2002. *Une grammaire électronique du français*. CNRS Editions, Paris.

M. A. Alonso and V. J. Díaz. 2003. Variants of mixed parsing of TAG and TIG. *Traitement Automatique des Langues (T.A.L.)*, 44(3):41–65.

M.-H. Candito. 1999. *Organisation modulaire et paramétrable de grammaires électroniques lexicalisées*. Ph.D. thesis, Université Paris 7.

J. Carroll, N. Nicolov, M. Smets, O. Shaumyan, and D. Weir. 1998. Grammar compaction and computation sharing in automata-based parsing. In *Proceedings of Tabulation in Parsing and Deduction (TAPD'98)*, pages 16–25, Paris (FRANCE).

Benoît Crabbé. 2005. *Représentation informatique de grammaires d'arbres fortement lexicalisées : le cas de la grammaire d'arbres adjoints*. Ph.D. thesis, Université Nancy 2.

Ch. Doran, D. Egedi, Beth Ann Hockey, B. Srinivas, and Martin Zaidel. 1994. XTAG system — a wide coverage grammar for English. In *Proc. of the 15th International Conference on Computational Linguistics (COLING'94)*, pages 922–928, Kyoto, Japan.

D. Duchier, J. Leroux, and Y. Parmentier. 2004. The metagrammar compiler: An nlp application with a multi-paradigm architecture. In *2nd International Mozart/Oz Conference*.

K. Harbusch and J. Woch. 2004. Integrated natural language generation with schema-tree adjoining grammars. In Christopher Habel and editors Thomas Pechmann, editors, *Language Production*. Mouton De Gruyter.

A. K. Joshi. 1987. An introduction to tree adjoining grammars. In Alexis Manaster-Ramer, editor, *Mathematics of Language*, pages 87–115. John Benjamins Publishing Co., Amsterdam/Philadelphia.

Laura Kallmeyer, Wolfgang Maier, Timm Lichte, Yannick Parmentier, Johannes Dellert, and Kilian Evang. 2008. TuLiPA: Towards a multi-formalism parsing environment for grammar engineering. In *proceedings of the 2nd workshop on Grammar Engineering Across Frameworks (GEAF 2008)*, Manchester, United Kingdom, August.

A. Kinyon. 2000. Hypertags. In *Proc. of COLING*, pages 446–452.

M.-J. Nederhof, G. Satta, and S. Shieber. 2003. Partially ordered multiset context-free grammars and free-word-order parsing. In *In 8th International Workshop on Parsing Technologies (IWPT'03)*, pages 171–182.

Patrick Paroubek, Isabelle Robba, Anne Vilnat, and Christelle Ayache. 2008. Easy, evaluation of parsers of french: what are the results? In *Proceedings of the 6th International Conference on Language Resources and Evaluation (LREC)*, Marrakech, Morroco.

Carlos A. Prolo. 2002. Generating the xtag english grammar using metarules. In *Proceedings of the 19th international conference on Computational linguistics*, pages 1–7, Morristown, NJ, USA. Association for Computational Linguistics.

Y. Schabes and R. C. Waters. 1995. Tree insertion grammar: a cubic-time, parsable formalism that lexicalizes context-free grammar without changing the trees produced. *Fuzzy Sets Syst.*, 76(3):309–317.

Discontinuity and Non-Projectivity: Using Mildly Context-Sensitive Formalisms for Data-Driven Parsing

Wolfgang Maier and **Laura Kallmeyer**
SFB 833, University of Tübingen
{wmaier,lk}@sfs.uni-tuebingen.de

Abstract

We present a parser for probabilistic Linear Context-Free Rewriting Systems and use it for constituency and dependency treebank parsing. The choice of LCFRS, a formalism with an extended domain of locality, enables us to model discontinuous constituents and non-projective dependencies in a straight-forward way. The parsing results show that, firstly, our parser is efficient enough to be used for data-driven parsing and, secondly, its result quality for constituency parsing is comparable to the output quality of other state-of-the-art results, all while yielding structures that display discontinuous dependencies.

1 Introduction

It is a well-known fact that Context-Free Grammar (CFG) does not provide enough expressivity to describe natural languages. For data-driven probabilistic CFG parsing, some of the information present in constituency treebanks, namely the annotation of non-local dependencies, cannot be captured by a CFG. It is therefore removed before learning a PCFG from the treebank and must be re-introduced in a post-processing step (Johnson, 2002; Levy and Manning, 2004). Non-projective dependencies also lie beyond the expressivity of CFG. Current dependency parsers are able to parse them (McDonald et al., 2005; Nivre et al., 2007). However, the corresponding parsing algorithms are not grammar-based.

We propose to use a grammar formalism with an extended domain of locality that is able to capture the non-local dependencies both in constituency and dependency treebanks. We chose Linear Context-Free Rewriting Systems (LCFRS),

a mildly context-sensitive extension of CFG that allows non-terminals to span tuples of discontinuous strings. The reason why we think LCFRS particularly well-suited is that treebanks with a direct annotation of discontinuous constituents (with crossing branches as in the German Negra treebank) allow a straight-forward interpretation of the trees as LCFRS derivation structures, without the necessity of inducing linguistic knowledge.[1] This considerably facilitates the extraction of probabilistic LCFRSs (Maier and Søgaard, 2008). The same holds for non-projective dependency structures, which can also straight-forwardly be interpreted as LCFRS derivation structures (Kuhlmann and Satta, 2009). Previous approaches that have used non-context-free formalisms for data-driven constituency parsing (Plaehn, 2004; Chiang, 2003) are either too restricted (Kallmeyer et al., 2009) or do not allow for an immediate interpretation of the treebank trees as derivation structures. Grammar-based non-projective dependency parsing has, to our knowledge, not been attempted at all.

First results for PLCFRS constituency parsing with a detailed evaluation have been presented in Maier (2010). The contribution of this article is to present the first results for data-driven dependency parsing on the dependency version of the German NeGra treebank and on the Prague Dependency Treebank. Furthermore, we give greater detail on the parser and the experimental setup. We also additionally investigate the effect on manually introduced category splits for PLCFRS constituency parsing.

---

[1]Treebank trees in which non-local dependencies are annotated differently, such as with trace nodes in the Penn Treebank, could also be interpreted as LCFRS derivations given an appropriate transformation algorithm.

The remainder of this paper is structured as follows. In the following section, we present the formalism and our parser. Sect. 3 is dedicated the experimental setup, Sect. 4 contains the experimental results. In Sect. 5, we present a conclusion.

2 A Parser for Probabilistic Linear Context-Free Rewriting Systems

We notate LCFRS with the syntax of *simple Range Concatenation Grammars* (SRCG) (Boullier, 1998), a formalism that is equivalent to LCFRS.

2.1 PLCFRS

A LCFRS (Vijay-Shanker et al., 1987) is a tuple $G = (N, T, V, P, S)$ where a) N is a finite set of non-terminals with a function $dim\colon N \to \mathbb{N}$ that determines the *fan-out* of each $A \in N$; b) T and V are disjoint finite sets of terminals and variables; c) $S \in N$ is the start symbol with $dim(S) = 1$; d) P is a finite set of rewriting rules

$$A(\alpha_1, \ldots, \alpha_{dim(A)}) \to A_1(X_1^{(1)}, \ldots, X_{dim(A_1)}^{(1)})$$
$$\cdots A_m(X_1^{(m)}, \ldots, X_{dim(A_m)}^{(m)})$$

for $m \geq 0$ where $A, A_1, \ldots, A_m \in N$, $X_j^{(i)} \in V$ for $1 \leq i \leq m, 1 \leq j \leq dim(A_i)$ and $\alpha_i \in (T \cup V)^*$ for $1 \leq i \leq dim(A)$. For all $r \in P$, every variable X occurring in r occurs exactly once in the left-hand side (LHS) and exactly once in the right-hand side (RHS).

For a given rule, the length of the RHS is called the *rank* of the rule. The maximal fan-out of all non-terminals in an LCFRS G is called the *fan-out* of G, and the maximal rank of all rules in an LCFRS G is called the *rank* of G.

$$
\begin{aligned}
&A(ab, cd) \to \varepsilon && (\langle ab, cd \rangle \text{ in yield of } A) \\
&A(aXb, cYd) \to A(X, Y) && (\text{if } \langle X, Y \rangle \text{ in yield of } A, \\
& && \text{then also } \langle aXb, cYd \rangle \text{ in yield of } A) \\
&S(XY) \to A(X, Y) && (\text{if } \langle X, Y \rangle \text{ in yield of } A, \\
& && \text{then } \langle XY \rangle \text{ in yield of } S)
\end{aligned}
$$

$$L = \{a^n b^n c^n d^n \mid n > 0\}$$

Figure 1: Sample LCFRS

A rewriting rule describes how to compute the yield of the LHS non-terminal from the yields of the RHS non-terminals. The yield of S is the language of the grammar. See Fig. 1 for a sample LCFRS.

A *probabilistic LCFRS* (PLCFRS) is a tuple $\langle N, T, V, P, S, p \rangle$ such that $\langle N, T, V, P, S \rangle$ is a

LCFRS and $p : P \to [0..1]$ a function such that for all $A \in N$: $\Sigma_{A(\vec{x}) \to \vec{\Phi} \in P} p(A(\vec{x}) \to \vec{\Phi}) = 1$.

2.2 PLCFRS Parsing

Our parser is a probabilistic CYK parser (Seki et al., 1991), using the technique of weighted deductive parsing (Nederhof, 2003). We assume without loss of generality that our LCFRSs are binary (i.e., have rank 2) (Gómez-Rodríguez et al., 2009) and do not contain rules where some of the LHS components are ε (Boullier, 1998; Seki et al., 1991). Our binarization algorithm is given in Section 3.4.

Furthermore, we make the assumption that POS tagging is done before parsing. The POS tags are special non-terminals of fan-out 1.

Scan: $\dfrac{}{0 : [A, \langle\langle i, i+1 \rangle\rangle]}$ A POS tag of w_{i+1}

Unary: $\dfrac{in : [B, \vec{\rho}]}{in + |log(p)| : [A, \vec{\rho}]}$ $p : A(\vec{\alpha}) \to B(\vec{\alpha}) \in P$

Binary: $\dfrac{in_B : [B, \vec{\rho_B}], in_C : [C, \vec{\rho_C}]}{in_B + in_C + log(p) : [A, \vec{\rho_A}]}$
where $p : A(\vec{\rho_A}) \to B(\vec{\rho_B})C(\vec{\rho_C})$ is an instantiated rule.
Goal: $[S, \langle\langle 0, n \rangle\rangle]$

Figure 2: Weighted CYK deduction system

add SCAN results to $\mathcal{A}$
while $\mathcal{A} \neq \emptyset$ **do**
    remove best item $x : I$ from $\mathcal{A}$
    add $x : I$ to $\mathcal{C}$
    if I goal item **then**
        stop and output true
    else
        for all $y : I'$ deduced from $x : I$ and items in $\mathcal{C}$
        do
            if there is no z with $z : I' \in \mathcal{C} \cup \mathcal{A}$ **then**
                add $y : I'$ to $\mathcal{A}$
            else
                if $z : I' \in \mathcal{A}$ for some z **then**
                    update weight of I' in $\mathcal{A}$ to $max(y, z)$
                end if
            end if
        end for
    end if
end while

Figure 3: Weighted deductive parsing

For a given input w, our items have the form $[A, \vec{\rho}]$

where $A \in N$, $\vec{\rho} \in (Pos(w) \times Pos(w))^{dim(A)}$ the vector of ranges characterizing all components of the span of A. We specify the set of weighted parse items via the deduction rules in Fig. 2. An instantiated rule is a rule where variables have been replaced with corresponding vectors of ranges. Our parser performs weighted deductive parsing, based on this deduction system. We use a chart C and an agenda A, both initially empty, and we proceed as in Fig. 3. For more details of the parser, see also Kallmeyer and Maier (2010).

3 Experimental Setup

3.1 Data

Our data sources are the NeGra treebank (Skut et al., 1997) and the Prague Dependency Treebank 2.0 (PDT) (Hajič et al., 2000).

We create two different data sets for constituent parsing. For the first one, we start out with the unmodified NeGra treebank. We preprocess the treebank following common practice (Kübler and Penn, 2008), attaching all nodes which are attached to the virtual root node to nodes within the tree such that ideally, no new crossing edges are created. In a second pass, we attach punctuation which comes in pairs (parentheses, quotation marks) to the same nodes. For the second data set we create a copy of the preprocessed first data set, in which we apply the usual tree transformations for NeGra PCFG parsing, i.e., moving nodes to higher positions until all crossing branches are resolved. The first 90% of both data sets are used as the training set and the remaining 10% as test set.

For dependency parsing, we also create two data sets. For the first one, we convert the NeGra constituent annotation to labeled dependencies using Lin's (1995) algorithm and Hall and Nivre's (2008) labeling scheme. For the second dependency data set, we use the training sections 1 to 5 of the PDT for training and the first 1,300 sentences for testing. Czech is a language with a rich morphology, which is reflected by a high number of POS tags with additional morphological information in the PDT. As in previous work, we use a simplified tag set in order to avoid data sparseness problems (Collins et al., 1999; McDonald et al., 2005).

We only include sentences with a maximal length of 25 words.[1] This leads to a size of 14,858, resp. 1,651 sentences for the NeGra training, resp. test sets and to 13,935, resp. 1,300 sentences for the PDT training, resp. test set.

3.2 Grammar Extraction

From all of our data sets, we extract PLCFRSs. For the constituent sets, we use the algorithm from Maier and Søgaard (2008), for the dependencies the algorithm from Kuhlmann and Satta (2009). For reasons of space, we restrict ourselves here to the examples in Fig. 4–6.

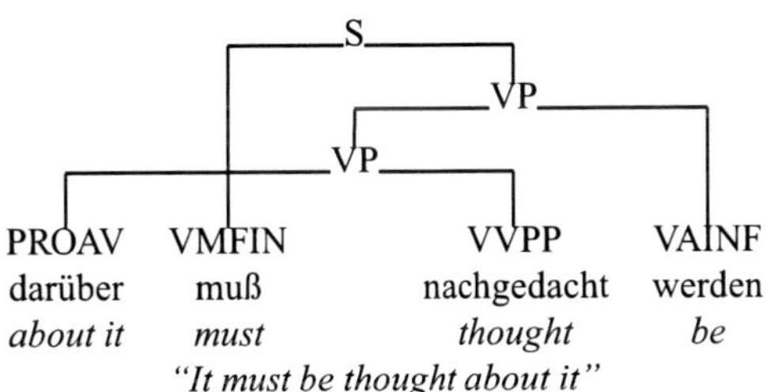

Figure 4: A sample tree from NeGra

$$\text{PROAV(Darüber)} \rightarrow \varepsilon$$
$$\text{VVPP(nachgedacht)} \rightarrow \varepsilon$$
$$\text{VMFIN(muß)} \rightarrow \varepsilon$$
$$\text{VAINF(werden)} \rightarrow \varepsilon$$
$$S_1(X_1X_2X_3) \rightarrow \text{VP}_2(X_1, X_3)\,\text{VMFIN}(X_2)$$
$$\text{VP}_2(X_1, X_2X_3) \rightarrow \text{VP}_2(X_1, X_2)\,\text{VAINF}(X_3)$$
$$\text{VP}_2(X_1, X_2) \rightarrow \text{PROAV}(X_1)\,\text{VVPP}(X_2)$$

Figure 5: LCFRS rules for the tree in Fig. 4

3.3 Grammar Annotation

Grammar annotation (i.e., manual enhancement of annotation information through category splitting) has previously been successfully employed in parsing German (Versley, 2005). In order to see if such modifications can have a beneficial effect in PLCFRS parsing, we will apply the following category splits to the Negra constituency data sets with unmodified labels (inspired by Petrov and Klein (2007)): We split the category S ("sentence") into SRC ("relative clause") and S (all other categories S). Relative clauses mostly occur in a very specific

---

[1] This length restriction can be greatly alleviated by using an estimate of outside probabilities of parse items which speeds up parsing (Kallmeyer and Maier, 2010)

Dependency tree:

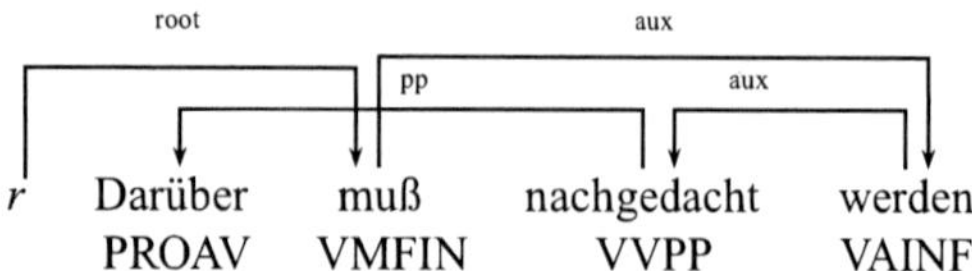

r Darüber   muß   nachgedacht   werden
PROAV   VMFIN   VVPP   VAINF

Corresponding LCFRS rules:

$$\begin{aligned}
\text{PROAV(Darüber)} &\rightarrow \varepsilon \\
\text{VVPP(nachgedacht)} &\rightarrow \varepsilon \\
\text{VMFIN(muß)} &\rightarrow \varepsilon \\
\text{VAINF(werden)} &\rightarrow \varepsilon \\
\text{pp}(X) &\rightarrow \text{PROAV}(X) \\
\text{root}(X_1X_2X_3) &\rightarrow \text{aux}(X_1,X_3)\,\text{VMFIN}(X_2) \\
\text{aux}(X_1,X_2) &\rightarrow \text{pp}(X_1)\,\text{VVPP}(X_2) \\
\text{aux}(X_1,X_2X_3) &\rightarrow \text{aux}(X_1,X_2)\,\text{VAINF}(X_3) \\
\text{top}(X_1) &\rightarrow \text{root}(X_1)
\end{aligned}$$

Figure 6: LCFRS rules extracted from a dependency tree[3]

context, namely as the right part of an NP or a PP. This splitting should therefore speed up parsing and increase precision.

The other category split we introduce concerns the VP category and the POS tags of verbs selecting for a VP. We distinguish between VP-PP ("VP with participle verb form"), VP-INF ("VP with infinitive without *zu*") and VP-ZU ("VP with *zu* infitive").

Apart from the *S* and *VP* splits, we also use both splits together ($S \circ VP$).

3.4 Binarization

Before parsing, we binarize the LCFRS rules of the extracted grammars. The transformation is similar to the transformation of a CFG into Chomsky Normal Form (CNF). The result is an LCFRS of rank 2. As in the CFG case, in the transformation, we introduce a non-terminal for each RHS longer than 2 and split the rule into two rules, using this new intermediate non-terminal. This is repeated until all RHS are of length 2.

For the presentation of the transformation algorithm, we need the notion of a *reduction* of a vector $\vec{\alpha} \in [(T \cup V)^*]^i$ by a vector $\vec{x} \in V^j$ where all variables in $\vec{x}$ occur in $\vec{\alpha}$. A reduction is, roughly,

<hr>

[3]An extra top rule is added in order to give the PLCFRS parser a unique start symbol in case more than one word has the root node as head, i.e., in case more than one rule with *root* as LHS label is extracted.

---

for all rules $r = A(\vec{\alpha}) \rightarrow A_0(\vec{\alpha_0}) \dots A_m(\vec{\alpha_m})$ in P with $m > 1$ **do**
   remove r from P
   $R := \emptyset$
   pick new non-terminals $C_1, \dots, C_{m-1}$
   add the rule $A(\vec{\alpha}) \rightarrow A_0(\vec{\alpha_0})C_1(\vec{\gamma_1})$ to R where $\vec{\gamma_1}$ is obtained by reducing $\vec{\alpha}$ with $\vec{\alpha_0}$
   for all $i, 1 \leq i \leq m - 2$ **do**
     add the rule $C_i(\vec{\gamma_i}) \rightarrow A_i(\vec{\alpha_i})C_{i+1}(\vec{\gamma_{i+1}})$ to R where $\vec{\gamma_{i+1}}$ is obtained by reducing $\vec{\gamma_i}$ with $\vec{\alpha_i}$
   end for
   add the rule $C_{m-1}(\vec{\gamma_{m-2}}) \rightarrow A_{m-1}(\vec{\alpha_{m-1}})A_m(\vec{\alpha_m})$ to R
   for every rule $r' \in R$ **do**
     replace RHS arguments of length > 1 with new variables (in both sides) and add the result to P
   end for
end for

Figure 7: Algorithm for binarizing a LCFRS

obtained by keeping all variables in $\vec{\alpha}$ that are not in $\vec{x}$. This is defined as follows: Let $\langle N, T, V, P, S \rangle$ be an LCFRS, $\vec{\alpha} \in [(T \cup V)^*]^i$ and $\vec{x} \in V^j$ for some $i, j \in \mathcal{N}$. Let $w = \vec{\alpha}_1 \$ \dots \$\vec{\alpha}_i$ be the string obtained form concatenating the components of $\vec{\alpha}$, separated by a new symbol $\$ \notin (V \cup T)$. Let w' be the image of w under a homomorphism h defined as follows: $h(a) = \$$ for all $a \in T$, $h(X) = \$$ for all $X \in \{\vec{x}_1, \dots \vec{x}_j\}$ and $h(y) = y$ in all other cases. Let $y_1, \dots y_m \in V^+$ such that $w' \in \$^*y_1\$^+y_2\$^+ \dots \$^+y_m\$^*$. Then the vector $\langle y_1, \dots y_m \rangle$ is the *reduction* of $\vec{\alpha}$ by $\vec{x}$.

For instance, $\langle aX_1, X_2, bX_3 \rangle$ reduced with $\langle X_2 \rangle$ yields $\langle X_1, X_3 \rangle$ and $\langle aX_1X_2bX_3 \rangle$ reduced with $\langle X_2 \rangle$ yields $\langle X_1, X_3 \rangle$ as well.

The binarization algorithm is given in Fig. 7. Fig. 8 shows an example. In this example, there is only one rule with a RHS longer than 2. In a first step, we introduce the new non-terminals and rules that binarize the RHS. This leads to the set R. In a second step, before adding the rules from R to the grammar, whenever a right-hand side argument contains several variables, they are collapsed into a single new variable.

The equivalence of the original LCFRS and the binarized grammar is rather straight-forward. Note however that the fan-out of the LCFRS can increase because of the binarization.

Original LCFRS:
$$S(XYZUVW) \rightarrow A(X,U)B(Y,V)C(Z,W)$$
$$A(aX,aY) \rightarrow A(X,Y) \qquad A(a,a) \rightarrow \varepsilon$$
$$B(bX,bY) \rightarrow B(X,Y) \qquad B(b,b) \rightarrow \varepsilon$$
$$C(cX,cY) \rightarrow C(X,Y) \qquad C(c,c) \rightarrow \varepsilon$$

Rule with right-hand side of length > 2:
$$S(XYZUVW) \rightarrow A(X,U)B(Y,V)C(Z,W)$$
For this rule, we obtain
$$R = \{S(XYZUVW) \rightarrow A(X,U)C_1(YZ,VW),$$
$$C_1(YZ,VW) \rightarrow B(Y,V)C(Z,W)\}$$

Equivalent binarized LCFRS:
$$S(XPUQ) \rightarrow A(X,U)C_1(P,Q)$$
$$C_1(YZ,VW) \rightarrow B(Y,V)C(Z,W)$$
$$A(aX,aY) \rightarrow A(X,Y) \qquad A(a,a) \rightarrow \varepsilon$$
$$B(bX,bY) \rightarrow B(X,Y) \qquad B(b,b) \rightarrow \varepsilon$$
$$C(cX,cY) \rightarrow C(X,Y) \qquad C(c,c) \rightarrow \varepsilon$$

Figure 8: Sample binarization of a LCFRS

In LCFRS, in contrast to CFG, the order of the RHS elements of a rule does not matter for the result of a derivation. Therefore, we can reorder the RHS of a rule before binarizing it. In practice, we perform a head-outward binarization where the head is the lowest subtree. It is extended by adding first all sisters to its left and then all sisters to its right. Consequently, before binarizing we reorder the RHS of the rules extracted from the treebank such that first, all elements to the right of the head are listed in reverse order, then all elements to the left of the head in their original order and then the head itself.[4]

Furthermore, we add additional unary rules when introducing the highest new binarization non-terminal and when deriving the head. This allows for an additional factorization that has proved itself useful in parsing. Fig. 9 shows a sample binarization of a tree in the NeGra format.

For the LCFRSs extracted from dependency tree-banks, we perform the same type of binarization. The head daughter is always the daughter with the POS tag non-terminal.

3.5 Markovization

Markovization (Collins, 1999) is achieved by introducing only a single new non-terminal for the new

___
[4] One could also add first the sisters to the right and then the ones to the left which is what Klein and Manning (2003) do. However, this has only a negligible effect on parsing results.

Tree in NeGra Format:

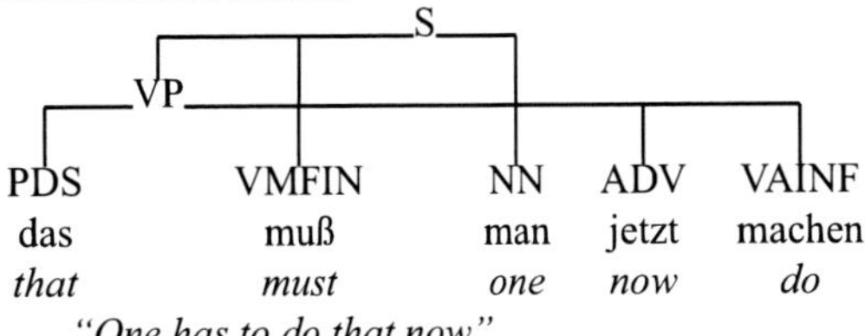

"One has to do that now"

Rule extracted for the S node:
$$S(XYZU) \rightarrow \text{VP}(X,U)\ \text{VMFIN}(Y)\ \text{NN}(Z)$$
Reordering for head-outward binarization:
$$S(XYZU) \rightarrow \text{NN}(Z)\ \text{VP}(X,U)\ \text{VMFIN}(Y)$$
New rules resulting form binarizing this rule:
$$S(X) \rightarrow S_{bin\,1}(X)$$
$$S_{bin\,1}(XYZ) \rightarrow S_{bin\,2}(X,Z)\ \text{NN}(Y)$$
$$S_{bin\,3}(X) \rightarrow \text{VMFIN}(X)$$
$$S_{bin\,2}(XY,Z) \rightarrow \text{VP}(X,Z)\ S_{bin\,3}(Y)$$

Tree after binarization:

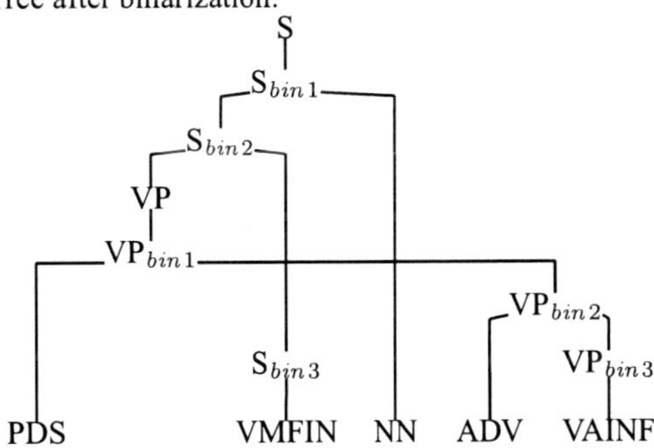

Figure 9: Sample binarization

rules introduces during binarization and adding vertical and horizontal context from the original trees to each occurrence of this new non-terminal. As vertical context, we add the first v labels on the path from the root node of the tree that we want to binarize to the root of the entire treebank tree. The vertical context is actually collected during grammar extraction and then taken into account during binarization of the rules. As horizontal context, during binarization of a rule $A(\vec{\alpha}) \rightarrow A_0(\vec{\alpha_0}) \ldots A_m(\vec{\alpha_m})$, for the new non-terminal that comprises the RHS elements $A_i \ldots A_m$ (for some $1 \leq i \leq m$), we add the first h elements of $A_i, A_{i-1}, \ldots, A_0$.

Figure 10 shows an example of a markovization of the tree from Fig. 9 with $v = 1$ and $h = 2$. Here, the superscript is the vertical context and the subscript the horizontal context of the new non-terminal X.

The probabilities are then computed based on the

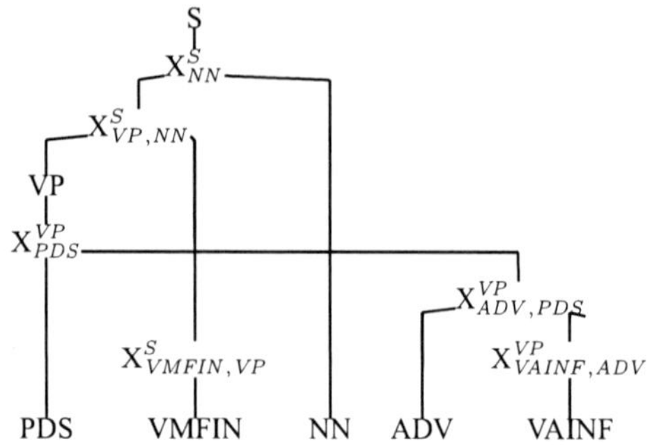

Figure 10: Sample Markovization with $v = 1, h = 2$

frequencies of rules in the treebank, using a Maximum Likelihood estimator (MLE). Such an estimation has been used before (Kato et al., 2006).

3.6 Properties of the Grammars

	unbin.	bin.	bin. lab.
NeGra LCFRS	13,858	16,904	4,142
S sp.	13,953	17,033	4,179
VP sp.	14,050	18,362	4,952
$S \circ VP$ sp.	14,144	18,503	4,995
NeGra PCFG	12,886	15,563	3,898
NeGra Dep.	18,520	68,847	49,085
PDT	12,841	38,312	24,119

Table 1: PLCFRSs extracted from training sets

Tab. 1 contains the properties of the grammars: The number of rules in the unbinarized grammar, the number of rules in the binarized and markovized grammar and the number of labels (including POS tags) in the binarized and markovized grammar.

4 Experiments

We run the parser on all data sets described above, providing gold POS tags in the input. In order to relate the costs of parsing for each of the data sets, we include Fig. 11, which shows the numbers of produced items for each data set.

4.1 Constituency Parsing

For the evaluation of the constituent parses, we use an EVALB-style metric. For a tree over a string w, a single constituent is represented by a tuple $\langle A, \vec{\rho} \rangle$ with A a node label and $\vec{\rho} \in (Pos(w) \times$

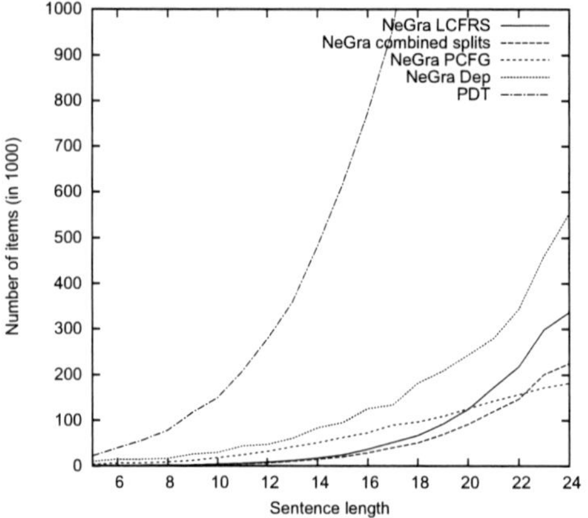

Figure 11: Number of items

$Pos(w))^{dim(A)}$.[5] We compute precision, recall and F_1 based on these tuples from gold and parsed test data. Despite the shortcomings of such a measure (Rehbein and van Genabith, 2007, e.g.), it still allows to some extent a comparison to previous work in PCFG parsing. For a more detailed evaluation of NeGra PLCFRS constituent parsing results, see Maier (2010). We use the previously successfully employed markovization settings $v = 2$ and $h = 1$ for all constituent experiments.

	LCFRS	w/ category splits			PCFG
		VP	S	$S \circ VP$	
LP	73.24	73.24	73.98	74.02	74.10
LR	73.56	73.91	74.17	74.45	74.83
LF_1	73.40	73.57	74.07	74.24	74.46
UP	77.12	76.98	77.47	77.39	78.08
UR	77.46	77.68	77.68	77.84	78.84
UF_1	77.29	77.33	77.58	77.62	78.46

Table 2: NeGra constituent parsing

	K 05	here	R&M 08	P&K 07
Labeled F_1	69.94	**74.46**	77.20	80.1

Table 3: Previous NeGra PCFG parsing

Tab. 2 presents the constituent parsing results for both data sets with (LCFRS) and without (PCFG) crossing branches. For the sake of comparison, we

---

[5]Note that our metric is equivalent to the corresponding PCFG metric for $dim(A) = 1$.

report PCFG parsing results from the literature[6] in Tab. 3, namely for PCFG parsing with a plain vanilla treebank grammar (Kübler, 2005), for PCFG parsing with the Stanford parser (Rafferty and Manning, 2008) (markovization as in our parser), and for the current state-of-the-art, namely PCFG parsing with a latent variable model (Petrov and Klein, 2007). We see that the LCFRS parser output (which contains more information than the output of a PCFG parser) is competitive. The PCFG (1-LCFRS) parsing results are even closer to the ones of current systems. Recall that these are just first results, much optimization potential is left.

Before we evaluate the experiments with category splits, we replace all split labels in the parser output with the corresponding original labels. The results show that the category splits are indeed beneficial, both in terms of output quality and speed (cf. the number of produced items in Fig. 11). We will continue to explore this approach using an automated split-and-merge approach in the style of Ule (2003).

Literature on parsing with discontinuous constituents is sparse. Hall and Nivre (2008) reconstruct the crossing branches of NeGra. They parse a (non-projective) dependency version of the German TIGER treebank (which follows the same annotation principles as NeGra) and convert the result back to constituents. For sentences up to length 40 and perfect tagging, they report a labeled F_1 of 70.79. While not directly comparable to our result, we still lie in the same range. Plaehn (2004) also reports results for direct parsing of the discontinuous constituents using Probabilistic Discontinuous Phrase Structure Grammar (DPSG). See Maier (2010) for details.

4.2 Dependency Parsing

In this section, we present the first grammar-based non-projective dependency parsing results. As Kuhlmann and Satta (2009) note, the principal advantage of grammar-based non-projective dependency parsing is that edge probabilities can be fine-tuned while staying polynomially parseable. This is not possible in the Maximum Spanning Tree approach (McDonald and Satta, 2007). For compar-

ison of our dependency parser output, we report labeled and unlabeled attachment score and completely correct graphs (punctuation included). As markovization setting for the PDT set, we choose $v = 2$ and $h = \infty$.

	NeGra		PDT	
	Grammar	MST	Grammar	MST
UAS	78.98	87.96	51.44	76.01
LAS	71.84	82.62	67.09	40.54
UComp	32.65	42.16	14.92	28.92
LComp	25.03	29.56	9.46	17.23

Table 4: Dependency parsing

Tab. 4 contain the dependency parsing results for our parser and the MSTParser (McDonald et al., 2005) for NeGra and PDT. As an overall observation, the fact that our results are far off the MSTParser's results is certainly surprising. The most prominent difference between the NeGra and the PDT set is the number of edge labels. It leads to grammars with 922 non-terminals for NeGra and only 51 non-terminals for the PDT. While the MSTParser is almost not affected by this difference, the fact that our NeGra results are superior to our PDT results allows the conclusion that for grammar-based parsing, more informative edges labels are an advantage. This is also confirmed by the higher number of items for PDT (cf. Fig. 11). We expect therefore that automated category splitting will lead to a large improvement. This will be tackled in future work.

5 Conclusion

We have presented a parser for Probabilistic Linear Context-Free Rewriting Systems and have used it to parse NeGra, a German constituency treebank with directly annotated crossing branches. Furthermore, we have applied our parser to a dependency version of NeGra, and to the Prague Dependency Treebank. To our knowledge, grammar-based parsing of non-projective dependencies has not been attempted before. Experiments have shown that PLCFRS parsing is feasible and that the results for constituency parsing lie in the vicinity of the state-of-the-art.

In future work, we will concentrate particularly on the optimization potential for the parsing results. Especially dependency parsing offers many possibilities of optimization.

---

[6]The results from the literature were obtained on sentences longer than 25 words and would most likely be better for our sentence length.

References

Pierre Boullier. 1998. A Proposal for a Natural Language Processing Syntactic Backbone. Technical Report 3342, INRIA.

David Chiang. 2003. Statistical parsing with an automatically extracted Tree Adjoining Grammar. In *Data-Oriented Parsing*. CSLI Publications.

Michael Collins, Jan Hajič, Lance Ramshaw, and Christoph Tillmann. 1999. A statistical parser for Czech. In *Proceedings of ACL 1999*.

Michael Collins. 1999. *Head-driven statistical models for natural language parsing*. Ph.D. thesis, University of Pennsylvania.

Carlos Gómez-Rodríguez, Marco Kuhlmann, Giorgio Satta, and David Weir. 2009. Optimal reduction of rule length in linear context-free rewriting systems. In *Proceedings of NAACL-HLT*, Boulder, Colorado.

Jan Hajič, Alena Böhmová, Eva Hajičová, and Barbora Vidová-Hladká. 2000. The Prague Dependency Treebank: A Three-Level Annotation Scenario. In A. Abeillé, editor, *Treebanks: Building and Using Parsed Corpora*. Amsterdam:Kluwer.

Johan Hall and Joakim Nivre. 2008. Parsing discontinuous phrase structure with grammatical functions. In *Proceedings of GoTAL 2008*.

Mark Johnson. 2002. A simple pattern-matching algorithm for recovering empty nodes and their antecedents. In *Proceedings of ACL 2002*.

Laura Kallmeyer and Wolfgang Maier. 2010. Data-driven parsing with probabilistic linear context-free rewriting systems. Unpublished manuscript.

Laura Kallmeyer, Wolfgang Maier, and Giorgio Satta. 2009. Synchronous rewriting in treebanks. In *Proceedings of IWPT 2009*.

Yuki Kato, Hiroyuki Seki, and Tadao Kasami. 2006. Stochastic multiple context-free grammar for rna pseudoknot modeling. In *Proceedings of TAG+8*.

Dan Klein and Christopher D. Manning. 2003. Accurate unlexicalized parsing. In *Proceedings of ACL 2003*.

Sandra Kübler and Gerald Penn, editors. 2008. *Proceedings of the Workshop on Parsing German at ACL 2008*.

Sandra Kübler. 2005. How do treebank annotation schemes influence parsing results? Or how not to compare apples and oranges. In *Proceedings of RANLP 2005*.

Marco Kuhlmann and Giorgio Satta. 2009. Treebank grammar techniques for non-projective dependency parsing. In *Proceedings of EACL*.

Roger Levy and Christopher D. Manning. 2004. Deep dependencies from context-free statistical parsers: correcting the surface dependency approximation. In *Proceedings of ACL 2004*.

Dekang Lin. 1995. A dependency-based method for evaluating broad-coverage parsers. In *Proceedings of IJCAI 1995*.

Wolfgang Maier and Anders Søgaard. 2008. Treebanks and mild context-sensitivity. In *Proceedings of Formal Grammar 2008*.

Wolfgang Maier. 2010. Direct parsing of discontinuous constituents in German. In *Proceedings of the First Workshop on Statistical Parsing of Morphologically Rich Languages (SPMRL 2010) at NAACL 2010*.

Ryan McDonald and Giorgio Satta. 2007. On the complexity of non-projective data-driven dependency parsing. In *Proceedings of IWPT 2007*.

Ryan McDonald, Fernando Pereira, Kiril Ribarov, and Jan Hajič. 2005. Non-projective dependency parsing using spanning tree algorithms. In *Proceedings of HLT/EMNLP 2005*.

Mark-Jan Nederhof. 2003. Weighted Deductive Parsing and Knuth's Algorithm. *Computational Linguistics*, 29(1).

J. Nivre, J. Hall, J. Nilsson, A. Chanev, G. Eryigit, S. Kübler, S. Marinov, and E. Marsi. 2007. MaltParser: A language-independent system for data-driven dependency parsing. *Natural Language Engineering*, 13(2).

Slav Petrov and Dan Klein. 2007. Improved inference for unlexicalized parsing. In *Proceedings of HLT-NAACL 2007*.

Oliver Plaehn. 2004. Computing the most probable parse for a discontinuous phrase-structure grammar. In *New developments in parsing technology*. Kluwer.

Anna Rafferty and Christopher D. Manning, 2008. *Parsing Three German Treebanks: Lexicalized and Unlexicalized Baselines*. In Kübler and Penn (2008).

Ines Rehbein and Josef van Genabith. 2007. Evaluating evaluation measures. In *Proceedings of NODALIDA 2007*.

Hiroyuki Seki, Takahashi Matsumura, Mamoru Fujii, and Tadao Kasami. 1991. On multiple context-free grammars. *Theoretical Computer Science*, 88(2).

Wojciech Skut, Brigitte Krenn, Thorten Brants, and Hans Uszkoreit. 1997. An Annotation Scheme for Free Word Order Languages. In *Proceedings of ANLP*.

Tylman Ule. 2003. Directed treebank refinement for PCFG parsing. In *Proceedings of TLT 2003*.

Yannick Versley. 2005. Parser evaluation across text types. In *Proceedings of TLT 2005*.

K. Vijay-Shanker, David J. Weir, and Aravind K. Joshi. 1987. Characterizing structural descriptions produced by various grammatical formalisms. In *Proceedings of ACL 1987*.

Sentence Generation as Planning with Probabilistic LTAG

Daniel Bauer
Department of Computer Science
Columbia University
1214 Amsterdam Ave.
New York, NY 10027, USA
`bauer@cs.columbia.edu`

Alexander Koller
Cluster of Excellence
Saarland University
Campus C7 4
66041 Saarbrücken, Germany
`koller@mmci.uni-saarland.de`

Abstract

We present PCRISP, a sentence generation system for probabilistic TAG grammars which performs sentence planning and surface realization in an integrated fashion, in the style of the SPUD system. PCRISP operates by converting the generation problem into a metric planning problem and solving it using an off-the-shelf planner. We evaluate PCRISP on the WSJ corpus and identify trade-offs between coverage, efficiency, and accuracy.

1 Introduction

Many sentence generation systems are organized in a pipeline architecture, in which the input semantic representation is first enriched, e.g. with referring expressions, by a *sentence planner* and only then transformed into natural language strings by a *surface realizer* (Reiter and Dale, 2000). An alternative approach is *integrated* sentence generation, in which both steps are performed by the same algorithm, as in the SPUD system (Stone et al., 2003). An integrated algorithm can sometimes generate better and more succinct sentences (Stone and Webber, 1998). SPUD itself gives up some of this advantage by using a greedy search heuristic for efficiency reasons. The CRISP system, a recent reimplementation of SPUD using search techniques from AI planning, achieves high efficiency without sacrificing complete search (Koller and Stone, 2007; Koller and Hoffmann, 2010).

While CRISP is efficient enough to perform well on large-scale grammars (Koller and Hoffmann, 2010), such grammars tend to offer many different ways to express the same semantic representation. This makes it necessary for the generation system to be able to compute not just grammatical sentences, but to identify which of these sentences are *good*. This problem is exacerbated when using treebank-derived grammars, which tend to underspecify the actual constraints on grammaticality and instead rely on statistical information learned from the treebank. Indeed, there have been a number of systems for statistical generation, which can exploit such information to rank sentences appropriately (Langkilde and Knight, 1998; White and Baldridge, 2003; Belz, 2008). However, to our knowledge, all such systems are currently restricted to performing surface realization, and must rely on separate modules to perform sentence planning.

In this paper, we bring these two strands of research together for the first time. We present the PCRISP system, which redefines the SPUD generation problem in terms of probabilistic TAG grammars (PTAG, (Resnik, 1992)) and then extends CRISP to solving the probabilistic SPUD generation problem using metric planning (Fox and Long, 2002; Hoffmann, 2003). We evaluate PCRISP on a PTAG treebank extracted from the Wall Street Journal Corpus (Chen and Shanker, 2004). The evaluation reveals a tradeoff between coverage, efficiency, and accuracy which we think are worth exploring further in future work.

Plan of the paper. We start by putting our research in the context of related work in Section 2 and reviewing CRISP in Section 3. We then describe PCRISP, our probabilistic extension of CRISP, in

Section 4 and evaluate it in Section 5. We conclude in Section 6.

2 Related Work

Statistical methods are popular for surface realization, but have not been used in systems that integrate sentence planning. Most statistical generation approaches follow a generate-and-select strategy, first proposed by Knight and Hatzivassiloglou (1995) in their NITROGEN system. Such systems generate a set of candidate sentences using a (possibly overgenerating) grammar and then select the best output sentence by applying a statistical language model. This family includes systems such as HALogen (Langkilde and Knight, 1998; Langkilde, 2000) and OpenCCG (White and Baldridge, 2003). The FERGUS system (Bangalore and Rambow, 2000) is a variant of this approach which, like PCRISP, employs TAG. It first assigns elementary trees to each entity in the input sentence plan using a statistical tree model and then computes the most likely derivation using only these trees with an n-gram model on the output sentence. An alternative to the n-gram based generate and select approach is to use a probabilistic grammar model, like PTAG, trained on automatic parses (Zhong and Stent, 2005). A related approach uses a model over local decisions of the generation system itself (Belz, 2008). Both models can either be used to discriminate a set of output candidates, or more directly to choose the next best decision locally. Our approach is similar in that it uses PTAG to find the most likely output structure. However, the previous work discussed so far addresses surface realization only. We extend this to a statistical NLG algorithm which does surface realization and sentence planning at the same time.

Our treatment of integrated sentence planning and surface realization as planning is inherited directly from CRISP (Koller and Stone, 2007). Planning has long played a role in generation, but has focused on discourse planning instead of specifically addressing sentence generation (Hovy, 1988; Appelt, 1985). The applicability of these ideas was limited at that time because efficient planning technology was not available. Recently the development of more efficient planning algorithms (Hoffmann and Nebel, 2001) spawned a renewed interest in planning for NLG. CRISP uses such algorithms to efficiently solve the sentence generation problem defined by SPUD (Stone et al., 2003). SPUD, which instead uses an incomplete greedy algorithm, is based on a TAG whose trees are augmented with semantic and pragmatic constraints. Given a communicative goal, a solution to the SPUD problem realizes this goal and simultaneously selects referring expressions. The next section explores CRISP in more detail.

3 Sentence Generation as Planning

In this section we review the original non-statistical CRISP system (Koller and Stone, 2007). Following SPUD (Stone et al., 2003), CRISP is based on a declarative description of the sentence generation problem using TAG. Given a knowledge base, a communicative goal and a grammar, we require to find a grammatical TAG derivation that is consistent with this knowledge base and satisfies a communicative goal. A number of semantic and pragmatic constraints that must be satisfied by the solution can be added, for instance to enforce generation of unambiguous referring expressions. Koller and Stone (2007) describe how to encode this problem into an AI planning problem which can be solved efficiently by off-the-shelf planners. We describe the general mechanism in the following section and then review the encoding into planning in section 3.2.

3.1 Sentence Generation in CRISP

Like SPUD, CRISP uses an LTAG in which elementary trees are assigned semantic content. Each node in a CRISP elementary tree is associated with a semantic role. Semantic content is expressed as a set of literals, encoding relations between these roles. All nodes that dominate the lexical anchor are assigned the role 'self', which intuitively corresponds to the event or individual described by this tree. Fig. 1(a) shows an example grammar of this type.

In a derivation we may only include elementary trees whose semantic content has an instantiation in the knowledge base. For each substitution and adjunction, the semantic role associated with the role of the target node is unified with the 'self' role of the child tree. For example, given the knowledge base

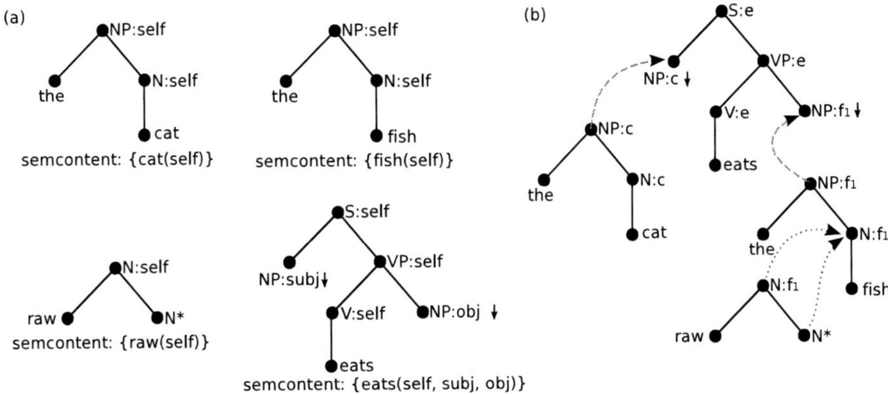

Figure 1: (a) An example grammar with semantic content. (b) A derivation for "the cat eats the raw fish".

$\{\mathrm{cat}(c), \mathrm{fish}(f_1), \mathrm{raw}(f_1), \mathrm{fish}(f_2), \mathrm{eats}(e, c, f_1)\}$ and the grammar in 1(a), CRISP could produce the derivation in 1(b). Notice that CRISP can generate the unambiguous referring expression 'the raw fish' for f_1, to distinguish it from f_2.

3.2 CRISP Planning Domains

Before we describe CRISP's encoding of sentence generation as planning, we briefly review AI planning in general. A planning state is a conjunction of first order literals describing relations between some individuals. A planning problem consist of an initial state, a set of goal states and a set of planning operators that describe possible state transitions. A *plan* is any sequence of actions (instantiated operators) that leads from the initial state to one of the goal states. Planning problems can be solved efficiently by general purpose planning systems such as FF (Hoffmann and Nebel, 2001).

In CRISP, planning states correspond to partial TAG derivations and record open substitution and adjunction sites, semantic individuals associated with them, and parts of the communicative goal that have not yet been expressed. The initial state also encodes the knowledge base and the communicative goal. Each planning operator contributes a new elementary tree to the derivation and at the same time can satisfy part of the communicative goal, as described in the previous section. In a goal state there are no open substitution sites left and all literals in the communicative goal have been expressed.

Fig. 2 shows planning operators for part of the

subst-t28-eats-S(u, x1, x2, x3):
Precond: referent(u, x1),
                subst(S, u), eats(x1, x2, x3)
Effect: ¬needtoexpr(pred-eats, x1, x2, x3),
                ¬subst(S, u),
                subst(NP, subj), subst(NP, obj),
                referent(subj, x2), referent(obj, x3)
                adj(VP, u), adj(V, u), adj(S, u)

subst-t3-cat-NP(u, x1):
Precond: referent(u, x1),
                subst(NP, u), cat(x1)
Effect: ¬needtoexpr(pred-cat, x1),
                ¬subst(NP, u),
                adj(N, u), adj(NP, u)

adj-t5-raw-N(u, x1):
Precond: referent(u, x1),
                adj(N, u), raw(x1)
Effect: ¬needtoexpr(pred-raw, x1),
                ¬adj(N, u)

Figure 2: CRISP operators for some of the elementary trees in Fig. 1.

grammar in Fig. 1(a). The operators are simplified for lack of space, and in particular we do not show the preconditions and effects that enforce uniqueness of referring expressions; see Koller and Stone (2007) for details. The preconditions of the operators require that a suitable open substitution node (i.e. of the correct category) or internal node for adjunction exists in the partial derivation. In the operator effect, open substitution nodes are closed and new identifiers are created for each substitution node and internal node in the new tree. Given the knowledge base from above, a plan corresponding to the derivation in

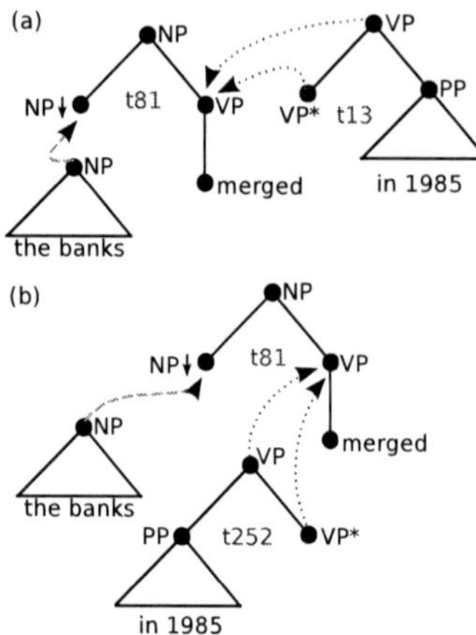

Figure 3: Two derivations with a large grammar, that satisfy the same communicative goal. Sentence (b) is dispreferred by most readers.

Fig. 1 would be subst-t28-eats-S-eats$(root, e, c, f_1)$; subst-t3-cat-NP$(subj, c)$; subst-t3-fish-NP(obj, f_1); adj-t5-raw-N(obj, f_1). This plan can be automatically decoded into a derivation tree for Fig. 1b.

3.3 CRISP and Large Grammars

Koller and Hoffmann (2010) report on experiments that show CRISP can generate sentences with the large-scale XTAG grammar (XTAG Research Group, 2001) quite efficiently. However, because CRISP has no notion of how "good" a generated sentence is compared to other grammatical alternatives, it will sometimes compute dispreferred sentences with large grammars. This is especially true for treebank-induced grammars, which tend to overgenerate and rely on statistical methods to rank good sentences highly. Fig. 3 illustrates this problem. Assuming a (treebank) grammar that includes trees for both right adjoining (t13) and left adjoining PPs (t252), both derivations (a) and (b) are *grammatical* derivations that satisfy the same communicative goal. However, most readers disprefer the reading in (b). Clearly, to use CRISP with such a grammar we need a method of distinguishing good derivations from bad ones.

4 Statistical Generation as Planning

We now extend CRISP to statistical generation (PCRISP). The basic idea is to add a statistical gram-

mar model while leaving the sentence generation mechanism untouched. This way we can select the highest scoring derivation which satisfies all constraints (grammaticality, expresses the communicative goal, uses unambiguous referring expressions, etc.).

As a straightforward probability model over LTAG derivations we choose probabilistic TAG (PTAG) (Resnik, 1992). Our choice of PTAG for sentence generation is motivated by a number of attractive properties. PTAG is lexicalized and therefore does not only assign probabilities to operations in the grammar (as for example plain PCFG), but also accounts for binary dependencies between words. Unlike n-gram models however, these co-occurrences are structured according to local syntactic context as a result of TAG's extended domain of locality. The probability model describes how the syntactic arguments of a word are typically filled. Furthermore, as TAG factors recursion from the domain of dependencies, the probability for core constructions remains the same independent of additional adjunctions. We review PTAG in section 4.1.

While we leave the basic sentence generation mechanism intact, we need to modify the concrete formulation of CRISP planning operators to accommodate bilexical dependencies. Likewise, we need to take the step from classical planning to *metric* planning systems which can use the probabilities. In metric planning (Fox and Long, 2002), planning actions can modify the value of numeric variables in addition to adding and deleting logical literals from the state. The goal state specifies constraints on this variable. In the simplest case the variable can only be increased by a static cost value in each action, and the goal state contains the objective to minimize the total cost. While systems such as Metric-FF (Hoffmann, 2003) do not guarantee optimality, they do generally offer good results. We address our encoding of sentence generation with PTAG as metric planning in section 4.2.

4.1 Probabilistic TAG

PTAG (Resnik, 1992) views TAG derivations as sequences of events of three types: initial events, substitution events, and adjunction events.

The probability distribution for initial events describes how likely it is to start any derivation with a given initial tree. It is defined over all initial trees $\alpha \in I$ with their possible lexicalizations $w \in W_\alpha$:

$$\sum_{\alpha \in I} \sum_{w \in W_\alpha} P_i(init(\alpha, w)) = 1$$

For substitution events, there is a probability distribution for each substitution node n of each elementary tree τ lexicalized with v, which describes how likely it is to substitute it with an initial tree α lexicalized with w.

$$\sum_{\alpha \in I} \sum_{w \in W_\alpha} P_s(subst(\tau, v, \alpha, w, n)) = 1$$

Similarly for each internal node there is a distribution that describes the probability to adjoin an auxiliary tree $\beta \in A$ lexicalized with w. In addition some probability mass is reserved for the event of not adjoining anything to such a node at all.

$$P_a(noadj(\tau, v, n)) +$$
$$\sum_{\beta \in A} \sum_{w \in W_\beta} P_a(adj(\tau, v, \beta, w, n)) = 1.$$

PTAG assumes that all events occur independently of each other. Therefore it defines the total probability for a derivation as the product of the probability of its individual events.

4.2 PCRISP Planning Domains

Using the definition of PTAG, we now reformulate the CRISP planning operators described in section 3.2. The independence assumption in PTAG allows us to continue to model each addition of a single elementary tree to the derivation (with a certain probability score). However, while CRISP planning operators can add an elementary tree to any site of the correct category, PTAG substitution and adjunction events are binary events between lexicalized trees at a specific node. We therefore adapt the literals that record open substitution and adjunction sites in partial derivations accordingly and create one operator for each node in each possible combination of lexicalized trees. Fig. 4 shows an example planning operator for each type.

Finally, we set the cost of an operator to be its negative log probability. For example

$$Cost(\text{subst-t3-cat-t28-eats-n1}) =$$
$$- \log P_s(subst(\text{t3}, \text{'cat'}, \text{t28}, \text{'eats'}, \text{n1}))).$$

subst-t3-cat-t28-eats-n1(u, x1):
Precond:	referent(u, x1),
	subst(t28-eats, n1, u), cat(x1)
Effect:	¬needtoexpr(pred-cat, x1),
	¬subst(t-28-eats, n1, u),
	adj(t3-cat, n2 u)
Cost:	4.3012

adj-t5-raw-t3-fish-n2(u, x1):
Precond:	referent(u, x1),
	adj(t28-eats,n2, u), raw(x1)
Effect:	¬needtoexpr(pred-raw, x1),
	¬adj(t-28-eats, n2, u)
Cost:	6.9076

init-t28-eats(u, x1, x2, x3):
Precond:	referent(u, x1),
	eats(x1, x2, x3)
Effect:	¬needtoexpr(pred-eats, x1, x2, x3),
	subst(t-28-eats, n1,subj), subst(t28-eats, n4,obj),
	adj(t-28-eats, n2, u), adj(t-28-eats, n3, u)
Cost:	8.5172

noadj-t28-eats-n3(u):
Precond:	adj(t-28-eats, n3,u)
Effect:	¬ adj(t-28-eats, n3, u)
Cost:	0.1054

Figure 4: Some PCRISP operators for the grammar from Fig. 1.

This way the plan which minimizes the sum of the costs of its actions corresponds to the TAG derivation with the highest probability.

4.3 Dealing with Data Sparseness

The event definition of PTAG is very-fine grained. Substitution and adjunction events depend on specific parent and child trees with specific lexicalizations and on a node in the parent tree, as illustrated in Fig. 5, B.1. When we estimate a probability model from training data, we cannot expect to observe evidence for all combinations of trees. Derivations that include such unseen events have zero probability and are therefore impossible. As we show in section 5, this gives rise to a massive data sparseness problem.

A straightforward way to deal with data sparseness is to drop all lexicalizations from event definitions, as illustrated in Fig. 5, A. Unfortunately this model no longer accounts for bilexical dependencies between words. Since our system has to add a lexicalized tree in each step, lexicalizations for this child tree should always be taken into account by the probability model, if available. Despite these drawbacks, we perform experiments with the unlexical-

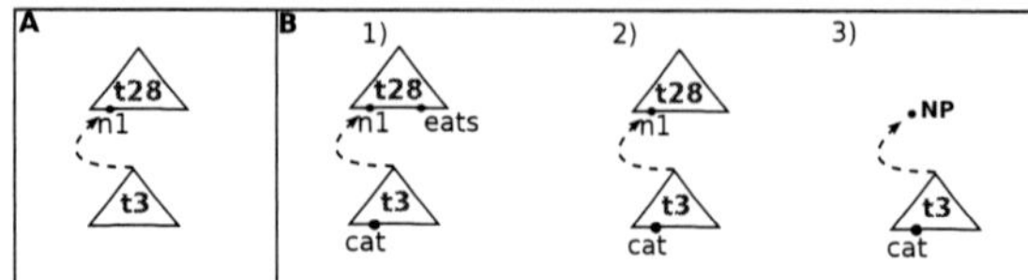

Figure 5: Illustration of the unlexicalized probability model (A) and the three back-off levels of the linear interpolation model (B).

ized model as a baseline. This allows us to investigate if purely syntactic information is sufficient to achieve high quality generation output.

An alternative model computes linear interpolation between three back-off levels. The first level is just standard PTAG (Fig. 5, B.1), for the second level the lexicalizations of the parent tree is dropped (Fig. 5, B.2), for the third level the model describes only the distribution of lexicalized child trees over each category (Fig. 5, B.3). Notice also that the third level is similar in spirit to a probabilistic version of original CRISP operators (compare Fig. 5, B.3 and Fig. 2).

5 Evaluation

We now report on some experiments with PCRISP. We are interested in the output quality and runtime behavior of different combinations of planning systems and probability models. Like CRISP, PCRISP is an integrated sentence generation system capable of generating referring expressions during surface realization. However, for lack of an appropriate evaluation dataset for full sentence generation, we only evaluate PCRISP on a realization task here. Further experiments and more details can be found in Bauer (2009).

5.1 Evaluation Data

For our experiments we use an LTAG grammar and treebank that was automatically extracted from the Wall Street Journal using the algorithm described by Chen and Shanker (2004).

This algorithm outputs a grammar that allows multiple adjunctions at the same node. For such a grammar PTAG is not a suitable probability model. Models that can deal with multiple adjunction are discussed by Nasr and Rambow (2006), but em-

ploying them would require non-trivial modifications to our encoding as a metric planning problem. We therefore preprocess the treebank by linearizing multiple adjunctions. Furthermore, we reattach prepositions to the trees they substitute in, to increase the expressiveness of the bilexical probability distribution.

We then automatically create semantic content for all lexicalized elementary trees by assigning a single semantic literal to each tree in the treebank, using the lexical anchor as the predicate symbol and variables for each substitution node and the 'self' role as arguments. We calculate the role associated with each node in each tree by assigning role names to each substitution node ('self' is assigned to the lexical anchor) and then percolating the roles up the tree, giving preference to the 'self' role.

We estimate our probability models on section 1 to 23 of the converted WSJ using maximum likelihood estimation. We use section 0 as a testing set. However, since the number of PCRISP operators grows quadratically with the grammar size, generating long sentences requires too much time to run batch experiments. We therefore restrict our evaluation to the 416 sentences in Section 0 that are shorter than 16 words.

For this testing set we automatically create semantic representation for each sentence, by instantiating the semantic content of each elementary tree used in its derivation. We use these representations as input for our system and compare the system output against the original sentence.

5.2 Generation tree accuracy

To evaluate the output quality of our statistical generation system we compare the system output O against the reference sentence R in the treebank from which the input representation was generated. We adopt the **generation tree accuracy** (GTA) measure discussed by (Bangalore et al., 2000). This measure is computed by first creating a list of all 'treelets' from the reference derivation tree D. A 'treelet' is a subtree consisting only of a node and its direct children. For each treelet we calculate the edit distance, sum the distances over all treelets and then divide by the total length of the reference string:

$$1 - \frac{\displaystyle\sum_{d \in treelets(D)} editDist(O|_d, R|_d)}{length(R)},$$

where D is the reference derivation tree and $S|_d$ are the tokens associated with the nodes of treelet d in the order they appear in S (if at all). Edit distance is modified to treat insertion-deletion pairs as single movement errors. Compared to a purely string-based metric like BLEU, GTA penalizes swapped words less harshly if they can be explained by local tree movements.

5.3 Results

Table 1 presents the results of the experiment for five different generation systems. We compare three variants of PCRISP: the fully lexicalized PTAG model ("PTAG"), the fully unlexicalized model ("unlexicalized"), and a linear interpolation model ("interpolation") in which we (manually) set the weight of level 2 to 0.9 and the weight of level 3 to 0. We also list results for the non-statistical CRISP system of Koller and Stone (2007) ("CRISP") and the greedy search heuristic used by SPUD. All these systems are based on a reimplementation of the FF planner (Hoffmann and Nebel, 2001), to which we added a search heuristic that takes action costs into account for the PCRISP systems.

For each system, we determine the proportion of sentences in the test set for which the system produced an output ("success"), did not find a plan ("fail"), and exceeded the five-minute timeout ("timeout"). The column "gta" records the mean generation tree accuracy for those sentences where the system produced an output.

The table confirms that the non-statistical CRISP system has considerable trouble reconstructing the original sentences from the treebank, with a mean GTA of 0.66. This is still better than our reimplementation of SPUD, which fails to recover from early mistakes of its greedy search heuristic for every single sentence in the test set.

By contrast, the fully lexicalized PCRISP model achieves a much better mean GTA. However, this comes at the cost of a very low success rate of only 10%, reflecting a serious data sparseness problem on unseen inputs. The data sparseness problem

System	gta	success	fail	timeout
SPUD	n/a	0%	100%	0%
CRISP	0.66	45%	42%	13%
PTAG	0.90	10%	88%	2%
unlexicalized	0.74	62%	16%	22%
interpolation	0.88	19%	74%	7%

Table 1: Results for the realization experiment.

is reduced in the unlexicalized version of PCRISP but this comes at the cost of decreased accuracy and much increased runtimes. The linear interpolation model strikes a balance between these two, by improving the success rate over the lexicalized model while sacrificing only a small amount of accuracy. This suggests that smoothing is a promising approach to balancing coverage, efficiency, and accuracy, but clearly further experimentation is needed to substantiate this.

6 Conclusion

We have described PCRISP, an approach to integrated sentence generation which can compute the best derivation according to a probabilistic TAG grammar. This brings two strands of research – statistical generation and integrated sentence planning and realization – together for the first time. Our generation algorithm operates by converting the generation problem into a metric planning problem and solving it with an off-the-shelf planner. An evaluation on the WSJ corpus reveals that PCRISP, like PTAG in general, is susceptible to data sparseness problems. Because the size of the planning problem is quadratic in the number of lexicalized trees in the grammar, current planning algorithms are also too slow to be used for longer sentences.

An obvious issue for future research is to apply improved smoothing techniques to deal with the data sparseness. Planning runtimes should be improved by further tweaking the exact planning problems we generate, and will benefit from any future improvements in metric planning. It is interesting to note that the extensions we made to CRISP to accommodate statistical generation here are compatible with recent work in which CRISP is applied to situated generation (Garoufi and Koller, 2010); we expect that this will be true for other future extensions to CRISP as well. Finally, we have only evaluated PCRISP on a surface realization problem in this paper. It would be interesting to carry out an extrinsic, task-based evaluation of PCRISP that also addresses sentence planning.

Acknowledgments. We are grateful to Owen Rambow for providing us with the Chen WSJ-TAG corpus and to Malte Helmert and Silvia Richter for their help with running LAMA, another metric planner with which we experimented. We thank Konstantina Garoufi and Owen Rambow for helpful discussions, and our reviewers for their insightful comments.

References

D. Appelt. 1985. *Planning English Sentences*. Cambridge University Press, New York, NY.

S. Bangalore and O. Rambow. 2000. Exploiting a probabilistic hierarchical model for generation. In *Proceedings of ACL-2000*.

S. Bangalore, O. Rambow, and S. Whittaker. 2000. Evaluation metrics for generation. In *Proceedings of INLG-2000*.

D. Bauer. 2009. Statistical natural language generation as planning. Master's thesis, Department of Computational Linguistics, Saarland University, Saarbrücken, Germany. `http://www.coli.uni-saarland.de/ ~dbauer/documents/MSc_Bauer2009.pdf`.

A. Belz. 2008. Automatic generation of weather forecast texts using comprehensive probabilistic generation-space models. *Natural Language Engineering*, 14(4):431–455.

J. Chen and V.K. Shanker. 2004. Automated extraction of TAGs from the Penn treebank. In Bunt H., J. Carrol, and G. Satta, editors, *New Developments in Parsing Technology*, pages 73–89. Kluwer, Norwell, MA.

M. Fox and D. Long. 2002. The third international planning competition: temporal and metric planning. In *Proceedings of the International Conference on Artificial Intelligence Planning and Scheduling (AIPS-02)*, pages 333–335.

K. Garoufi and A. Koller. 2010. Automated planning for situated natural language generation. In *Proceedings of ACL-2010*.

J. Hoffmann and B. Nebel. 2001. The FF planning system: fast plan generation through heuristic search. *Journal of Artificial Intelligence Research*, 14:253–302.

J. Hoffmann. 2003. The Metric-FF planning system: Translating "ignoring delete lists" to numeric state variables. *Journal of Artificial Intelligence Research*, 20:291–341.

E. Hovy. 1988. *Generating Natural Language Under Pragmatic Constraints*. Lawrence Erlbaum, Hillsdale, NJ.

K. Knight and V. Hatzivassiloglou. 1995. Two-level, many-paths generation. In *Proceedings of ACL-1995*.

A Koller and J. Hoffmann. 2010. Waking up a sleeping rabbit: On natural-language generation with FF. In *Proceedings of ICAPS-2010*.

A. Koller and M. Stone. 2007. Sentence generation as planning. In *Proceedings of ACL 2007*.

I. Langkilde and K. Knight. 1998. Generation that exploits corpus-based statistical knowledge. In *Proceedings of ACL-1998*.

I. Langkilde. 2000. Forest-based statistical sentence generation. In *Proceedings of NAACL-HLT 2000*.

A. Nasr and O. Rambow. 2006. Parsing with lexicalized probabilistic recursive transition networks. In *Finite State Methods and Natural Language Processing*, volume 4002 of *Lecture Notes in Computer Science*, pages 156–166. Springer.

Ehud Reiter and Robert Dale. 2000. *Building Natural Language Generation Systems*. Cambridge University Press, Cambridge, UK.

P. Resnik. 1992. Probabilistic tree-adjoining grammar as a framework for statistical natural language processing. In *Proceedings of COLING-1992*.

M. Stone and B. Webber. 1998. Textual economy through close coupling of syntax and semantics. In *Proceedings of INLG-98*.

M. Stone, C. Doran, B. Webber, T. Bleam, and M. Palmer. 2003. Microplanning with communicative intentions: The SPUD system. *Computational Intelligence*, 19(4):311–381.

M. White and J. Baldridge. 2003. Adapting chart realization to CCG. In *Proceedings of ENLG-2003*.

XTAG Research Group. 2001. A lexicalized tree adjoining grammar for english. Technical Report IRCS-01-03, IRCS, University of Pennsylvania.

H. Zhong and A. Stent. 2005. Building surface realizers automatically from corpora. *Proceedings of UC-NLG05*.

Cosubstitution, derivational locality, and quantifier scope[*]

Chris Barker
New York University
chris.barker@nyu.edu

Abstract

Quantifier scope challenges the mantra of Tree Adjoining Grammar (TAG) that all syntactic dependencies are local once syntactic recursion has been factored out. The reason is that on current TAG analyses, a quantifier and the furthest reaches of its scope domain are in general not part of any (unicomponent) elementary tree. In this paper, I consider a novel basic TAG operation called COSUBSTITUTION. In normal substitution, the root of one tree (the argument) replaces a matching non-terminal on the frontier of another tree (the functor). In cosubstitution, the syntactic result is the same, leaving weak and strong generative capacity unchanged, but the derivational and semantic roles are reversed: the embedded subtree is viewed as the functor, and the embedding matrix is viewed as its semantic argument, i.e., as its nuclear scope. On this view, a quantifier taking scope amounts to entering a derivation at the exact moment that its nuclear scope has been constructed. Thus the relationship of a quantifier and its scope is constrained by DERIVATIONAL LOCALITY rather than by elementary-tree locality.

1 Introduction

The main claim of the present paper is that among the major grammatical frameworks, Tree Adjoining Grammar (TAG) offers a uniquely simple and direct way to understand the relationship between a quantifier and its scope.

[*]Thanks to Robert Frank and Chung-chieh Shan.

There are at least two well-developed approaches to scope in TAG. One is due to Kallmeyer and Romero and their collaborators (e.g., Joshi, Kallmeyer and Romero 2008). They use Multi-Component TAG (MC-TAG), and emphasize semantic underspecification, so that a single derivation corresponds to multiple quantifier scope construals. Another approach due to Nesson and Shieber (e.g., 2006) uses a Synchronous TAG to relegate the multi-component part to the semantic side of the derivation.

The view here is not intended as a competing approach, so much as a competing perspective on what other accounts are already doing—an alternative conceptualization. However, there are some differences between the analyses that I will mention below.

The basic idea here relies on flexibility in the order in which the components of a TAG derivation combine. That is, substitutions and adjunctions can be interleaved and reordered with considerable freedom. This flexibility makes it possible to build a partial derivation that exactly corresponds to the material over which a quantifier takes scope:

(1) a. John left with no one.

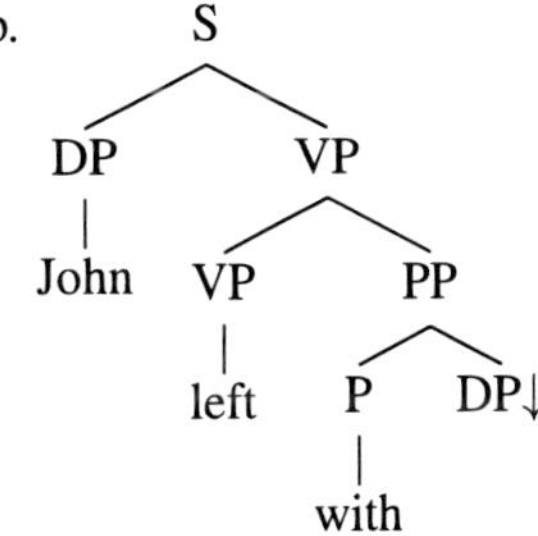

Normally, we might choose to substitute *no one* into

the auxiliary tree projected by *with*, and then adjoin the derived tree *with no one* at the VP node dominating *left*. But we might just as well adjoin the incomplete auxiliary tree first, resulting in the (still incomplete) tree in (1b). The point of interest is that this derivational constituent corresponds in a natural way to the nuclear scope of *no one*: just abstract over the substitution location to get the property λx.John-left-with x.

Thus the reason that managing scope in TAG is a challenge is that quantifiers and their scope domain are not local in the usual TAG sense. That is, it is not possible to factor out recursion in such a way that the quantifier and its scope are safely included within a single elementary tree. For instance, in (1), the quantifier never shares an elementary tree with the S node it take scope over.

Yet although quantifiers and their scope are not elementary-tree local, quantifiers and their scope are never discontinuous. At the end of a derivation, if we shade in the portion of the tree that corresponds to the material a quantifier takes scope over, it will always be a contiguous portion of the tree, and in addition, it will also immediately dominate (in general, surround) the quantifier.

Making sense out of the derivational approach considered here requires rethinking the tree-merging operation that combines the quantificational DP *no one* with its nuclear scope. Instead of regarding the quantifier DP as plugging a hole in the argument structure of *with*, we would like to reverse the roles, and think of the incomplete tree in (1b) as the semantic argument of the quantifier. Call this desired operation COSUBSTITUTION (details below).

If we allow cosubstitution as a basic TAG operation, we recognize quantificational scope as an example of a different kind of local dependency, namely, the dependence of a functor on its (co)substitution argument. The result is that we need to recognize two kinds of locality: structural locality, i.e., sharing the same elementary tree, and derivational locality, participating in the same derivational step.

The late substitution contemplated in (1) would not be innocent in a Multi-Component TAG. Allowing one component of a tree set to substitute into the lower DP position in (1) at the same time that another element (think: the scope-taking part) adjoins into the original initial tree is non-local, and allowing such non-local operations in MC-TAG increases its generative capacity. Therefore it's important that I'm considering ordinary TAG here, not MC-TAG. In some sense, of course, all analyses of quantifier scope are an attempt to simulate just this kind of non-local operation, as discussed further below.

Treating scope-taking as cosubstitution is a version of the continuation-based approaches to scope-taking of Barker 2002, de Groote 2001, and Bernardi and Moortgat 2010, among others. A continuation is (a portion of) the computational future of an expression. In (1), the computational future of the quantifier *no one* is that it will serve as the argument of the preposition *with*, and the result of that computation will serve to modify the verb phrase *left*, and so on. The central insight I'm aiming for in this paper is that in TAG, the computational future of a DP can be viewed as the same thing as its derivational past.

2 Preliminaries

2.1 Syntax

A Tree Adjoining Grammar is a finite set of elementary trees closed under two derivational operations: substitution and adjunction.

Elementary trees are finite ordered labeled trees. Nonterminals on the frontier of an elementary tree are substitution targets, and are decorated with a downarrow. Some elementary trees have a distinguished node on their frontiers called the FOOT (marked with a star) that match the root node in syntactic category. Such trees are auxiliary trees, and participate in adjunction.

Substitution: Nodes with downarrows on their labels can be replaced via substitution with any non-auxiliary tree whose root node has a matching label. The substitution operation amounts to replacing the target node with the root of the substitution tree.

(2)
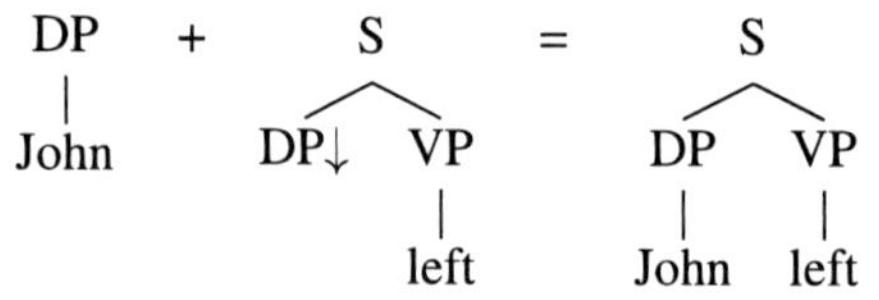

Adjunction: Interior nodes whose labels match the root label of an auxiliary tree can be adjunction targets. Adjunction is accomplished by replacing the adjunction target node with the root of the auxiliary tree, at the same time that the foot of the adjunction tree is replaced by the subtree rooted in the adjunction target node. In effect, the auxiliary tree is inserted into the tree at the adjunction target node.

(3)

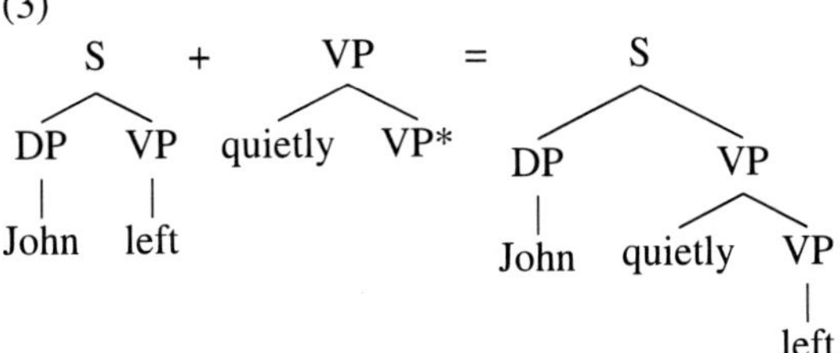

This is the familiar TAG story, simple and elegant. Technical details are available in may places, e.g., Joshi and Schabes 1997.

2.2 Semantics

I will use a Synchronous TAG (Shieber and Schabes 1990) to specify semantic representations. Instead of elementary trees, STAG uses pairs of elementary trees connected by a linking relation. Any operation targeting a node in the left element of a pair must be matched by a parallel operation targeting the linked node in the right element of the pair.

In general, then, STAG is a tree transduction system. Here, as in Nesson and Shieber 2006, each pair will be interpreted as the syntax and the corresponding semantics for an expression. The syntactic component will use syntactic categories for labels, and the semantic component will use semantic types for labels.

So for [syntax, semantics] pairs we might have:

(4)

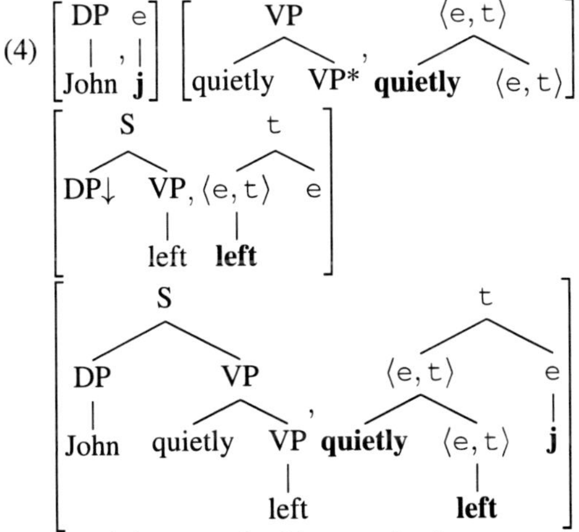

Not much happens in this transduction, except that the compositional order of the VP and the sub-

ject are reversed to conform to the conventions for function/argument order in the lambda calculus. Throughout the paper, I've left the linking relation between syntactic nodes and semantic nodes implicit, since the intended relation is particularly simple and, I hope, obvious.

3 Cosubstitution

The basic idea of using cosubstitution to handle scope is that we can build the nuclear scope of a quantifier before the quantifier enters the derivation.

In the normal substitution case, we have a tree t_1 containing a substitution target, that is, a node x whose label B is decorated with a downarrow. We also have a separate tree t_2 whose root r has a matching label, B. We replace x with r, and the tree rooted in r becomes a subtree of t_1 (first column of (5)).

In cosubstitution, we reverse the roles: now t_2 contains the (co)substitution target, (which can only be) the root node r. In recognition that the root is now a cosubstitution target, we annotate its label with an uparrow. As long as t_1 contains a frontier node x with a matching label (matching except that it is still decorated with a downarrow rather than an uparrow), cosubstitution may occur. Conceptually, we replace (only!) the target node r with x, and the tree footed in x becomes a supertree of t_2. (So the operation probably should be called "superstitution".)

(5)

Substitution: Cosubstitution:

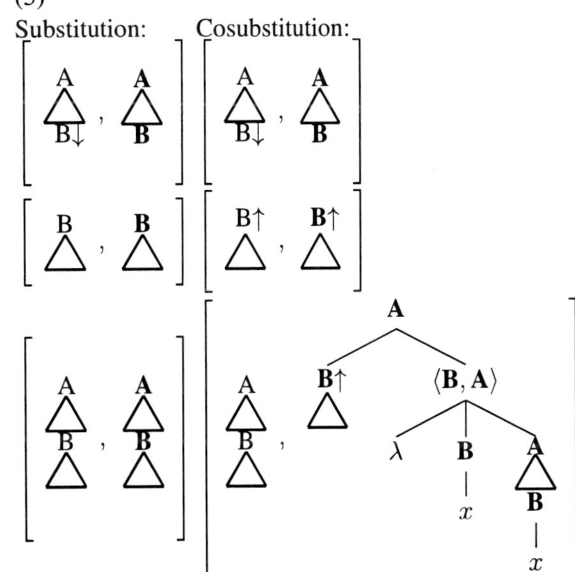

In the diagrams, bolded symbols (e.g., **A**) represent the semantic type of the corresponding syntactic category (A). In general, **A**↑ will be $\langle\langle\mathbf{A}, t\rangle, t\rangle$; in particular, **DP**↑ $= \langle\langle e, t\rangle, t\rangle$, the type of a generalized quantifier. I'll use **Q** as shorthand for $\langle\langle e, t\rangle, t\rangle$.

Note that the syntactic trees after substitution and after cosubstitution are identical. There is a difference in the semantics, however, since we must abstract over the substitution argument expression.

As usual (e.g., Nesson and Shieber 2006:5) the abstraction variable (in the diagram, x) should be chosen fresh with respect to all previous choices of abstraction variables in the derivation, though it may be identical with the translation of pronouns in order to accomplish quantificational binding.

In the simplest case, the cosubstitution argument is the lexical projection of a predicate.

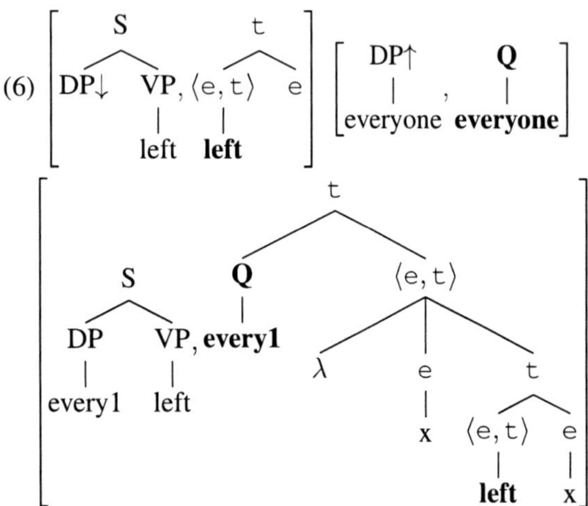

If **everyone** $= \lambda P \forall x.(Px)$, then the semantics for *everyone left* beta-reduces to $\forall x.(\mathbf{left}\ x)$.

In general, however, nuclear scopes can be complex, as in (1):

(7)

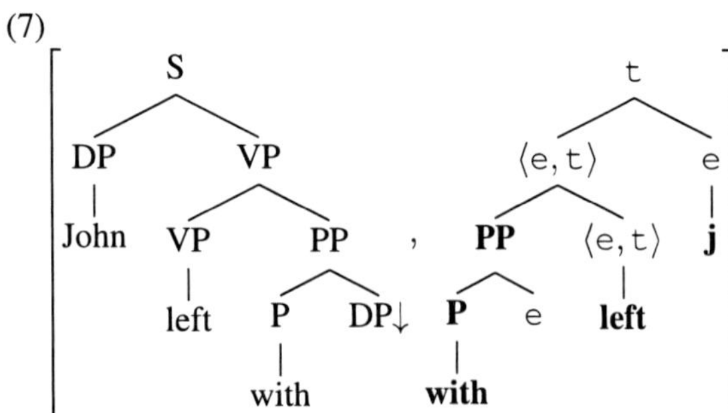

If we cosubstitute (7) onto the quantifier *no one*, we get **no one**$(\lambda x.(\mathbf{with}\ x\ \mathbf{left})\ \mathbf{j})$.

Thus the dependence of *no one* on its nuclear

scope is not local in the usual sense of forming part of the same elementary tree. However, it is derivationally local: the quantifier and its nuclear scope are the two participants in a single derivational step, a cosubstitution step.

4 Inverse scope

As in previous TAG work, inverse scope makes a good test case for illustrating how the system works.

(8) Some person from every city left.

Near the beginning of the derivation, *some person* undergoes cosubstitution with *left*, essentially as in (6). After adjunction with *from* at the NP node, we have:

(9) a. Some person from every city left.

b.

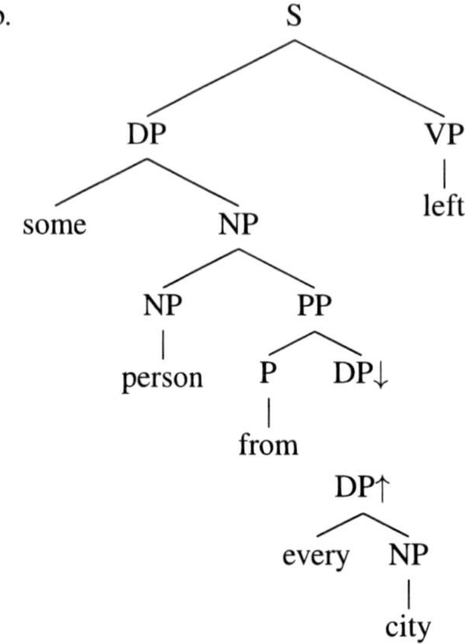

At this point, we have a cosubstitution opportunity for *every city* in which its scope corresponds to *Some person from __ left*.

In other words, the nuclear scope of a quantifier is quite simply and quite literally its syntactic and semantic argument.

The fact that the embedded quantifier has the entire verb phrase in its scope explains how it can bind a pronoun in the verb phrase, as in *Someone from every$_i$ city loves it$_i$*.

Getting the opposite scoping requires supposing that prepositions project structure at which a quantifier can take scope internal to the enclosing DP. This strategy is used by May 1985, Heim and Kratzer 1998, Barker and Shan 2006, among others, and, in the TAG literature, by Nesson and Shieber 2006. For the sake of concreteness, we can approximate this analysis (more work is needed to make it fully general) by allowing *from* to take a quantificational DP as its argument:

(10)

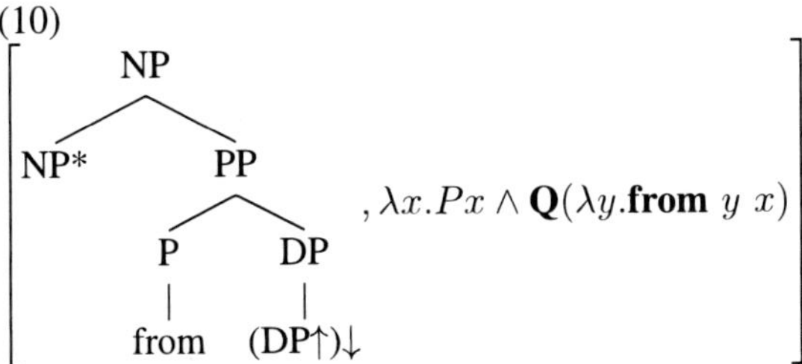

After substitution (not cosubstitution!), the generalized quantifier denoted by *every city* substitutes for the semantic non-terminal **Q**.

One advantage of this strategy is that when *some* takes scope over *every*, *every* has only the prepositional phrase in its scope, so it can't bind a pronoun in the verb phrase (this agrees with the facts).

A second advantage of this strategy is that whenever the scope of the embedded quantifier is trapped inside of the larger DP, there is no way for quantifiers external to the DP to intervene in scope between *some* and *every*.

(11) Two politicians spied on some person
         from every city.

The truth conditions of such a reading for (11) would require that there be some specific person from every city, a single pair of politicians, and at least one spying event for each city. As discussed in detail in Joshi, Kallmeyer and Romero 2008 and in Nesson and Shieber, there is a general consensus that this scoping should be ruled out by the grammar.

However, the system here does allow external quantifiers to intervene in scope between *some* and *every* on the inverse linking reading. That is, it is possible to cosubstitute the *spied on* tree onto *some person*, then cosubstitute the result onto *two politicians*, then cosubstitute the result of that operation onto *every city*, giving as a scoping *every > two > some*. As Nesson and Shieber note, there is less of a consensus on whether this reading should be considered ungrammatical. My position is that it is grammatical, but unusually hard to process.

5   Scope ambiguity and derivation trees

Thus on the cosubstitution approach, quantifier scope ambiguity is a matter of timing: quantifiers that enter later in the derivation take wider scope.

(12) Someone saw everyone.

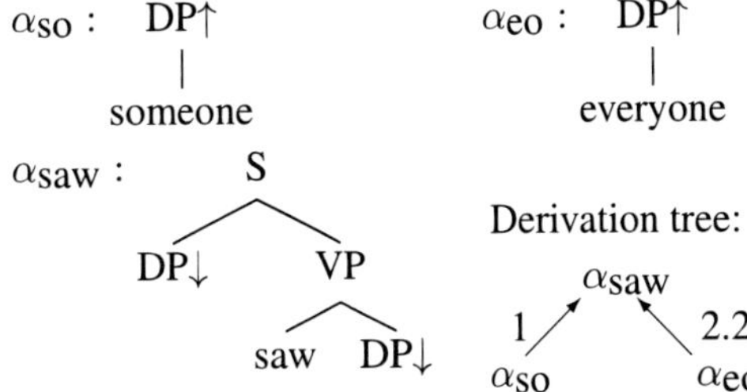

As Nesson and Shieber point out, if we use the usual kind of derivation tree, we end up with a derivation tree that does not disambiguate scope. In the derivation tree in (12), I have even added arrowheads to distinguish substitution (downward-pointing arrowhead) from cosubstitution (upward), but the derivation tree still does not reveal which quantifier takes wide scope.

(13) Linear scope:

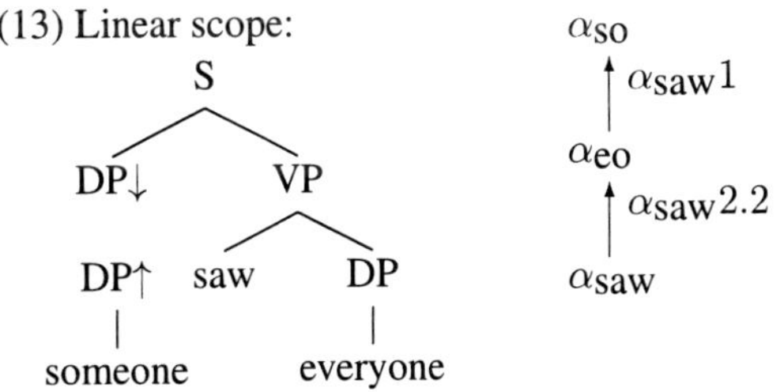

(14) Inverse scope:

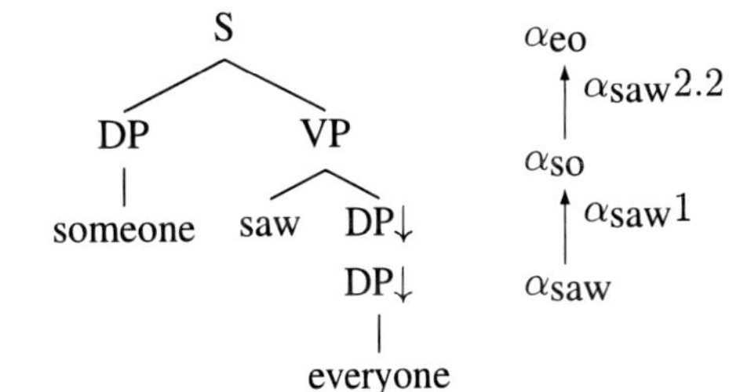

But if we take the conceptualization of cosubstitution seriously, we have to treat the derived scope as the argument of the quantifier. That means that the quantifier conceptually is the target for the cosubstitution. The correct derivation trees, then, have the quantifier dominating their nuclear scope.

These derivation trees contain full information about the order in which the quantifiers were added to the derivation, and which takes wider scope.

Usually, derivation links are labelled with the Gorn address of the substitution location. This is uninformative here, since the only possible cosubstitution location is the root of the cosubstitution target, whose Gorn address is always 0. Therefore I have labeled the cosubstitution links with the address of the node that cosubstitutes onto the cosubstitution target.

6 Comparison with other approaches

6.1 TAG approaches

In the MC-TAG approaches, quantifiers contribute a pair of trees to the derivation. One part corresponds to the visible DP, and the other corresponds to the scope-taking part. The scope-taking component floats upwards in the derivation until it finds the top of the scope domain. In the version of Kallmeyer and Romero and collaborators, the multiple components are part of the syntax: the scope part is a degenerate, single-node S tree that eventually attaches to the top of the scope domain. In the STAG version of Nesson and Shieber, the syntax contains a simple DP, and the multiple components are part of the semantics.

In both accounts, the scope-taking part of a quantifier must potentially remain unattached (i.e., part of one component in a tree set) over an unbounded number of TAG operations until the full scope domain is in view. To see this, note that in *A raindrop fell on the tire near the right corner of the hood of every car* there is a reading that entails that there is at least one raindrop-falling event per car. That means that it is possible for *every car* to take scope over the entire clause. Similar examples show that adjunctions (*on, near*) and substitutions (*of*) can be added between the quantifier and its scope without any grammatical limit.

The claim of the MC-TAG approach is that quantifiers and their scope domains are at most only tree-set local. Another way to interpret the MC-TAG analyses is to say that the relationship between a quantifier and its scope is local, but they are (at least temporarily) discontinuous, a kind of long-distance scrambling.

On the cosubstitution view here, the entire scope (*a raindrop fell on the tire near to the right corner of the hood of __*) is composed before the quantifier enters the derivation. There is no need to resort to multicomponent tree sets. The relationship between the quantifier and its scope is entirely local, since it is nothing more than the relationship between a predicate and its cosubstitution coargument.

6.2 Delimited continuations

In systems with delimited continuations (Felleisen 1988, Shan 2005, etc.), there are typically two elements: shift and reset (prompt). Shift is analogous to the uparrow used here to mark cosubstitution targets; it corresponds to the bottom of a scope domain. The reset marks the top of the scope domain. One common challenge in shift/reset systems is indexing occurrences of shift with matching occurrences of reset. In the TAG system here, there is no need for a separate reset element. Instead, the state of the derivation implicitly delimits the continuation that is captured by the uparrow (shift). The continuation will always contain the derivation up to the point at which the cosubstitution occurs, and we achieve delimitation without needing an explicit reset operator.

In other systems with delimited continuations such as Barker and Shan 2008, delimitation is accomplished by a system of optional typeshifting operators. Once again, the interleaving of the cosubstitution with the derivation makes typeshifting unnecessary here.

7 Generalized scope-taking

Most work in TAG semantics, including this paper so far, assumes that scope-taking elements all take scope over a sentence (S) and produce as a result a (quantified) sentence. More general scoping mechanisms allow these parameters to vary independently. Thus in Moortgat 1997, q(A,B,C) is a type that functions syntactically as an expression of type A, takes scope over a constituent of type B, and returns a result of type C, so the quantifiers discussed above would all be type q(DP, S, S). Barker and Shan 2008, Morrill et al. 2007, and others provide directly analogous general scope-taking categories.

This more general approach allows new kinds of linguistic analyses. For instance, I argue in Barker 2008 that in *two men with the same name*, the word *same* is a scope-taking quantifier that functions locally as an adjective and takes scope over a nominal, in this case, *men with the __ name*. Thus *same* has category q(Adj, NP, NP).

For a second instance due to Moortgat (in teaching materials circa 2000), in order to handle the bracketed phrase in *a book [the author of which] I know*, we can analyze *which* as having category q(DP, DP, RelPn): it behaves syntactically as a DP, it takes scope over a DP (the bracketed phrase), and the result functions as a relative pronoun.

It would probably be straightforward to allow existing TAG accounts to accommodate non-S scope targets, though perhaps at the cost of increased generative power. It is far from clear, however, how these accounts would allow scope-takers to return arbitrary result categories. This would require allowing a deeply embedded constituent to change the syntactic category of the constituent in which it is embedded.

The cosubstitution account here, however, was created with the general case in mind. We simply refine the definition of cosubstitution to require that if a cosubstitution target has category q(A,B,C), the surrounding cosubstitution argument must have category A on its foot, B on its root, and the result of the cosubstitution operation is treated as a tree of category C. Perhaps in the TAG tradition of split categories, the root of the resulting tree would have B as its lower category and C as its upper category.

8   Conclusions

A fully general system for scope-taking requires providing a scope-taking element with its delimited continuation. Derivational flexibility in TAG allows construction of delimited continuations on the fly. Adding the operation of cosubstitution as dual to substitution makes for a strikingly simple but fully general scope-taking system.

Still, after all is said and done, there is something multicomponent-ish about the cosubstitution approach. The semantics of cosubstitution expands the DP node on the frontier of the tree at the same time that it also adds semantic material at the top of the tree. As I mentioned, I don't view cosubstitution as a competitor to the MC-TAG approaches, but rather as a reconceptualization. Given that scope-taking requires associating distant locations in a tree, just what is the nature of the required dependency? Exactly what sort of multicomponent-ness is required? What expressive power is needed, and what extra generative capacity?

In the system as described above, the answer to the generative capacity question is simple. For every co-TAG grammar, there is an ordinary TAG grammar in which each root labeled X↑ is replaced with the label X. For every derivation in the co-TAG grammar, there is a derivation in the ordinary TAG grammar that generates the same tree with the same string. Furthermore, cosubstitution is defined in every situation in which ordinary substitution would be defined. As a result, syntactically, co-TAG is both weakly and strongly equivalent to TAG.

Of course, even though cosubstitution is defined when the root of the cosubstitution argument is not of type t (e.g., an S node), the lambda term constructed by the semantics may be ill-typed. In effect, we've only been interested so far in a subclass of derivations, the ones in which uparrowed constituents are combined with arguments rooted in S.

Building ill-typed lambda terms is clearly not satisfactory. However, it is easily fixed. We restrict the version of cosubstitution defined above to cases in which the cosubstitution argument is rooted in S, and we add two new cosubstitution definitions to cover cases in which the argument is rooted in some category A where A is distinct from S.

For the first new version, the syntax will be the same, except that now the category of the resulting derived tree will be A↑ instead of A. The semantics will be $\lambda\kappa\lambda\gamma.\mathbf{Q}(\lambda x.\gamma(\kappa x))$, where κ is a function of type $\langle \mathbf{B}, \mathbf{A}\rangle$, γ is a function of type $\langle \mathbf{A}, t\rangle$, $\mathbf{Q}$ is the semantics of the B↑ tree (and so has type $\langle\langle \mathbf{B}, t\rangle, t\rangle$), and x is a variable of type $\mathbf{B}$. This rule says that if a scope-taking element does not find its scope, it turns the constituent it combines with into a new scope-taking element. When this new, complex scope-taker finally finds its scope, meanings compose in such a way that the original scope-taker takes scope over the entire domain.

This rule in effect allows a scope-taking expression to combine bottom-up if desired, much in the way that the MC-TAG scope analyses work. In the full system, then, we can either accumulate a scope domain piecemeal, layer by layer, in the style of the MC-TAG analysis, or we can jump directly to the top layer in one swoop. See Barker 2007 for a discussion of a type-logical system in which these two conceptions of scope-taking coexist in a single grammar.

The second new version of the cosubstitution

rule covers cases in which the cosubstitution argument is rooted in a scope-taking category A↑ to begin with. This will happen if there are already scope-taking elements incorporated into the cosubstitution argument. In this case, the syntactic result is unchanged (A↑ again), and the semantics is $\lambda\kappa\lambda\gamma.\mathbf{Q}(\lambda x.(\kappa x)\,\gamma)$, where κ now has type $\langle\mathbf{B},\mathbf{A}{\uparrow}\rangle$. This rule gives the newest scope-taker scope over all of the other scope-taking elements already present in the (partial) domain.

As long as there aren't any initial trees rooted in S↑, or internal nodes with arrows, it is easy to see that the final co-TAG tree will have no arrows in it. Clearly, for every co-TAG derivation, there is a derivation in the corresponding de-arrowed TAG in which the final tree is identical, and vice-versa. Furthermore, with the new cosubstitution rules in place, every derviation in the co-TAG has a well-typed (and sensible) semantic interpretation. Finally, note that all TAG grammars are also co-TAG grammars.

In other words, co-TAG has exactly the same weak and strong generative capacity as TAG.

References

Barker, Chris. 2002. Continuations and the nature of quantification. *Natural Language Semantics* **10.3**: 211–242.

Barker, Chris. 2007. Direct Compositionality on Demand. In Chris Barker and Pauline Jacobson (eds). *Direct Compositionality*. Oxford University Press. 102–131.

Barker, Chris. 2008. Parasitic Scope. *Linguistics and Philosophy*. **30.4**: 407–444.

Barker, Chris, and Chung-chieh Shan. 2006. Types as graphs: continuations in Type Logical Grammar. *Journal of Logic, Language and Information* **15.4**: 331–370.

Barker, Chris, and Chung-chieh Shan. 2008. Donkey anaphora is in-scope binding. *Semantics and Pragmatics* **1.1**: 1–42.

Bernardi, Raffaella and Michael Moortgat. 2010. Continuation semantics for the Lambek-Grishin calculus. *Information and Computation* **208.5**: 397–416.

Felleisen, Mattias. 1988. The theory and practice of first-class prompts. In *Popl 88: Proceedings of the 15th acm sigplan-sigact symposium on principles of programming languages*. 180–190.

de Groote, P.: 2001, Continuations, type raising, and classical logic, in R. van Rooy and M. Stokhof (eds.), *Thirteenth Amsterdam Colloquium*, pp. 97–101. Institute for Logic, Language and Computation, Universiteit van Amsterdam.

Heim, Irene and Angelika Kratzer. 1998. *Semantics in Generative Grammar*. Blackwell.

Joshi, Aravind, Laura Kallmeyer, and Maribel Romero. 2008. Flexible composition in LTAG: quantifier scope and inverse linking. In H. Bunt and R. Muskens (eds). *Computing Meaning*, vol. 3, Springer. 233–256.

Joshi, Aravind and Yves Schabes. 1997. Tree-Adjoining Grammars. In *Handbook of Formal Languages, Beyond Words*, vol. 3. 69–123.

May, R.: 1985, *Logical Form: Its Structure and Derivation*, MIT Press, Cambridge, MA.

Morrill, Glyn, Mario Fadda and Oriol Valentn. 2007. Nondeterministic Discontinuous Lambek Calculus. In *Proceedings of the Seventh International Workshop on Computational Semantics, IWCS7*. Tilburg.

Nesson, Rebecca and Stuart Shieber. 2006. Simpler TAG semantics through synchronization. In *Proceedings of the 11th Conference on Formal Grammar*. CSLI.

Shan, Chung-chieh. 2005. *Linguistic side effects*. Harvard PhD.

Shieber, Stuart and Yves Schabes. 1990. Synchronous tree-adjoining grammars. In *Proceedings of the 13th International Conference on Computational Linguistics*, vol. 3, 253–258.

Binding Variables in English: An Analysis Using Delayed Tree Locality[*]

Dennis Ryan Storoshenko
Department of Linguistics
Simon Fraser University
8888 University Drive
Burnaby, BC V5A 1S6, Canada
dstorosh@sfu.ca

Chung-hye Han
Department of Linguistics
Simon Fraser University
8888 University Drive
Burnaby, BC V5A 1S6, Canada
chunghye@sfu.ca

Abstract

This paper presents an analysis of bound variable pronouns in English using Synchronous Tree Adjoining Grammar. Bound variables are represented as multi-component sets, composing in delayed tree-local derivations. We propose that the observed anti-locality restriction on English bound variables can be formalised in terms of a constraint on the delay in the composition of the bound variable multi-component set. While most cases are captured in a derivation making use of two simultaneous delays, maintaining weak equivalence with flexible composition, our analysis is open to derivations with an unlimited number of simultaneous delays.

1 Introduction

The English pronouns in (1a) and (1b) do not have the same function as referential pronouns. Instead, they function as bound variables, their references determined by the c-commanding antecedent. The relationship between the antecedent (binder) and the bound variable is difficult to capture in standard TAG, as the dependency between them is necessarily non-local. The predicate in (1a) intervenes between the variable and its binder, and this dependency is even further stretched in (1b) where two predicates intervene.

(1) a. Every girl$_i$ loves **her**$_i$ father.

   b. Every girl$_i$ knows that **she**$_i$ is smart.

To capture these cases, a TAG variant is needed which will allow for this type of non-local derivation without excessively increasing generative capacity. In this paper, we show that Delayed Tree-Local Multi-Component (MC) TAG, demonstrated

---

[*]We thank the anonymous reviewers of TAG+10 for their insightful comments. All remaining errors our ours. This work was partially supported by NSERC RGPIN/341442 to Han.

by Chiang and Scheffler (2008) to be weakly equivalent to standard TAG, permits exactly this kind of non-local derivation. We show that 2-delayed tree-local derivation is sufficient to handle core cases such as in (1), though a generalization to k-delayed tree-local derivation is needed to handle complicated cases where a bound variable is embedded in a DP that has another bound variable. Our analysis of bound variable anaphora in English also makes use of Synchronous Tree Adjoining Grammar (STAG) as formulated by Shieber (1994), augmented with syntactic feature agreement (Vijay-Shanker and Joshi, 1988). In Section 2, we show our analysis of the core cases such as (1a) and (1b). We then show, in Sections 3 and 4, how semantic and syntactic well-formedness constraints work together to rule out certain ungrammatical cases, and argue for the necessity of an anti-locality constraint based on the size of delays. In Section 5, we briefly discuss the cases that require generalization to k-delayed tree-local derivation.

2 The Analysis of Core Cases

Elementary trees for (1a) are presented in Figure 1. In the semantic trees, nodes are labelled as (T)erms, (R)elations, and (F)ormulae. Indices are included on substitution sites not only as a mark of syntactic movement, but also to identify substitution sites in derivation trees.

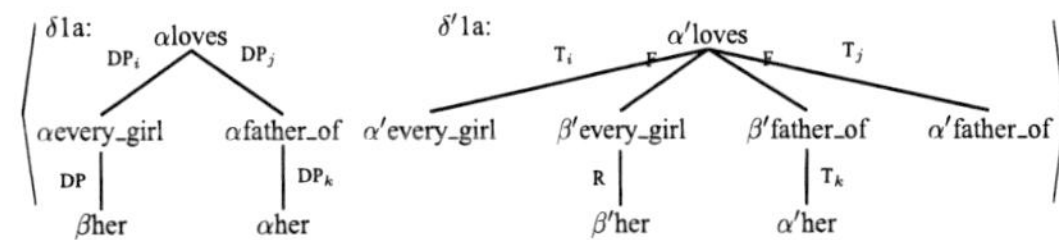

Figure 2: Derivation trees for *Every girl$_i$ loves her$_i$ father.*

Derivation trees for (1a) are shown in Figure 2. The syntactic tree (αevery_girl) treats the quantifier as a single DP, but crucially, the semantic side

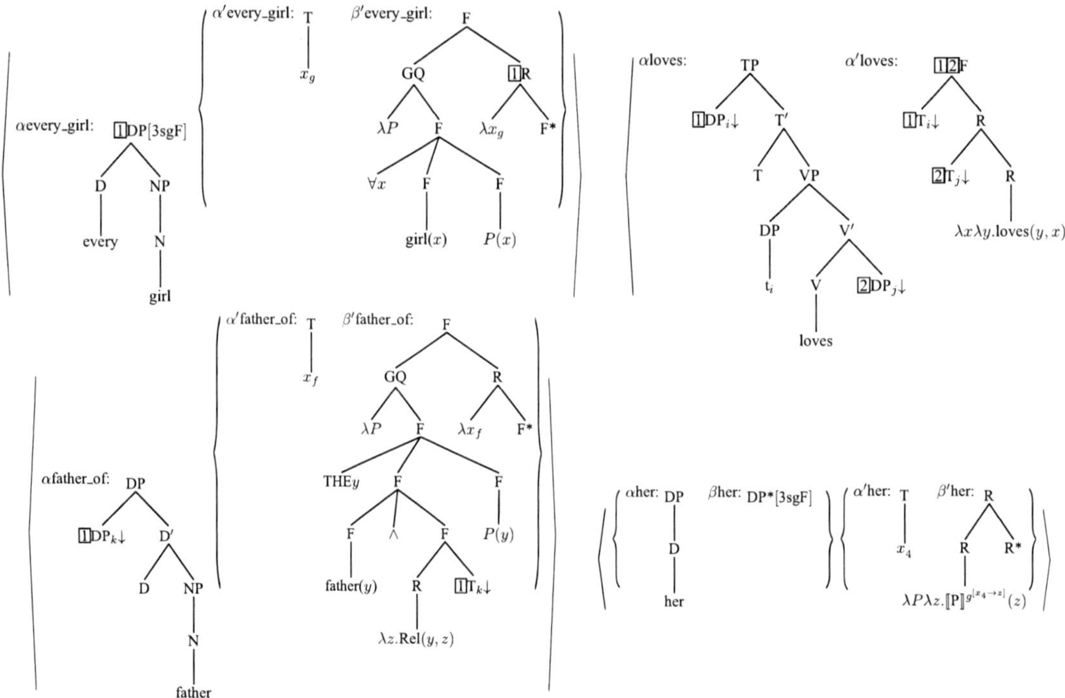

Figure 1: Elementary trees for *Every girl$_i$ loves her$_i$ father.*

is an MC set. (α'every_girl) is a variable which substitutes into an argument position in (α'loves). (β'every_girl) is an auxiliary tree which adjoins at the root of (α'loves), taking advantage of the multiple links (indicated by boxed numerals) between the syntax and semantics trees. A syntactic argument position links to two positions in the semantics: one for the argument variable, and another at the predicate's root where scope is calculated. In this way, isomorphism of the derivations is maintained despite one syntactic tree corresponding to an MC set in the semantics. (β'every_girl) presents a generalised quantifier (GQ) analysis (Barwise and Cooper, 1981), as implemented for STAG in Han et al. (2008). The trees for *father_of* are similar, implementing a GQ analysis for possession. Following Shieber and Schabes (1990) and Kallmeyer and Joshi (2003), we leave unspecified the order of adjoining for the scope portions of the GQs at the root of (α'loves). The possessor is the bound variable *her*, an MC tree set in both syntax and semantics. (αher) is a DP, which substitutes into (αfather_of). There is a defective auxiliary tree (βher) which adjoins at the root of (αevery_girl); syntactic agree-

ment is captured in the union of ϕ features at this adjoining site. The semantic side follows the same derivation: (α'her) substitutes into the linked argument position in (β'father_of), and (β'her) adjoins into (β'every_girl), between the GQ and the binder, λx_g. (β'her) contains a condensed representation of the binder index evaluation rule presented in Büring (2005), using one function to show both steps of altering the assignment function on the relation created by the binder portion of (β'every_girl), and then re-binding the remaining variable inside. This derivation is licit under the definition of 2-Delayed Tree-Local MC-TAG, in that there are no more than two simultaneous delays. Delays are defined as sets of derivation tree nodes along the shortest path between members of an MC set, excluding the lowest node dominating both members of the MC set. As shown in (2), there are three delays in the semantic derivation, but no one node in the derivation tree participates in more than two delays.

(2)   Delay for *every_girl*:
        $\{\alpha'$every_girl, β'every_girl$\}$
    Delay for *father_of*:

$\{\alpha' \text{father\_of}, \beta' \text{father\_of}\}$
Delay for *her*:
$\{\alpha' \text{her}, \beta' \text{her}, \beta' \text{father\_of}, \beta' \text{every\_girl}\}$

In the syntactic derivation, only one delay is present:

(3) Delay for *her*:
$\{\alpha \text{her}, \beta \text{her}, \alpha \text{father\_of}, \alpha \text{every\_girl}\}$

While this delay is not identical to the semantic one, it is set-isomorphic in that both delays for *her* contain members of the *father_of* and *every_girl* sets. The difference is that on the syntax side, composition of (βher) is with (αevery_girl) while (β'her) is composed with (β'every_girl), which has no equivalent in the syntax.

The final derived trees are shown in Figure 3. Recalling the ambiguous ordering of adjoining at the root of (α'loves), we only show the derived semantic tree for the ordering where (β'father_of) adjoins before (β'every_girl); though the alternate order is available, it results in the x_4 variable remaining unbound, and we assume this is blocked by a constraint against unbound variables. Semantic composition on the tree in (γ1a) yields the formula in (4), showing the binding relationship between *every girl* and *her*.

(4) $\forall x[\text{girl}(x)][\text{THE}y[\text{father}(y) \wedge \text{Rel}(y,x)][\text{loves}(x,y)]]$

A similar derivation is possible for the example in (1b), with additional trees shown in Figure 4. Following the derivation in Figure 5, we arrive at the derived trees in Figure 6. Again, the derivation has no more than two simultaneous delays. The final semantic form is shown in (5), and the expected variable binding comes through the derivation.

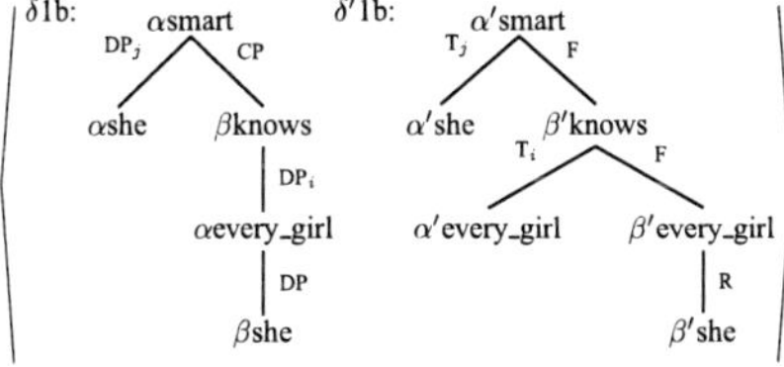

Figure 5: Derivation trees for *Every girl$_i$ knows that she$_i$ is smart.*

(5) $\forall x[\text{girl}(x)][\text{knows}(x, \text{smart}(x))]$

3 Blocking Spurious Derivations

There are some derivations which our analysis must block, shown in (6). For the case of (6a), the standard explanation is that the variable is not c-commanded by its quantifier. Making use of previously-presented elementary trees, the derivation of (6a) is shown in Figure 7.

(6) a. * **She**$_i$ thinks that every girl$_i$ is smart.

b. * Every girl$_i$ loves **her**$_i$

c. Every girl$_i$ loves **herself**$_i$

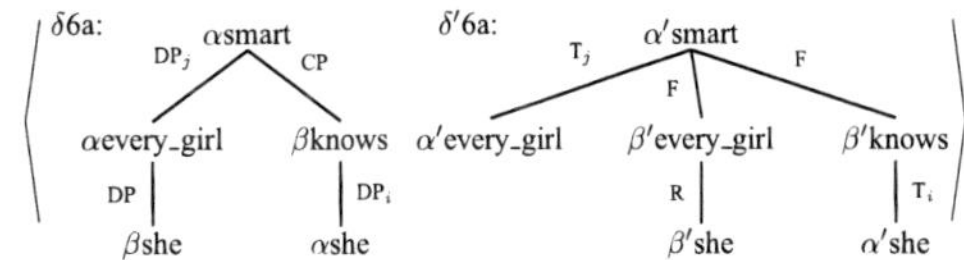

Figure 7: Derivation trees for *She$_i$ knows that every girl$_i$ is smart.*

Note that there is nothing about the derivation itself which blocks (6a): the same delays are observed as in (1b). However, performing semantic composition on the derived semantic tree in Figure 8 yields (7), which leaves the x_2 variable unbound, similar to the blocked derivation for (1a).

(7) $\text{thinks}(x_2, \forall x[\text{girl}(x)][\text{smart}(x)])$

The situation in (6b) is more complex. This example can be derived using familiar elementary trees, with derivation trees shown in Figure 9. The derived trees in Figure 10 result in the semantic form given in (8); all variables are bound, and the intended reading comes out, yet the example is ungrammatical.

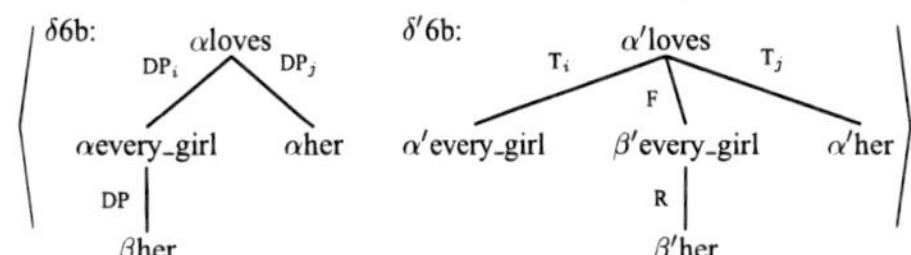

Figure 9: Derivation trees for *Every girl$_i$ loves her$_i$.*

(8) $\forall x[\text{girl}(x)][\text{loves}(x, x)]$

For this, we propose a constraint on the derivation itself, based on the delays. Nesson and Shieber (2009) propose that locality on MC sets can be measured in terms of the size of a delay. For all the previous examples, the cardinality of a delay for a

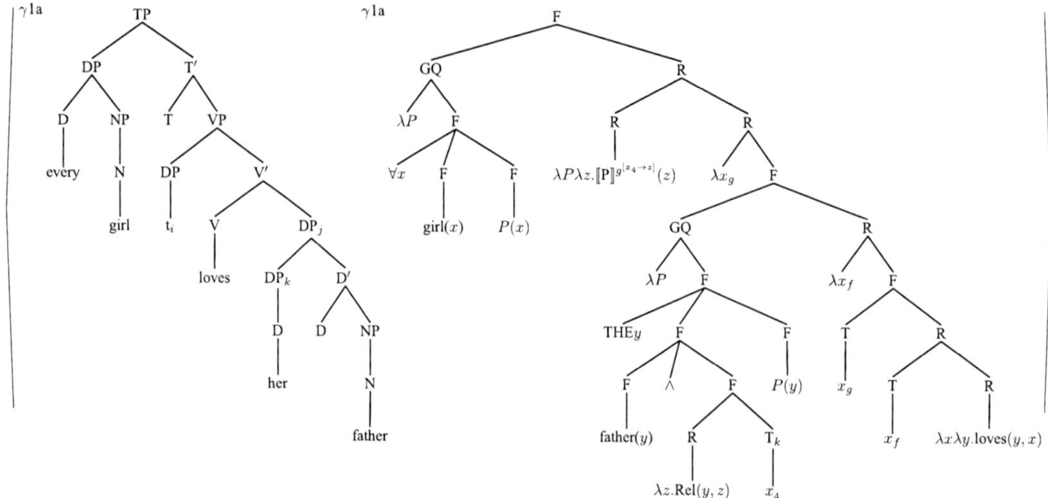

Figure 3: Derived trees for *Every girl$_i$ loves her$_i$ father.*

bound variable was at least four. For (6b), the delay is smaller, with a cardinality of only three. We thus propose a constraint on derivations containing bound variable trees in English: the cardinality of the delay of an MC set for a bound variable must be at least four, imposing a minimum distance between the variable and its antecedent. The grammatical equivalent of (6b), using a reflexive in (6c), can be captured with the analyses of either Frank (2008) or Storoshenko et al. (2008).

4 Capturing Crossover

In the literature on bound variable anaphora, a widely-known constraint is that against crossover, coming in two flavours, weak and strong. For both cases, the analysis is that an antecedent in a derived position binds a variable it did not originally c-command. Looking at the examples in (9), crossover will result after quantifier raising. In strong crossover, the variable c-commands the quantifier's base position, shown in (9a), but in weak crossover, the (9b) case, this is not so.

(9) a. * **She**$_i$ loves every girl$_i$

 b. * **Her**$_i$ father loves every girl$_i$

(9a), derived according to Figure 11, is semantically identical to (6b) after all composition has been completed on the derived trees in Figure 12. The same constraint on the delay will rule out this example, as the cardinality of the delay of the MC set for

the bound variable is again just three. Furthermore, Condition C, implemented for STAG, would rule out such an example.

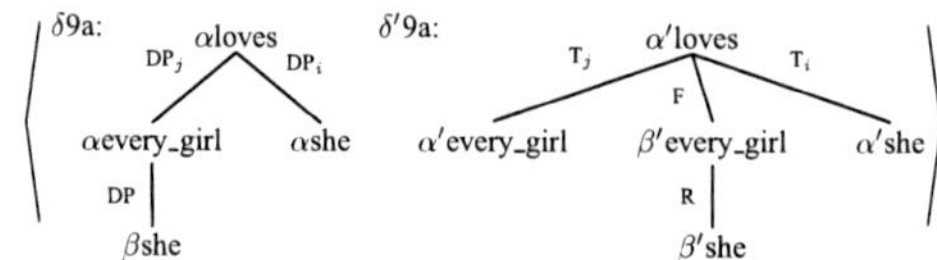

Figure 11: Derivation trees for **She$_i$ loves every girl$_i$.*

However, the same constraints will not account for (9b). Recalling the discussion of (1a), there are two possible derivations where there are two GQs, one of which leaves the variable contributed by (α'her) unbound. However, a perfectly legitimate derivation is possible, shown in Figure 13. This example cannot be blocked on the basis of the delay size constraint, as the delay of the MC set for the bound variable has a cardinality of four. Semantic composition from the derived trees in Figure 14 results in the semantic form in (10) with the variable bound, and the intended meaning intact.

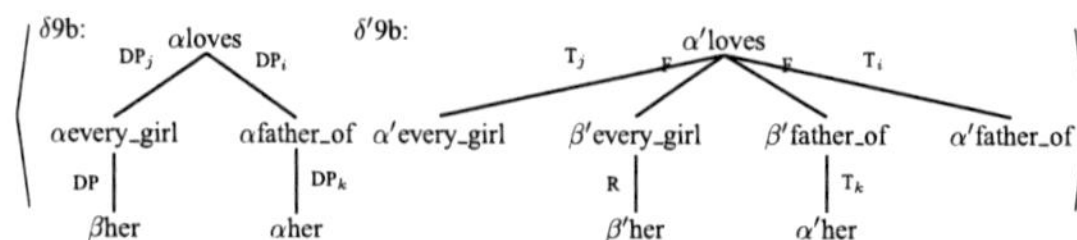

Figure 13: Derivation trees for **Her$_i$ father loves every girl$_i$.*

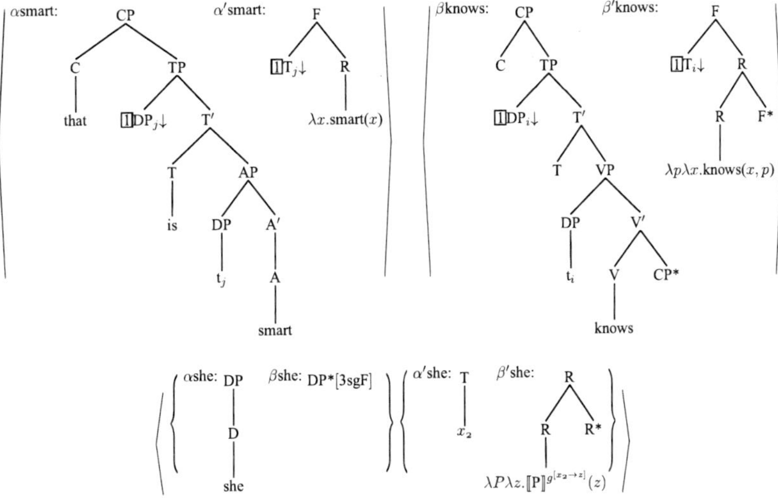

Figure 4: Additional elementary trees for *Every girl$_i$ knows that she$_i$ is smart.*

(10) $\forall x[\text{girl}(x)][\text{THE}y[\text{father}(y) \wedge \text{Rel}(y, x)][\text{loves}(y, x)]]$

To block this, we impose one final constraint on the syntax of the bound variable, a c-command constraint between the elementary trees of the bound variable MC set: in the derived syntactic tree, the defective DP* elementary tree must c-command the argument DP tree. In (9b), (βher) is adjoined at the root of (αevery_girl), while (αher) substitutes at a higher position in (αloves); the necessary c-command relation does not hold, ruling out this sentence. The same constraint will also rule out (9a), and it will likewise rule out (6a), both of which violated other constraints as well.

5   Complicated Cases

The examples presented in this paper so far have all been restricted to 2-delayed tree-local derivations. There are however examples which, if treated under our present analysis, will require more than 2 simultaneous delays in the derivation. These are cases where more than one bound variable is embedded in a DP, as in (11).[1]

(11)   a. Every girl$_i$ showed a boy$_j$ some picture of him$_j$ by her$_i$.

b. Every girl$_i$ told a boy$_j$ that some professor$_k$ liked a picture of him$_j$ that she$_i$ gave him$_k$.

For instance, as can be seen from the semantic derivation tree of (11a) in Figure 15, (α'some_picture_of) occurs in 3 delays, those of *some_picture_of*, *him* and *by_her*. And in (11b), it occurs in 4 delays, those of *some_picture_of*, *him$_j$*, *she*, and *him$_k$*. So, as the number of bound variables embedded in a DP increases, so does the number of simultaneous delays in the derivation. As embedding is in principle unbounded, we cannot put a formal bound on the number of simultaneous delays required to handle bound variables, though Tatjana Scheffler (p.c.) points out that the number of elementary trees will ultimately limit the number of delays in a given derivation—it's not the case that any one derivation will have an unbounded number of delays. Still, we speculate that as the number of simultaneous delays increases, so does the processing load in deriving the sentence. Speakers encountering a 4-delay example such as (11b) may have difficulty in reaching the desired interpretation.[2]

---

[1]Thanks to a TAG+10 reviewer for pointing this out to us and providing us with these examples.

[2]Chiang and Scheffler (2008) has shown that 2-delayed tree-local MC-TAG is weakly equivalent to MC-TAG with flexible composition. The existence of such examples as in (11) which require even further simultaneous delays can be argued to show that delayed tree local derivations are preferable to derivations using flexible composition in that they permit such sentences to be formed.

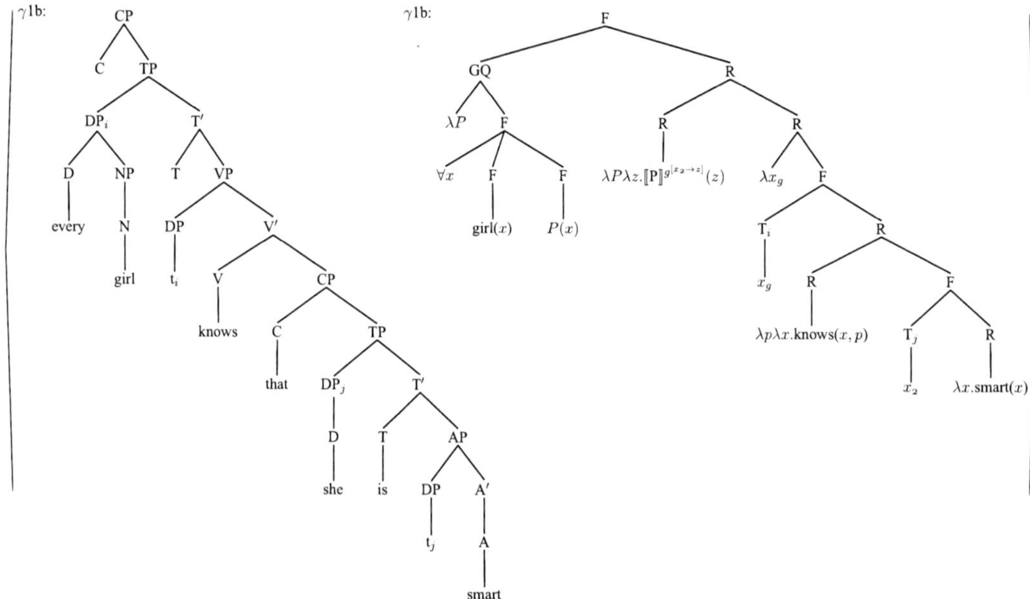

Figure 6: Derived trees for *Every girl$_i$ knows that she$_i$ is smart*.

6 Conclusion and Implications

In this paper, we have presented an analysis of bound variable anaphora for English in STAG. This analysis presents the bound variable as an MC set in the syntax and the semantics, and crucially makes use of delayed tree-locality in the derivation. We have proposed three different constraints on the derivations: a syntactic constraint which was necessary to rule out weak crossover, a semantic constraint against derivations with unbound variables, and a derivation constraint which enforces a degree of anti-locality, to account for the case where a reflexive must be used. While some derivations violate multiple constraints, each constraint is vital in ruling out at least one ungrammatical example. The syntactic and semantic constraints are quite standard in the literature on bound variables, and are relatively uncontroversial. In future work, we hope to explore possible parametric variation in the delay constraint, accounting for languages where bound variables are either more strictly local, or more flexible in their use than in English. Our analysis has not touched on co-referential, rather than bound, uses of English pronouns. These we assume to be captured under an STAG implementation of Condition B, possibly along the lines of the LTAG binding theory proposed in Champollion (2008). Finally, acknowledging that our present analysis requires a c-command constraint between the variable and its antecedent, we leave for future work English cases such as *Someone from every city$_i$ is proud of its$_i$ history*, in which a pronoun with a bound variable interpretation is not c-commanded by its antecedent.

References

Barwise, Jon, and Robin Cooper. 1981. Generalized quantifiers and natural language. *Linguistics and Philosophy* 4:159–219.

Büring, Daniel. 2005. *Binding theory*. Cambridge University Press.

Champollion, Lucas. 2008. Binding theory in LTAG. In *Proceedings of TAG+9*, 1–8.

Chiang, David, and Tatjana Scheffler. 2008. Flexible composition and delayed tree-locality. In *Proceedings of TAG+9*, 17–24.

Frank, Robert. 2008. Reflexives and TAG semantics. In *Proceedings of TAG+9*, 97–104.

Han, Chung-hye, David Potter, and Dennis Ryan Storoshenko. 2008. Compositional semantics of coordination using Synchronous Tree Adjoining Grammar. In *Proceedings of TAG+9*, 33–41.

Kallmeyer, Laura, and Aravind K. Joshi. 2003. Fac-

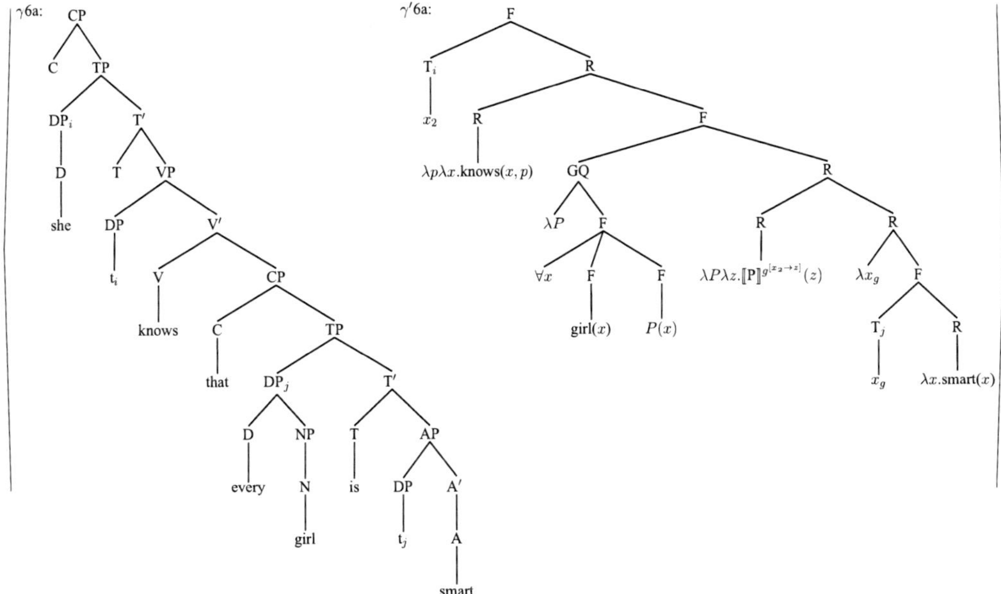

Figure 8: Derived trees for *She$_i$ knows that every girl$_i$ is smart.*

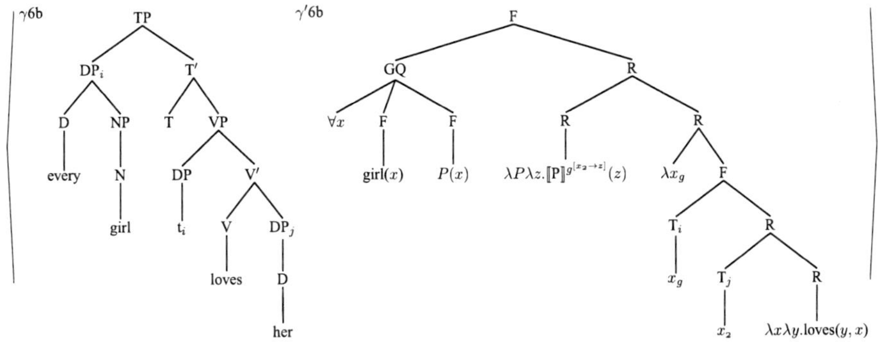

Figure 10: Derived trees for *Every girl$_i$ loves her$_i$.*

toring predicate argument and scope semantics: Underspecified semantics with LTAG. *Research on Language and Computation* 1:3–58.

Nesson, Rebecca, and Stuart M. Shieber. 2009. Efficiently parsable extensions to Tree-Local Multicomponent TAG. In *Proceedings of NAACL 2009*, 92–100.

Shieber, Stuart, and Yves Schabes. 1990. Synchronous Tree Adjoining Grammars. In *Proceedings of COLING'90*, 253–258.

Shieber, Stuart M. 1994. Restricting the weak generative capacity of Synchronous Tree Adjoining Grammars. *Computational Intelligence* 10:371–385.

Storoshenko, Dennis Ryan, Chung-hye Han, and David Potter. 2008. Reflexivity in English: An STAG analysis. In *Proceedings of TAG+9*, 149–157.

Vijay-Shanker, K., and Aravind Joshi. 1988. Feature structure based Tree Adjoining Grammars. In *Proceedings of COLING'88*, 714–719.

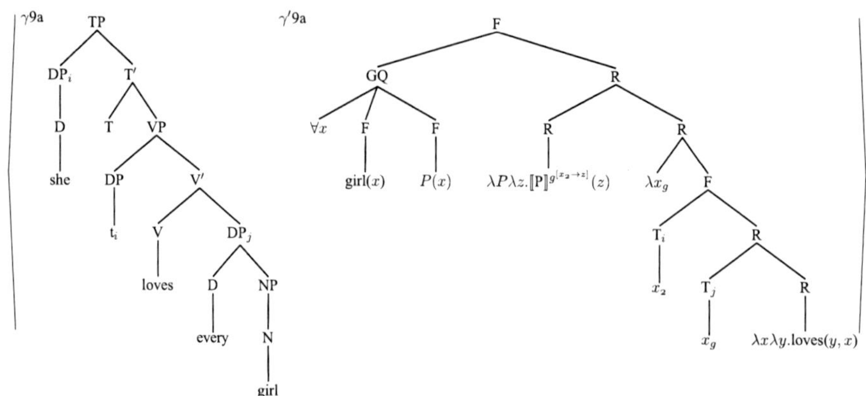

Figure 12: Derived trees for *She_i loves every girl_i*.

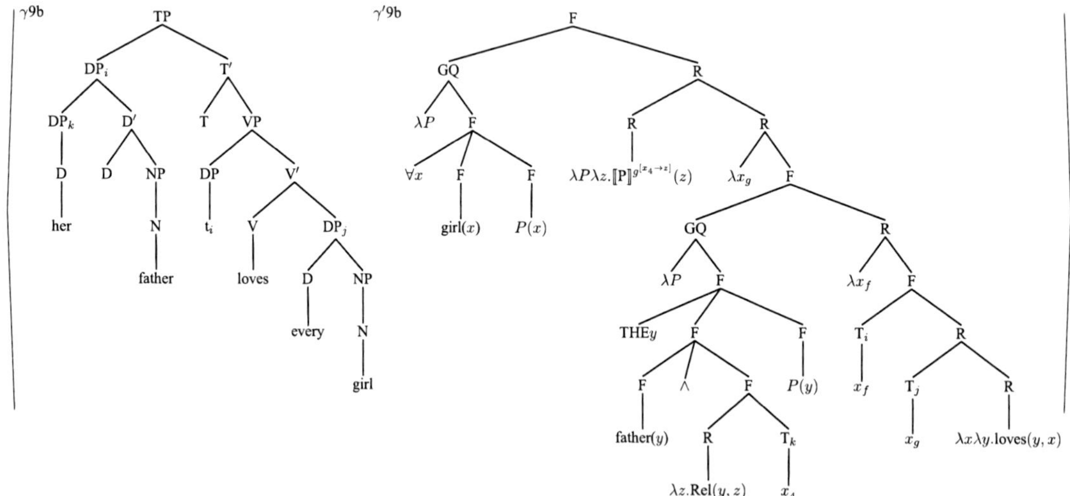

Figure 14: Derived trees for *Her_i father loves every girl_i*.

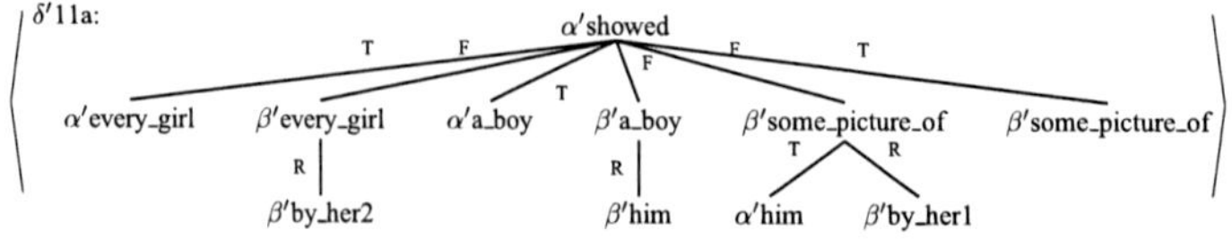

Figure 15: Semantic derivation tree for *Every girl_i showed a boy_j some picture of him_j by her_i*

TAG Analysis of Turkish Long Distance Dependencies

Elif Eyigöz
University of Rochester
Computer Studies Bldg.
Rochester, NY 14627, USA
eyigoz@cs.rochester.edu

Abstract

All permutations of a two level embedding sentence in Turkish is analyzed, in order to develop an LTAG grammar that can account for Turkish long distance dependencies. The fact that Turkish allows only long distance topicalization and extraposition is shown to be connected to a condition -the coherence condition- that draws the boundary between the acceptable and inacceptable permutations of the five word sentence under investigation. The LTAG grammar for this fragment of Turkish has two levels: the first level assumes lexicalized and linguistically appropriate elementary trees, where as the second level assumes elementary trees that are derived from the elementary trees of the first level, and are not lexicalized.

1 Introduction

The formal power of lexicalized TAG (LTAG) (Joshi et al., 1975; Schabes et al., 1988; Schabes, 1990) is adequate to assign appropriate structural descriptions to Turkish long distance scrambling. This provides an uncomplicated ground for the investigation of the mechanisms behind long distance scrambling in Turkish. In this paper, all permutations of a five word two level embedding structure are analyzed and an LTAG grammar is developed for this fragment of Turkish. Sentences involving scrambling from more than two levels of embedding are difficult to interpret, therefore the optimum compromise between the complexity of the structure and the validity of the analysis is determined by restricting the number of the words in the structure under investigation, which as a result limits the number of permutations to a manageable quantity.

The use of the adjunction operation to explain several linguistic phenomena such as raising, extraction, and long distance dependencies has been demonstrated in (Kroch and Joshi, 1985; Kroch and Joshi, 1987; Kroch and Baltin, 1989; Frank, 2000; Frank, 1992). However, it has been shown that German long distance scrambling can not be adequately described within the framework of lexicalized TAGs, as elements from subordinate clauses can scramble to any position in the matrix clause in German (Becker et al., 1991; Becker et al., 1992; Rambow, 1994). As a consequence, multi-component TAG (MC-TAG) (Weir, 1988; Becker et al., 1991; Rambow, 1994) grammars have been proposed for German and Korean scrambling (Rambow and Lee, 1994). Since Turkish, unlike German, allows only long distance topicalization and long distance extraposition, the formal power of LTAG is adequate to explain Turkish long distance dependencies.

The detailed analysis of the two level embedding sentence in section 2 brings forth a condition -the coherence condition- that draws the boundary between the acceptable and inacceptable permutations of the five word sentence. The LTAG grammar for this fragment of Turkish developed in section 3 and 4 serves multiple purposes. First, it was complied into a linear indexed grammar as explained in (Schabes and Shieber, 1992), and parsed with a parser written in Prolog (Shieber et al., 1995). Second, it shows that the set of derivations can be meaningfully partitioned according to the coherence condition. Finally, it reveals a connection between the coherence condition and the semantic function of long distance scrambling in Turkish.[1]

2 Turkish Long Distance Scrambling

Turkish is an head-final SOV language. Yet, there is no restriction on the order of arguments and adjuncts of simple sentences, as long as they are not referentially dependent and the sentence does not contain non-specific NPs or WH-phrases (Kural, 1992). Scrambling in Turkish causes different semantic interpretations. Scrambling to the sentence initial position marks the constituent as the *topic*, the immediately preverbal position marks it as the *focus*, and the post-verbal position as the *background* information (Ergüvanlı, 1984). Scrambling of case marked

---

[1]Following the literature on the free word order phenomena in Turkish, the term *scrambling*, in this paper, refers to any word order variation from the unmarked word order.

arguments and adjuncts out of subordinate clauses to sentence initial and sentence final positions, i.e. long distance topicalization and extraposition are also grammatical. Long distance scrambling to positions other than these two, i.e. scrambling without a *semantic function* is unnatural, and is considered ungrammatical.

This section gives an analysis of the two level embedding structure in (1) to determine the grammatical, acceptable and inacceptable permutations this five word sentence. This structure has two subordinate clauses, the subject positions of which are empty.[2] The sentence has two noun phrases: the most embedded verb has an NP complement *NP3*, and the matrix sentence has an NP subject *NP1*. The matrix verb *V1* has an infinitival complement (INF) with an ablative case (ABL). Likewise, *V2* has a verbal noun (VN) complement with accusative case (ACC). The most embedded verb *V3* has an NP complement with accusative case (ACC).[3]

(1) **Unmarked Order**

Mary çocukları   susturmayı   denemekten
Mary children-ACC silence-VN-ACC try-INF-ABL
yoruldu.
tired-PAST

'Mary is tired of trying to silence the children.'
NP1 NP3 V3 V2 V1

(2) *Çocukları*   Mary susturmayı   denemekten
children-ACC Mary silence-VN-ACC try-INF-ABL
yoruldu.
tired-PAST

[NP3] NP1 V3 V2 V1

(3) Mary susturmayı   denemekten yoruldu
Mary silence-VN-ACC try-INF-ABL   tired-PAST
çocukları.
children-ACC

NP1 V3 V2 V1 [NP3]

(4) ? *Çocukları   susturmayı*   Mary denemekten
children-ACC silence-VN-ACC Mary try-INF-ABL
yoruldu.
tired-PAST

[NP3 V3] NP1 V2 V1

(5) ? Mary denemekten yoruldu *çocukları*
Mary try-INF-ABL   tired-PAST *children-ACC*
susturmayı.
silence-VN-ACC

NP1 V2 V1 [NP3 V3]

The most embedded argument *NP3* is long distance topicalized in (2), and is long distance extraposed in (3). *[NP3 V3]*, which is the complement of *V2*, is long distance topicalized in (4) and is long distance extraposed in (5).

(6) shows an ungrammatical sentence in which *NP3* extraposes and *V3* topicalizes. If *NP3*, *V2* and *V3* are separated into three as in (6), then the sentence not only becomes ungrammatical but also becomes inacceptable. Such a sentence is not more informative than a 'word salad' with respect to pragmatic inference. The coherence condition in (7) is proposed to rule out such inacceptable sentences.

(6) * *uğraşmaktan* Mary *bırakmaya* bıktı
try-INF-ABL   Mary quit-VN-DAT tire-PAST-3SG
Sigarayı.
Cigarette-ACC

[V3] NP1 [V2] V1 [NP3]

'Mary is tired of trying to quit smoking.'

(7) *The Coherence Condition*
In acceptable sentences, [[NP3 V3] V2] is separated as [NP3 V3] - V2 or NP3 - [V3 V2].

It is not the case that all sentences that do not violate the coherence condition are grammatical. The sentence in (8a) exemplify long distance topicalization of *NP3* when *[V3 V2]* is extraposed. Similarly in (8b), *[NP3 V3]* is topicalized and *V2* is extraposed. In both cases, an element of a subordinate clause is topicalized when its verb is extraposed, which results in an ungrammatical sentence.

(8) a. *? *Çocukları*   Mary yoruldu
children-ACC Mary tired-PAST
susturmaya   uğraşmaktan.
silence-VN-DAT try-INF-ABL

[NP3] NP1 V1 [V3 V2]

b. *? *Çocukları   susturmaya*   Mary
children-ACC silence-VN-ACC Mary
yoruldu *uğraşmaktan.*
tired-PAST try-INF-ABL

[NP3 V3] NP1 V1 [V2]

Since Turkish is a head-final language, embedding a sentence inside another one creates a center embedding structure. Moreover, long distance scrambling creates center embedding with crossing dependencies. Psycholinguistics studies indicate that such sentences in-

---

[2]Since the discussion on long distance scrambling does not hinge upon the existence of the silent PRO, it is left out in the analysis for the sake of the clarity of the presentation.

[3]The analysis proposed in this paper is independent of the choice of the verbs, the case markers on their complements, and the type of subordination. The analysis is intended to explain the least pragmatically restricted cases, the sentences that in fact can undergo long distance scrambling described in this work.

1	Long Distance Left Scrambling of NP3	• NP3 • [V3 V2]
	Long Distance Left Scrambling of [NP3 V3]	• [NP3 V3] • V2
2	Long Distance Right Scrambling of NP3	[V3 V2] NP3 • •
		[V3 V2] • NP3 •
		• [V3 V2] NP3 •
	Long Distance Right Scrambling of [NP3 V3]	V2 • [NP3 V3]•
3	Local Extraposition of [NP3 V3]	• V2 [NP3 V3] •
		V2 [NP3 V3] • •

Table 1: Permutations without a Semantic Function

crease processing load, which results in low acceptability judgments associated with these sentences. As indicated with the judgment '?' for (4) and (5), long distance topicalization and extraposition of *[V3 V2]* is more marked than long distance topicalization and extraposition of *NP3*.

Both the tendency to group the verbs as *[V3 V2 V1]*, and the coherence condition are reminiscent of the 'clause union' account of German and Dutch verb constructions (Evers, 1975). According to the 'clause union' hypothesis, verbs undergo a process by which they form a single complex verb. Similarly, the coherence condition seems to collapse the two level embedding structure into a one level embedding structure by either combining the *[V3 V2]* into one complex verb, or freezing *[NP3 V3]* as one complex object.

2.1 Semantic Function of Scrambling

Among the 120 permutations of the sentence in (1), only 42 word orders do not violate the coherence condition. However, 16 more sentences have to be ruled out because scrambling without a semantic function, i.e scrambling to positions other than the sentence initial *topic* and sentence final *background* positions is ungrammatical in Turkish. Therefore, only 26 out of 120 word orders are left to be accounted for.

The word orders that have to be ruled out are given in Table 1. The • shows the positions of the two elements of the matrix clause. In row one, a constituent from a subordinate clause is scrambled to the left, but it is not at the sentence initial position. In row two, a constituent from a subordinate clause is scrambled to the right, but it is not at the sentence final position. In row three, *[NP3 V3]* undergoes local extraposition.

The following section presents an LTAG grammar for the word orders that do not violate the coherence condition *and* involve scrambling with a semantic function. The grammar, through the adjunction operation, reveals a relation between the coherence condition and the semantic function of long distance scrambling. However, local extraposition cannot be related to the coherence condition in the same way, because derivation of local extraposition does not involve the adjunction operation.

Moreover, local extraposition of the subject in a one level embedding sentence is grammatical, as exemplified below. (9) shows the unmarked order. *S1* refers to the subject of the matrix clause, *S2* to the subject of the embedded clause, *O2* to the object of the embedded clause, *V1* and *V2* to the verbs of the matrix and the embedded clauses respectively. *S2* is extraposed in (10). Local extraposition of the subject in a subordinate clause places the subject in the preverbal *focus* position of the matrix clause, therefore it is not semantically vacuous. Local extraposition of a direct object in a subordinate clause, however, may be semantically vacuous because the object is already in a preverbal focus position at its base position.

(9)　Elif Ali'nin Ankara'dan geldiğini
　　Elif Ali-GEN Ankara-ABL come-NOM-P2SG-ACC
　　biliyor.
　　know-PROG
　　S1 [S2 O2 V2] V1
　　'Elif knows that Ali came from Ankara.'

(10)　Elif Ankara'dan geldiğini　　　　　Ali'nin
　　Elif Ankara-ABL come-NOM-P2SG-ACC Ali-GEN
　　biliyor.
　　know-PROG
　　S1 [O2 V2 S2] V1
　　'Elif knows that Ali came from Ankara.'

Since local extraposition is ungrammatical in the structure under investigation, the sentences in row three of Table 1 are omitted in the LTAG grammar developed in the following section.

	SOV	OSV	OVS	SVO	VSO	VOS
V2-0 V3-0 Unmarked	√	√	√	√	√	√
V2-0 V3-1 Topicalization of [NP3]	√	SE	SE	A	A	A
V2-0 R3-1 Extraposition of [NP3]	√	A	A	A	A	A
V2-1 V3-0 Topicalization of [NP3 V3]	√	SE	SE	A	A	A
R2-1 V3-0 Extraposition of [NP3 V3]	√	A	A	A	A	A

Table 2: The summary of the 26 legitimate derivations

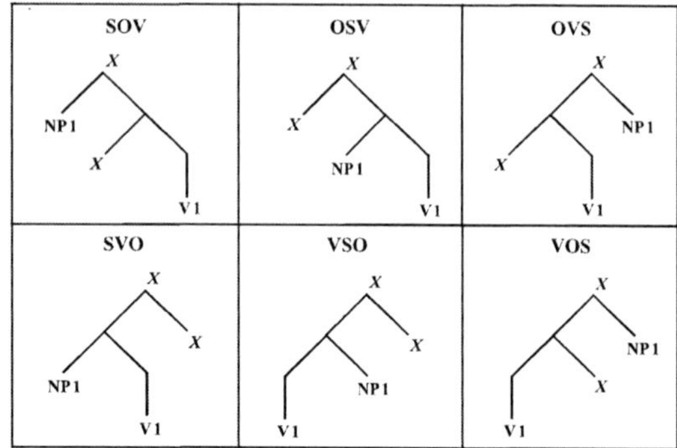

Figure 1: Elementary Matrix Trees

Figure 2: Elementary Trees

3   LTAG Grammar

The elementary structures that participate in the derivation of the two level embedding sentence are the clausal trees shown in Figure 1 and 2. Figure 1 and 2 show all word orders for each clause, only one of which participates in the derivation. The initial tree is the tree of the most subordinate clause, which is headed by *V3*. The two possibilities for the initial tree are shown in Figure 2: the head-initial tree is represented as 'R3', the head-final tree as 'V3'. Likewise, the head-final and head-initial auxiliary trees headed by *V2* are shown in 2. The matrix verb *V1* is a transitive verb, so there are six possible orders on the matrix clause, as shown in Figure 1. An MC-TAG grammar for Turkish local scrambling was demonstrated in (Eyigöz, 2007). Therefore, the elementary trees in Figure 1 and 2 are presumably derived by a set internal merge operation.

Adjoining a tree at a node below the root node may result in topicalization or extraposition of the arguments that are higher than the node of adjunction. The elements above the node of adjunction may be topicalized or extraposed depending on their *directionality* with respect to the node of adjunction. To derive this effect, clausal sub-categorization is indicated by a footnode, as opposed to a substitution node.

A matrix *V1* tree adjoins into a tree of its subordinate clause headed by *V2* through its root and foot nodes, labeled *X* in Figure 1. A tree headed by *V2* adjoins into a tree of its subordinate clause headed by *V3* through its *Root* and *Foot* nodes. Since there is no clause that matrix *V1* is subordinate to, nothing adjoins into *V1* trees. As for *V2*, *R2*, *V3*, *R3* trees, it is assumed that adjoining does not take place at a foot node or a substitution node. Therefore, keeping track of the *level* of the node of adjunction is sufficient, as there is at most one possible node of adjunction at each level. As shown in Figure 2, adjunction at level 0 takes place at a root node, adjunction at the level 1 takes place at the sister of the *Foot* node on *V2/R2* trees, and at the sister of *NP3* on *V3/R3* trees. Finally, there is no possible node of adjunction at the third level. Therefore, there are two nodes of adjunction per tree, one at level 0 and one at level 1.

3.1   Restricting the Derivations

Two possible nodes for adjunction per tree means that there are 16x6 possible TAG derivations that could be performed with the grammar in Figure 1 and 2. However, some of these derivations result in word orders that violate the coherence condition. Adjunction at the trees of *V2/R2* and *V3/R3* both at the first level results in word orders that either violate the coherence condition, or word orders that are string equivalent to the word orders derived by other derivations. Likewise, adjoining at the *R3* tree at the root level yields word orders that violate the coherence condition. Ruling out such derivations decreases the number of derivations to 6x6.

An interesting result of eliminating the derivations that violate the coherence condition is that only the derivations that involve long distance scrambling to the sentence initial and the sentence final positions, and local extraposition are left as legitimate derivations.

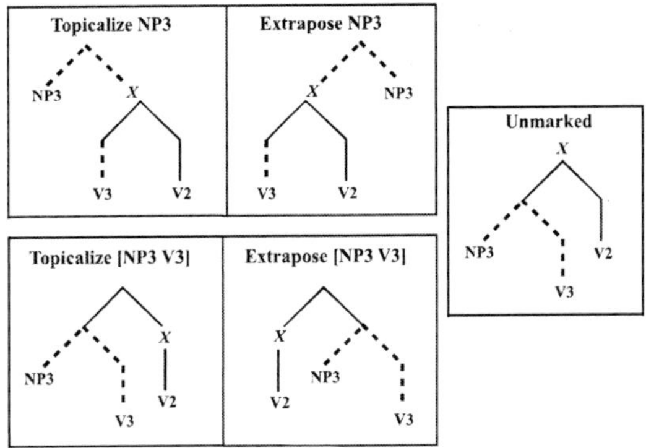

Figure 4: Revised Initial Trees

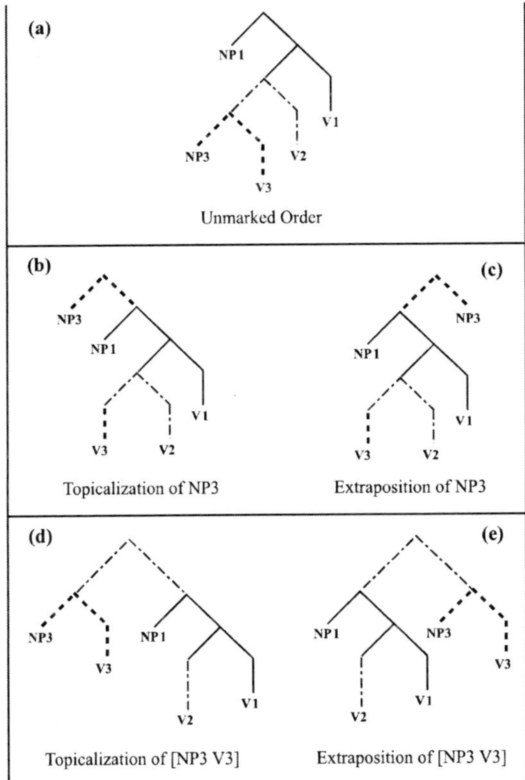

Figure 3: Derivation Examples

As argued in section 2, local extraposition in subordinate clauses has to be ruled out on grounds independent of the coherence condition. Adjoining at the root of the head-initial tree headed by *V2* (R2 in Figure 2) results in the local extraposition of its argument *[NP3 V3]*. Therefore, this derivation is also eliminated, which decreases the number of derivations from 6x6 to 5x6.

Figure 3 shows the results of the five legitimate derivations on the SOV order of the matrix clause. The trees in Figure 3 yield grammatical sentences. Figure (a) shows the unmarked order. Comparing (b) with the unmarked order in (a), we can see that adjoining the tree headed by *V2* into the tree headed by *V3* at level 1 results in topicalization of its argument *N3*. Figures (b) and (c) illustrate the derivation of topicalization and extraposition based on the directionality of the tree headed by *V3* (head-initial vs. head-final). Likewise, the trees in (d) and (e) show topicalization and extraposition of the argument *[NP3 V3]* based on the directionality of the tree headed by *V2*.

Table 2 summarizes the 5x6 legitimate derivations and acceptability judgments associated with them. Not all 30 possibilities are realized because topicalization out of a topicalized constituent is string vacuous topicalization. Therefore, topicalization does not apply to OSV and OVS word orders on the matrix clause, because the foot node is already at the sentence initial topic position in these trees. Accordingly, *SE* in Table 2 stands for sentences that are string equivalent to sentences derived by other derivations. $\sqrt{}$ in Table 2 stands for the grammatical sentences. Finally, *A* stands for sentences that are not grammatical but acceptable.

In section 2.1, the number of permutations that do not violate the coherence condition and involve scrambling with a semantic function was determined to be 26. Table 2 shows the linguistically appropriate derivations of these 26 word orders.

4   TAG Grammar Revisited

The coherence condition is enforced on the LTAG grammar developed in section 3 by restricting the set of possible derivations. In order to move from restrictions placed on derivations to restrictions placed on elementary trees, there are alternative paths to pursue. Motivated by the grammaticality judgments listed in Table 2 and the coherence condition, the revised TAG grammar comprises of the revised initial trees in Figure 4 and the auxiliary matrix trees in Figure 1. Adjunction takes place at the nodes with the label *X* on the initial trees, through the nodes with the same label on the auxiliary trees.

The revised grammar comprises of two sets of trees to be combined. The first set -the initial trees in Figure 4- corresponds to the five rows of Table 2. The second set -the auxiliary matrix trees in Figure 1- corresponds to the six columns of Table 2. The combination of the unmarked SOV tree with any tree in Figure 4 results in a grammatical sentence. Similarly, the combination of the unmarked *[NP3 V3 V2]* tree with any tree in Figure 1 results in a grammatical sentence. The combination of the unmarked SOV tree with the unmarked *[NP3 V3 V2]* tree derives the unmarked word order at the upper left corner of Table 2.

As argued in section 2, the coherence condition is reminiscent of the 'clause union' hypothesis for German and Dutch verb constructions, in that the coherence condition seems to collapse the two level embedding structure into a one level embedding structure by either combining the *[V3 V2]* into one complex verb, or freezing *[NP3 V3]* as one complex object. The trees in Figure 4 reflect the merger expressed by the coherence condition.

5 Conclusion

The LTAG grammar proposed in this work has two levels: the first level assumes lexicalized and linguistically appropriate elementary trees, where as the second level assumes elementary trees that are derived from the elementary trees of the first level, and are not lexicalized. The choice of the grammar proposed in this work, especially the introduction of the second level, is motivated mainly by how conveniently the grammar expresses the special status of the unmarked order and how the grammar relates the unmarked order to the other grammatical word orders of the same sentence. Moreover, the coherence condition, which is a filter on the acceptable permutations of the two level embedding sentence, seems to express the merger that results in the second level of the LTAG grammar.

References

Tilman Becker, Aravind K. Joshi, and Owen Rambow. 1991. Long-distance scrambling and tree adjoining grammars. In *ACL*, pages 21–26.

Tilman Becker, Owen Rambow, and Michael Niv. 1992. The derivational generative power of formal systems or scrambling is beyond lcfrs. Technical Report IRCS-92-38, Institute for Research in Cognitive Science, University of Pennsylvania, Philadelphia, PA.

Emine E. Ergüvanlı. 1984. *The Function of Word Order in Turkish Grammar*. University of California Press, Los Angeles, California.

Arnold Evers. 1975. *The Transformational Cycle in Dutch and German*. Ph.D. thesis, University of Utrecht.

Elif Eyigöz. 2007. Tag analysis of turkish scrambling. Master's thesis, UCLA, Los Angeles, CA.

Robert Evan Frank. 1992. *Syntactic locality and Tree Adjoining Grammar: grammatical, acquisition and processing perspectives*. Ph.D. thesis, University of Pennsylvania, Philadelphia, PA, USA.

Robert Frank. 2000. *Phrase Structure Composition and Syntactic Dependencies*. MIT Press.

Aravind K. Joshi, Leon S. Levy, and Masako Takahashi. 1975. Tree adjunct grammars. *J. Comput. Syst. Sci.*, 10(1):136–163.

Antony Kroch and Mark Baltin, editors, 1989. *Asymmetries in Long Distance Extraction in a Tree Adjoining Grammar*. University of Chicago Press.

Anthony Kroch and Aravind Joshi. 1985. Linguistic relevance of tree adjoining grammar. Technical Report MS-SC-85-16, Department of Computer and Information Sciences, University of Pennsylvania.

Antony Kroch and Aravind Joshi, 1987. *Analyzing Extraposition in a Tree Adjoining Grammar*, page 107149. Syntax and semantics. Academic Press, New York.

Murat Kural. 1992. Properties of Turkish scrambling. Master's thesis, UCLA.

Owen Rambow and Young-Suk Lee. 1994. Word order variation and tree-adjoining grammar. *Computational Intelligence*, 10:386–400.

Owen Rambow. 1994. *Formal and Computational Aspects of Natural Language Processing*. Ph.D. thesis, University of Pennsylvania.

Yves Schabes and Stuart M. Shieber. 1992. An alternative conception of tree-adjoining derivation. In *ACL*, pages 167–176.

Yves Schabes, Anne Abeille, and Aravind K. Joshi. 1988. Parsing strategies with 'lexicalized' grammars: application to tree adjoining grammars. In *Proceedings of the 12th conference on Computational linguistics*, pages 578–583, Morristown, NJ, USA. Association for Computational Linguistics.

Yves Schabes. 1990. *Mathematical and computational aspects of lexicalized grammars*. Ph.D. thesis, University of Pennsylvania.

Stuart M. Shieber, Yves Schabes, and Fernando C. N. Pereira. 1995. Principles and implementation of deductive parsing. *J. Log. Program.*, 24(1&2):3–36.

David Weir. 1988. *Characterizing Mildly Context-Sensitive Grammar Formalisms*. Ph.D. thesis, University of Pennsylvania, Philadelphia.

A TAG-derived Database for Treebank Search and Parser Analysis

Seth Kulick and **Ann Bies**
Linguistic Data Consortium
University of Pennsylvania
3600 Market St., Suite 810
Philadelphia, PA 19104
{skulick,bies}@ldc.upenn.edu

Abstract

Recent work has proposed the use of an extracted tree grammar as the basis for treebank analysis, in which queries are stated over the elementary trees, which are small chunks of syntactic structure. In this work we integrate search over the derivation tree with this approach in order to analyze differences between two sets of annotation on the same text, an important problem for parser analysis and evaluation of inter-annotator agreement.

1 Introduction

In earlier work (Kulick and Bies, 2009; Kulick and Bies, 2010; Kulick et al., 2010) we have described the need for a treebank search capability that compares two sets of trees over the same tokens. Our motivation is the problem of comparing different annotations of the same data, such as determining where gold trees and parser output differ. Another such case is that of comparing inter-annotator agreement files during corpus construction. In both cases the typical need is to recognize which syntactic structures the two sets of trees are agreeing or disagreeing on.

For this purpose it would be useful to be able to state queries in a way that relates to the decisions that annotators actually make, or that a parser mimics. We refer to this earlier work for arguments that (parent, head, sister) relations as in e.g. (Collins, 2003) are not sufficient, and that what is needed is the ability to state queries in terms of small chunks of syntactic structure.

The solution we take is to use an extracted tree grammar, inspired by Tree Adjoining Grammar

(Joshi and Schabes, 1997). The "elementary trees" and the derivation trees of the TAG-like grammar are put into a MySql database, and become the objects on which queries can be stated. The "lexicalization" property of the grammar, in which each elementary tree is associated with one or more tokens, allows for the the queries to be carried out in parallel across the two sets of trees.

We show here how this approach can be used to analyze two types of errors that occur in parsing the Arabic Treebank. As part of this analysis, we show how search over the derivation tree, and not just for the elementary trees, can be used as part of this analysis of parallel annotations over the same text.

2 Elementary Tree Extraction

The work described and all our examples are taken from the Arabic Treebank, part 3, v3.2 (ATB3-v3.2) (Maamouri et al., 2010).

As discussed above, we are aiming for an analysis of the trees that is directly expressed in terms of the core syntactic constructions. Towards this end we utilize ideas from the long line of TAG-based research that aims to identify the smaller trees that are the "building blocks" of the full trees of that treebank, and that are then used for such purposes as training parsers or as a basis for machine translation systems (Chen, 2001; Chiang, 2003; Xia, 2001). However, as far as we know this approach has not been utilized for searching within a treebank, until the current line of work.

As in the earlier TAG work we use head rules to decompose the full trees and then extract out the "elementary trees", which are the small syntactic chunks. This decomposition of the full tree results

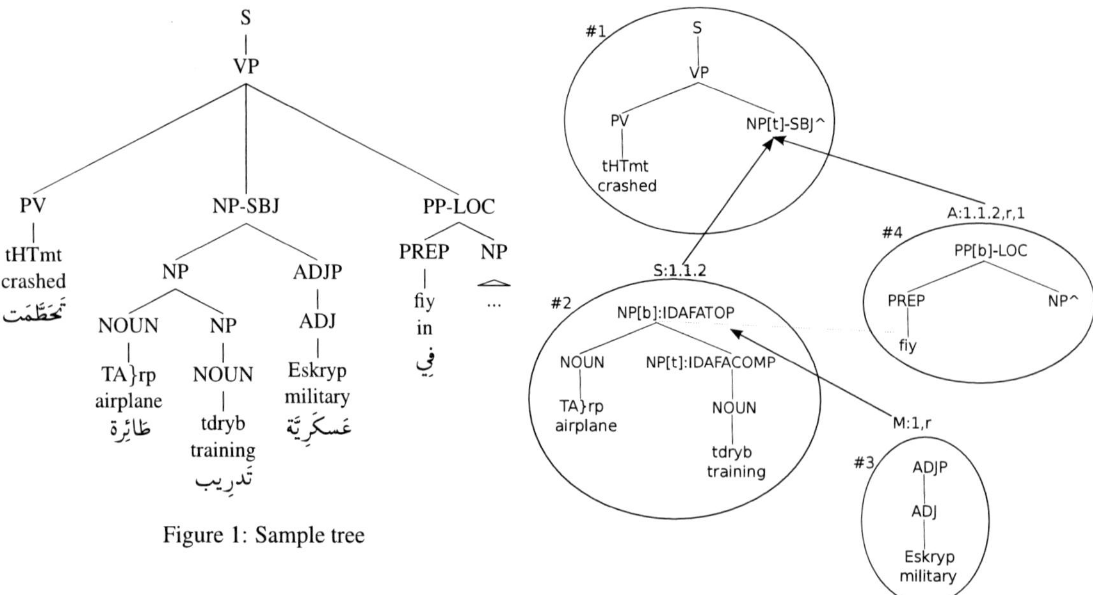

Figure 1: Sample tree

Figure 2: Elementary Trees and Derivation Tree for the Tree Decomposition in Figure 1

not just in these elementary trees, but also records how the elementary trees relate to each other, and therefore how they can be recombined to form the original full tree. For our grammar we use a TAG variant with tree-substitution, sister-adjunction, and Chomsky-adjunction (Chiang, 2003).

A small example is shown in Figures 1 and 2.[1] The full tree is shown in Figure 1, and the extracted elementary trees[2] and derivation tree in Figure 2. (The ˆ symbol at the node NP[t]-SBJ in tree #1 indicates that it is a substitution node.) The extracted trees are the four trees numbered #1–#4. These trees are in effect the nodes in the derivation tree showing how the four elementary trees connect to each other.

We briefly mention three unusual features of this extraction, and refer the reader to (Kulick and Bies, 2009) for detail and justification.[3]

1. The function tags are included in the tree extraction, with the syntactic tags such as SBJ treated as a top feature value, and semantic tags such as LOC treated as a bottom feature value, extending the traditional TAG feature

system (Vijay-Shanker and Joshi, 1988) to handle function tags.

2. Etree #2 consists of two anchors, rather than splitting up the tree decomposition further. This is because this is an instance of the idafa ("construct state") construction in Arabic, in which two or more words are grouped tightly together.

3. During the extraction process, additional information is added to the nodes in some cases, as further attributes for the "top" and "bottom" information, parallel to the function tag information. In this case, the root of etree #2 has the "bottom" attribute IDAFATOP, meaning that it is the top of an idafa structure, and the lower NP has the "top" attribute IDAFACOMP, meaning that it is the complement within an idafa structure.[4] Such added attributes can be used by the search specifications, as will be done here.

The derivation tree for this tree decomposition

---

[1] We use the Buckwalter Arabic transliteration scheme http://www.qamus.org/transliteration.htm for the Arabic.

[2] We will sometimes use "etree" as shorthand for "elementary tree".

[3] See (Habash and Rambow, 2004) for an earlier and different approach to extracting a TAG from the ATB. As they point out, there is no one correct way to extract a TAG.

[4] At the root node, the IDAFATOP information is in the "bottom" attribute because it is part of the structure from below. The IDAFACOMP is a "top" attribute because it is a consequence of being a child of the higher node.

shows how the relations of substitution, sister-adjunction, and Chomsky-adjunction relate the etree instances. For example, etree instance #2 substitutes at address $1.1.2^5$ of etree instances #1, as indicated by the $\mathtt{S:1.1.2}$ above instance #2. Etree instance #3 Chomsky-adjoins at the root of etree instance #2, as indicated by the $\mathtt{M:1,r}$ above instance #3. The $\mathtt{M}$ indicates Chomksy-adjunction, the $\mathtt{1}$ indicates the root, and the $\mathtt{r}$ indicates that it is to the right.[6] Etree instance #4 sister-adjoins to node 1.1.2 in Etree #1, as indicated by the $\mathtt{A:1.1.2,r,1}$, becoming a sister of node $\mathtt{NP[t]-SBJ\hat{}}$. The $\mathtt{A}$ indicates sister-adjunction, and the $\mathtt{r}$ is again the direction, and the $\mathtt{1}$ indicates the ordering, in case there was more than one such sister-adjunction at a node.

It is of course often the case that the same elementary tree structure will be repeated in different elementary trees extracted from a corpus. To make our terminology precise, we call each such structure an "etree template", and a particular instance of that template, together with the "anchors" (tokens) used in that instance of the template, is called an "etree instance". For example, in tree #2, the template is $\mathtt{(NP[b]:IDAFATOP\ A1}$ $\mathtt{(NP[t]:IDAFACOMP\ A2))}$, where $\mathtt{A1}$ and $\mathtt{A2}$ stand for the anchors, and this particular etree instance has that template and the anchors $\mathtt{(NOUN}$ $\mathtt{TA\}rp)}$ and $\mathtt{(NOUN\ tryb)}$.

3 Query Processing

We are concerned here with showing the analysis of parallel sets of annotations on the same text, and as mentioned in Section 1, we compare gold and parser output. However, we are interested in exploring differences between different parser runs, in which aspects of the parser model are changed. Therefore we use a training/dev/test split[7], and work here with the dev section. We do not include here all the details of the parser setup, since that is not the focus here,[8] but

we work with two settings. For both "Run 1" and "Run 2", the parser is supplied with the gold tags for each word. For "Run 2 ", the parser is forced to use the given tags for every word. For "Run 1", the parser can use its own tags, based on the training data, for words that it has seen in training. We are interested in exploring some of the consequences of this difference.

We therefore carry out the extraction procedure described in the previous section on each of three versions of trees for the same tokens: (a) the gold dev section trees, (b) the parser output for Run 1, and (c) the parser output for Run 2. Each has (the same) 17882 tokens. The gold version has 14370 etree instances using 611 etree templates, Run 1 has 14208 etree instances and 489 etree templates, and Run 2 has 14215 etree instances using 497 etree templates. This gives some indication of the huge amount of duplication of structure in a typical treebank representation. From the perspective of database organization, the representation of the etree templates can be perhaps be viewed as a type of database "normalization", in which duplicate tree structure information is placed in a separate table.

A significant aspect of this decomposition of the parse output is that the tree decomposition relies upon the presence of function tags to help determine the argument status of nodes, and therefore what should be included in an elementary tree. We therefore use a modification of Bikel parser as described in (Gabbard et al., 2006), so that the output contains function tags. However, inaccuracy in the function tag recovery by the parser could certainly affect the formation of the elementary trees resulting from Runs 1 and 2. We do not include empty categories for the parser output, while they are present in the Gold trees.[9] There are 929 etree templates in total, combining those for the three versions, with those for Run 1 and Run 2 overlapping almost entirely.

The extracted tokens, etree templates, etree instances, and derivation trees are stored in a MySQL database for later search. The derivation tree is implemented with a simple "adjacency list" representation, as is often done in database representations of

---

[5]The addresses are Gorn addresses, with the root as 1.

[6]Since we do not store such directional information in the actual tree adjoining in in the traditional TAG way, by including the appropriate root and foot node, the directional information needs to be specified in the derivation tree.

[7]http://nlp.stanford.edu/software/parser-arabic-data-splits.shtml. We also include only sentences of length <= 40.

[8]We used the Bikel parser, available at www.cis.upenn.edu/~dbikel/software.html

[9]On a brief inspection, this is likely the reason for the greater number of templates used for the gold version of the data, since the templates then include the empty categories as well.

Lexical restrictions:

```
L1: text="Ean"
```

Etree queries:

```
E1) [NP{b:IDAFATOP}  (A1,)]
    [NP{t:IDAFACOMP}  (A2,)]
E2) [NP{b:IDAFATOP}  (A1,)]
    [NP{t:IDAFAMID}   (A2,)]
    [NP{t:IDAFACOMP}  (A2,)]
...
E6 [VP (A1,PP[t]-CLR^{dta:1})]
E7 [PP (A1{lex:L1},)]
```

Dtree queries:

```
# two-level idafa (NP A1 (NP A2))
D1) E1
# three-level idafa
# (NP A1 (NP A2 (NP A3)))
D2) E2
# four-level idafa
# (NP A1 (NP A2 (NP A3 (NP A4))))
D3) E3
# five-level idafa
D4) E4
# six-level idafa
D5) E5
# VP with PP substituting into PP-CLR
D6) (sub{dta:1} E6 E7)
```

Figure 3: Examples of Etree and Dtree queries

hierarchical structure. We do not have space here to show the database schema, but it is organized with appropriate indexing so that a full tree is represented by a derivation tree, with integers pointing to the etree instance, which in turn use integers to represent the etree template in that etree instance and also point to the anchors of that etree instance.

This tree extraction and database setup only needs to be done once, as a preliminary step, for all of the queries on the corpus, as stored in the database. We now illustrate how queries can be specified, and describe the algorithm used for searching on the database with the extracted tree grammar.

3.1   Query Specification

Queries are specified as "Etree queries" and "Dtree queries". Sample queries are shown in Figure 3. Etree queries determine a set of etree instances, by specifying conditions on the structure of a etree instance (and therefore on the etree template that the etree instance uses), and, optionally, lexical constraints on the anchor(s) of that etree instance. The

Dtree queries specify a relationship in the derivation tree of etree instances that satisfy certain etree queries.

Each Etree query is in the form of a list of pairs, where each pair is `(node-label, children-of-node-label)`, where the node labels identify nodes on the spine from the root down. We forgo a rigorous definition here of the query language here in favor of focusing on the example queries.

Etee query E1 specifies that an etree instance is a match for E1 if it has a path with a `NP{b:IDAFATOP}` node and then another node `NP{t:IDAFACOMP}`. Each such node further has a child that is an anchor, A1 for the first, and A2 for the second. There are no lexical restrictions specified for these anchors, so any etree instance with an etree template that satisfies that condition satisfies E1. Etree query E2 is similar except that it matches a three-level idafa, using the attribute `IDAFAMID` to do so. By repeating the number of nodes in the spine with `IDAFAMID`, idafas of various sizes can be found, as in Etree queries E3-E5, which we leave out.

Etree query E6 specifies that an etree instance is a match for E6 if it has a VP node, with children A1 and substitution node `PP-CLR^`. Etree query E7 simply finds all templates with node `PP`, for which the anchor satisfies lexical restrction L1, which is specified to mean that its text is `Ean`.

Some Dtree queries, such as `D1`−`D5`, are as simple as possible, corresponding to a single node in the derivation tree, and are identical to a specified Etree query. Here, `D1`−`D5` just return the results of Etree queries `E1`−`E5`, respectively. Other Dtree queries involve two nodes in the derivation, such as `D6`, which specifies that is is selecting pairs of Etree instances, one satisfying Etree query `E6`, and the other `E7`, with the latter substituting into the former. This substitution has to be at a certain location in the parent etree instance, and `dta:1` (for "derivation tree address') is this location. It arises from the search of etree templates for the parent query, here `E6`, in a manner described in the following Step 1.

3.2   Step 1: Etree Template Search

The etree templates are searched to determine which match a given etree query. For the current data, all

929 etree templates are searched to determine which match queries E1–E7. It's currently implemented with simple Python code for representing the templates as a small tree structure. While this search is done outside of the database representation, the resulting information on which templates match which queries is stored in the database.[10]

This step does not search for any lexical information, such as `lex:L1` in E7. That is because this step is simply searching the etree templates, not the etree instances, which are the objects that contain both the etree template and lexical anchor information. So this step is going through each template, without examining any anchors, to determine which have the appropriate structure to match a query. However, in order to prepare for the later steps of finding etree instances, we store in another table the information that for a (template,query) to match it must be the case that an anchor at a particular address in that template satisfies a particular lexical restriction, or that a particular address in that template will be used in a derivation tree search.

This additional information is not necessarily the same for different templates that otherwise match a query. For example, the two templates

```
(1)  (S (VP A1 NP[t]-SBJ^ PP[t]-CLR^))
(2)  (SBAR WHNP^
        (S (VP A1 (NP[t]-SBJ (-NONE- *T*))
              PP[t]-CLR^)))
```

both match query E6, but for (1) the stored address `dta:1` is 1.1.3, while for (2) the stored address is 1.2.1.3, the address of `PP[t]-CLR^` in each template. Likewise, the stored information specifies that an etree instance with the template `(PP A1 NP^)` matches the query E7 if the anchor has the text `Ean`.

This step in effect produces specialized information for the given template as to what additional restrictions apply for that (query,template) pair to succeed as a match, in each etree instance that uses that etree template.

To summarize, this step finds all (Etree query, etree *template*) matches, and for each case stores the additional lexical restriction or `dta` information for

that pair. This information is then used in the following steps to find the etree *instances* that match a given Etree query Eq, by also checking the lexical restriction, if any, for an etree instance that has a template that is in the pair (Eq, template), and by using in a derivation tree search the `dta` information for that pair.

3.3   Step 2: Dtree Search and Etree Instances

For each Dtree query, it first finds all etree instances that satisfy the etree query (call it Eroot here) contained in the root of the Dtree query. This is a two-part process, by which it first finds etree instances such that the (Eroot, etree template) is a match for the instance's etree template, which is the information found in Step 1. It then filters this list by checking the lexical restriction, if any, for the anchor at the appropriate address in the etree instance, using the information stored from Step 1.

For single-node Dtree queries, such as D1–D5 this is the end of the processing. For two-node Dtree queries, such as D6, it descends down the derivation tree. This is similar to the two-part process just described, although the first step is more complex. For the Etree query specified by the child node (call it Echild here), it finds all etree instances such that (Echild, etree template) is a match for the instance's etree template, and, in addition, that the etree instance is a child in the derivation tree for a parent that was found to satisfy Eroot, and that the address in the derivation tree is the same as the address `dta` that was identified during Step 1 for the template of the parent etree instance. Note that the address is located on the parent tree during Step 1, but appears in the derivation tree on the child node.

4   Search over Pairs of Trees

As discussed in the introduction, one of the motivations for this work is to more easily compare two sets of trees for structures of interest, arising from either two annotators or gold and parser output. We construct confusion matrices showing how corresponding tokens across two different annotations compare with regard to satisfaction of the queries of interest. We do this by associating each token with satisfaction results for queries based on the etree instance that the tree token belongs to (this is related to the

---

Gold:

```
(PP-PRP  (PREP  <17>li)                                          for/to
         (NP  (NOUN+CASE_DEF_GEN  <18>waDoE+i)                   laying down
              (NP
                   (NP  (NOUN+CASE_INDEF_GEN   <19><iTAr+K)      framework
                        (ADJ+CASE_INDEF_GEN    <20>EAm~+K)       general
                   (SBAR ....
```

Run1:   Run2:

```
(PP-PRP  (PREP  <17>li)                  (PP-PRP  (PREP  <17>li)
         (NP                                      (NP
              (NP  (NOUN  <18>waDoE+i)                   (NP  (NOUN  <18>waDoE+i)
                   (NP  (NOUN  <19><iTAr+K)                    (NP
                        (NP  (NOUN  <20>EAm~+K)                     (NP  (NOUN  <19><iTAr+K)
                   (SBAR                                                (ADJ  <20>EAm~+K)
                                                                   (SBAR
              ...
```

Figure 4: Token <18> is an example entry from cell (D1, D2) in Table 1, showing that the gold tree satisfies query D1 (a two-level idafa) while the Run 1 parse tree satisfies, incorrectly, query D2 (a three-level idafa). Token <18> in Run 2 correctly satisfies query D2.

"lexicalization" property of TAG). To prevent the same query from being counted twice, in case it is satisfied by an etree instance with more than one anchor, we associate just one "distinguished anchor" as the token that counts as the satisfying that instance of the query.[11] Similarly, for a Dtree query such as D6 that is satisfied by two etree instances together, each one of which would have its own distinguished anchor, we use just the anchor for the child etree instance. For D6, this means that the token that is associated with the satisfaction of the query is the preposition in the child elementary tree.

As discussed in Section 3, we have three sets of trees to compare over the same data, (a) the gold, (b) Run 1, and (c) Run 2. We constructed confusion matrices measuring (a) against (b), (a) against (c), and (b) and against (c). The latter is particularly helpful of course when identifying differences between the two parser runs. However, due to space reasons we only present here sample confusion matrices for (a) the gold vs. (b) Run 1, although our examples also show the corresponding tree from Run 2.

It is often the case that some queries are logically grouped together in separate confusion matrices. For the queries in Figure 3, we are interested in comparing the idafa queries (D1−D5) against each

gld\Rn1	N	D1	D2	D3	D4	D5	Total
N	0	66	30	6	0	0	102
D1	81	1389	13	3	1	0	1487
D2	21	4	285	1	1	0	312
D3	1	0	1	42	0	0	44
D4	0	0	0	0	5	0	5
D5	0	0	0	0	0	1	1
Total	103	1459	329	52	7	1	1951

Table 1: Confusion matrix showing results of queries D1-D5 for Gold trees and Run 1

other, with the PP-CLR case (D6) in isolation.

Table 1 shows the confusion matrix for queries D1−D5 for the gold vs. Run 1. The row N contains cases in which the token for the gold tree did not satisfy any of query D1−D5, and likewise the column N contains cases in which the token for the parse output did not satisfy any of queries D1−D5. The cell (N, N) would consist of all tokens which do not satisfy any of queries D1−D5 for either the gold or the parse, and so are irrelevant and not included.

For example, the cell (1, 2) consists of cases in which the token in the gold tree is a distinguished anchor for an elementary tree that satifies query D1, while the corresponding token in the parse output is a distinguished anchor for an elementary tree that satisfies query D2. An example of an entry from this cell is shown in Figure 4. The token

---

[11]This is just the anchor that is the head.

Gold:

```
(S
   (VP  (PV+PVSUFF_SUBJ:3MS   <13>Eab~ar+a)          express + he
        (NP-SBJ (DET+NOUN+CASE_DEF_NOM   <14>Al+|bA'+u)     the fathers/ancestors
        (PP-CLR (PREP <15>Ean)                        from/about/of
              (NP
                 (NP  (NOUN+CASE_DEF_GEN   <16>qalaq+i)    unrest/concern/apprehension
                      (NP (POSS_PRON_3MP <17>him)          their
                 (PP (PREP <18>min)                        from
                    (NP ...
```

Run1:   Run2:

```
(S                                          (S
   (VP (PV <13>Eab~ar+a)                        (VP (PV <13>Eab~ar+a)
       (NP-SBJ                                      (NP-SBJ (DET+NOUN <14>Al+|bA'+u)
             (NP                                     (PP-CLR (PREP <15>Ean)
                (NP (DET+NOUN <14>Al+|bA'+u)            (NP (NOUN <16>qalaq+i)
                (PP (PREP <15>Ean)                         (NP (POSS_PRON <17>him)
                (NP                               (PP (PREP <18>min)
                   (NP (NOUN <16>qalaq+              (NP ....)
                   (NP (POSS_PRON <17>him)
                (PP (PREP <18>min)
                (NP ...)
```

Figure 5: Token <15> is an example entry from cell (D6,N) in Table 2, showing that the gold tree satisfies query D6 (a verbal structure with a PP-CLR argument that is headed by Ean), while the Run 1 parse tree fails to satisfy this. Token <15> in the Run 2 parse does correctly satisfy query D6.

<18>waDoE+i satisfies query D1 in the gold tree because it is the distinguished anchor for the two-level idafa structure consisting of tokens <18> and <19>:

```
(NP (NOUN+CASE_DEF_GEN <18>waDoE+i)
    (NP (NOUN+CASE_INDEF_GEN <19><iTAr+K)))
```

The modifier at <20> does not interfere with this identification of the two-level idafa structure, since it is a modifier and therefore a separate etree instance in the derivation tree.

However, token <18> in the Run 1 output is the distinguished anchor for a 3-level idafa, consisting of the tokens at <18>, <19>, <20>. Note that these identifications are made separately from the incorrect attachment level of the SBAR (at <19> in the gold tree, at <18> in Run 1), which is a separate issue from the idafa complexity, which is of concern in this query. One can see here the effect of the parser choosing the wrong tag for token <20>, a NOUN instead of ADJ, which causes it to mistakenly build an extra level for the idafa structure. Figure 4 also shows the corresponding part of the parse output for Run 2 (in which the parser is forced to use the given tags), which is correct. Therefore if we also

gold\Run 1	N	D6	Total
N	0	152	152
D6	76	258	334
Total	76	410	486

Table 2: Confusion matrix showing results of query D6 for Gold trees and Run 1

showed the confusion matrix for gold/Run 2, token <18> would be an entry in cell (D1,D1). Also, in a confusion matrix for Run1/Run2 it would appear in cell (D2,D1). (This is analogous to comparing annotations by two different anotators.)

Table 2 shows the confusion matrix for Dtree query D6, which simply scores the satisfaction of D6 compared with a lack of satisfaction. An example entry from cell (D6,N) is shown in Figure 5, in which token <15>Ean in the gold tree is the distinguished anchor for the child etree instance that satisfies query D6, while the corresponding token <15>Ean in Run 1 does not. For Run 2, token <15> does satisfy query D6, although the attachment of the PP headed by <18>min is incorrect, a separate issue.

5 Future Work

Our immediate concern for future work is to use the approach described for inter-annotator agreement and work closely with the ATB team to ensure that the queries necessary for interannotator comparisons can be constructed in this framework and integrated into the quality-control process. We expect that this will involve further specification of how queries select etree templates (Step 1), in interesting ways that can take advantage of the localized search space, such as searching for valency of verbs. We also aim to provide information on where two annotators agree on the core structure, but disagree on attachment of modifiers to that structure, a major problem for corpus annotation consistency.

However, there are many topics that need to be explored within this approach. We conclude by mentioning two.

(1) We are not using classic TAG adjunction, and thus cannot handle any truly (i.e., not auxiliaries) long-distance dependencies. Related, we are not properly handling coindexation in our extraction. The consequences of this need to be explored, with particular attention in this context to extraction from within an idafa construction, which is similar to the extraction-from-NP problem for TAG in English.

(2) We are also particularly interested in the relation between query speed and locality on the derivation tree. In general, while searching for etree instances is very efficient, complex searches over the derivation tree will be less so. However, our hope, and expectation, is that the majority of real-life dtree queries will be local (parent,child,sister) searches on the derivation tree, since each node of the derivation tree already encodes small chunks of structure. We plan to evaluate the speed of this system, in comparison to systems such as (Ghodke and Bird, 2008) and Corpus Search[12].

Acknowledgements

We thank David Graff, Aravind Joshi, Anthony Kroch, Mitch Marcus, and Mohamed Maamouri for useful discussions. This work was supported in part by the Defense Advanced Research Projects Agency, GALE Program Grant No. HR0011-06-1-0003 (both authors) and by the GALE program, DARPA/CMO Contract No. HR0011-06-C-0022 (first author). The content of this paper does not necessarily reflect the position or the policy of the Government, and no official endorsement should be inferred.

References

John Chen. 2001. *Towards Efficient Statistical Parsing Using Lexicalized Grammatical Information.* Ph.D. thesis, University of Delaware.

David Chiang. 2003. Statistical parsing with an automatically extracted tree adjoining gramar. In *Data Oriented Parsing.* CSLI. http://www.isi.edu/~chiang/papers/chiang-dop.pdf.

Michael Collins. 2003. Head-driven statistical models for natural language parsing. *Computational Linguistics*, 29:589–637.

Ryan Gabbard, Seth Kulick, and Mitchell Marcus. 2006. Fully parsing the Penn Treebank. In *HLT-NAACL*, pages 184–191.

Sumukh Ghodke and Steven Bird. 2008. Querying linguistic annotations. In *Proceedings of the Thirteenth Australasian Document Computing Symposium.*

Nizar Habash and Owen Rambow. 2004. Extracting a Tree Adjoining Grammar from the Penn Arabic Treebank. In *Traitement Automatique du Langage Naturel (TALN-04)*, Fez, Morocco.

A.K. Joshi and Y. Schabes. 1997. Tree-adjoining grammars. In G. Rozenberg and A. Salomaa, editors, *Handbook of Formal Languages, Volume 3: Beyond Words*, pages 69–124. Springer, New York.

Seth Kulick and Ann Bies. 2009. Treebank analysis and search using an extracted tree grammar. In *Proceedings of The Eigth International Workshiop on Treebanks and Linguistic Theories.*

Seth Kulick and Ann Bies. 2010. A treebank query system based on an extracted tree grammar. In *HLT-NAACL (short paper)*.

Seth Kulick, Ann Bies, and Mohammed Maamouri. 2010. A quantitative analysis of syntactic constructions in the Arabic Treebank. Presentation at GURT 2010 (Georgetown University Roundtable).

Mohamed Maamouri, Ann Bies, Seth Kulick, Sondos Krouna, Fatma Gaddeche, and Wajdi Zaghouani. 2010. Arabic treebank part 3 - v3.2. Linguistic Data Consortium LDC2010T08, April.

K. Vijay-Shanker and A. K. Joshi. 1988. Feature structures based tree adjoining grammars. In *COLING*.

Fei Xia. 2001. *Automatic Grammar Generation From Two Different Perspectives.* Ph.D. thesis, University of Pennsylvania.

[12]http://corpussearch.sourceforge.net.

Automated Extraction of Tree Adjoining Grammars
from a Treebank for Vietnamese

Phuong Le-Hong[1,2]**, Thi Minh Huyen Nguyen**[2]**, Phuong Thai Nguyen**[2]**, Azim Roussanaly**[1]
[1] LORIA, Nancy, France, [2] Vietnam National University, Hanoi, Vietnam
{lehong,azim}@loria.fr, huyenntm@hus.edu.vn, thainp@vnu.edu.vn

Abstract

In this paper, we present a system that automatically extracts lexicalized tree adjoining grammars (LTAG) from treebanks. We first discuss in detail extraction algorithms and compare them to previous works. We then report the first LTAG extraction result for Vietnamese, using a recently released Vietnamese treebank. The implementation of an open source and language independent system for automatic extraction of LTAG grammars is also discussed.

1 Introduction

Grammars in general and lexicalized tree adjoining grammars in particular are one of the most important elements in the natural language processing (NLP). Since the development of hand-crafted grammars is a time consuming and labor intensive task, many studies on automatic and semi-automatic grammar development have been carried out during last decades.

After decades of research in NLP mostly concentrated on English and other well-studied languages, recent years have seen an increased interest in less common languages, notably because of their growing presence on the Internet. Vietnamese, which belongs to the top 20 most spoken languages, is one of those new focuses of interest. Obstacles remain, however, for NLP research in general and grammar development in particular: Vietnamese does not yet have vast and readily available constructed linguistic resources upon which to build effective statistic resources upon which to build effective statistical models, nor reference works against which new ideas may be experimented.

Moreover, most existing research so far has been focused on testing the applicability of existing methods and tools developed for English or other Western languages, under the assumption that their logical or statistical well-foundedness guarantees cross-language validity, while in fact assumptions about the structure of a language are always made in such tools, and must be amended to adapt them to different linguistic phenomena. For an isolating language such as Vietnamese, techniques developed for flexional languages cannot be applied "as is".

The primary motivation to develop a system that can automatically extract an LTAG grammar for the Vietnamese language is the need of a rich statistical information and wide-coverage grammar which may contribute more effectively in the development of basic linguistic resources and tools for automatic processing of Vietnamese text.

We present in this article a system that automatically extracts lexicalized tree adjoining grammars from treebanks. We first discuss in detail the extraction algorithms and compare them to previous works. We then report the first LTAG extraction result for Vietnamese, using the recently released Vietnamese treebank. The implementation of an open source and language independent system for automatic extraction of LTAG grammars from treebanks is also discussed.

2 Previous works on extracting grammars from treebanks

There has been much work done on extracting treebank grammars in general and LTAG grammars in particular from annotated corpora, all of these works are for common languages. Xia developed the uniform method of grammar extraction for English, Chinese and Korean (Xia et al., 2000; Xia, 2001). Chiang developed a system for extracting an LTAG grammar from English Penn Treebank and used it for statistical parsing with LTAG (Chiang, 2000). Chen extracted TAGs from English Penn Treebank (Chen and Vijay-Shanker, 2000; Chen et al., 2006) and there are other works based on Chen's approach such as Johansen (Johansen, 2004) and Nasr (Nasr, 2004) for French, and Habash for Arabic (Habash and Rambow, 2004). Neumann extracted lexicalized tree grammars for English from English Penn Treebank and for German from NE-GRA treebank (Neumann, 2003). Bäcker extracted an LTAG gramar for German, also from the NEGRA corpus and used it for supertagging (Bäcker and Harbusch, 2002). Park extracted LTAG grammars for Korean from Korean Sejong Treebank (Park, 2006).

3 Vietnamese treebank

Recently, a group of Vietnamese computational linguists has been involved in developing a treebank for Vietnamese (Nguyen et al., 2009), and it is also the first treebank on which our extraction system was used.

The construction of a Vietnamese treebank is a branch project of a national project which aims to develop basic resources and tools for Vietnamese language and speech processing[1]. The raw texts of the treebank are collected from the social and political sections of the Youth online daily newspaper. The corpus is divided into three sets corresponding to three annotation levels: word-segmented, POS-tagged and syntax-annotated set. The syntax-annotated corpus, a subset of the POS-tagged one, is currently composed of $10,471$ sentences ($225,085$ tokens). Sentences range from 2 to 105 words, with an average length of 21.75 words. There are $9,314$ sentences of length 40 words or less. The tagset

No.	Category	Description
1.	S	simple declarative clause
2.	VP	verb phrase
3.	NP	noun phrase
4.	PP	preposition phrase
5.	N	common noun
6.	V	verb
7.	P	pronoun
8.	R	adverb
9.	E	preposition
10.	CC	coordinating conjunction

Table 1: Treebank tags in examples.

of the treebank has 38 syntactic labels (18 part-of-speech tags, 17 syntactic category tags, 3 empty categories) and 17 function tags. For details, please refer to (Nguyen et al., 2009).

The meanings of the tags that appear in this paper are listed in Table 1.

4 Extraction algorithms

In general, our work on extracting an LTAG grammar for Vietnamese follows closely the method of grammar extraction originally proposed by Xia (Xia, 2001). The extraction process has three steps: first, phrase-structure trees are converted into LTAG derived trees; second, the derived trees are decomposed into a set of elementary trees conforming to their three predefined prototypes; and third, invalid extracted elementary trees are filtered out using linguistic knowledge.

4.1 Building LTAG derived trees

The phrase structures in the Vietnamese treebank follow the English Penn Treebank bracketed style format which are not based on the LTAG formalism. They may have different formats from the LTAG derived trees which distinguish heads, arguments and adjuncts. Therefore, we first have to convert the phrase structures of the treebank into derived trees.

In this step, we first classify each node in a phrase-structure tree into three types, head, argument or modifier, and then build a derived tree by adding intermediate nodes so that at each level of the tree, the nodes satisfy exactly one of the following relations (Xia, 2001):

- *predicate-argument relation*: there are one or

---

[1]Project "Vietnamese Language and Speech Processing"

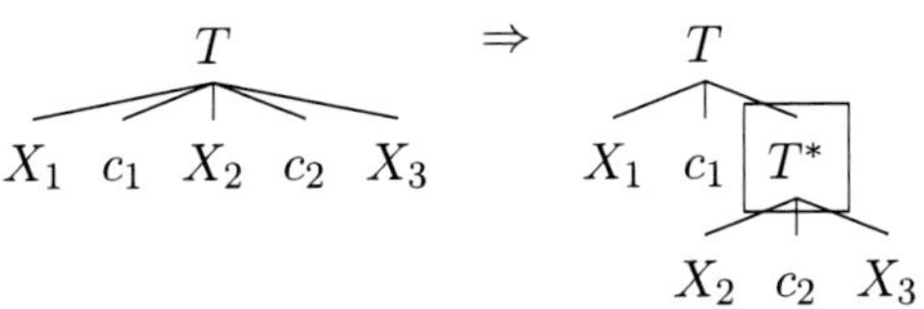

Figure 1: Conjunction groups transformation by Algorithm 1.

more nodes, one is the head, the rest are its arguments;

- *modification relation*: there are exactly two nodes, one node is modified by the other;

- *coordination relation*: there are exactly three nodes, in which two nodes are coordinated by a conjunction.

In order to find heads of phrases, we have constructed *a head percolation table* (Magerman, 1995; Collins, 1997) for the Vietnamese treebank. This table is used to select the head child of a node. In addition, we have also constructed *an argument table* to determine the types of arguments that a head child can take. The argument table helps explicitly mark each sibling of a head child as either an argument or an adjunct according to the tag of the sibling, the tag of the head child, and the position of the sibling with respect to the head child. Together with *the tagset table*, these three tables constitute the Vietnamese treebank-specific information that is required for the extraction algorithms[2].

Since the conjunction structures are different from the argument and modifier structures, we first recursively bracket all conjunction groups of a treebank tree by Algorithm 1 and then build the full derived tree for the resulting tree by Algorithm 2.

Figure 1 shows a tree with conjunction groups before and after being processed by Algorithm 1 where c_i are coordinating conjunctions and X_i are conjunction groups. Figure 2 shows a realisation of Algorithm 2 where A_i are arguments of the head child H of T and M_i are modifiers of H.

These two algorithms use the function INSERT-NODE$(T, \mathcal{L})$ shown in Algorithm 3 to insert an intermediate node between a node T and a list of its child

---

Algorithm 1 PROCESS-CONJ(T)

Require: A tree T
Ensure: T with conjunctions processed
1: **for** $K \in T.\texttt{kids}$ **do**
2:   **if** IS-PHRASAL(K) **then**
3:     $K \leftarrow$ PROCESS-CONJ(K);
4:   **end if**
5: **end for**
6: $(\mathcal{C}_1, \ldots, \mathcal{C}_k) \leftarrow$ CONJ-GROUPS$(T.\texttt{kids})$;
7: **for** $i = 1$ to k **do**
8:   **if** $\|\mathcal{C}_i\| > 1$ **then**
9:     INSERT-NODE$(T, \mathcal{C}_i)$;
10:   **end if**
11: **end for**
12: **if** $k > 2$ **then**
13:   **for** $i = k$ **downto** 3 **do**
14:     $\mathcal{L} \leftarrow \mathcal{C}_{i-1} \cup c_{i-1} \cup \mathcal{C}_i$;
15:     $T^* \leftarrow$ INSERT-NODE$(T, \mathcal{L})$;
16:     $\mathcal{C}_{i-1} \leftarrow T^*$;
17:   **end for**
18: **end if**
19: **return** T;

---

nodes $\mathcal{L}$. This new node is a child of T, has the same label as T and has $\mathcal{L}$ as the list of its kids. The function CONJ-GROUPS$(\mathcal{L})$ returns k groups of components $\mathcal{C}_i$ of $\mathcal{L}$ which are separated by $k - 1$ conjunctions $c_1, \ldots, c_{k-1}$. The function NEW-NODE(l) returns a new node with label l.

The Algorithm 2 uses several functions that are relatively self-explained. The function HEAD-CHILD(X) selects the head child of a node X according to a head percolation table. The head percolation table for the Vietnamese treebank is shown in the Table 4. The function IS-LEAF(X) checks whether a node X is a leaf node or not. The function IS-PHRASAL(X) checks whether X is a phrasal node or not.[3] The function ARG-NODES$(H, \mathcal{L})$ (respectively, MOD-NODES$(H, \mathcal{L})$) returns a list of nodes which are arguments (respectively modifiers) of a node H. The list $\mathcal{L}$ contains all sisters of H.

For example, Figure 3 shows the phrase structure of a sentence extracted from the Vietnamese treebank "*Họ sẽ không chuyển hàng xuống thuyền vào*

---

[2]To our best knowledge, this is the first time such tables are published for the Vietnamese treebank.

[3]A phrasal node is defined to be a node which is not a leaf or a preterminal. This means that it must have two or more children, or one child that is not a leaf.

Algorithm 2 BUILD-DERIVED-TREE(T)

Require: A tree T whose conjunctions have been processed
Ensure: A derived tree whose root is T
  1: **if** (not IS-PHRASAL(T)) **then**
  2:   **return** T;
  3: **end if**
  4: $H \leftarrow$ HEAD-CHILD(T);
  5: **if** not IS-LEAF(H) **then**
  6:   **for** $K \in T$.kids **do**
  7:     $K \leftarrow$ BUILD-DERIVED-TREE(K);
  8:   **end for**
  9:   $\mathcal{A} \leftarrow$ ARG-NODES$(H, \mathcal{L})$;
  10:   $\mathcal{M} \leftarrow$ MOD-NODES$(H, \mathcal{L})$;
  11:   $m \leftarrow \|\mathcal{M}\|$;
  12:   **if** $m > 0$ **then**
  13:     $\mathcal{L} \leftarrow \{H\} \cup \mathcal{A}$;
  14:     $T^* \leftarrow$ INSERT-NODE$(T, \mathcal{L})$;
  15:   **end if**
  16:   $(M_1, M_2, \ldots, M_m) \leftarrow \mathcal{M}$;
  17:   **for** $i = 1$ **to** $m - 1$ **do**
  18:     $\mathcal{L} \leftarrow \{M_i, T^*\}$;
  19:     $T' \leftarrow$ INSERT-NODE$(T, \mathcal{L})$;
  20:     $T^* \leftarrow T'$;
  21:   **end for**
  22: **end if**
  23: **return** T;

ngày mai."[4] The head children of phrases are circled.

The derived tree of the sentence given by Algorithm 2 is shown in Figure 4, the inserted nodes are squared.

4.2 Building elementary trees

At this step, each derived tree is decomposed into a set of elementary trees. The recursive structures of the derived tree are factored out and will become auxiliary trees, the remaining non-recursive structures will be extracted as initial trees.

Extracted elementary trees fall into one of three prototypes according to the relation between the anchor and other nodes, as shown in Figure 5.

The extraction process involves copying nodes from the derived tree for building elementary trees. The result of extraction process is three sets of el-

Algorithm 3 INSERT-NODE$(T, \mathcal{L})$

Require: A tree T and its children list $\mathcal{L}$
Ensure: A new child node T^* of T whose kids are $\mathcal{L}$
  1: $T^* \leftarrow$ NEW-NODE$(T$.label$)$;
  2: T^*.kids $\leftarrow \mathcal{L}$;
  3: T.kids $\leftarrow T$.kids $\setminus \mathcal{L}$;
  4: T.kids $\leftarrow T$.kids $\cup \{T^*\}$;
  5: **return** T^*;

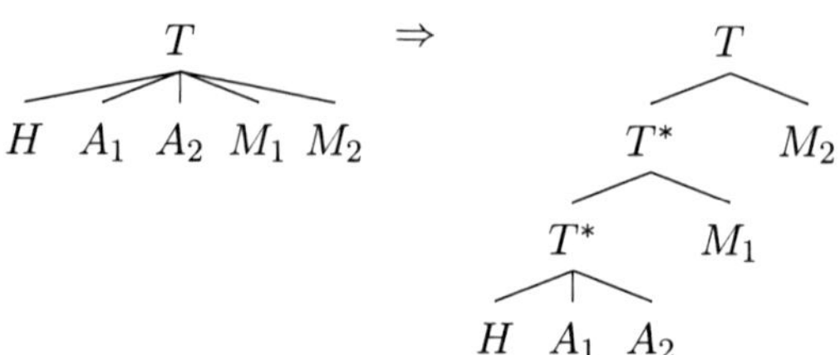

Figure 2: An example of derived tree realisation

ementary trees: $\mathcal{S}$ contains spine trees, $\mathcal{M}$ contains modifier trees and $\mathcal{C}$ contains conjunction trees.

To build elementary trees from a derived tree T, we first find the head path[5] $\{H_0, H_1, \ldots, H_n\}$ of T. For each parent P and its head child H, we get the list $\mathcal{L}$ of sisters of H and determine the relation between H and $\mathcal{L}$. If the relation is coordination, a conjunction tree will be extracted; if the relation is modification, a modifier tree will be extracted; otherwise, the relation is predicate-argument and a spine tree will be extracted. Algorithm 4 shows the extraction algorithm.

Algorithm 5 shows the function for building a spine tree. The function MERGE-LINK-NODES(T) merges all link nodes of a spine tree into one node (see Figure 7). Algorithms 6 and 7 are functions which respectively build modifier and conjunction trees.

For example, from the derived tree shown in Figure 4, 9 trees are extracted by algorithms as shown in Figure 6 and Figure 7.

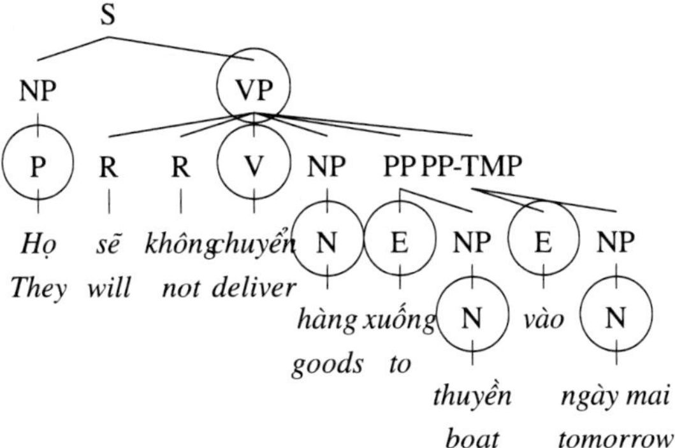

Figure 3: A treebank tree.

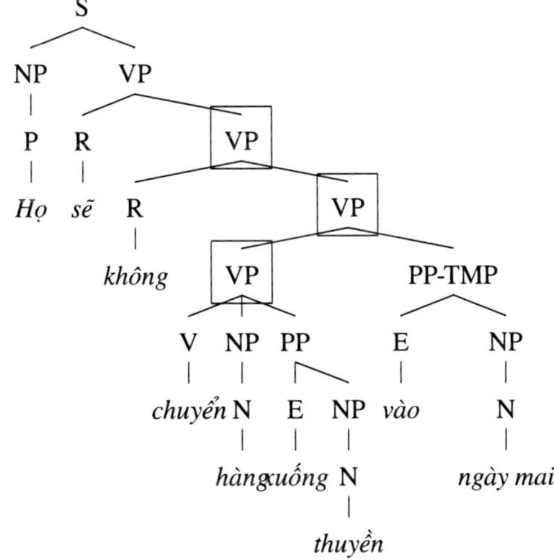

Figure 4: The derived tree of the treebank tree in Figure 3.

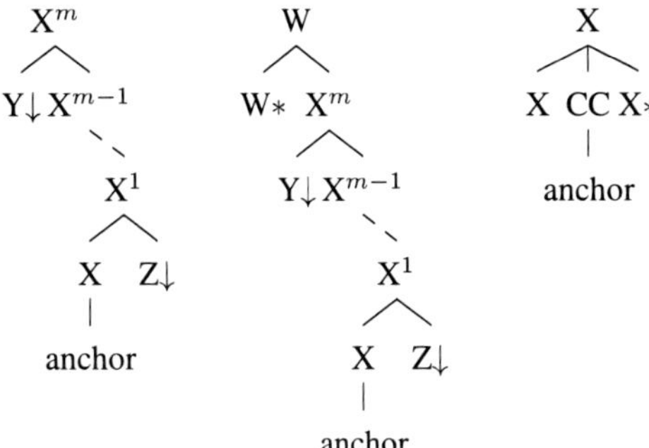

Figure 5: Prototypes of spine trees (predicate-argument relation) and auxiliary trees (modification and coordination relation).

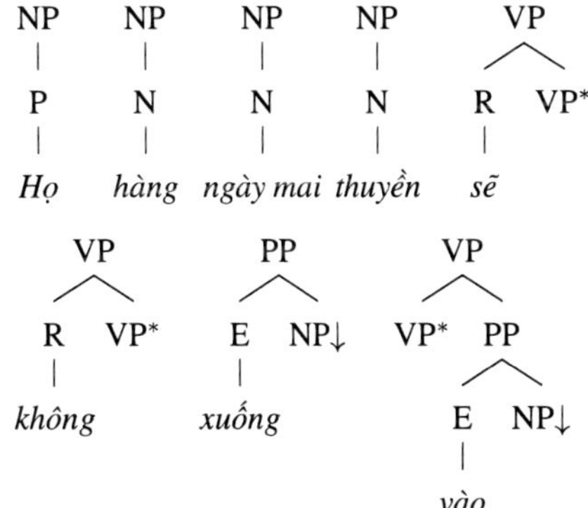

Figure 6: Extracted elementary trees.

4.3 Filtering out invalid trees

Annotation errors are inevitable for any treebank. The errors in parse trees will result in wrong elementary trees. An elementary tree is called invalid if it does not satisfy some linguistic requirement. We have construct some linguistic rules for filtering out invalid elementary trees. For example in Vietnamese, an adjective (or an adjectival phrase) can be an argument of a noun (or a noun phrase), however, they must be always on the right of the noun. Thus if there is an adjective on the left of a noun of an extracted spine tree, the tree is invalid and it must be filtered out.

4.4 Comparison with previous work

As mentioned above, our approach for LTAG extraction follows the uniform method of grammar extraction proposed by Xia (Xia, 2001). Nevertheless, there are some differences between our design and implementation of extraction algorithms and that of Xia.

First, in the building derived tree step, we first recursively bracket all conjunction groups of the tree before fully bracketing the arguments and modifiers of the resulting tree. We think that this approach is easier to understand and implement since conjunction structures are different from argument and modifier structures. Second, in the elementary tree decomposition step, we do not split each node in the derived tree into the top and bottom parts as it was done in the approach of Xia. In our implementation, the nodes are directly copied to build extracted trees. Third, the tree extraction process is broken into func-

Algorithm 4 BUILD-ELEMENTARY-TREES(T)

Require: T is a derived tree
Ensure: Sets $\mathcal{S}, \mathcal{M}, \mathcal{C}$ of elementary trees.
1: **if** (not IS-PHRASAL(T)) **then**
2:     **return** ;
3: **end if**
4: $\{H_0, H_1, \ldots, H_n\} \leftarrow$ HEAD-PATH(T);
5: $ok \leftarrow$ false;
6: $P \leftarrow H_0$;
7: **for** $j \leftarrow 1$ **to** n **do**
8:     $\mathcal{L} \leftarrow$ SISTERS(H_j);
9:     **if** $|\mathcal{L}| > 0$ **then**
10:         Rel $\leftarrow$ GET-RELATION($H_j, \mathcal{L}$);
11:         **if** Rel = Coordination **then**
12:             $\mathcal{C} \leftarrow \mathcal{C} \cup$ BUILD-CONJ-TREE(P);
13:         **end if**
14:         **if** Rel = Modification **then**
15:             $\mathcal{M} \leftarrow \mathcal{M} \cup$ BUILD-MOD-TREE(P);
16:             **if** $j = 1$ **then**
17:                 $\mathcal{S} \leftarrow \mathcal{S} \cup$ BUILD-SPINE-TREE(P);
18:                 $ok \leftarrow$ true;
19:             **end if**
20:         **end if**
21:         **if** Rel = Argument **then**
22:             **if** not ok and not IS-LINK-NODE(P) **then**
23:                 $\mathcal{S} \leftarrow \mathcal{S} \cup$ BUILD-SPINE-TREE(P);
24:                 $ok \leftarrow$ true;
25:             **end if**
26:         **end if**
27:     **else**
28:         **if** not IS-LINK-NODE(P) and IS-PHRASAL(P) **then**
29:             $\mathcal{S} \leftarrow \mathcal{S} \cup$ BUILD-SPINE-TREE(P);
30:         **end if**
31:     **end if**
32:     $P \leftarrow H_j$;
33: **end for**

Algorithm 5 BUILD-SPINE-TREE(T)

Require: T is a derived tree
Ensure: a spine tree
1: $T_c \leftarrow$ COPY(T);
2: $P \leftarrow T_c$;
3: $H \leftarrow$ NULL;
4: **repeat**
5:     $H \leftarrow$ HEAD-CHILD(P);
6:     $\mathcal{L} \leftarrow$ SISTERS(H);
7:     **if** $|\mathcal{L}| > 0$ **then**
8:         Rel $\leftarrow$ GET-RELATION($H, \mathcal{L}$);
9:         **if** Rel = Argument **then**
10:             **for** $A \in \mathcal{L}$ **do**
11:                 BUILD-ELEMENTARY-TREES(A);
12:                 A.kids $\leftarrow \emptyset$;
13:                 A.type $\leftarrow$ Substitution;
14:             **end for**
15:         **else**
16:             **for** $A \in \mathcal{L}$ **do**
17:                 P.kids $\leftarrow P$.kids $\setminus A$;
18:             **end for**
19:         **end if**
20:     **end if**
21:     $P \leftarrow H$;
22: **until** ($H =$ NULL)
23: **return** MERGE-LINK-NODES(T_c);

Algorithm 6 BUILD-MOD-TREE(T)

Require: T is a derived tree
Ensure: a modifier tree
1: $T_c \leftarrow$ COPY(T);
2: $H \leftarrow$ HEAD-CHILD(T_c);
3: H.kids $\leftarrow \emptyset$;
4: H.type $\leftarrow$ Foot;
5: $M \leftarrow$ MODIFIER(H);
6: $T' \leftarrow$ BUILD-SPINE-TREE(M);
7: **if** $|M$.kids$| > 1$ **then**
8:     BUILD-ELEMENTARY-TREES(M);
9: **end if**
10: $M \leftarrow T'$;
11: **return** T_c;

tions, each function builds a type of elementary trees and they can be called mutually by each other to repeat the extraction process for the subtrees whose roots are not yet visited. In spite of using recursive functions, our extraction algorithms are carefully designed so that there is no redundant or repeating function calls: each node is assured to be visited one time. The "divide and conquer" approach in algorithm design has been shown to be efficient and easy to optimise.

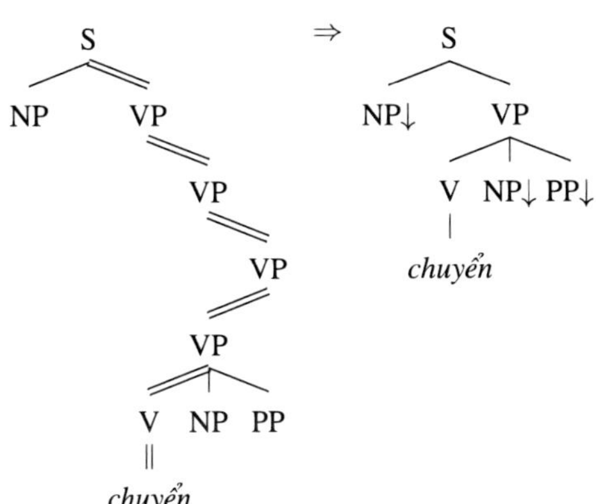

Figure 7: Merge link nodes to get a spine tree. The head path of the tree is marked by double lines.

Category	Original tags	Tags in G_2
noun phrases	NP/WHNP	NP
adjective phrases	AP/WHAP	AP
adverbial phrases	RP/WHRP	RP
preposition phrases	PP/WHPP	PP
clauses	S/SQ	S

Table 2: Some tags in the Vietnamese treebank tagset are merged into a single tag.

5 Experiments

We ran extraction algorithms on the Vietnamese treebank and extracted two treebank grammars. The first one, G_1, uses the original tagset of the treebank. The second one, G_2, uses a reduced tagset, where some tags in the treebank are merged into a single tag, as shown in Table 2. The grammar G_2 is smaller than G_1 and it is presumable that the sparse data problem is less severe when G_2 is used. Furthermore, it was shown that the size of the extracted grammar is important for Lightweight Dependency Analysis (LDA) and supertagging (Bangalore and Joshi, 1999).

We count the number of elementary trees and tree templates. The sizes of the two grammars are in Table 3. Recall that a template is an elementary tree without the anchor word.

Type	# of trees	# of templates
G_1	**46,382**	**2,317**
Spine trees	$24,973$	$1,022$
Modifier trees	$21,309$	$1,223$
Conjunction trees	100	72
G_2	**46,102**	**2,113**
Spine trees	$24,884$	952
Modifier trees	$21,121$	$1,093$
Conjunction trees	97	68

Table 3: Two LTAG grammars extracted from the Vietnamese treebank.

There are $15,035$ unique words in the treebank and the average number of elementary trees that a word anchors is around 3.07. We also count the number of context-free rules of the grammars where the rules are simply read off the templates in an extracted LTAG. The extracted grammar G_1 and G_2 respectively has 851 and 727 context-free rules.

Algorithm 7 BUILD-CONJ-TREE(T)

Require: T is a derived tree
Ensure: a conjunction tree
1: $T_c \leftarrow \text{COPY}(T)$;
2: $H \leftarrow \text{HEAD-CHILD}(T_c)$;
3: BUILD-ELEMENTARY-TREES(H);
4: $K \leftarrow \text{COORDINATOR}(H)$;
5: BUILD-ELEMENTARY-TREES(K);
6: $H.\text{kids} \leftarrow \emptyset$;
7: $H.\text{type} \leftarrow \text{Foot}$;
8: $K.\text{kids} \leftarrow \emptyset$;
9: $K.\text{type} \leftarrow \text{Substitution}$;
10: **return** T_c;

In order to evaluate the coverage of the Vietnamese treebank, we count the number of extracted tree templates with respect to size of the treebank. Figure 8 shows the number of templates converges very slowly as the size of the corpus grows, implying that there are many unseen templates. This experiment also implies that the size of the current Vietnamese treebank is not large enough to cover all the grammatical templates of the Vietnamese language.

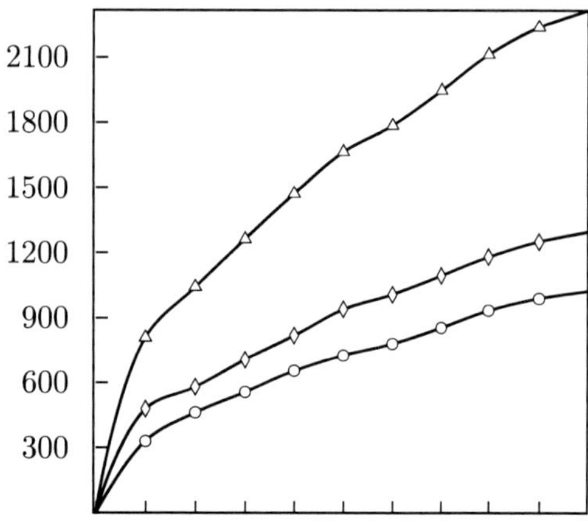

Figure 8: The growth of tree templates. The x axis shows the percentage of the corpus used for extraction, the y axis shows the number of extracted templates ($\triangle$), initial templates (o) and auxiliary templates ($\diamond$).

We have developed a software package that implements the presented algorithms for extracting an LTAG for Vietnamese. The software is written in the Java programming language and is freely distributed under the GNU/GPL license[6]. The software is very efficient in term of extraction speed: it takes only 165 seconds to extract the entire grammar G_1 on an ordinary personal computer. It is very easy to extend the software for use to extract LTAGs from treebanks of other languages since the language-specific information is intensionally factored out of the general framework. In order to use the software on a treebank of a language, user needs to provide the treebank-specific information for that language: a tagset, a head percolation table, and an argument table.

---

[6]*http://www.loria.fr/~lehong/tools/vnLExtractor.php*

6 Conclusions

We have presented a system that automatically extracts LTAGs from treebanks. The system has been used to extract an LTAG for the Vietnamese language from the recently released Vietnamese treebank. The extracted Vietnamese LTAG covers the corpus, that is the corpus can be seen as a collection of derived trees for the grammar and can be used to train statistical LTAG parsers directly.

The number of templates extracted from the current Vietnamese treebank converges slowly. This implies that there are many new templates outside the corpus and the current Vietnamese treebank is not large or typical enough to cover all the grammatical templates of the Vietnamese language.

Preliminary experimental parsing results using the LLP2 LTAG parser (Crabbé et al., 2003) show a high complexity of Vietnamese parsing in term of number of parses produced. For example, a test involving 70 sentences of length 15 words or less, parsed using an extracted LTAG grammar gives an average number of parses of 49.6 for a sentence, in which 14 sentences having unique parse. In future work, we plan to evaluate and extend the coverage and performance of both the grammar and parser for Vietnamese in greater detail.

We are currently experimenting the extraction of a French LTAG from a French treebank (Abeillé et al., 2003). We also plan to compare quantitatively syntactic structures of French and Vietnamese. We believe that a quantitative comparison of the two grammars may reveal interesting relations between them since, due to historical reason, by being in contact with the French language, Vietnamese was enriched not only in vocabulary but also in syntax by the calque of French grammar.

Acknowledgement

This work has been carried on in the framework, and with the support of the project QT-09-01, Vietnam National University of Hanoi.

References

Anne Abeillé, Lionel Clément, and François Toussenel. 2003. Building a treebank for French. In *Treebanks:*

Tags	Direction	Priority List
S	Left	S VP AP NP
SBAR	Left	SBAR S VP AP NP
SQ	Left	SQ VP AP NP
NP	Left	NP Nc Nu Np N P
VP	Left	VP V A AP N NP S
AP	Left	AP A N S
RP	Right	RP R T NP
PP	Left	PP E VP SBAR AP QP
QP	Left	QP M
XP	Left	XP X
YP	Left	YP Y
MDP	Left	MDP T I A P R X
WHNP	Left	WHNP NP Nc Nu Np N P
WHAP	Left	WHAP A N V P X
WHRP	Left	WHRP P E T X
WHPP	Left	WHPP E P X
WHXP	Left	XP X

Table 4: Head percolation rules for the Vietnamese treebank.

Building and Using Parsed Corpora. Kluwer, Dordrecht.

Jens Bäcker and Karin Harbusch. 2002. Hidden Markov model-based supertagging in a user-initiative dialogue system. In *Proceedings of TAG+6*, pages 269–278, Universita di Venezia.

Srinivas Bangalore and Aravind K. Joshi. 1999. Supertagging: An approach to almost parsing. *Computational Linguistics*, 25(2):237–265.

John Chen and K. Vijay-Shanker. 2000. Automated extraction of TAGs from the Penn treebank. In *Proceedings of the Sixth International Workshop on Parsing Technologies*.

John Chen, Srinivas Bangalore, and K. Vijay-Shanker. 2006. Automated extraction of tree-adjoining grammars from treebanks. *Natural Language Engineering*, 12(3):251–299.

David Chiang. 2000. Statistical parsing with an automatically-extracted tree adjoining grammar. In *ACL'00*, pages 456–463, Morristown, NJ, USA.

Michael Collins. 1997. Three generative, lexicalised models for statistical parsing. In *Proceedings of ACL*.

Benoît Crabbé, Bertrand Gaiffe, and Azim Roussanaly. 2003. Représentation et gestion de grammaires d'arbres adjoints lexicalisées. *Traitement Automatique des Langues*, 44(3):67–91.

Nizar Habash and Owen Rambow. 2004. Extracting a tree adjoining grammar from the Penn Arabic treebank. In *Proceedings of TALN'04*, Morocco.

Ane-Dybro Johansen. 2004. Extraction des grammaires LTAG à partir d'un corpus étiquetté syntaxiquement. Master's thesis, Université Paris 7.

David M. Magerman. 1995. Statistical decision tree models for parsing. In *Proceedings of ACL*.

Alexis Nasr. 2004. *Analyse syntaxique probabiliste pour grammaires de dépendances extraites automatiquement*. Habilitation à diriger des recherches, Université Paris 7.

Günter Neumann. 2003. A uniform method for automatically extracting stochastic lexicalized tree grammar from treebank and HPSG. In *Treebanks: Building and Using Parsed Corpora*. Kluwer, Dordrecht.

Phuong Thai Nguyen, Luong Vu Xuan, Thi Minh Huyen Nguyen, Van Hiep Nguyen, and Phuong Le-Hong. 2009. Building a large syntactically-annotated corpus of Vietnamese. In *Proceedings of the 3rd Linguistic Annotation Workshop, ACL-IJCNLP*, Singapore.

Jungyeul Park. 2006. Extraction of tree adjoining grammars from a treebank for Korean. In *COLING ACL'06 Student Research Workshop*, pages 73–78, Morristown, NJ, USA.

Fei Xia, Martha Palmer, and Aravind Joshi. 2000. A uniform method of grammar extraction and its applications. In *Proceedings of the joint SIGDAT conference on empirical methods in NLP and very large corpora*, pages 53–62, Morristown, NJ, USA.

Fei Xia. 2001. *Automatic grammar generation from two different perspectives*. Ph.D. thesis, University of Pennsylvania.

174

Index of Authors